Viva South America!

Oliver Balch is a UK freelance journalist specialising in business and world affairs. His work has appeared in a wide range of international publications, including the *Guardian*, the *Financial Times*, *Condé Nast Traveller* and *The Traveller*. His first book, *Viva South America!* was shortlisted as Book of the Year at the UK Travel Press Awards and his second book, *India Rising: Tales from a Changing Nation*, was published in 2012.

Further praise for *Viva South America!*:

'A stimulating dive into this large and gamey continent.'
Literary Review

'Balch's eye for detail is impressive, personalising the book beyond the academic and painting vivid, affecting pictures of the poverty that blights the continent . . . A clear, colourful account of people whose liberation from their colonisers has yet to provide them with the kind of freedom that Bolívar envisioned.' *Irish Times*

'*Viva!* is both funny and serious . . . A vivid, enjoyable book about one of the few areas that offer any real hope for socialists today.'
New Statesman

'The reader is left hungry to hear more, for the author is adept at giving vivid pictures . . . A brilliant series of snapshots of life and struggle in this seething continent.' *Tablet*

'Wittily observant, and with a good eye for the absurd, he can find himself one moment sitting alongside the Chilean president Michelle Bachelet at an all-female lunch, and the next taking a "four-night break in Rio's premier favela hotel".' *Independent*

The Journey of
Viva South America!

Land over 2000m

CUBA

VENEZUELA

COLOMBIA

A m a z o n

basin

Amazon

ECUADOR

Napo

PERU

BRAZIL

BOLIVIA

PARAGUAY

ARGENTINA

CHILE

PARAGUAY

URUGUAY

Uruguay

1 Mar del Plata
2 La Paz
3 Chapare
4 Cochabamba
5 Potosí
6 Oruro
7 Santa Cruz
8 Copacabana
9 Santiago
10 Elqui Valley
11 Concepción
12 Valparaíso
13 Buenos Aires
14 Santa Cruz province
15 Gualeguaychú
16 Mendoza
17 Asunción
18 Santa María de Fé
19 Ciudad del Este
20 Alto Paraná
21 Sao Paulo
22 Rio de Janeiro
23 Recife
24 Salvador
25 Ayaviri
26 Cusco
27 Lima
28 Iquitos
29 Cajamarca
30 Coca
31 Cuenca
32 Quito
33 La Sierra
34 Otavalo
35 Bogotá
36 Meta province
37 Upper Cauca Valley
38 Cali
39 Medellín
40 Mutatá
41 Cartagena
42 Santa Marta
43 Los Rastrojos
44 Maracaibo
45 Coro
46 Caracas
47 Mérida
48 Ciudad Bolívar
49 Havana

Viva South America!

A Journey through a Surging Continent

OLIVER BALCH

FABER & FABER

For Emma, *con doble 'm'*

by the same author

INDIA RISING: TALES FROM A CHANGING NATION

First published in 2009
by Faber & Faber Ltd
Bloomsbury House, 74–77 Great Russell Street
London WC1B 3DA
This updated paperback edition first published in 2014

Typeset by Faber & Faber Limited
Printed in the UK by CPI Group (UK) Ltd, Croydon, CR0 4YY

A CIP record for this book
is available from the British Library

ISBN 978–0–571–31246–7

10 9 8 7 6 5 4 3 2 1

CONTENTS

SIMÓN BOLÍVAR

Revolutionary, state-builder, philosopher and ladies' man, Simón José Antonio de la Santísima Trinidad Bolívar y Palacios represents the archetypal South American hero. He's Fidel Castro, Che Guevara and the Incan Túpac Amaru all rolled into one.

Born into the upper echelons of Venezuelan aristocracy in 1783, he enjoyed a privileged childhood and a golden youth in Europe. Orphaned and widowed before his twentieth birthday, he also had his share of tragedy.

On his return to his homeland in 1807, Bolívar dedicated his life to winning independence for Hispanic America. A master strategist and charismatic general, he's credited with liberating modern-day Colombia, Venezuela, Panama, Ecuador, Peru and Bolivia.

Ever since his death in 1830, the Great Liberator has become the subject of nationalistic pride and literary fable. To schoolchildren, he is the man who vanquished the Spanish and held high the torch of liberty. To political theorists, he is the visionary who mapped out a unified future for the free Americas. To everyday South Americans, he is the bronze statue sitting high on a horse in the town square, model citizen, die-hard romantic and martyr to his cause.

Today, the first President of Greater Colombia enjoys a cult following across the continent. Ardent patriot, American hero, macho male, faithful Catholic – Bolívar's image is used to fit them all. He has a country named after him. Heads of state espouse his ideas. Poets and artists evoke his memory.

But Bolívar, like South America itself, remains little known to the outside world. Even the great emancipator once described his own continent as 'shrouded in darkness'. For those after a torch to light their way, there's none brighter than the Liberator's own life and legacy.

INTRODUCTION

Headlong into chaos

We threw ourselves headlong into the chaos of revolution.
SIMÓN BOLÍVAR, 'THE JAMAICA LETTER', 6 SEPTEMBER 1815

Mar del Plata, Argentina, 4 November 2005

A carnival mood brightens the rain-soaked skies above Mar del Plata's football stadium. I shoulder my way through the cheering crowd to the security rail at the front, squeezing into a space between a student anarchist and a vocal group of Falklands veterans.

On stage, an ageing protest singer is warming up the audience with a repertoire of rock and revolution.

'*Viva la libertad!*' the front man hollers, prompting thirty-five thousand voices to scream back in unison.

'Long live freedom!'

The order of play is reversed, with the spectators on the pitch and the performers on a temporary platform above the lower-tier seating. Flags and banners carpet the playing field. An assault of three-letter acronyms flutters in the wind: MSP, MST, MTR, PCR. The members of the Revolutionary Patriotic Movement are the only ones with sufficient calligraphy skills to protest in longhand. Above them all, dangling from the roof, hangs a fifty-foot banner of Che Guevara, the South American revolutionary icon.

Amid the lashings of an Atlantic squall, the Argentine seaside resort is reverberating with the hopes of a continent. Unionists cry out for better wages. Socialists bellow for workers' rights. The sixties rocker dreams of a future without war. The veterans want their islands back. The long-haired anarchist shouts for nothing and everything all at once. Deafening and desperate, their collective clamour shakes the open-seater stadium.

The battle-worn vocalist is done with giving peace a chance. He passes the microphone to a diminutive indigenous woman from Ecuador. Hidden beneath a cerulean shawl and a persistent drizzle, the strident-voiced activist reads out the conclusions of a four-day 'People's Summit'. She retires to rapturous applause.

On the seat beside her in the front row sits Diego Maradona, Argentina's all-time soccer legend. A picture of George W. Bush is stamped across his T-shirt, the words 'War Criminal' scribbled in English above. The barrel-chested football star raises a clenched fist to the crowd. The stadium erupts a second time at the gesture of their home-grown hero.

The true star of the show then takes the stage: '*Viva* the people of South America!'

'*Viva!*' we all shout back. The roar rebounds around the stadium like a war cry.

'*Viva* life!

'*Viva!*' Raw and visceral sounds our response.

'*Viva* the Fatherland!'

'*Viva!*' Louder the echo grows.

The television cameras are rolling. The protestors are rapt. There, in the rain, on the stage, before his public, Hugo Chávez is in his element.

'Just over an hour ago,' the charismatic Venezuelan president tells the crowd, 'a Cuban companion came up to me and passed me the phone, and I was like, "Well, who am I talking to?"' Calling collect from Havana, no less, was Fidel Castro.

'*Viva* Fidel!'

'*Viva!*'

'Our Cuban brother regrets not making it in person to this "historic event", but, let us be in no doubt, he's watching every minute via satellite television. We're going to make a racket! *Viva* the new world! *Viva* the *pueblos* of the world!'

'*Viva!*'

'Do you know how the goodbye went?' The showman is gearing up his act, living up to his billboard hype.

'His voice signed off like a thunderclap that crossed the Caribbean, the Orinoco, the Amazon, the River Plate and arrived here, telling me: "Chávez. Hell, *Viva* Che!"'

'*Viva!*' The poster child of political revolution earns the loudest shout so far.

The bad weather worsens as the speech unfolds, Heaven and orator competing in torrents. As a baptism into South American revolutionary politics, it feels appropriate that I should be getting soaked to the skin.

Chávez is supposedly in town to hobnob with his fellow heads of state. Up for discussion is the ALCA (Área de Libre Comercio de las Américas), a continental free-trade agreement proposed by the USA. In a barricaded conference hall across town wait thirty-three American presidents from north and south. Mar del Plata has been put on a war footing in preparation. Shops shelter behind metal grilles. A security cordon blocks off downtown's evacuated streets. Police riot divisions brush off their body armour and truncheons.

The combative Venezuelan premier has already decided how the presidential summit will end: 'We have come here today for many reasons, to march, to sing, to shout, to fight, but . . . each one of us has brought a spade, a gravedigger's spade, because here in Mar del Plata is the tomb of the ALCA!'

The crowd drinks it in, and the media has its soundbite.

'Who has buried the ALCA?'

The self-proclaimed 'twenty-first-century socialist' needn't ask, and he tells us the answer anyway.

'The people of the Americas, we are burying the ALCA, today, here in Mar del Plata!' General jubilation and flag-waving ensue.

But this is more than just political theatre. For Chávez, world history is at stake. Between the anecdotes and insults, he lectures us about fascism and climate change ('in one hundred years, there'll be no ice in the Arctic'), about Malcolm X and Mao Zedong, about globalisation and Judas Iscariot ('the first great capitalist, who sold Christ for a few coins').

The man who keeps Noam Chomsky's *Hegemony or Survival* by his bedside table sees a planet that's diverging: the greed of capitalism pulling it one way, the will of its citizens yanking it the other.

'The people of the world must choose which destiny we want for our descendants.' More clapping, more shouting.

'Never again will we be a colony of North America!' Maradona is now on his feet too, applauding wildly.

'*Viva el pueblo! Viva* the people!'

'*Viva!*' we scream.

The pulpit president then transports us to the backwaters of Venezuela, reminding us of his proletarian roots among the pork-eating *campesinos* in the fields.

'There they have a saying that goes, "Every pig has its Saturday." Here, too, we are *campesinos*. For every empire, a Saturday arises too . . . It's our duty to destroy the empire, all the empires.'

The verbal volley fires into the top of the net. Elation spreads from goalmouth to goalmouth. This is better than a football cup final.

Then he's steadying us, calming our excitement, playing our emotions like puppets on a string.

'*Ojo,* be aware, today is only Thursday. The light of Friday's dawn is just rising. Battles lie ahead. We must take up once more the victorious standard of the liberators.'

Rare is the sermon in which the political evangelist doesn't touch on the prophets of South American independence. Anticipating the president's conclusion, the protest organisers have rigged up some visual aids. From the front of the elevated stage fall the portraits of two distinguished-looking gentlemen. Their bearing is military, their countenance solemn and their sideburns impressive in both length and fullness. They're models for bank notes and stone carvings. On the left hangs the chiselled side profile of Simón Bolívar, the Venezuelan who chased off the Spanish from the north. Next to him flaps José de San Martín, the Argentine who booted them out from the south. Both men set out to liberate a continent. Here in the stadium, Chávez reminds us, their legacy lives on.

In case anyone remains in doubt about what the liberators stood for, the president and former history lecturer provides a recap:

'The project was to create republics of equal and free men, republics in liberty and equality.' *A roar goes up from the crowd.*

'To eliminate slavery, to eliminate misery, to eliminate poverty, exploitation.' *A contagious ovation.*

'Now is the new hour, now is the new moment that we are living.' *Palms hit palms in ecstatic applause.*

'Two hundred years ago, our father liberators couldn't achieve it.' *And? He keeps us waiting.*

'The strategy of Bolívar . . .' – *the anticipatory silence builds* – 'has even more relevance today than yesterday.' *Thousands of voices whooping in delight.* This is the revolutionary talk we've come to hear.

Time is of the essence. Thanks to 'neo-liberal capitalism', two hundred and twenty-two million people are now living in poverty across the continent. Twenty-seven in every thousand babies are born with curable illnesses.

'Every day there is more hunger, more misery.' The people of America must unite for a 'Bolívarian alternative'. It's the task of all of us: of the working class, of the indigenous, of the *campesinos,* of the farmers, of the students, of the women, of the African descendants, of the professionals, of the artists, of the singers, of the poets. The new order for South America 'must be built from below'.

Regrettably, the clock has run on. The 'other summit' calls. The President must preside. But we can rest assured. Our voice will be heard. He, Hugo Chávez, will personally deliver it.

The ex-military man looks around for his own memorable farewell. He finds inspiration in a quote from José Martí, the Cuban revolutionary poet: 'The hour has arrived for the second independence of the peoples of the Americas.'

Hysteria breaks out across the sodden stadium.

'*Hasta la Victoria, siempre!*' 'Until Victory, forever!'

A wall of security personnel closes in around the rebel president. 'Hell, *viva* Che Guevara!'

He's whisked off stage. '*Viva!*' we yell back, electricity streaming through our veins.

Outside the gates, the first rioters are already congregating. Balaclava-clad protestors set their minds to smashing windows and looting stores. The armed police file out across the city's main boulevard. Bricks and paving stones rain down on them. A bank is set on fire. Tear-gas cartridges slip into gun barrels. My throat burns at the gas's toxic taste.

By nightfall, calm is eventually restored. The street fires are put out. The glass is being swept up. And, under the glass chandeliers of the hotel banqueting hall, the tuxedoed presidents are just sitting down to dinner.

The newspaper I was filing for wasn't especially interested in the speech or the riot. The foreign desk already had enough real wars to cover, the editors told me. They didn't need a rhetorical one. Anyway, in a land of despots and dictators, another loudmouth revolutionary was hardly news. Street skirmishes in South America didn't do it for them either. Unless I could promise bloodshed, of course, and then they'd think about it. Coups and kidnappings were what the newspaper really wanted. On quiet weeks, perhaps a gun battle in the slums of Brazil. Or a grisly drugs murder in Colombia. But a continent simmering in discontent? A liberator rising from the ashes? No, they were sorry, but that wouldn't cut it. Wouldn't cut it at all.

During my initial months in Buenos Aires, the fortunes of Falklands fisheries and the finance markets kept my bills paid and a roof over my head. Skirmishes over shrimp quotas and battles against inflation weren't exactly the front-line reporting I'd had in mind when I quit my job in London to try my hand as a freelance foreign correspondent. But it was difficult to see an alternative. The international press just didn't seem to care.

And then, almost overnight, it did. It was strange. One minute, South America was the forgotten continent. Next, it was the new world. It was as if word of Columbus's discovery had just reached CNN. International journalists began arriving. Foreign bureaus opened. Newswires were hiring.

Their interest was sparked by immediate events. The continent was going to the polls. Over a twelve-month period, only Paraguay and Argentina found themselves in midterms. Every other sizeable country was holding elections. Each campaign threw up its stories. Rumours of vote-rigging circulated in Venezuela. A cash-for-favours scandal blew up in Brazil. Indigenous uprisings broke out in Bolivia. But it was the results that sustained the hype. Every month, more red splotches stained the political map. The trend was undeniable: South America was heading left. Colombia and Peru alone bucked the tide. Washington was justifiably looking worried. Its backyard was turning boisterous.

At the centre was that man Chávez. He took his Chomsky to the United Nations and his revolution to the people. The news channels focused on the first. President of the publicity stunt, his antics kept them more than busy. If the Venezuelan 'firebrand' wasn't expropriating oil fields, he was denouncing CIA plots to assassinate him. Dressed in a Che-style beret, it all made great TV.

The media circus suited me just fine. It left me room to explore the story behind the story: the people and their revolution. In a post-ideological world, it all seemed a fraction absurd. Mao was dead. Lenin was loathed. Marx was mincemeat. The battle for ideas was supposed to have been buried with the Berlin Wall. Yet, here was a continent in thrall to rehashed rhetoric about hegemonies and empires. Voters were buying in to notions of wars between classes and prowling robber barons in their midst.

South America was angry. I'd seen it on the streets of Mar del Plata. I'd felt it rumbling somewhere deep beneath the turf in the football stadium. People wanted someone or something to blame. But why? What was it that fuelled their fury? What was making them so eager to tread the perilous path of revolution? Answer these questions, I sensed, and this strange land might begin explaining itself.

7

Casting around for a starting point, my mind kept returning to Chávez's farewell phrase. The hour for the continent's 'second independence' had, apparently, arrived. But what need had South America of a fresh fight for freedom? Their Old World colonialists had been booted out two centuries ago. Sovereign, democratic governments held power from Bogotá to Buenos Aires. What greater independence did they need?

I went back to my recording of Chávez's speech in search for clues. Between the yelps of the crowd, talk of Simón Bolívar's strategy stopped me short: 'republics in liberty and equality'.

It was a utopian dream, a goal the Enlightenment made people believe possible. Bolívar and his fellow liberators had fallen short. The orator reminded us as much. Republics had been formed, but not fully liberated. Is that what was angering South Americans? The sense of a job half finished? Cheering erupted from my tape recorder. The thirty-five thousand protestors certainly felt that way. I found myself wondering how many others around the continent might agree.

Liberty and equality come in many guises. Deciphering who strove for which and why would be no small job. I drew up a provisional list of issues. It filled half a page: economics, politics, gender, race, culture, religion, law, security, human rights and so forth. On the remainder of the page, I scribbled an outline of South America's largest countries. For each issue, I identified a resonant nation. By matching list with map, I eventually struck on a rough route. In Chávez's roll-call of bottom-up revolutionaries, I also had my test-bed of opinion: the working class, the indigenous, the *campesinos,* the farmers, et cetera.

As methodologies go, more scientific approaches might exist. But I had a year at my disposal and a territory four times the size of the European Union to cover. If South America really was buzzing with the ideas of the liberators, I felt confident my strategy would turn up the evidence.

To be sure, I decided to take a guide, someone who could point out the way and help me navigate. Simón Bolívar seemed the obvious choice. No one knew the terrain of independence better than Chávez's revolutionary muse. Into my bag, I packed a single-volume edition of the Liberator's political writings and letters. Where it was silent, I would turn to the phalanx of Bolívar's fellow liberators for guidance.

A journey in Bolívar's footsteps could only feasibly begin in one place: the country that bore his name. I bought a one-way ticket to Bolivia.

1

THE BEGGAR ON THE GOLDEN THRONE

Bolivia and economics

Only God had the power to name this land Bolivia.
SIMÓN BOLÍVAR, BOLIVIAN CONSTITUTION

La Paz

La Paz must be the most topographically bizarre city on the planet. Any sensible urban planner would order the city's immediate demolition. The air is too thin, the winds too cold and the gradient too steep. Inhabiting the top of the world means learning to live with a permanent nagging hangover. Consent to a life of morning afters without the nights before and you'll be granted lifetime residency in Bolivia's hilltop capital.

These truths occur to me as I stumble down the hill from the bus station, my head spinning and a vague sense of nausea settling in my lower gut. I'd spent the previous night not only sober but also in the less-than-sweet embrace of a snoring farmer. We'd shared seats 14A and 14B. Our night-time proximity had concerned me even before his spluttering body mass shifted onto my shoulder. There the wool-wrapped pastoralist remained, as stubbornly immobile as a mule on sedatives.

Being wide awake at dawn on a La Paz-bound bus has its benefits though. Brushing your teeth or relieving your bladder are not among them. Ten minutes into the overnight journey and a 'not working' sign was already hanging on the toilet door. This was thoughtful advice from the management but entirely unnecessary. The stench from the closet latrine was potent enough for even the flies to give it a wide berth.

The merits lie beyond the confines of the bus, a kilometre down in the creased fissures of a prehistoric crater. As the coach driver veers towards the seared city limits, the Bolivian capital presents itself bathed in the rose pink of dawn. Splayed out across the volcanic valley below, the mountainous metropolis clambers up the hillsides and snakes down the ravines. As views go, La Paz in the first light of day is worth a sleepless night.

Architectural bravado aside, the city would make a more fitting site for a mountaineers' base camp than a national capital. Enthroned majestically above the citadel gates looms the imperious bulk of Mount Illimani. Neat files of white-wigged courtiers avidly guard her virgin white slopes. Equipped with snow-tipped bayonets and jagged-edged scimitars, her noble guard protects her modesty with the impenetrable attention of a sharp-toothed chastity belt.

Perhaps because the *Pazeños* leave her be, Queen Illimani has allowed them to clutter her lower foothills with freeways and apartment blocks and pavements and football stadiums and parks and markets and hospitals and shopping centres. Or perhaps she's biding her time, waiting for a minor earth shudder to send the entire edifice crashing down the mountainside. Either way, La Paz sprouts from the Earth's bowels as an undeniable urban reality. Its neighbourhoods cling to sloping precipices with the determined resolution of barnacles on a ship's hull. Earthquake insurance must be an exorbitant luxury.

After a few days of heavy-legged sightseeing, it becomes apparent that the gravity-challenging capital has its geological curiosities too. Like no other city in the world, La Paz's postcodes are arranged by palaeontology. Amid the lower strata, compressed beneath millennia of accumulated sediment, lives the slender vein of Bolivia's wealthy. In defiance of their surroundings, they hose their barren backyards until grass lawns sprout. They surround their lots with electric gates and cameras, little kings in the folds of Illimani's flowing robes.

Above them, halfway up the capital's exposed rock-face walls, reside those who work for them: their office managers and accountants, their car salesmen and bank clerks, the teachers of their children and vendors of their security systems.

On the higher ground, toppling on the crater's crust, where the wind tousles the sandy topsoil in bilious clouds, lives the teeming remnant. El Alto, a hilltop community of over one million inhabitants, is so cold that water pipes crack and the rocks are said to split in two. Its residents suffer the extremes of poverty too, a poverty that dates back centuries, as entrenched as the geological gradations beneath their feet. A steady job here is the exception, electricity a boon and crime the norm.

In Murillo Square, between the cathedral and the Congress Building, stands the Presidential Palace. On this cool February evening, a bossy corporal dripping in silver-plated epaulettes is overseeing a change of guard. He's so busy with his duties that I pass through the gateway unobserved.

Bolivians have a new king to reign over them. It is carnival, and the recently elected president is dancing. Throwing back his head, he grabs a pretty girl and skips around the open fire in the palace's main ballroom. Wearing a bright pink pleated skirt and white bowler hat, the doll-like *indígena* whirls dizzily on his arm. The tall, flop-haired president proves light on his feet. He swaps partners. Immediately entwined, the new pair swivels and swirls around the flickering flames. Dutiful ministers join the throng. Everywhere, loyal retainers clap and cheer as loyal retainers should.

A band of flautists joins the dance. Their music gathers pace. Colourful eightsomes twirl in interweaving circles, the movement unremitting. More dancing partners for the president. Arms join. A riotous reel unfolds around the bonfire, swaying this way, then that. Swaying bodies blur the room. The minstrels increase the tempo. Boiled sweets, confetti and coca leaves, tossed in the air, now sprinkle the floor. Flowered garlands dangle delightedly around necklines. Beads of sweat gather on foreheads. The music quickens, faster and faster. Drums now too. Towards a crescendo the dancers head. Roars of merriment. The final twirl. A kiss. A bow. The president takes a breather.

Into the balconied hall step three *yatiris,* elders from the historic Inca town of Tiwanaku. Like Macbeth's three witches, they huddle together over the ritual pyre, chanting and praying. With rice and petals and incantations, the Aymara priests feed the flames. A wispy spiral of white smoke drifts up towards the high, gilded ceiling. With it climb words of blessing, for king and country. Never before has the *cha'lla,* the ancient consecration ceremony of the Incas, been held in the Presidential Palace. From their painted friezes, the mounted heroes of Bolivia's independence look down in mild confusion.

A beautiful, slender nymphet jumps forward from the crowd. Dressed in a flimsy, figure-hugging tunic, mountain flowers adorn her flowing black hair. Solemnly, she holds the curled shape of a cow horn to her delicate mouth. Eyes closed, head arched back, her full lips purse. An imperceptible breath.

Then it comes, echoing eerily through the vaulted room, the slow, drawn-out wail of prehistory. Haunting, primordial, the cow horn wakens the palace to a new dawn. And then, amid the flash of camera bulbs, the president is gone.

Villa Tunari

Evo Morales has come a long way. Born into poverty in Bolivia's arid highlands, the former sheep-herder now proudly presides over Illimani's mountain kingdom. It took a near revolution to get him there. Unfortunately, the country's first indigenous president has arrived late on the scene. Half a millennium late, some would argue. Centuries of rape and ransacking have left his citizens disenfranchised and his state coffers drained. Evo's Movement Towards Socialism hopes to salvage what it can.

Hurtling downhill in the back of a cramped minibus, I set off to the tropical lowlands of Chapare to discover where Evo's journey began. With every eastward mile, the humidity becomes stickier and the vegetation more boundless. After we have driven for two and a half hours around sharp mountain chicanes, a uniformed policeman steps into the middle of the road. With an open palm, the moustached official orders us to halt.

The two-lane, eastward highway from the city of Cochabamba in the central sierras is dotted with drug checkpoints. But this is not one of them. Recent heavy rains have caused a landslide on the bend ahead. Five hundred metres of road are now swilling in the river down below. The khaki-clad policeman tells us to alight. All those who wish to continue will be doing so on foot. Bags hauled onto our backs, we trudge for half an hour across a muddy path cut from the debris of the destroyed road. 'Unstable Geological Zone' reads a sign on the other side. A prize for that far-sighted transport engineer.

Ahead, a sinuous train of stranded lorries winds its way along the twisting jungle road. Their stinking cargo is rotting after a week in the sun. The drivers lounge in hammocks under their trailers, sleeping, snoring, chatting, bored. Enterprising motorbike owners wait for us on the other side, their engines revving. Side-saddle, we race around a dozen hair-raising bends. The roadside bushes reverberate with rustles and squawks. A parked minibus further down the road meets the caravan of straggling passengers. I throw my rucksack in the back. After five hours of potholes and semi-penetrable jungle, we arrive in Evo's old stomping ground. The president did well to fight his way out of Chapare, let alone make it to La Paz.

A yellow concrete arc stretching over the road announces our arrival in Villa Tunari, Chapare's capital. 'Paradise of ethno-eco-tourism', it proclaims. The slogan is a ruse. Everyone knows the welcome notice should read, 'Capital of Coca'. At a push, the small Parque Machia animal reserve at the bottom of the town could justify the 'eco' label. 'Ethno' is harder to place. Perhaps the phrase's creators had quaint images of Chapare's predominantly Quechua population in mind. Closer to the mark is the legion of bug-bitten backpackers who fill the volunteers' dormitories in the reserve.

But the term 'paradise' is at least well chosen. Chapare is a dreamland when it comes to growing coca, the base ingredient for cocaine. The pest-averse coca plant thrives in the region's tropical temperatures and nutrient-poor soils. In a good year, farmers can bank on up to four harvests. Narcotics manufacturers like it too. Remote and inaccessible, the Chapare jungles provide them with an ideal location for their canopy-covered laboratories.

By the 1970s, Villa Tunari was competing with Colombia as the narcotics nexus of South America. Bolivian coca farmers accounted for more than a third of world production, most of which was destined for the USA. By the mid-1980s, Bolivia's cocaine exports were worth over twice the country's legal exports put together.

The party was never going to last for ever. Uncle Sam, for one, would not allow it. As early as 1950, an investigation by a US banker, Howard Fonda, concluded that 'the chewing of coca is responsible for mental slowness and poverty in Andean Countries'. His report influenced world leaders, who, under the Geneva Convention of 1961, lumped the humble coca leaf together with heroine, cocaine and other banned Class-A drugs.

With billions of dollars in US aid conditioned on fighting the narcotics trade, the Bolivian authorities began cracking down. Their main target was Chapare's coca-growers. For decades, the province became one large boot camp. The war on drugs went into overdrive in the late 1990s. President Hugo Banzer, a former dictator turned drugs tsar, pledged to wipe out every last coca plant within five years. His 'zero coca' policy shaped the battle lines that, over the coming years, would lead to dozens of deaths on both sides.

The veterans of that war are today sitting pretty in Villa Tunari's Town Hall. I pay a visit the next morning. The two-storey building is crammed with parents who've come to hear about a new school breakfast programme. The initiative is being sponsored by the mayor, a front-line combatant alongside Evo in the fight to preserve coca production. Shrapnel from an old gun battle with anti-narcotics police is lodged in his foot, a sure election-winner in this coca-growing corner of Bolivia.

I make my introductions and am pointed towards José Roni's office. A nameplate with the words 'Top Official' is hammered above the door. In his thirties and casually dressed, the baby-faced man who opens the door little resembles the grand job description. He grew up fighting at Evo's side, evidently a compulsory criterion for public office in Chapare. During a month-long protest march by the province's *cocaleros* (coca growers), he'd even dressed up as the future president, 'to put the secret police off the scent'. The memory brings a contented look to his face, as though it were a childhood game of hide-and-seek that he's recalling.

As well as old war stories, the curricula of Villa Tunari's politicians share another factor in common: they were all educated at the university of life. No elitist degree certificate will be found after their names, only sweat and toil. José came late to politics, he wants me to know. Before Evo, he earned his crust as a job-hopping day labourer. Not a single one of Chapare's nine municipal representatives is a *profesional* (shorthand for 'graduate', 'manager', 'capitalist' and a host of other sins). In Chapare, the doctrine of class war reigns.

'Like Evo, our politicians know the problems of the people because they've lived through them. They're not out of touch like the political elites of the past,' the Top Official says, repeating his political liturgy with the passion of a faithful acolyte.

He laughs. Did I know that the ex-minister of agriculture didn't even know how much a kilo of tomatoes cost? That would never happen under *compañero* Evo. *What else is different now?* Chapare's farmers no longer have to worry about crop-sprayers indiscriminately destroying their harvests. Coca is not cocaine, I should know. A remonstrating finger is raised. Bolivians have been using unprocessed coca for centuries: as a stimulant, an anaesthetic, a hunger suppressant and a cure for stomach aches and all manner of everyday ills. Incan brain surgeons even used it. *And as a narcotic?* No, never. Drugs are for coke-sniffing *gringos*. 'For us Bolivians, no.'

The Top Official has some bullet points he feels obliged to share. Was I aware that all Bolivians up to the age of twenty-one now get free medical care? I shake my head. Had I been told about the bonus payments for parents who keep their children in school? Nope. Did

I know the minimum wage had been increased and a nationwide literacy programme instigated? Vaguely. I must have heard how contracts with foreign energy multinationals had been renegotiated and their excessive profits curbed? Yes, now *that* I was familiar with. With the second largest gas reserves in South America, it was a subject that had preoccupied the international media during the first months of Evo's presidency. That and the alpaca wool jumper he'd worn every day during his first world tour.

José watches me making rapid notes on everything he's saying. Running out of steam with his list-making, he falls silent and starts toying with a protracted whisker on his chin. He wants to finish with something statesmanlike.

'Evo will not abandon us,' he spells out with careful deliberation. I should be getting this down, the Top Official indicates, waggling his finger at my notebook. 'Like a good president, Evo submits to the majority.' He pauses for me to write. 'And the majority in Bolivia is rural, poor and indigenous.' Like a good president, Evo knows where the votes lie too.

After our conversation, José points me down the corridor to the office of the coca-growers' union. It was through this same union's ranks that Evo's star had risen, first as a local sports secretary and finally as its combative leader. I knock and enter, and Julio Salazar waves me to be seated. Dressed in muddy sandals and with his jeans rolled up to just below his knees, the battle-scarred unionist is wrapping up a phone call in brisk Quechua.

I cast my eye over the room as the phone call continues. A flyer advertising the union's last annual conference is pinned to the back of the door. 'To resist is to survive – never surrender' runs the event's catchy title. One of its key themes is simply entitled 'Yankis'.

'Here are Evo's roots as a politician,' Julio Salazar intones, after replacing the receiver. 'Chapare is where our president's character and his thinking were formed.'

Could he elaborate? Bolivia is not a poor country. It is a country that has been impoverished. The world should know the difference. The United States and other foreign imperialists have always dictated Bolivia's internal economic and political affairs. The fight against coca is just another pretext to protect their interests.

The union man is now on a roll. Savage capitalism is to blame for everything: for Bolivia's foreign debt problem, for the country's failure to industrialise, for the marginalisation of its indigenous people. Did I know that as recently as two generations ago, certain districts of La Paz were out of bounds to those of Aymara or Quechua descent? By electing Evo, Bolivians were voting for a break with the 'oligarchies' of the past.

'Evo is with us,' the *cocalero* militant finishes, 'he won't let us down.'

The local bus leaves from a police checkpoint on the far side of town. A huge billboard featuring a healthy-looking teenage girl looms above the roadside. 'We are in the fight against drugs,' the caption reads. 'Welcome to drug-free Chapare.'

I'd been reliably informed that Evo once lived somewhere down the northbound jungle track. My inquiries around Villa Tunari for a more precise location had returned inconclusive. The advert at least implies that I'm starting in the right direction: into the heart of coca country.

The police wave us through, and exuberant foliage greets us. Jolting up and down along the single-lane road, progress is painfully slow. One-room chipboard shacks line the roadside, most with chicken pens and washing lines out back. We cross over several languid streams, their gullies bubbling with soap suds and the giggles of washerwomen. The sight of the familiar bus attracts gleeful waves from dirty-kneed children. Dogs bark. At one stage, a cyclist gives chase. Occasionally, the bus driver stops to let someone off. They step out, and the undergrowth eats them up.

The bus pulls in at a dilapidated garage in the dusty settlement of 14 de Septiembre. Passengers disembark and shuffle off home. The driver disappears after them. I climb down too.

Stewed under the midday sun, the village has retired indoors. A handful of hard-working market vendors, up since dawn, are packing away their produce into balsa-wood crates. Pedalling past me on an adult's bicycle rides a teenage boy in plastic sandals. Two pensioners sit beside each other on a wooden bench in the square, silently, enjoying the shade of the trees and the sensation of not being alone. A pack of scrounging street dogs sniff at an overturned dustbin. Otherwise, the streets are empty. Only Evo can bear the heat, his campaign smile grinning out from behind a hundred unwashed window panes.

The president's house lies a way off still, the driver has assured me. So I return to the bus and await his return. The scorch of the black plastic seat burns the back of my thighs. I fashion an improvised fan from my notebook to offset the heaviness of the saturating humidity. Sweating bodies board in ones and twos, small bundles of children and shopping dragged up behind them.

After half an hour, the driver reappears. Ambling along the pavement from his house, his shirt hangs out at the back of his trousers, and his hair has the ruffle of a short siesta. With a turn of the key, the engine wheezes into gear without enthusiasm. Chugging slowly out of sleepy 14 de Septiembre, we once more pick up the bumpy road northwards. Gradually, the bus empties until only three of us remain.

For long stretches now, we pass nothing. No shacks, no hamlets, no side roads, only creepers and thickets and lush jungle frondescence. Then, without warning, the driver pulls up and starts jabbing a finger at the foliage. No one stirs.

'Here we are!' There's a tickle of jaded amusement in his voice. Is he speaking to me? He'd told me he'd point out the house when we passed it. Could this be it? 'Kilometre Twenty-One'. The words mean nothing to me, a fact that obviously annoys the driver, who's now turned around to eyeball me. 'Well, are you going to get off or not?' I remain in my seat. Through the bus's open window, I can see nothing but a wall of thick, impenetrable bushes. There's no way I'm getting out.

Muttering to himself, the irritated driver cuts the engine, climbs out and beckons me to follow him. Confident now that the bus cannot leave without me, I get up from my seat. My involuntary guide is walking towards a ditch ten metres back along the roadside. I jog to catch him up. Across the narrow trench lies a thin plank, hidden under the tall grass and invisible from the bus. We inch across it and then push, shoulder first, through a gap in the forest hedge. After twenty paces or so, we emerge from the dense shrubbery into a grassy clearing. I brush the leaves and briers from my clothes.

The house catches me by surprise, suddenly jumping out at us from the tropical woodland. I'd not expected anything grand, but I'd reckoned on something with walls. Resting high above the plant life on sixteen wooden stilts, the head of state's former residence comprises a raised wooden platform beneath a sloping, moss-stained roof.

Adopting the air of an estate agent, the bus driver takes me around the property pointing out its selling points. Furniture is not one of them. As with the walls, it has none. 'Bolivian hardwood,' the amateur realtor notes approvingly, tapping his knuckle against one of the stilted beams.

Access to the first and only floor is via a sturdy wooden ladder. The ground underneath is covered with waist-high grass. When in use, the empty space would double as a storeroom and a stable during the dry season. The driver is without his tape measure but reckons the building is probably thirty feet long. It's half that in width. Alongside stands a miniature version of the same building. An outdoor kitchen apparently, all very *nouveau*. If there had ever been a lavatory, it's been lost to the encroaching jungle.

From behind the overgrown hedgerow, the beep of a horn sounds. The abandoned trio are growing impatient in the oven-like bus. I take a couple of photos for memory's sake and clamber back through the undergrowth. The driver remains behind a moment, taking advantage of our stop to empty his bladder on the president's front lawn.

Down the track in Puerto San Francisco, the siesta hour has rolled over into the afternoon. Nothing and no one stirs in the one-street hamlet. It's the end of the road for the bus. The remaining passengers alight, and the paint-stripped bus with its rattling bumper trundles back the way it came. The driver waves from the open window and then disappears in a cloud of dust and exhaust fumes. As the bus swings around the final corner, he beeps the horn three times.

A few curtains ruffle. The proprietor at the corner store peers out from a hammock on his front porch. His face is unshaven and his serving counter unmanned. I wander across towards him. Two deep-set, suspicious eyes observe my approach. There are no chairs outside the store, and I make do with a log. *Does he have a fizzy drink?* Begrudgingly, he swings his feet out of the hammock and pads across in bare feet to a rusty industrial refrigerator. He flips the cap of a glass bottle of Pepsi and hands it to me with a straw. 'What brings me to San Francisco?' There's an interrogatory note to his question. 'Evo, I heard he was from round here.'

'You a journalist?'

'Yes.'

A pause. He heads back to the folds of his hammock.

'Evo was here, but long before my time.' Another break. He seems to be weighing something up. 'Try Don Santiago,' he suggests eventually. 'He's out back.'

I find the seventy-four-year-old don bent double with a hoe in his vegetable plot. He'll talk, but before he does he'd like to see my identification as a journalist. The precondition surprises me. Rarely am I asked for my professional credentials in South America, and hardly ever outside formal media events. But I have a press card in my wallet, which I dutifully dig out and hand over. Forgive the photo, I joke, trying to lighten the mood. He doesn't laugh. Instead, he turns the card over with his dirt-ingrained hands and examines the small print.

'*Policia*,' he barks, a moment later. 'Why does it say *policia*?'

I take it back from him, suddenly flustered. In truth, I suspected Don Santiago of being illiterate. More than one in eight Bolivians cannot read or write, most of whom are elderly and live in backwater spots not unlike Puerto San Francisco. Reading the card for myself, I identify the source of his suspicion.

'If found,' I translate back to him, 'please hand in at the nearest *police* station.' The explanation seems to satisfy him, but he remains stiff and monosyllabic. Two decades of military intervention have evidently left the coca heartlands wary of outsiders.

He guesses correctly that I'm interested in *compañero* Evo.

'What is it you'd like to know exactly?'

I ask if it's true that they were friends.

'Sure,' he says. He'd got to know the current premier as soon as he moved to Chapare.

When was that? Don Santiago couldn't remember exactly. Late 1970s, perhaps. Evo was only a young lad back then.

'Lived with his brother, Hugo.' He's a teacher now, if Don Santiago wasn't mistaken.

The two brothers lived down near the swamp, the old man explains, waving his skinny hand to a boggy wetland beyond the village limits. It flooded, so they had to abandon the house. That would explain the new property back down the road. And the stilts too.

What was he like, Evo, as a person? 'A hard worker,' comes the reply. Don Santiago used to buy produce from the brothers and sell it on at the local market. 'Always popular with the locals.' An afterthought occurs to him. 'Fine footballer as well. The best striker that Real Porteño, the village team, ever had.'

The memory of Evo charging down the wing with a football at his feet loosens the old farmer's tongue. The *compañero* was always involved in the union movement, did I know? That was back when the coca clampdown was just picking up. There were always clashes with the police. One time, the anti-drugs squad arrested the future president and bundled him into the back of their van. The villagers were incensed. For the first time, a smile appears on Don Santiago's wrinkled face. They rushed the van. The police had to throw Evo out of the back. Then they fled into the forest. Don Santiago is laughing uproariously now. Could I guess where the van ended up? In the river. The villagers upended it and tipped it in. He claps his hands at the memory, rocking back and forth, convulsed with laughter as though hearing his own story for the first time.

Evo's star was rising, and in the mid-1980s he moved away to Cochabamba, a larger and more temperate city in the Andean foothills. Don Santiago has not heard from his 'intimate friend' since. He wants to get his phone number.

Why? He'd like to request a nurse for the village and a couple more teachers. A downcast expression replaces his good humour. People are saying Evo has forgotten his roots. Don Santiago won't tolerate such talk. But a full-time nurse, he admits, wouldn't go amiss.

Cochabamba

Four peasant farmers are waiting for *compañero* Omar at the roadside. When the local senator steps from the mud-splashed taxi, they greet him with gap-toothed smiles and the bear hugs of old veterans in arms. These are the survivors of the Water War.

On the drive out to Vinto Chico, Omar had provided me with a potted version of their conflict. The villain of the piece was the evil-sounding Bechtel, a multinational utility company based in California. Allied with them were the collaborators in Cochabamba's municipal government. Together, they hatched up a covetous plan to privatise the water system, bump up prices and sit back as the money rolled in. Only, the peasants revolted and spoilt their plans. With pitchforks and roadblocks, they held the city under siege. First in the barricade was the ace striker from Real Porteño. Omar certainly has the script off pat.

The senator's companions lead us along a path of clogging mud alongside a flat-bellied field of carrots. To our left, the snow-sprinkled *cordillera* sweeps upwards from the Arcadian valley floor, curving gently skywards like a quarterpipe jump ramp in a skateboard park. Rivulets of melting ice trickle down its serpentine slopes. A freshly dug ditch runs parallel to the squelching pathway, terminating at a new wellhead.

'Not bad, eh?' says Evaristo, the sprightliest of the peasant delegation and its apparent spokesperson, as he points at the brick pump house.

Omar appears impressed. He inquires about technicalities such as valve pressure and irrigation channels. The farmers answer in exact terms, keen to evidence the professionalism of their construction to the senatorial inspector. All that's required is a connection to the electric grid. Without that, the pump won't work.

'I'm sure we can twist some arms,' the senator responds jovially. It's the answer the delegation is hoping for. With satisfied expressions, the group plods back along the gluey walkway towards the road.

As we walk, I fall into conversation with Evaristo. He's not easy to understand. Accustomed to speaking in Quechua, his Spanish is laboured. Coupled with that, he has a masticated ball of coca leaves the size of a large gobstopper wedged into the side of his mouth.

'We practise somehing we cawl *usos y costumbres* here,' he slurs.

'*Usos y costumbres*?' I respond, unclear whether I've heard him right.

'Exactwe. It's somehing our grandpawents passed down to us. It dates bwack phousands of years.'

He spits, and a globule of brackish green saliva arches through the air, splattering on the sprouting leafs of a carrot. Ridding his mouth of excess coca mucus temporarily improves his pronunciation: 'For the Incas, water was a community good, a gift of God. We believe it should be shared by everyone. How can a Yankee company say they own what has always been free and communal?' The notion baffles him.

'Even if the water's free, surely the well isn't?'

It's an argument I'd heard the defenders of water privatisation use. Collecting, cleaning, delivering and disposing of water requires money. Its finances forever veering on bankruptcy, the Bolivian Government can't or won't pay. Private investors therefore put up the cash to make it happen, collecting their money back through tariffs and charges. It's a lucrative business.

'Of course de well cwosts money,' responds Evaristo, his diction regressing towards the incomprehensible with every extra chew.

He appears mildly exasperated by my failure to grasp basic economics. Slowly, the Quechua-speaking farmer spells it out for me. The well set them back fifteen thousand US dollars. All the families on their side of the village chipped in equally towards the cost. Labour was also dished out evenly among the community, with each household allotted its quota of trench to dig: 'Phat way, we dwon't conswede the wight to our water.'

The irrigation trench is ready bar one short stretch. We pass a bare-chested man and his son, ankle-deep in soggy mud, shovelling away in earnest. Theirs is the last section. Laggards, it seems, are common to all workplaces, whether capitalist or communitarian.

We exit the path onto the tarmac road at the very top of the village. Immediately across from us lies a lopsided brick building that houses the local radio station. Only one in thirty Bolivians has a television, but almost every house, however humble, has a radio. Today, Radio Vinto Chico is mostly airing dreamy Andean pipe music. During the Water War and subsequent mobilisations, stations such as these turned into military-like nerve centres of information.

In an open yard behind the two-storey station, a trestle table has been erected on an open-air veranda. Three chairs and a bench surround it. The table is laid with two plastic washing-up bowls and a bucket. The delegation sits round expectantly. A salad of onions and tomatoes fills one bowl. Boiled potatoes with flaking skins steam in the other. The senator spears a spud with a fork and swallows it whole. Greedily, we tuck in after him.

Evaristo picks up a flat wooden bowl from a nearby shelf, runs his hand over it in a feigned concern for cleanliness and dunks it in the bucket. His hand emerges dripping with a sweet-smelling, snot-yellow liquid.

'Aah, *chicha!*' the senator exclaims heartily. The spokesman hands his congressional colleague the brimming bowl. He tips a fraction on the floor for Pachamama, Mother Earth, and downs the rest in one swig. The senator is not one for half measures. Nor is the delegation. Long after the potatoes have grown cold, the bowl is still being dunked and the bucket refilled.

Between the shouting and singing, someone brings up the subject of a letter to the electricity company. Omar had suggested the idea back at the well as a precursor to more violent arm-twisting.

'Yes, *compañeros,*' the sozzled senator bellows, 'To business!' Letting out a well-fed belch, he reaches for his leather computer bag. Onto the messy tabletop, strewn now with discarded potato peelings and spilt *chicha,* he plonks a state-of-the-art laptop.

It takes a moment or two for him to find the 'on' button. Once he does, the machine starts whirring, and the senatorial scribe finds his stride.

'*Estimado Señor Gerente . . .*' he starts.

'Very good, *compañero,*' Evaristo opines.

'Yes,' nods Don Pascual, the oldest and shrewdest of the peasant delegates, 'that's the tone.'

The senator reads as he types, a laboured affair of fingers and thumbs and regular deletes. 'On behalf of the Vinto Chico division of the Provincial Federation of Regantes and Community Systems of Drinking Water' – *drunken applause* – 'kindly request . . .'

'Wouldn't "demand" be better?'

'No, the *compañero* knows best. Best to "request".'

'*Chicha,* anyone?'

' . . . at your earliest convenience . . .'

Amid a noisy hubbub of comments and clapping, the one-page letter eventually gets written. Evaristo's full name and identification number is included at the bottom beside those of the senator. A time is set for him to pass by the office to sign the request. More *chicha* arrives, and the success of the letter is toasted with an extra large portion for Pachamama.

His computer still open, the senator double-clicks the Google Earth icon. He ushers the farmers to gather round. Inebriated, they stagger to their feet and form a semi-circle around the screen. Childlike hoots of amusement go up as the cursor on the downloaded satellite-mapping programme zooms in: Bolivia, Cochabamba, Vinto Chico, the stream at the bottom of the lane. The group's excitement frightens the fattened gerbils, who peer nervously through the wire meshing of their cage across the yard.

Seeing the halcyon village paraded from space has got the delegation all worked up. In a frenzy of excitement, they clamour to know what else the wonder machine can do. Pointing fingers smudge starchy prints across the computer's screen. 'Go on, go on, show us.' Enjoying the attention, the senator clicks on a folder of his recent holiday photos to London. The pixels of a snapshot unscramble themselves to reveal a double-decker bus. The farmers think it's hysterical and laugh raucously. Big Ben. The River Thames. A beefeater outside Buckingham Palace. Each photo meets with guffaws and a flurry of comments in animated Quechua. The laughter stops with the picture of a gravestone.

'Karl Marx's tomb. Been there?' The politician is horrified to learn that I haven't and switches folders immediately.

Snaps of the senator's trip to southern Chile appear next on screen. The Mapuche Indians are losing their traditional lands to commercial foresters, Omar comments. The delegates grunt in gruff solidarity as he scans through pictures of the pony-tailed Patagonians and their endangered woodland. For a brief moment, sobriety reigns. Then the laptop's battery packs up, and the joking ribaldry returns.

As darkness descends and the bucket empties itself once more, the battle stories begin. The friends laugh and bicker, their tales growing longer and more lavish with each telling. The name 'Bechtel' incites drunken jeers around the table. The *compañero* senator is explaining how the company issued a multi-million-dollar claim for breach of contract. Everyone boos, as if the villain in a children's play has just walked on stage. The case was then withdrawn. Bawdy mockery breaks out. Bechtel eventually washed its hands of the troublesome concession, selling it for the token sum of one *boliviano* (0.002 pence). Evaristo burps, unleashing infectious, thigh-slapping laughter throughout the group.

The senator needs to go. His wife has supper ready and will box his ears if he's any later or any drunker than he already is. Wobbling to his feet, he reaches into his pocket and pulls out a bronze coin. Slamming it on the tabletop, he shouts defiantly into the night. 'Here's your one, lousy *boliviano*, Mr Bechtel!'

We all cheer, and the cry goes up for another bucket of *chicha*.

Jim Schultz, an American with a long face and a sharp mind, is checking the proofs of his new book. Its pages deal with the modern-day looting of Bolivia by foreign companies. A long-term resident of Bolivia, Jim runs a think-tank from a third-floor office not far from Cochabamba's central square. He'd had a bird's-eye view of the Water War.

After my outing with Omar and his fellow critics of capitalism, I pop by the next day to ask his opinion on what economic system is best for Bolivia. His starting position is clear: Bolivia needs foreign investment. No sensible economist would say otherwise. What matters are the 'rules of the game.' In Bolivia's case, the rules have always been skewed. The rich get richer, and the poor get to eat potatoes.

For two decades, the country became the lab rat of technocrats in Washington. Suited executives from lending organisations such as the World Bank would fly down, business class, to preach 'free-market fundamentalism'. The experiment failed. Bolivia emerged from privatisation poorer than before. And without its family silver.

'Imagine two people buy a car, but only one of the two gets to drive it.'

As with Evaristo, Jim believes in putting things simply.

'The other pays for the petrol, yet still has to walk. That, in essence, was the deal Bolivia struck with its foreign creditors.'

The exasperation of everyday Bolivians has been a long time in coming. For centuries, the deal was even worse. They not only had to pay in full for the car, they had to build it, polish it and even push it when their master wanted to go for a drive.

The reason why Bolivia remains stubbornly at the bottom of all wealth-creating indices is not because its citizens are stupid, Jim insists. It is because they got ripped off – truly, royally, superlatively ripped off. To understand the full extent of the swindle, I only had to visit the Cerro Rico, the Rich Mountain, in Potosí.

'Never has a mountain been more aptly, or more tragically, named.'

I head off to buy a bus ticket.

Potosí

Simón Bolívar's entry into Potosí was somewhat more dramatic than mine. Three grim-faced taxi drivers comprised my welcoming party at the bus station. The Great Liberator had been met with a troupe of dancing natives, pealing church bells and a triumphal march through the city.

Never one to pass up a party, Bolívar threw himself into the victory celebrations with gusto. He deserved it. Spanish America lay at his feet. After the fabulous festivities began to fade, the patriot leader set off up the Cerro Rico to survey the spoils. Accompanied by his full entourage, he travelled over the mountain's lower reaches by mule. Beside him rode Antonio José de Sucre, vanquisher of the last royalist army at Ayacucho and Bolívar's successor as president of the independent republic of Bolivia.

Nearing the summit, the party was forced to dismount. Scrambling up the loose shingle, panting for breath in the thin mountain air, they finally reached the summit. Heads in the clouds, a toast was called. The flags of independence were hoisted and blew like foresails in the ice-cold wind. Standing there on the spine of the Andes, nothing but barren mountain ridges as far as the eye could see, Bolívar had arrived at his own zenith. The fact was not lost on him:

As for me, with my feet on this mountain called Potosí, whose enormously rich veins were for three hundred years the treasury of Spain, I regard this opulence as nothing when I compare it to the glory of having carried the standard of freedom victoriously from the burning shores of the Orinoco to fix it here, on the peak of the mountain, whose breast is the wonder and the envy of the universe.

Today, there is little to envy about Potosí. Among the poorest provinces in South America's poorest country, life doesn't get much grimmer. The grey, grassless slagheap of Cerro Rico, specked with dirt browns and rust iron reds, looms ever present over the cowering town. Brittle, impoverished housing stretches up the hillsides, built intentionally low to ward off the worst of the cold. The narrow streets are modelled on a pinball machine, all sharp corners and plunging gradients.

Ageing cars creak up and down the mountainside. Small boys yell unintelligible directions from bus doorways. Men urinate in the street. Babies stare at the world from shoulder level, wrapped tight in their mothers' deliriously patterned shawls. Pigs snort in the rubbish. Skeletal animal foetuses, destined for religious rituals, hang like dried fish from market stalls. The town's forty-plus churches stand forlorn and empty, traces of a past that *Potosinos* would prefer to forget.

The city is at its grimmest in San Cristóbal, the poor man's hillside district where the miners live and their wives mourn. Potosí is a city of widows. Few husbands make it into middle age, their wheezing lungs eaten away by asbestos and silicosis.

At the district's dilapidated health centre, a queue of patients waits wearily outside. A harried nurse checks their papers at the door. Inside, a baby with tuberculosis coughs plaintively into his mother's breast. A gaunt old woman, weak with malnutrition, sits slumped on a bench. The dank waiting room is crowded despite the early hour. Abscesses await lancing. Rotting teeth ache. Stomach cramps and skin diseases hold out hope for the proper pills and medicine.

No one has money to pay. A paunchy consultant doctor, whose limbs are shivering in spite of an Arctic duffel coat and homemade fingerless mittens, calls for the next patient. Cuban and not yet acclimatised, the Havana exile is one of the free medics gifted by his socialist homeland in exchange for cheap Bolivian gas.

Through the waiting room's cracked window sounds the deep boom of a distant explosion. Not a soul flinches. The residents of San Cristóbal have grown deaf to the detonation of dynamite.

The noise takes me back to my first visit to Potosí, ten years earlier. A bright-eyed backpacker, with a misplaced attachment to tie-dye trousers, I'd followed Bolívar up the Cerro Rico. As I stopped by a mine shaft, a scraggly ten-year-old offered to guide me inside. I remember it as if it were yesterday; the wet touch of the slimy walls, the infernal heat, the myriad tunnels, the open shafts, the thin air, the rasp in my throat, the ache in my back, the sense of claustrophobia, the soot-faced miners. I survived an hour. Most shifts last eight or more.

Stamped foremost in my memory is the ghoulish figure of *El Tio*, The Uncle. God of the Underworld, the diabolic figure was tucked away in the murky nook of a cavernous shrine. Ringed with unlit candles, his feet were covered in curling coca leaves and empty beer bottles, gifts from his miner supplicants. A pair of red horns poked from his grotesquely malformed head. From his grinning, toothless mouth drooped the stubs of unfiltered cigarettes. Evil staring eyes of broken coloured glass bored into his skull.

As naked as the day he was sculpted, the black stone Lucifer was equipped with an enormous, bulbous penis. Two foot long and pointing insolently at the heavens, *El Tio*'s erect member symbolised the mountain's supposed virility. The days of dallying with the Devil are long gone though. He may still be stiff as a young buck, but *El Tio*'s seed is sadly spent. No longer do streams of silver and gold flow down Cerro Rico's flanks. Tin, zinc and misers' metals are all that remain after a night's carousing with the washed-out Beelzebub.

From San Cristóbal, I retrace my steps up the desolate mountainside. On the way, I dawdle a while at a flat-roofed shed selling mining materials. The lower shelves are stocked with the usual fare: hard hats, electric lamps, battery packs, matches, plastic overalls, ninety-six-proof spirits. Lurking on the higher shelves is a veritable terrorist treasure trove. For the princely sum of seventeen *bolivianos* (£1.20), the proprietor hands me two eight-inch sticks of dynamite, a bag of ammonium nitrate, a detonator and a metre-length fuse. As gift-bearing goes, I feel well armed.

Climbing up a gravel path that skirts the Cerro Rico, I stop by one of the bleak rabbit-hole entrances that perforate the mountain's slopes. Standing in for my young guide of yesteryear is another scrawny youngster. A blackened cap hides his face. Two holes in the knees of his ragged trousers wink open and closed as he walks.

Thirteen years old, Julio is employed by the Unificara Cooperative at the Candelaria mine. His job is to transfer the excavated rocks from the tunnel opening to a nearby collection point. The miners' findings arrive in open-cast wagons weighing half a tonne, which Julio shoves and shoulders to the end of a wobbly twin-rail track. There they are tipped into an aggregates lorry by two adult men, and the contents are taken off for sorting. Deep within the mountain, his three older brothers are digging diligently.

Miners start young in Potosí. In school holidays, as now, the number of child labourers shoots up. In good years, when metal prices are high, their teachers even join them.

Basillo is another of Cerro Rico's school-age navvies. The eldest son of a now fatherless family, his career as a miner began soon after his fifteenth birthday. Although he suffers back pain and his nose sometimes bleeds for days, he still heads off to the mine every morning. He knows that if he doesn't his mother and three siblings will go hungry.

On my third day in Potosí, I travel back up the mountain to speak with him. Elena, his older sister, answers the door of their shack. Basillo is not at home, she informs me, a nine-month-old baby suctioned fast to her breast. He's on the early shift this week. He'll be back after lunch if I'd like to wait. What did I want with her brother anyway?

I'd heard about Basillo's starring role in a recent documentary about child miners. I was hoping he might speak with me. My aspiration brings a shake of the head from his single-mum sister: 'He wants nothing more to do with foreigners, I'm afraid.' The response takes me by surprise. It's not her place to explain why.

Was I a journalist? 'Yes.' Well, perhaps her mother might offer more details. Leaving me at the door, she wanders off behind the house to find her.

Elena returns several minutes later with a frail old lady leaning on her arm. The woman's hands are covered in soot, and she offers me her forearm to shake. Appearing more frail than her fifty years would suggest, Basillo's mother is dressed in the traditional garb of a Bolivian *cholita:* a girded, thigh-length skirt above a hip-enhancing mound of lace petticoats; a discoloured white apron over a wool-knit jumper; thick brown socks pulled up to her knees; navy square-toed sandals caked with dirt; and a black broad-rimmed bowler hat on her head. Both women wear their long black hair in carefully woven plaits.

The sun is high, and we sit on a dusty ledge outside her house. Twenty feet away lies the mine's entrance, a sepulchral hole in the mountainside. In the absence of any seats, we make do with some bench-sized boulders. Elena recounts how her mother was taken on by the mining cooperative as a watchwoman after her husband's death. She's paid to clean the mine site and guard the entrance, keeping an eye out for the pilferers and wastrels who roam the mountain after dark. The job comes with accommodation, which comprises one half of the cooperative's single-room storeroom. Her guard duty earns her a paltry stipend. She tops this up with scraps from the miners' wagons. Together with Elena's help, the two women can collect enough surplus rubble to fill a lorry-load three or four times a year. All the same, without Basillo's income, the family would more than likely starve.

As Elena's mother moves to say something, a group of monosyllabic miners saunters over. On their morning break, they want the boulders back. Without a word, the women concede the space in the sun and withdraw to their storeroom hovel.

The doorway is so low that even the diminutive Elena has to bend at the knees to avoid knocking her head. With an inconsonant propriety, her mother removes her hat as she crosses the threshold. According to the blue lettering painted on the mantle, the multi-purpose building also doubles as an emergency health station.

Constructed from concrete breeze blocks and corrugated plastic, the squalid room reeks of damp. Not only is there no medical equipment, but there's no running water, heating or natural light either.

A dirty brown sheet held up by a piece of string separates the family's half of the house from the miners' spades and oil drums. We sit facing one another on the room's two beds. Their paper-thin mattresses are covered with sheets of clear plastic to keep off the dust that hangs thick in the air. The family's sleeping arrangements occupy most of the floor space. Filling the remainder of their cramped quarters are a small gas stove, a rack for vegetables, a wooden shelf and a low, single-door cupboard. Dirty pots and pans lie jumbled in a bucket of puddle-brown water beneath the shelf. A frying pan, half full of leftover rice, hangs by a nail on the wall. Beside it, a colourful baby chair is suspended from a second nail. Amid so much gloom, the wall hangings are almost decorative.

Elena's mother speaks only Quechua, so her daughter translates. When the film-makers came, she says, they promised the family a small house of their own and provisions to start a simple corner-shop. A year on and neither has materialised.

The elderly widow begins to cry. Between her sniffled sobs, she explains how her neighbours further down the mountain suspect her of pocketing a small fortune. A jealous gang of them even tried attacking her recently. Now she's too afraid to leave the mine site. Did I think she'd stay in this windowless shack one day more if she had a hoard of cash under the bed? The film, she blurts, has brought them nothing but bad luck.

So they've received no money at all, then? A few months ago, Basillo did get a cheque for $30. It came in an envelope with a postage stamp from the United States of America. Inside was a photo. She shows me a snapshot of a smiling mom and pop from Iowa with two identikit children, all sitting with backs straight on a garden bench. The bank tellers in town told Basillo it would cost $59 to cash the cheque. He still keeps it folded up in his wallet, just in case their policy changes.

Later, back at my hostel, I check the documentary's promotional website. *Devil's Miner* has helped raise more than 1 million euros in charitable donations. A six-year programme is apparently being launched to get four hundred and fifty children 'out of the mines for good.' My mind turns to Basillo and the loss-making cheque he guards so preciously. If and when the promised assistance arrives, Elena's brother will probably be too old to qualify. Even *El Tio* would be challenged to come up with a more diabolical irony.

Oruru Province

Away from Potosí, life is little better in Bolivia's other mining towns. Drudgery broken by occasional drunkenness is the norm. Carnival provides the only escape in the miners' annual calendar. For a week, they can relax and dance and eat their fill. Fireworks stand in for dynamite. Headdresses replace hard hats. And all the while, the ninety-six-proof bottles fly off the shelves.

Nowhere are the festivities more lavish than in the usually bleak altiplano town of Oruru, the proud possessor of Bolivia's only commercial smelter. For a week, its dingy sidewalks are lit up with silvery bunting, dancing dragons and mini-skirted carnival queens. From early morning until sundown, twenty thousand dancers pass below the tiered stand where I'm sitting. Their joyful, dancing marches whisk them down the twisting streets. On their tails stride their private carnival bands, accompanying their every twirl with blasting trumpets and clashing cymbals.

To add spice to the spectacle, rival groups of spectators keep up an unremitting water fight. Multicoloured balloons, filled from the tap, sail above the dancers in an arching rainbow of dampness. Dizzy from the dancing and drenched from the battery of balloons, I leave the spectacle around midnight. The carnival continues until the early hours. By dawn, three miners are dead from alcohol poisoning. The rest of the town is in bed nursing a shared hangover.

A hardened group of stalwarts make it onto the midday bus with me to nearby Llallagua. As we pull out of bleary-eyed Oruru, a middle-aged woman with workhorse thighs and a curly bouffant steps on. She is carrying a satchel and is smartly attired in a dark blue nylon trouser suit.

'Esteemed passengers,' she shouts out, in the commanding voice of a sports coach, 'with the utmost gratitude for your patience . . .'

Throughout South America, the sales pitches all start the same. On local buses, most vendors get on at one stop and off at the next, content to have sold a stick of chewing gum or a bar of chocolate in the interim. On intercity buses, their natural loquaciousness has time for fuller expression.

Bolivians certainly blag with the best of them. A multipurpose vegetable peeler or compendium of aphrodisiac recipes can keep their silvery tongues wagging for hours. The suited saleswoman to Llallagua is no exception. Elbowing a stage for herself among the standing passengers, she begins with the build-up for her one-time-only deal. Can we all see the sachet in her hand? Within this humble packet lies a herbal oil sourced from the depths of the Amazon. Its healing properties, she need hardly point out, are nothing short of miraculous. Apply twice a day and we judicious travellers can say goodbye to arthritis and acne, farewell to leg cramps and varicose veins.

The captive audience gradually becomes a captivated one too. Spurious test results are quoted. Technical terms are thrown in. Volunteers are called on. The lotion burns, madam? Very good: it's a sign the worm extract is working. Cat's Nail might not appear on any medical registries, but the saleswoman knows her audience well. Homoeopathy and hope both sell well in the altiplano.

As the peddler pharmacist dishes out samples, I seek distraction in a thin autobiographical volume I'd purchased at a second-hand bookshop in Oruru. *If You Allow Me to Speak* describes the life and times of Domitila Barrios, a miner's wife from Llallagua. Her days start at 4 a.m. and her husband's shortly afterwards. They live in a workers' compound of paper-thin walls, communal lavatories and numbing poverty. In her mid-twenties, she joined the Housewives Committee. Far from baking cakes and apple pies, as the name might imply, their coffee mornings were spent thrashing through the collected works of Marx and Engels. A convert to militant socialism, her new-found beliefs bring her abuse from the 'company' and stints behind bars. When the miners went on strike, she saw her husband's comrades mown down by soldiers' bullets.

Domitila's political convictions also led her to a solitary conclusion: that Bolivia's liberation rests in freeing itself from the 'yoke of imperialism' and putting 'a worker like us in power'. Only then, she predicted, 'will we have the conditions to achieve a complete liberation'.

Nearly three decades have passed since Domitila's account, and her working-class president is in power. Stepping off in Llallagua, though, the liberated masses are hard to spot. The only triumphant workers are those in the propagandistic murals that coat the town's walls. There are no Stakhanovites in Llallagua's sorry streets, only morose market sellers and the great unemployed. The company-built compounds remain in place, although sinking now with subsidence. The town's water supplies only operate half the week, and then just for three hours at a time.

Up on the hillside, in the severed crevice of the Siglo Veinte mine, the workers are at least free. Yet the term is relative. Laid off when the state mining company went bust, they are now free to organise themselves, free from oppressive paymasters and free of the state crackdowns that so dogged Domitila. But they are still bound by poverty. They are still slaves to the mountain. And, most depressing of all, they are still trapped in accursed Llallagua with only a tub of Cat's Nail for hope.

I call in on Héctor Solis, Llallagua's one-time mayor and a lobbyist for the town's development. The bearded former official is sitting in his office at the Centre for the Promotion of Mining, a non-governmental agency burdened with a task of Kafkaesque absurdity. At the turn of the last century, Llallagua was home to the richest mine in the world, he explains. But even the optimistic Señor Solis has to admit that Llallagua's days are numbered. Yields are low, technology dismal and safety standards atrocious. But, yes, the workers are technically free.

Up the road and over the mountains, conditions in Huanuni are little better. A town of open sewers and stray dogs, only the engorged carrion birds look to be doing well. The mine is easy enough to find, located as it is at the source of Huanuni's pestilent, rubbish-strewn river. I cadge a tour from Roman Manzano, the chief safety officer. He is anxious to expound the security precautions around the newly nationalised site. As if on cue, a group of workers appear from the ventilated mineshaft in standard-issue helmets and anti-toxic mouth guards. 'And the soldiers?' I ask, having spotted several armed units of military personnel dotted around the mine.

'Oh, they're here to protect the workers,' the safety officer responds. And there was me thinking that was his job.

Government control of the Huanuni mine had not come easy. Four months beforehand, sixteen people had been killed in clashes between miners and the Army. Evo had ordered the troops in. On the steps of the union office, beneath a mural of Che Guevara, Simón Tito gives me his version of events. Until recently, the mountain was divvied up between a British-owned company and worker-led cooperatives. For thirty years, Simón belonged to the latter. Long-standing conflicts between the *cooperativistas* and the company eventually bubbled over. The government decided to step in. Overnight, miners like Simón were obligated to join the state payroll. He misses not working independently but admits the set hours and regular monthly wage make for a welcome change. The pension, he hopes, might be better too. A foghorn signals the start of his shift. The Devil calls. He'd best be off.

Nicolas Collareta is less content with the new arrangement. Forty years old, he's been working the upper levels of Huanuni mine since he was twelve. I find him in his cooperative's headquarters, playing cards with friends on a bug-infested mattress. He and fifteen hundred fellow miners refused to accept the government's new conditions.

The warehouse headquarters nowadays serves as part dormitory, part soup kitchen. The disgruntled miners are digging in for the long haul. A week later, I'd see them on hunger strike on the steps of San Francisco church in La Paz. Five men would climb up beside the baroque carvings and chain themselves to the windowsills. A grandmother would station herself in an open coffin with the epitaph 'Give Us Back Our Work!' engraved on the lid.

At the time of my visit, the protestors are busy strategising their next step. They are listening to radio reports of current negotiations with the government. The news is not good. The likes of Simón are 'spineless turncoats' in Nicolas's mind.

'We'd rather die than live as slaves to the company again.' Defiantly, the redundant cooperative member throws down a King of Clubs to win the trick. He scoops up the playing cards, the back of which are designed to look like $100 bills.

Skirmishes in the mountains are not the worst of Evo's worries. In the eastern lowlands, his socialist reforms are brewing civil war.

Santa Cruz

Landslides and floods still bedevil the highways heading east. Bolívar and his indomitable troops would have waded across dauntlessly. I take advantage of the travel revolution and hop on a plane.

In the city of Santa Cruz, the heartbeat of Bolivia's oil-rich east, the great and the good are sitting in rows of white plastic chairs. Stubbornly refusing to sweat, bejewelled wives and their daughters are stoically fanning themselves against the sticky night air. The men pull at their collars and pat their foreheads with folded handkerchiefs.

A deep voice crackles out over the loudspeaker. We are invited to stand. A pre-recorded band strikes up, and the three hundred distinguished guests break out in a rousing version of the provincial anthem. Returning to our seats again, we watch this year's successful graduates of the Pro-Santa Cruz Civic Committee's School of Leadership step up to collect their certificates. Blessed with the confidence of youth and high-yield trust funds, they approach the rostrum with purposeful strides. Diploma in hand, each smiles professionally at the cub reporter from the local paper. Barely out of high school, the cream of the Santa Cruz crop is already primed for the public stage.

Santa Cruz has the good fortune of being a resource-rich province in a dirt-poor country. After the ceremony, Mario Suarez, the refined doyen of the Civic Committee's culture department, takes me through the numbers. The province occupies over two-fifths of the country's territory, represents more than a third of its industrial activity and produces in excess of half its exports. The charming Señor Suarez doesn't mention that its residents are also predominantly of European stock. He doesn't need to. The aquiline noses, clear eyes and blond rinses of the graduates' families say it all.

The eastern province might boast an enviable opulence today, but a century ago it was a ramshackle outpost rotting in the heat. And then it struck oil. The black gold propelled it from a tropical backwater to Bolivia's petrodollar capital. Today, chunky four-by-four jeeps ply up the capital city's handsome avenues, and business parks spread like lichen through its suburbs.

Under Evo, the pro-indigenous Movement Towards Socialism thinks it is high time the *Cruceños* started sharing. The white folk in Santa Cruz aren't convinced. Pedro Youhio, for one, won't budge an inch. The portly president of the province's main business lobby derides the government's meddling. He's looking out from his ninth-floor office, a self-righteous sense of ownership about him, as if he'd built the glass tower himself. Santa Cruz's success is all to do with its entrepreneurial spirit. Where was the central government when his forefathers were breaking their backs in this wilderness? An answer pops into my head. *In the land department, signing over vast tracts of indigenous land.* I leave it unsaid. It's not the answer he has in mind anyway.

'Nowhere,' he clarifies for me. Now the province has built itself up with its own bare hands, the bloodsucking ingrates in La Paz want in on the action. Not only is it unfair, it's bad for business. What foreign companies will invest when the government could just come along and rip up their contracts at any moment?

In the coffee shop at the corner of Santa Cruz's main square, more questions are being asked. The silver-haired representative for Camba Nation wants to know what the citizens of Santa Cruz have in common with Evo's Bolivia.

They're both Bolivians? For the second time in one morning, I judge it best to keep my thoughts to myself. Camba Nation is not big on national patriotism. Flag-burning is more its style.

'Nothing at all,' confirms Angel Sandoval, the spokesperson.

Very occasionally, *Cruceños* don't just answer with an obstinate negative. When it comes to the theme of political autonomy, referendums and spot polls always return with a near universal 'yes' vote. Greater regional freedom is what they want. In the civic committees and business lobbies they dress it up in democratic terms: bringing power closer to the people, cutting out wasteful bureaucracy, responding to local needs, et cetera. But behind closed doors, no one denies it's really about the money. Santa Cruz and its energy-rich neighbours are fed up with the taxman struggling back to La Paz under the weight of all their profits. If they have to pay up, they'd rather the collector didn't have to travel so far.

Señor Sandoval of Camba Nation bites into a cream éclair. The time for talking is over. Bolivia's eastern provinces should go it alone. Leave the *Collas,* the highlanders, to their llamas and Leninism. If Evo and his 'indigenous fundamentalists' wish to return to some pre-capitalist paradise, let them go. He and his lowland cohorts will cope just fine by themselves. A Bolivian Quebec, he has in mind.

When he sat down to write the country's first constitution, Bolívar had envisioned a harmonised system of government. 'Wealth was insignificant in the past,' the Liberator had lectured Bolivia's first legislators, 'even more so than in the present.' But then the state-builder hadn't had Mammon's servants hovering over him. Evo, on the other hand, does.

Bolivia's indigenous president has no diploma to wave at his opponents. What he learned about leadership, he picked up fighting beside his fellow *cocaleros* and *campesinos.* His qualifications rest in his personal charisma and the support of Bolivia's poor and marginalised. His first steps in power augmented both. He nationalised the country's gas fields and cut politicians' salaries. But five hundred years of exclusion cannot be turned around in an instant, especially with the non-cooperation of the rich eastern provinces.

Wealth *is* significant, maybe not for legislators, but certainly for the millions of Bolivians who struggle to feed their families. But significant too are hope and dignity. The day will come when Bolivia's impoverished majority wake up and realise they are still poor. But now they've tasted what it is to walk tall. No more will they stoop in subservience.

Copacabana

Back in La Paz, I take a day trip to the lakeside town of Copacabana on the craggy mountain border with Peru. Prayers ushered me into Bolivia, and prayers will usher me out.

On the shores of Lake Titicaca, a veritable sea in the sky, resides Bolivia's most revered virgin saint. Pilgrims travel from all over the country to have her bless their newly purchased automobiles. They park outside the Moorish cathedral, creating a car showroom on the sacred steps. Around the silver hubcaps and shining spoilers walks a circumambulatory priest. Reaching into his plastic wash bucket of holy water, he baptises each vehicle with a shower of sanctified sprinkles. At the end of each lap, the cassocked cleric orders the bonnet open and consecrates the engine. Then a short perfunctory prayer, for safe travelling and vigilance behind the wheel. Cocooned in the embrace of the Virgin of Copacabana, the devotees speed off home with horns tooting and wheels spinning.

On a rocky outcrop above the town, a group of six *cholitas* sit in a circle. A picnic rug is spread out between them, covered with coca leaves and glasses of beer. Wrapped in shawls of rough-hewn sheep wool, they are conducting their own private ceremony. If Pachamama, in her munificence, might only bless them with a bountiful harvest, a healthy family, a sober husband.

The chill breeze across Lake Titicaca carries tidings of transformation for Bolivia: a stir from Queen Illimani, a rumble from Mother Earth, a whisper from the Virgin of Copacabana. The female trinity is mobilising. But their ear is being pulled. Down the spine of the Andes, there are other women praying too.

2

SUFFERING SERVANTS
Chile and gender

The house of the Tyrant echoed with the howls and weeping of countless wretched women.
SIMÓN BOLÍVAR, 'MANIFESTO TO THE NATIONS OF THE WORLD', 1813

Santiago, Plaza de Armas

Below the Plaza de Armas, a molten pool of people is bubbling. Hot and bothered metro-goers gush from suffocating train carriages onto the crammed platform. Reluctantly, I step into the sweltering flow of human lava, squashing in behind a group of gingham-clad convent girls and their whiskery schoolmistress. The crowd is rumpling the teacher's equanimity and creasing her students' pressed blazers. Tucking into their slipstream, I edge slowly towards the elevator.

At the platform end, a frothing queue of overheated passengers is threatening to boil over. One by one, we escape skywards on the mechanised stairs, away from the station's simmering depths. From behind, the metallic screech of a braking train reverberates up the thick tunnel walls. The warm underground air tastes stale and recycled. It's a relief when we eventually spew out above ground and into the busy square above.

Sundays in South America are rarely so infernal. Across the continent, the Sabbath is guarded as a private, slow-paced affair; the preserve of late-morning lie-ins, long family lunches and snoozes in the shade. Faith, habit, illness or guilt might see a Mass thrown in too. But total inactivity is generally the ideal. Shops close, and public transport creaks along with a skeletal service. I know because these are the times on my travels that I feel most abandoned, when city centres turn into ghost towns and only homeless drunks join the tourists roaming the streets. It's a good day, in my experience, for long-distance bus journeys.

Chile guards its Sunday shutdown as jealously as the next. Only two motives can wrest it from its sacred slumbers. Both are religious rites: a local football derby (of which there are plenty) and a religious procession (of which there are even more). Nothing quite stirs South America's faithful as seeing their favourite saint on walkabout.

Today it's the Virgin of Carmen's chance for an airing. Christened 'Mother of Chile' by the independence hero, Bernardo O'Higgins, she's been faithfully watching over this coastline of a country for almost two centuries. As patron of the armed forces, she's also seen them through battles, border wars and, most recently, General Augusto Pinochet's seventeen-year dictatorship.

At the first gust of fresh air, my convent guides are swallowed up by the masses. Disorientated, I search out a vantage point above the crowd. Discovering one in the form of a sturdy iron dustbin, I climb up. Santiago's emblematic square opens out before me. Dominating its north corner, the capital's eighteenth-century cathedral spurts upwards with Romanesque arrogance towards overcast skies. A frightened cluster of white-robed priests huddle on its steps, a clerical island amid a sea of laity.

To my left, a giant-sized Pedro de Valdivia wades through the crowds astride a muscular bronze horse. In front, steering a shaky course through the waves of people, sail carts of candyfloss vendors and peanut roasters. The central bandstand, usually full of chess-playing pensioners, floats empty on the swell. Ensconced around the square's edge stand the courts of law and the command centres of government. Flags fly from their rooftop masts in the Virgin's honour.

The only person apparently oblivious to the commotion is the saint herself. From a raised dais in the centre of the square, she serenely surveys the hubbub around her. A spherical silver crown anoints her head. All curves and counterpoints, it reminds me of an ancient astronomer's measuring globe. Weighing down her delicate shoulders hangs a gold-embroidered robe, fit for a medieval queen.

Her auburn hair cascades in wavy locks onto a sequinned bodice.

She is dressed to excite the masses to veneration. Styled by the Church for the Church, the Virgin reflects the ecclesiastical vision of feminine perfection: as pure as snow, as timid as a deer, as dignified as a monarch – and as sexless as a eunuch.

In her right hand, Chile's guardian angel holds the beads of a rosary. In her left, she cradles the progeny of Heaven. The infant child is decked out in similar finery. On his immaculate head, squashing down a forest of curly golden hair, rests a smaller version of his mother's crown. His priestly outfitters have done him no favours with the dress, a frumpy christening gown rimmed with gold trimming and flouncing in lace. Nor have they spared him the make-up box, dabbing his chubby cherub cheeks with rouge until they glow like rose blossom. The overall effect is more doll-like than divine.

Apart from the Virgin and Child, only the archbishop is permitted to showboat on so dignified an occasion. The elderly churchman has opted for a white ankle-length number with a scarlet shoulder wraparound and matching coloured hat. A brass band strikes up the national anthem. At the song's close, the outdoor congregation falls silent, and the octogenarian archbishop fires off a solemn prayer. The request to Heaven serves as a starting pistol. On the stroke of '*Amén*,' the peregrinators are off.

Out in front race the marching bands. Slotting in behind charge the religious orders. On their heels, a close third, follow the Catholic schools (Cumbres, Maitenes, San Isidro, Santa Teresa, Mercedes, ad infinitum) and the Church charities. By the first corner, the chasing pack is taking shape: the city parishes nudging just ahead of the Red Cross; the federal constabulary fending off the armed forces; the local councils jostling in front of the municipal bigwigs; the priests getting the edge on the church wardens. Finally, bringing up the rear, stroll the Virgin and the arthritic archbishop.

Two hours it takes the procession to finish the eight-block circuit, time enough for me to speak with stragglers in the square. With notebook in hand, I hit the crowd. I'm interested to know whether or not the Virgin presents a model of the ideal woman. Amongst the infirm, the elderly, the latecomers and the lazy, there are several thousand women with whom to enquire. I draw stumps after twelve. All are in agreement. The Virgin does not simply symbolise the ideal woman; she *is* that woman.

Animated to have stumbled on my answer so soon, I push my female interviewees to be more specific.

How exactly does the Virgin represent the archetype of woman-hood? Which of her qualities do you most admire?

Fifty-something Lucia digs into her bag of adjectives and pulls out character traits such as 'humble', 'obedient' and 'persevering'.

'Her service for the needy,' says Elisa, a serious lady in her mid-forties with thick-rim glasses and a Legion of Mary badge on her lapel. Frizzy-haired Angelica stresses the Virgin's 'love for her child'. Beside her, in a wheelchair, sits her own daughter.

'Silence' and 'saintliness' opines pious Claudia, a mother of four. Working mum Cecilia pictures the saint as a 'mother who gave all for her family'. I close my notebook, sealing the long list of virtues in case the modest Virgin catch a glimpse and puff with pride.

The archbishop is now back and doddering up onto a temporary stage outside the cathedral. An open-air Mass commences.

'Mother of Chile! Patron of Chile! Queen of Chile!' A row of four septuagenarian priests sit either side of the chief celebrant, their bald spots covered by conical mitres shaped like flattened aces of diamonds.

'Mary, full of grace!' White handkerchiefs are waved by the crowd in the square.

'Our Eternal Guide!' Readings are read. A hymn is hummed. Thanks are given for the gift of so sacred a mother.

'Virgin of Carmen! Spiritual Mother!' Orange floodlights illuminate the basilica's spires. Bread is broken. Foreheads, breastbones and shoulders are crossed.

'Go with us now. Most perfect of women.'

Reading over my notes the next day, the women's responses begin to nag at me. The Virgin, in all her crystal purity and chasteness, does not make for an easy taskmaster. Could half the population really be striving to be mothers of God, flawless virgins, fountains of grace? Is it *really* feasible that Chilean women are toiling under the psychological and social burden of such saintly standards?

The more I think about it, the more far-fetched the idea seems. Yet, there's no denying that the ladies at the procession harboured just such aspirations. Perhaps that wasn't so peculiar? These were the matrons of the moral majority after all, the sort who saved their cherry for their husbands and their earthly desires for Heaven.

I'd met their type before. In the immediate aftermath of General Pinochet's death, I'd spent several days canvassing Chilean public opinion for a British newspaper. The ex-military leader was lying in state in Santiago's Military School, half hidden inside a coffin beneath the national flag. It was there that I'd found them, ashen-faced and swollen-eyed. Many had queued through the night to pay their last respects. Dressed head to toe in black, they spoke exclusively in eulogies: how their general had saved Chile from becoming 'another Cuba', how he'd stamped out 'Communism' (one of the few dirty words they permitted themselves), how he'd brought order out of chaos. Only one thought had consoled them, and this they wrote on their cardboard banners: 'Today, you'll be with God in Paradise.'

I am hoping Chile might reveal something about how South America's womenfolk perceive themselves and are perceived by others. Are they equal citizens or second-rate servants? Are they out burning their bras, or back home darning their husbands' socks? For answers, I realised I would have to look beyond the mainstream. So I hopped on a bus north, to the Elqui Valley.

In the Virgin, I'd found the saintly ideal of womanhood. In Gabriela Mistral, the most revered female in Chile's recent history, I hoped to uncover a mortal version of the same.

Elqui Valley

The bus's cheerful driver invited me to take a seat up front with him.

'Every day I drive this route, and it still gets me right here,' he said, whistling in wonder and punching his heart so hard he let out an involuntary splutter.

The bucolic valley inspired Gabriela Mistral in equal measure. Born in 1889 to a seamstress mother and a soon-to-be-absent father, she overcame her bad start in life to become Chile's foremost female poet. As well as her verse, she's remembered as South America's first female Nobel Prize winner, an accomplished diplomat, a life-long educator and a passionate defender of women's rights. The peregrinate writer never forgot the gravelly mountains and lush vales of her childhood, referring back to them continually in her work. When Chile's best-loved daughter died in 1957, the country pulled its curtains closed and went into three days of official mourning.

From the window, I watch the vineyards swish by. With the speed of the bus, the regimental rows of young vines fragment into disordered agricultural cross-stitch. Far, far ahead, where the road peters to a stop and the valley gives out, lies the Andean *cordillera*, capped with snow and silence. The Elqui Valley is so beautiful it could be a poem itself. As the bus tootles eastwards, I imagine full sonnets trickling down its babbling rivers and rhyming couplets inscribing themselves on the stems of its grapevines. The thought of Gabriela Mistral searching out doggerels on the bark of an orange tree or discovering a florid pentameter on the rind of a custard apple keeps me entertained.

Foreign tourists tend to skip over this picturesque corner of rural Chile. The omission is understandable, but regrettable. The Elqui Valley lacks the drama of the Atacama Desert in the north or the cobalt-blue glaciers of the south. Picturing Chile as a snake (which it feasibly resembles when looked at sideways on an inverted map), then it's the country's bulging eye and swishing tail that attract the visitor. Mistral's birthplace is more like the field mouse trapped in its belly, lodged down its digestive tract, going nowhere, just waiting on Nature to take its course.

It is the lunch hour – a misnomer in South America if ever there was one – that is taking its course when the bus finally trundles into the sedate, unruffled village of Montegrande. Mistral spent her first years in this tiny hamlet, living in the backroom of the schoolhouse where her sister taught. Today, the building acts as a museum in the poet's honour. The shutters are down. My friend the bus driver suggests we continue on to the next village.

'It'll open again after lunch. Come back at three o'clock.' It's midday. I carry on with him up the winding road to Elqui Pisco.

He drops me off on the corner of a botanical square overrun with flowers and cheerful palm trees. My eye immediately sets on the Mistral Pisco Distillery, located on a bend in the road directly in front of me. Thinking I might try a thimbleful of the region's famed liquor, I head towards the distillery gate. I'm just shy of the entrance when the short distance between me and a cool glass of *pisco* sour is suddenly barred. Blocking the way is a lady of a preposterously chatty disposition. Her name, I learn immediately and without inquiry, is Gabriela.

The poet's namesake owns a fine hostel, she herself informs me. I'm after a drink not a bed, I respond, hoping to shake her off. Aah, well, she has a juice bar too. Weakened by her exuberance and genuinely thirsty, I allow myself to be led away towards Gabriela's Cactus Bar. In the time it takes for the cheerful chatterbox to prepare a banana and orange smoothie, I become fully acquainted with her life story.

As a single mum, she moved to Elqui Pisco 'on a whim' twenty years ago. She'd been reading a women's magazine when she stumbled on an article about the tranquil valley. According to the glossy, the Earth's magnetic centre had recently shifted from the plateaus of Tibet to the dales of Elqui. The hippie inside her had decided to go and check it out. Though she's yet to see a UFO ('the valley's full of them, you know'), she's never regretted her impulsive relocation.

'Is it the energies that have brought you this way too?' she asks, finally pausing for breath.

'No, I'm here to find out about Gabriela Mistral.'

I explain a little about my investigation, how I'm interested in women ('in a research sense, I mean') and in whether the famous poet acts as a female role model of sorts. My more mundane, terrestrial quest doesn't dampen her spirits one bit. Far from it. It merely opens the floodgates to another stream of consciousness.

'Aah, in that case, an interesting fact you should know about Elqui Pisco is how many single women there are here.'

'Really? And how many are there?'

Well, the exact figure she doesn't know, but it's definitely 'plenty'. Gabriela is one of them, for example, which, as an aside, doesn't worry her as she's bound to suffer less and therefore live longer. Apparently, the high number has to do with all the dope that the local men smoke.

'They call it "the curse of Gabriela Mistral". The singleness that is, not the dope.'

Have I read much of the poet's work? Only fragments, I confess.

'I suppose it *could* be that she did dope,' the cosmic juice-maker ponders. 'The idea isn't altogether impossible.'

Anyway, if I was interested in Mistral, I ought to go see Widow Pinto. Word is that she was good friends with the poet in her youth. Gabriela draws me a map. Although the village only has two streets, the task somehow occupies five minutes and an entire sheet of A4 paper.

'Just tell her I sent you.'

With Gabriela's map in hand, I head off to find the pantomime-sounding dame.

On the lower of Elqui Pisco's two roads, halfway down the block opposite the Elke Restaurant, I reach the 'X' on the scrawled directions. Discovering a bungalow with walls as thick as ramparts and a goblin-sized door, I knock. A full minute passes before I hear the steps of shuffling feet through an open window. The door opens an inch to reveal a wrinkled nose in the semi-darkness.

'Dona Pinto?' I enquire of the nose.

'*Sí*, and who might be asking?' The voice is frail and brittle.

'Gabriela sent me,' I explain. The introduction doesn't have the Ali Baba touch I was hoping for, and the door fails to open further.

'Gabriela *who?*' the nose wants to know.

'Gabriela from the juice parlour.'

No reply, not so much as a sniff of recognition.

'Buck teeth, so high, talks non-stop.'

'No, never heard of her.'

'Oh, how odd. Well she told me you were friends with Gabriela Mistral. Is that right?'

'Of course.'

'Would you have five minutes to talk?' I explain my quest in brief. Slowly, the door slides open, revealing the nose to be attached to a little old lady in a short-sleeve woven dress and slippers.

Inside, the low ceilings give the house a pleasant coolness. Dona Pinto guides me to the rear conservatory, which, in contrast to the shadowy interior, is bright with sunshine. An overgrown vegetable patch is running riot in the back garden. Did I want to see the *maté* cup Gabriela Mistral drank from during her last visit? She bustles off into the pantry and returns with a delicate wicker basket. Pulling back a chequered tea towel, yellowed with age, she reveals the accoutrements of a seventy-five-year-old afternoon tea: china sugar bowl, matching receptacle for the *maté* leaves, a metal straw. Only Aladdin's lamp is missing.

'Very nice,' I remark, admiring the mouldering keepsake with as much gusto as I can muster. I endeavour to change track: 'What kind of woman was Gabriela Mistral, I wonder?'

'She'd call me *hijita* [little daughter] and we'd go for walks together along the river.'

'Ah, so you really were very close.'

'Yes, of course. We were very good friends. I was four years old at the time.'

The famed poet's friends were really Dona Pinto's parents. She'd come round in the afternoons to drink *maté* and chat in the cool of the veranda. That was back in the early 1930s. The Pintos knew her through family ties. The widow's grandmother had once worked for Gabriela's mother, Dona Pinto explains.

Her voice drops into a conspiratorial whisper. Few people knew this, but her grandfather's surname was Alcayada. I do my best to look impressed, imagining he must have been a local notable of some sort. Only later did I learn that Gabriela Mistral's half-sister carried the same surname.

'Do you remember much of her character?'

'Oh, she was a wonderful woman,' Dona Pinto responds without hesitation. 'A big heart, very kind. But reserved, not very openly affectionate. Serious, some people used to say.'

'Why was that, do you think?'

'Perhaps Chileans were slow to recognise her talent.'

The elderly grandmother's response doesn't surprise me. Before leaving Santiago, I'd spent an afternoon hunting around the capital's bookstores. For every one edition by Mistral, I found ten by Pablo Neruda, Chile's other (male) Nobel Prize winner. Neither wounded pride nor career frustrations seem reason enough for the poet's remoteness.

Her icy reputation lies in her suffering, Widow Pinto asserts: 'Hers was a tragic life really.'

Mistral's father walked out when she was only a baby, my host goes on to explain. As a schoolgirl, the poet was branded a Communist for writing a feminist tract and duly expelled. Then her childhood sweetheart committed suicide.

'Gabriela never loved again. No children of her own. Only sadness.'

Dona Pinto carries the pain as though the suffering were her own. Years later, Mistral's godson, who she'd raised from his youth, also took his own life.

'Imagine, the two most important men in her life, both killing themselves?' The pantomime had taken a heart-rending turn.

I check my watch. It's almost three o'clock. I take my leave of Widow Pinto, who's carefully packing away her keepsake, and make my way back to the bus stop. Arriving in Montegrande for a second time, I find the museum doors open. Betica, the elderly curator, is enjoying a catnap in her chair by the door. The sound of my step wakes her, and she collects her entrance fee.

The adobe-brick schoolhouse consists of two rooms. Classes took place in the front one, being the larger and better lit of the two. The rows of miniature wooden desks have not been moved. Nor have the slate blackboard ingrained with chalk dust or the wooden abacus by the door or the faded maps of Chile on the walls. It's as if the pupils popped out for recess and never came back.

The second of the two rooms is connected to the first by an outside patio. The walls are bare and whitewashed. It contains three iron-framed beds, which lend the room a sanitised, hospital feel. Mistral, the young girl, is survived by the meanest of possessions: a chipped porcelain water jug, her mother's sewing machine, a wooden trunk, a clunky washbasin and a dark religious painting in an untidy wooden frame.

A group of eighteen German tourists troop in and troop out, quadrupling Betica's takings for the day but upsetting her afternoon doze. She flusters about them taking photographs, issuing strained injunctions in Spanish to which they neither listen nor respond. Eventually, the white-haired curator shrugs her shoulders and gives up trying to explain herself. She sits back down in her chair. The hoot of a minibus sounds from outside, and the whirlwind of visitors sweeps back out the door.

I also turn to leave. As a final thought, I ask Betica if there's a particular volume of Mistral's poetry that she would recommend. The cane-carrying curator rattles off all the poet's published works, plus dates of publication, relevant biographical snippets and translation details for good measure. *And her favourite?* A shy smile. She's not read them all, she confesses. Getting hold of copies isn't easy, I have to understand. However, the snoozy curator does own an early version of the Nobel Prize-winner's first compilation, which Mistral wrote when she was only nineteen. I'd be sure to enjoy it.

'Great, what's it called?'

'*Desolation,*' Betica announces with curious delight. 'We Chilean women suffer a lot, you know?'

Outside, in Montegrande's otherwise empty square, the town's authorities have erected a statue of their brilliant but troubled

55

protégée. Mistral followed her sister into the teaching profession, and it's as such that the sculptor remembers her. Two cheerful pupils skip along at her side, clinging to the hemline of her sensibly straight skirt. Their smiling faces contrast with the formal expression bequeathed to their schoolmistress. Her lips turn down at the corners as though she's grimacing. The impression is one of joylessness, touching on sourness.

Perhaps the sculptor was aspiring to a lifelike image? Dona Pinto was not wrong in saying that the poet came across as serious. Surviving photos invariably show her straight-faced and soberlooking. Yet, I wonder if there isn't a degree of artistic licence too. The statue reminds me of Isabel Allende's throwaway comment about Chilean women.

'Most are martyrs by vocation,' she writes in *My Beloved Country,* a nostalgic reminiscence of her homeland. 'They take pride in suffering.'

Whether heavenly or human, silent stoicism seems to be the overwhelming virtue attributed to Chile's fairer sex. Allende paints her gender as willing victims. Maybe some are. The idea isn't altogether impossible, as the owner of the Cactus Bar would say. But while their willingness might be up for debate, their victim status all too often is not.

Concepción

I stamp my feet against the cold. Five hundred and twenty kilometres south of Santiago, and winter feels perpetual. I check my watch: 8.10 a.m.

'Class starts at eight o'clock sharp,' María had advised me. I'd arrived at the university medical faculty ten minutes early to be sure.

Four years living in South America, and I'm still to master Latino time-keeping. 'Sharp' is an occupationally arbitrary term. If it's the TV repair people, for example, it can mean anything from a morning's wait to a few days'. For the postal service, it could be weeks. Anything to do with the government, and you're looking at months, if not years. I'd taken a punt on women's-rights activists being punctual. Comparatively speaking, Maria doesn't let me down. Ten minutes later, I feel a tap on my numbed shoulder.

The youthful Maria is all bubbles and rosy cheeks. We walk along several corridors and up even more flights of stairs, she nattering all the while. The terrible weather. The traffic. The class ahead. Today's session is called 'First Support', she explains. Medical staff can be invaluable in the detection phase.

'Many women are ashamed about being beaten. They do everything to hide the fact.'

Eventually, we arrive at the remote classroom to which she's been assigned. Waiting for her at their desks are fifteen trainee nurses.

Coat, scarf, hat, gloves and ear mufflers removed, Maria takes the class through an initial slide presentation. It consists of statistics put together by the women's organisation where she works: ninety-six thousand reports of domestic abuse per year in Chile; fifteen thousand cases of sexual assault annually; 30 per cent of all women suffer physical abuse of some kind. Then, she opens the floor to discussion.

'Sixty per cent or more of women that are abused totally deny it. Anyone have any ideas why that might be?'

Hands shoot up.

'Fear,' says one of the two male students.

'Shame,' suggests the girl next to him.

'Worry that no one will believe them,' another.

'Concern for their children,' a fourth. Maria commends them on their answers.

'Often women believe they've brought it on themselves.' The lecturer turns into an impressionist. '"I provoked the situation," they'll say. "I know he gets angry when the food's not ready." Or they tell themselves it doesn't hurt so much. Over time, violence becomes normalised.'

The female students react indignantly.

'Any man hits me, and I'd be out the door straight away, no

question,' states a pretty student with long eyelashes. Her girl-friends are equally adamant. Maria tries to explain the psychological complexities that come with domestic abuse.

'It's important to appreciate that each woman needs her own time to confront the situation.' The class doesn't buy it.

'Gluttons for punishment, if you ask me,' an unsympathetic student remarks. I'm tempted to agree.

It's Alma who convinces me otherwise. We meet two days later in the fishing town of Tomé, a short drive towards the coast from the much larger city of Concepción. It's dark when I arrive, and the square is empty but for three sleeping dogs and a drunk slumbering on the bench. I get the impression that not much happens in Tomé, even during sunlight hours. That's exactly why Alma moved there. It's her refuge.

I find her in a long wooden shed just off the main square. Children's paintings decorate the walls, and a thin table stretches from one end to the other. Sitting eating ice cream are twenty or so adults with mental disabilities. Alma, round and gentle, like a cuddly school matron, is sitting at the head of the table. Her hair is cut short and prematurely grey. She helps coordinate activities at the shed, which serves as social centre for the local community. On Wednesdays, it's where her self-help group for battered women meets.

An art activity replaces the ice cream, giving us the opportunity to retire to a quiet side-office where we can talk more easily. Alma's voice is soft and gentle. Her story is the very opposite. She had only been married a few months when the violence started. Her husband was in the armed forces. It meant he knew how to beat her without leaving bruises. Banning her from having friends or money, the psychotic naval officer eventually took to locking her in the house when he left for work.

'After so many years of being told I was nothing, I'd ended up believing it.' Her words are free of resentment, the product of long years of counselling.

I ask after her children. She has two adult sons; both work in the police. Alma takes her glasses off and cleans them with a tissue from her pocket. It's a means of buying time, of preparing her thoughts: 'I had a daughter too.'

The past tense weighs heavy in the small office. For a tiny moment, her composure slips, and her bottom lip trembles ever so slightly. Then it's back to the measured, detached tone of before.

'She died.' Alma doesn't explain how; she doesn't need to. 'I took her to the Naval Hospital. I was screaming hysterically, telling everyone that it was my husband's fault.' In response, her authoritative spouse calmly advised the doctors that Alma was insane. His word won the day, and his wife was temporarily confined to a psychiatric unit.

Fast forward fifteen years, and she's back in the emergency ward again, this time fighting for her own life. She came through, just. During her recovery, a nurse told her about a support group for abused women. In twenty years, it was the first time she'd received an offer of help, she says. And the first time that she was ready to accept it.

No, Alma didn't strike me as the gluttonous type.

Back in the classroom, Maria's pen is hovering over a slide. Above its shadow reads the capitalised phrase, 'LAW ON DOMESTIC VIOLENCE'. Under Chilean legislation, all medical staff are legally bound to report cases of domestic abuse, she's telling the nurses.

'If you heard your neighbour's house being robbed, you'd call the police without hesitation, right? Abuse within a family should be no different. It's a crime, just like any other.'

Obediently, her students note down the point. It's difficult to determine how convinced they are. Nurses or not, everyone knows that in Chile what happens behind closed doors stays behind closed doors. 'Dirty clothes,' the saying goes, 'get washed inside the house.'

Maria brings the class to a close with a role-play. She picks out two students – a boy and a girl – and hands them a fictitious case study. They take a seat at the front of the class, which, for the purposes of the act, is now a mock consulting room. The atmosphere remains jovial as the pair settle into their invented characters.

NURSE: What do you do?
WOMAN: I'm a hairdresser. [*Nurse looks down at his sheet of paper and notes a deviation from the script.*]
WOMAN [*realising mistake*]: But I resigned.
NURSE: When?
WOMAN: Oh [*re-reads the brief*] about nineteen years ago, it appears.

The audience laugh. As the *woman who walked into a door* scene unfolds, a gradual change takes over the room. The two act surprisingly well: the girl flinching involuntarily every time she mentions her husband's name, the male nurse listening intently across the table. Discomfited, their classmates start shifting in their seats.

WOMAN [*still denying everything*]: He loves us. He's a good man really. He bought the children new shoes last week.
NURSE [*still probing*]: Do you experience violence at home?
WOMAN: No. My husband loves us.

The conversation bounces back and forth until the girl playing the battered wife finally breaks and confesses all. The class relaxes, the act finishes, and everyone applauds.

Maria asks for feedback. One joker recommends the pair give up nursing for roles in a *telenovela,* but otherwise no one says anything. Their instructor for the day makes some constructive criticisms of her own. Her comments focus mostly on the nurse's role.

'Listening? Yes, good. Advice? Again, good. Presented all the options. Be careful with the use of the term "violence" though. You need to remember, "violence" is a violent word.'

A professional counsellor, Maria leaves her most serious criticism for the end. She wants to know if anyone picked up on the nurse's one-liner about the children.

'No, no one? It came right at the end.' The class's collective memory refuses to be jogged.

'No one remembers the line?' She looks down at her notes to show she is reading it back verbatim:

Maria [as Nurse]: As an adult, you can take the odd hit, but if he starts hitting the little ones . . .?

The class looks down at their desks; pens start tapping lever-arch files; books are moved into straight-edged piles. Jointly, the students are shamed into silence. The words hang in the air, an ugly reminder of how desensitised Chileans are to domestic violence – even among the country's caring profession. The class is dismissed.

The Attention Centre forms the left-hand section of a small detached house. It's located opposite the town hall in San Pedro, another of Concepción's suburban overshoots. I knock, and a secretary in the single-room downstairs office ushers me in. I take a seat next to a thin, middle-aged woman with hunched shoulders and bobbed hair. Nervously, she taps a toe to a Madonna track over the radio, all the while twiddling the ring on her marriage finger. Her gaze is fixed blankly on the office printer's electronic key pad, two metres in front of her.

At the far end of the office, chunky box folders fill the shelves from floor to ceiling. Official-looking papers spill out of their sides: names, cases, psychiatric observations, doctors' notes. All are written out in black and white, women's stories reduced to standardised forms and catalogue entries. Each one of them officially normalised.

Ten minutes pass before Julia, the centre's harried coordinator, comes down from her upstairs office. She invites me into a tiny consulting room. Bags of tiredness hang under her eyes like swollen wineskins. The room has space enough for a desk and two chairs and little else. Damp is eating away at the roof. The 'No Smoking' sign has been pasted over with a 'No Drugs Permitted' notice. San Pedro is at the wrong end of town.

After yesterday's lecture, I'd asked Maria what she felt drove men to acts of domestic violence. The question had elicited a resigned shrug from the women's activist. No one really knew, it seemed. If they did, she'd admitted, the problem would be easier to counteract. Advocates of castration for rapists came to mind. Perhaps their fists could be permanently bound?

We had been sitting in a café close to the university campus, and Maria took a bite of apple pie.

'Identifying "risk factors" is as far as behavioural science can take us,' she'd said, munching slowly. 'Alcoholism, drug-taking, poverty, unemployment, multiple families living in a small space: all make some men more prone to beat their partners. But they don't *cause* violence as such.' A decade in the job, and she's concluded that some men are just 'brutes'.

I repeat the conversation to Julia, and she agrees. 'Some men are more prone to violence than others. That's true the world over. But Chile aids and abets its wife-beaters.'

'How so?'

'You need to be aware that Chile is a profoundly violent society,' she replies.

'It is?' The news came as a surprise to me. Chileans are reputed to be reserved and stable types, exceptions to the continent's volatile, passionate norm. The Swiss of South America, some jest.

'Of course it's violent,' Julia responds sharply, as if I've offended her professional credentials. She sets out to defend them.

'Do you know the motto on our national shield?' I didn't. '*Por la razon o la fuerza*' ('By reason or by force'). What's that if it's not a validation of violence? Wait there, I want to show you something.'

She pulls open a desk drawer and removes a stack of laminated cards large enough to fill both hands. Each card has a Chilean idiom written across it in black felt pen. Julia and her colleagues use them as part of a school outreach programme. She invites me to flick through them.

Many are polite ways of making a crude point. The wink/nudge encouragement for husbands to play the field, for example: '*Catedral hay una sola y parroquias muchas*' ('There's only one cathedral, but plenty of parishes'). Others are plain boorish, especially when it deals with men being men. '*Soltero maduro, fleto* seguro' ('Mature single man, must be gay') goes one. '*Los hombres no lloran*' ('Men don't cry') reads another.

There are clues to the denial dilemma as well. '*El amor lo soporta todo*' ('Love puts up with everything'), mothers are fond of counselling their unhappy daughters. '*Contigo pan y cebolla*' (the Chilean equivalent of 'With you in good times and bad') runs another pearl of maternal wisdom.

Julia has other examples in mind. She takes the pack from me and starts hunting through it herself. 'Here's one, for example.' A laminated card is placed face up on the table. '*Quien te quiere te aporea*' ('The person that loves you hits you'). 'And another.' It's a different thought on the same theme. '*Los celos son una prueba de amor*' ('Jealousy is proof of love'). The third comes from the classroom.

'We grew up with our teachers saying this,' Julia says, her eyes turned up in disbelief. '*La letra con sangre entra*' ('With blood, the letter enters') – a justification for caning slow learners.

'Chilean society is fundamentally patriarchal. Men inherit power over women here,' she continues. 'Worse, they inherit the belief that it's their *right* to abuse that power. If you don't get that, you'll never get why we're so tolerant of violence.'

She's made her point and begins clearing up the cards, which are now spread across the table top. As she does so, her eye catches a final phrase.

'Ah, this one's interesting.' The tired social worker instructs me to recover my pen and paper and make a note of it. '*La M de "Machismo" se escribe con M de "Mama"*' ('The M of "Machismo" is written with the M of "Mother"'). Dutifully, I write it down. The full sense, though, is lost on me. Julia explains.

'Women are responsible for the upbringing of their children, right?'

'Right,' I venture slowly, curious where her logic is leading.

'So, if their son turns out to be a macho thug, then whose fault do people say it is?'

'The mother's?' I suggest, more dubious still about the argument's final destination.

'Exactly. Women think it must be their fault. Do you see?'

I do, but it seems a little rich: women being responsible for male violence against them. I share my doubts.

'Of course, it's absurd!' she exclaims. 'Women turn the violence around and blame it on themselves. They ignore the fact that everything in our society encourages men to behave like this.'

She puts the cards back in the desk drawer. So ends my second class in as many days. Outside, the hunched-over woman is still tapping her toe, staring at the digitalised numbers on the electronic pad.

The road to Casa Hadewijch takes me westward out of Concepción along the built-up Bio Bio estuary. The streets are bordered by industrial sprawl: an electricity sub-station, faceless warehouse facilities, oil-stained mechanics' garages, anonymous haulage companies, rows of square, monotone apartment blocks.

My instructions are to get off at the 'container' when I reach the suburb of Haulpen. I give the unlikely sounding directions to the bus driver and settle down to read. Over the past few days, I'd picked up a variety of literature on domestic abuse in Chile. My reading pile proves even more depressing than the passing landscape. Among the information leaflets and lists of state services, I turn up a photocopied news article from Concepción's *Diario del Sur* newspaper. 'Machismo kills' runs the headline. I read on. In the past six years, over three hundred women have died at the hands of their male partners or ex-partners. The article includes a list of 'femicides' from the previous week: Katherine Casas, aged twenty-six years old, from Maipú, separated, stabbed; María Gallardo, forty-five years old, from Santiago, recently split from long-term partner, beaten to death; Karina Rojas, sixteen years old, from Renca, broken up with boyfriend, stabbed. In each case, the guilty party had a record of domestic abuse stretching back years. Another commonality is the recent end of the abusive relationship. Murder, a Chilean psychologist would later explain to me, represents the 'final act' of the male exertion of control. Another reason why Alma and thousands like her stay put for so long.

'Container!' the gruff driver barks.

I step down at the edge of a dusty playing field. Identical A-frame, semi-detached homes ring the lunar recreation ground. Fenced in behind metal bars, the buildings' chipped wood panelling cries out for a paint job. Haulpen is as drab and colourless as an army base. The metallic hulk of a cargo ship container sits incongruously beside a solitary football post. I walk across the deserted sports field towards it and find the Hadewijch women's shelter just a block away.

Oriana, a well-to-do woman in her late thirties, welcomes me at the door and offers me a brief tour around the halfway house. The neighbourhood's down-at-heel theme continues inside: the dining room in the garage, mismatched furniture in the living room, the hand-me-down bunk beds in the dormitories upstairs. The centre would be smarter, she says, if she accepted donations from the local drug dealers. But she'd prefer it to remain scruffy than take 'blood money'. Half a dozen women are participating in a yoga session in the kitchen in accordance with their rehabilitation programme. The less flexible of Hadewijch's female residents are doing the washing up.

We take a seat on a threadbare sofa, and Oriana invites Irma to join us. Short and diffident, with chipmunk cheeks, she's been at Hadewijch for a fortnight. We share the same age, I discover. Both of us are thirty-two. And there our stories diverge. At sixteen, she'd fallen in love with a man twice as old as her, a street vendor. The two married; she got pregnant; the beating started; and, sixteen years later, here she was, with two daughters, in the women's shelter.

Irma begins a detailed explanation of the legal battle in which she's currently engaged.

'He, of course, denies everything . . .'

As she describes the litany of abuse she's suffered, I find myself drifting off.

It's my fourth day on the trail of domestic assault in Concepción. I've heard a dozen or so testimonies, all of them gut-wrenching. Slowly, though, my initial anger and disgust at the depravity of their partners is softening. Better, perhaps, it's retreating – withdrawing behind an emotional wall of my own making. Each blow, each bruise, each broken rib, another brick. This sentiment – or lack of sentiment? – disturbs me. I am, I fear, normalising.

'Because of the injunction order, he sent my son to ransack the house . . .' Irma is still talking. Habit and manners keep me noting, but my mind has already turned to the next bus out of town.

Later that afternoon, with a one-way ticket to Valparaíso bought, my phone rings. It's Oriana. There's another woman she thinks that I should meet.

'Look, Oriana, it's very kind of you to think of me, but I think I've probably got enough information as it is.' It's not a lie, but neither is it the whole truth. It dawns on me that I'm running away, and the realisation shames me.

'I think you'll find her interesting,' Oriana persists. 'She was jailed for murdering her husband.'

Two hours later, I'm asking Blanca what she wants me to call her. It was Oriana's idea that we use a pseudonym. We're sitting in the second-floor cafeteria of the bus station. The overhead Tannoy is spouting out destinations in a mumbled baritone. 'Talca,' 'Valdivia,' 'Los Angeles,' 'Rancagua'. An electronically amplified *cumbia* band is shouting unintelligible lyrics from a wide-screen television. The plastic seats are fixed to the table and prevent me from nudging closer.

Sorry, could you repeat the name again? She spells it out a second time, letter by letter. B.E.T.Z.A.B.E.T.H.

Blanca looks older than her fifty-two years. Deep grooves spread out concentrically from the corners of her eyes like prongs on a garden rake. Her hair is dyed black and cut just below her jaw line. Dressed in a denim skirt and turtleneck jumper, she's wearing no jewellery other than two simple stud earrings. Her blue eyeliner has been applied crookedly, betraying an inexperienced hand.

She begins with her childhood, a period she describes as 'mostly happy'. Like Irma, her story takes a turn with a teenage romance. From the start, her father didn't approve of the local boy and banned the two from dating. They carried on seeing one another in secret. A year later, just shy of her nineteenth birthday, Blanca moved out of home. Shortly afterward, the pair married in a civil ceremony. That would have been 1974, she calculates, counting out the years on the fingers of her left hand. He was living with his parents, so she moved in there. For two years, life was good. Not great, perhaps, but good enough. In retrospect, she would have settled for that.

Everything changed when he adopted what he liked to call a 'bohemian' lifestyle. The word covered a multiple of sins: he gave up his job, started staying out all night and began taking drugs. Shuffled around enough, it came to include beatings, rape, whipping and general denigration too. He proved a lousy husband but an imaginative wordsmith.

Her parents-in-law eventually threw them out. Several temporary flats followed, until a squalid two-room shack became their permanent home. Into that 'bohemian' paradise, she gave birth to a son, Manuel. Over the years, she learned to get by with no windows and a wood-burning fire for a stove. For cups and bowls, they used empty tin cans. Money was always scarce. She took a job as a car-park attendant. Her wages would go straight into her husband's worsening drug habit. He started an affair with a neighbour, and he'd disappear for days. Around the house, he began keeping sticks, bats, chains, 'anything he could hit me with'. Several times, he threw Blanca naked into the street. Throughout, her neighbours remained stoically silent.

The waitress comes over and asks if we'd like more drinks. I'm grateful for the intervention and ask for an apple juice. Blanca waits for the orders to arrive before picking up the story. Her attitude is one of quiet composure. Patiently, she takes the time to clarify my questions and go back over details.

She restarts with the night of 18 May 1994. Manuel, now seventeen, had invited a friend to come over and stay. Daniel lived under their roof for about a fortnight. He saw at first hand the abuse meted out to Blanca.

'One night, my husband came home at three in the morning, totally off his head. I was sleeping but he forced me to get up and perform an erotic show in front of Daniel and my son.'

It was around 11 p.m. when her husband, son and his friend left the house together. Blanca says she had no idea where they were going. She didn't ask.

An hour later, Manuel came crashing through the door. He led her at a run to the nearby football field. There, in the light of the moon, she saw her husband lying in a pool of blood. Standing over him was Daniel. In his hand was a bloodstained kitchen knife.

'"He's killed him," I kept shouting. "Why's he killed him?"'

Years later, at the plastic table in the bus-station cafeteria, Blanca describes her husband's murder in a flat, matter-of-fact tone.

'"Open your eyes, Mum," Manuel yelled at me. "He did it for you."'

She takes a sip of her fruit juice.

If events unfolded as Blanca described, I wonder how it is that she ended up as a convicted murderer.

Blanca continues to slurp her drink, and it falls to the coordinator of the women's hostel to put the missing piece in place.

'Manuel and Daniel both got ten years, isn't that right?'

Putting down her straw, the ex-convict nods.

'Blanca got fifteen,' Oriana carries on.

'Why?' I ask, confused.

'The judge reckoned she masterminded the whole thing.'

For Oriana, who met Blanca during the last years of her sentence, there was a point of legal principle at stake: 'When men kill their wives, the courts call it an "act of passion". When it's the other way around, they call it "premeditation". It's just not fair.'

The precise tenets of the law don't seem to bother Blanca quite so much. Her defence is the same today as it was then.

'If I'd wanted to kill him,' she says, 'I would have done it a whole lot earlier.' There's a stifled irony in her voice.

Only when she begins describing her life in prison does her tranquillity finally begin to give way. Not for her own sake so much. Incarceration, she'd learn, was just another form of abuse, something she could learn to live with. Her tears she saved for her son. Manuel was a soft, introverted boy, not cut out for prison life. He would send her letters from the men's prison begging for help.

'They did terrible things to him there, terrible.'

Seven years into his sentence, he was moved to a smaller prison with lower security. There, mother and son spoke once a month by telephone. Excitedly he'd told her how the warden had granted him permission to pay her a visit. The date was set for a Sunday in December.

'On the Friday before, the warden called me into his office. There was a medic standing there too.' Blanca's whole appearance has suddenly changed. Her words emerge choked. She's breathing in gulps, as though an invisible noose were tightening around her neck.

'I remember like it was yesterday. Neither of them would speak to me at first. Eventually, the warden came out with it. "Your son's been killed." Just like that. Nothing more. I don't remember much of what happened next. I guess I went a little crazy.'

Manuel did arrive on the Sunday as arranged, but in a coffin. Blanca was put on suicide watch.

'He was my only child,' she says in a barely audible whisper, scraping at a stain on the tablecloth as fat tears stream down her lean face.

Oriana intervenes again, allowing Blanca time to collect herself. Through contacts at the prison, Blanca had heard about the Casa Hadewijch. She'd been given authorisation to attend a monthly self-help meeting. On learning her story, Oriana started petitioning the Appeals Court for Blanca's early release. Her persistence paid off. On Christmas Eve, thirteen years into her sentence, Blanca's cell door was opened and her liberty restored.

'I've been out of prison for just over a year now,' Blanca explains, her voice still a little shaky but her appearance visibly more composed.

Her life is beginning to take on some semblance of normality, she says. She has a weekend job at a women's shelter run by a Catholic charity, which she finds rewarding. A chance to redeem something good from all the bad, as she puts it. Blanca's also fallen in love again. It hadn't been her intention.

'My dream used to be to live the rest of my life alone, totally alone, all by myself,' she confides coyly.

But then Ivan came into her life. They'd met during her last year in prison. She used to work as a waitress at a local diner. The job was part of a weekend-release scheme. Ivan, an independent contractor, was a regular lunchtime customer.

'I'd always end up serving him. We gradually got to know each other. It was his smile that conquered me.'

Blanca's romance is by far the happiest thing I've heard in four days, and I thank her as sincerely as I know how.

'No problem,' she says, getting up out of her seat. She excuses herself. Her date's waiting. Both ladies gush.

'Oh, and forget about that Betzabeth nonsense. Call me Blanca. I don't like lies.'

Valparaíso

In Valparaíso, I take a room on Cerro Concepción in a run-down guesthouse overlooking the Lutheran church. Don Juan, the amiable seventy-seven-year-old proprietor, marks my name down in his ledger and shows me to a cubbyhole at the back of the building. The front rooms of Alojamiento Juan Carrasco look out onto the bay below, with its navy frigates in neat lines like a game of Battleships. My fleapit garret has a view of a wire-strangled telephone pole and a brick wall.

Don Juan and his wife Edita purchased the ramshackle old house on Abtao Street nearly four decades ago.

'Bought it from an English couple. Johnson, I think their name was.' The elderly owner is walking away down the threadbare stairs, feigning deafness to my request for a room change. The couple have been assiduous in making as few changes as possible to the sprawling town house.

The result of such thrift is the creation of an authentic Brighton boarding house, circa 1950. From the lurid plastic flowers to the stale-smelling carpets, there is little this accidental curator has over-looked. Peeling wallpaper spreads contagiously through the musty corridors. What the decorative ivy hasn't devoured, Don Juan has painted bright pink.

Appropriately enough, the only other guest is a Londoner. John, a retired architect with a bushy white beard and a two-berth dinghy, is on a quest to repeat Darwin's *Beagle* voyage. Unfortunately, the bank machine ate his credit card, shipwrecking the weatherworn mariner in the rambling old house until he gets it back.

'Rotten luck, really,' he grumbles over breakfast. 'Might have to wire old Aunt Judith for a couple of hundred quid to tide me over.' I wonder if he means to email his elderly relative or if he is genuine-ly going to go in search of a radio telegraph machine.

I leave the marooned seaman to his bacon and eggs and head down the hill into Valparaíso proper. Located on the coast directly west of Santiago, the city hosts the nation's parliament and its most important port. So many politicians and sailors in one place could only mean one thing, I figured: sex.

'*Tener relaciones*' ('to have relations') is the rather quaint way 'sexual intercourse' translates into Spanish. The phrase omits any sense of the carnal, as though it's something you might get up to over an afternoon cup of Earl Grey with Aunt Judith. Of course, words can be deceiving. Latinos certainly like to think of themselves as the world's great Lotharios – the macho male with all his cath-edrals and parishes, dedicated to filling confession booths with honour-stripped maidens.

Again, Chile provides the exception to the rule. Its serious citizens don't have sex. At least, if they do, it's for the strict purposes of introducing sperm to egg. Thus, *relaciones* – daughter, son, brother, sister, et cetera – are born.

Where sex is concerned, the virgin beats the vixen to the altar. In Chile, children grow up believing the birds and the bees is a genuine story. Teenagers get their sex education on the street, one health worker told me. What they can't find there, they look up on YouTube.

Official attitudes are positively prudish. Mention of the C word, for example, still causes Chile's Catholic majority to burst a collective organ valve. It took nine years before the term 'condom' could be used in the country's annual HIV-awareness campaign. And then it was only as a very distant third after abstinence and monogamy. If folk must fondle, then they're to do so with just one person and for the rest of their lives.

Abortion is another great reproduction-related taboo. Chile's three biggest pharmacy chains recently earned the Health Ministry's ire for refusing to stock the morning-after pill. The Spanish Inquisition was positively tolerant compared to Chile's pro-life lobby.

Pretend as they might, though, Chileans' prickliness about sex doesn't make them a nation of monks and nuns. Figures for teenage pregnancies and sexually transmitted diseases indicate they are at it as much as everywhere else.

The history books render a similar account. Spanish ships weren't built with women's quarters. The colonists left their families at home and quickly set about making American replacements. The chores of slave women and domestic staff lasted long after sundown. In fact, Chile owes its illustrious independence hero to a roll in the hay. The ginger-haired Bernardo O'Higgins came into the world thanks to a fling between his Irish-born father and a sixteen-year-old aristocrat. O'Higgins Senior rose through the ranks of the Spanish Civil Service to become Viceroy of Peru. The eminent post did not lend itself to bastard offspring; even less so when they start running around with revolutionaries. Young Bernardo took his father's rejection hard. Not that the lifelong bachelor was any better at acknowledging the illegitimate fruit of his own loins later on in life.

As in everything, Bolívar seems to have had a healthy disregard for the norms of his day. He was an avowed, unabashed philanderer. Short and thin, with a pointy aquiline nose and large forehead,

Bolívar didn't look the Hollywood heart-throb. But women were not indifferent to his charms. Nor he to theirs. Rarely did a triumphant march finish without the Liberator skulking off to his boudoir with one of the cheerleaders. Bedrooms and battlefields litter the Bolívarian campaign trail in equal measure; each new notch a testament to his glory, each fresh conquest a boost to his fame.

Time, not birth, established Bolívar's status as Liberator; so too his character as a libertine. As a seventeen-year-old student in Spain, the young Simón had fallen head over heels for the dark-eyed María Teresa Rodríguez del Toro y Alayza, two years his elder. In May 1802, the love-struck Venezuelan married his *novia,* and three weeks later the newly-weds set sail for home. Tragically, his virgin bride didn't take to the tropics. Seven months later, the fair-skinned María Teresa, Bolívar's 'jewel without a flaw', was dead of a malignant fever. On the pretext of completing his education, the inconsolable young aristocrat returned to Europe. His grief diminished gradually in the arms of various lovers. A raucous affair with Fanny du Villars, the wife of a Parisian count, sealed his reputation as an inveterate playboy. He returned to South America ready to sow the seeds of independence, in the full sense of the term.

Never did the Liberator marry again. Yet he did fall in love, regularly and recklessly. But among his infatuations and one-night stands, only one woman could be said to have mended his broken heart. Manuela Sáenz was young, beautiful, passionate – and married. The two met during his victorious entry into Quito in June 1822. His aides-de-camp probably gave the romance a fortnight, perhaps a month at most. Over seven years later, the two were still an item.

Their open affair scandalised the snobbish salons from Lima to Caracas. Wagging tongues didn't bother the love-struck couple though. Manuela was happy to be called a harlot as long she had the heart of her Liberator. A hot-blooded romantic, she drafted a letter to her middle-aged English husband to inform him as much. It was a put-down of the first order. 'You are boring,' she wrote, 'like your nation.' Now South America's most famous mistress, she thought it best he return to his homeland, a place 'which makes love without pleasure, conversation without grace . . . and jokes without laughing'. The recipient's response is not recorded, but the two quietly separated.

Few in Bolívar's age flaunted their sexuality so boldly. Little has changed. Sex remains a vicarious sport for most Chileans. Something others do. To compensate, they titillate themselves continually. The *café con piernas* ('coffee with legs') personifies the see-but-don't-touch phenomenon. Every morning, Santiago's office-goers casually drop into these ubiquitous coffee houses. Behind each percolator stands a buxom barista, scantily enough clad to make a lingerie model blush. The seedier joints even throw in a *minuto feliz,* a 'happy minute', the espresso version of a topless pole dance.

For those who can tear their eyes from the coffee grinder, there's always the paper to read. *La Cuarta* is Chile's most popular tabloid. Mechanics' yards and teenagers' bedrooms are plastered with posters of its Page Three girls. News is broken into three broad sections: sex-related scandals, sex-related crimes and sex-related gossip. *Ferandula* is the term Chileans give the latter. The country's favourite television show *SQP* is devoted to the theme. Any space left over after the silicon pin-ups and the 'He Slept with My Bridesmaid on Our Wedding Day' articles, *La Cuarta* devotes to adverts for twenty-four-hour sex lines.

Keeping sex a hands-off affair proves a boon for pornographers. My morning edition of *La Cuarta* informs me about Chile's Fourth Erotic Film Festival at the capital's Centro Arte Alameda. Leading the bill is *Nine Songs,* the story of how Matt and Lisa find romance during the course of their musically accompanied lovemaking.

On a Tuesday morning a few weeks before, I'd paid a visit to Santiago's burgeoning red-light district. Crowded along Paseo Huérfanos, at the base of the Cerro Santa Lucía hill, the country's first sex shops can be found. Passing by Gallery and Free Sex, I settled on Solo Adultos, a dingy joint at the end of the street. Thirty-six-year-old Tatiana was behind the counter in the store's video section. Sitting at the till, she was sifting through internet orders on a computer. She double-clicked on the photo of an eight-inch plastic dildo to check the price. The enlarged $24.50 penis then expanded alarmingly across the screen. Their collection of a thousand or more explicit videos filled the wall-to-wall shelving. Most had European or American titles. Solo Adultos relied on Argentina and Brazil for its small Latino section. Chile's film industry is still fighting shy of its own porno productions.

'Solo Adultos, Julieta speaking,' Tatiana had said, picking up the telephone. The cordless under her chin, she typed a title into her database. 'Sure, we have it in stock. It'll be with you within two hours.' The shop's online catalogue and confidential door-delivery service go down well with its sexually repressed clients. Tatiana replaced the phone set. '*Sweet Caramels 2*,' she shouted down to an invisible grunt working in the basement. She followed up the order with an address in the upmarket Las Condes district.

A small man in a raincoat and glasses came in. He glanced at the shelf nearest the door but was obviously self-conscious. Feeling himself watched, he snuck out almost as quickly as he'd snuck in.

'Do you get a lot of customers like that?' I asked.

'Sure, there are a lot of first-timers who feel embarrassed. But we get regulars too, who like to spend time browsing. Some come in couples too.'

Fridays and weekends are when Tatiana is at her busiest. As well as videos, men come in looking for a sexy outfit for their partners. Nurses' outfits sell the fastest. Women, meanwhile, tend to head straight for the vibrator counter. Even in the world of sexual fantasy, it seems Chileans drift towards the predictable.

'Sales go up in the summer,' Tatiana explained, 'when the wives and kids go off to the beach and the men are left in town by themselves.'

The sex vendor assured me her family aren't bothered about her line of work. She used to be an assistant to a senator, but she found that pornography pays better than politics. Now she only has to work mornings, leaving the afternoons free to look after her two school-age daughters. It was her husband who first got her into the business. Back in the 1990s, the bootlegger was importing illegal X-rated videos into the country. As soon as the government legalised pornography in 1998, he opened the store.

'One of his American actor friends recently visited from the States – a big star and all,' Tatiana said with a smile. 'We took him to a posh restaurant downtown. It was hilarious to see all these respectable folk double-take when they saw him.'

Tatiana put her liberal attitudes towards sex down to a stint in Holland when she was younger. As a business opportunity, it's served her well. She only knew of a dozen other sex shops in the whole of Chile. All the same, she had yet to tell her children where Mummy and Daddy work.

'It'd be difficult for them at school if word got out,' she reasoned.

Most Chileans, Tatiana conceded, are still very closed about sex. It saddened her, for example, when young girls came in asking for a vibrator, 'to lose their virginity'. But the ex-senator's assistant could laugh at Chile's prudishness too.

Giggling to herself, she recounted how a thief had stolen three vibrators several months ago.

'They were huge things, two kilos a time. The shop minder chased him down the street, yelling "Thief, thief" all the way down Alemada.' To speed his escape, the robber had thrown his spoils into the crowd.

'Lucky no one got hit,' snorted Tatiana. 'They could have been hospitalised.'

The phone rang again. Tatiana took two long breaths to control her laughter. A titter still in her voice, she picked up the receiver.

'Solo Adultos, Julieta speaking.'

In Valparaíso, I head off to see another expert in the secrets of Chile's shame-ridden sexual appetites.

It is an odd feeling waiting to be picked up by a transsexual. Sitting on a bench in Plaza Margarita, I eye up the passers-by. A man in a corduroy jacket with a flat head and thin wrists is reading a newspaper two benches down. He doesn't look the tran type, but my experience on these matters is limited. My date is only a little late and I hold off propositioning the stranger.

A tall woman with a flat chest then enters the shady square and starts walking towards me. Could this be her? But she continues straight by, studiously ignoring my attempts to catch her eye. Beginning to feel as though I must look like the park pervert, I resign myself to being found and concentrate on the view instead.

An oil tanker emerges around the southern coastline and turns in a slow arc towards the port below. Several huge blue cargo cranes can just be made out on the quayside from Cerro Baron, the poor hilltop district that houses the square. I watch a tug inching across the bay, leaving a foam trail behind it as it heads out to meet the larger vessel. Around the curve of the coastline, the white turrets of Viña del Mar's swanky high-rises blot the shore. One next to the other in varying heights, they remind me of the stubby columns of a bar chart. The day is crisp and clear. Not a cloud drifts across the turquoise sky. Spring cannot be far away, I reflect, picturing how pretty the square must be in blossom.

A tap on the shoulder shakes off all thoughts of springtime and romance. For a seasoned sex worker, Jimena is older, taller and considerably more haggard than I'd imagined. Her smile reveals two or three missing front teeth. She's wearing no make-up or jewellery. Plumes of dry, unbrushed red hair mushroom out from beneath her black plastic headband. The roots are white, as is the two-day stubble that sprouts from her neck and chin.

As for her wardrobe, it's mismatched and multilayered. A spotty apron skirt covers a pair of thin, plum-coloured linen trousers. From beneath a holey, grey woollen jumper emerges a red polo neck. On her feet, thick yellow socks peep through an old pair of off-white plastic sandals. Despite her breast implants and effeminate walk, her large hands and deep voice betray her original gender. She's a mix of Old Mother Hubbard and a longhaired vamp from the seventies. I get up and follow her to her house. The man on the bench lowers his paper and watches us leave together.

Jimena lives three or four minutes away in a poorly built shack on a bend in the road. Thirty short, precipitous steps lead up an almost vertical bank to her front door. Wet underwear drips from a line outside her four-room home. Ducking beneath the Y-fronts and knickers, she unlocks the tin door and invites me in.

Jimena has little to show for her four decades working the streets of Valparaíso. We sit at a glass-topped table in the living room, which leads into a kitchen at one end and a bedroom at the other. Two children's dolls sit propped up on a plastic sofa. A tea towel from Tenerife hangs on the wall next to a feather-strewn mask from a costume ball. Her bootlegged cassette collection is stacked up on a crudely made wooden tape deck. Two empty bottles of rum serve as bookends on a bookshelf with no books. The draughty house has no heating and, without the sunshine of the morning, is chilly.

Before we sit down to speak, Jimena vanishes into the kitchen to finish preparing her dinner. I ask to use the lavatory.

'Sure, it's just here,' she says, pointing to a crooked wooden door close to the kitchen. The door has a carpet stapled to it and string for a handle. In the dim light, I edge towards the lavatory mindful of wide gaps in the floorboards. The seatless lavatory doesn't flush, I discover. Nor is there water in the tap. By the door, I spot a large washing machine. Other than the gas stove in the kitchen, it's the only domestic appliance in the house.

As with Blanca, Jimena kicks off her tale with her childhood. In her case, though, it wasn't a happy time. Brought up in a small town, her habit of dressing up in women's clothes was not well received. Following the break-up of her parents' marriage, her mother – 'God rest her soul' – packed her off at age nine to live with her father in Valparaíso. Unsympathetic to Jimena's suggestion that he'd sired a girl in a boy's body, he sent her to a Catholic boarding school.

'I think he thought the nuns could beat it out of me,' she chuckles, her giggle husky from a heavy cigarette habit.

The plan didn't work. Jimena was expelled. By fifteen, she was working on the streets as a prostitute. Her beat was along Calle

Francia and Calle Brasil, just beside the national Congress Building. The girl prostitutes would occupy one corner and the transsexuals another.

'Who were your clients in general?' I ask.

'Lots of politicians, as you might imagine. But we'd service all sorts: doctors, lawyers, teachers and the like. Many hold a very high social standing.'

'Why's that?' I enquire, my curiosity sparked by her customers and their class.

'Socially, it's much harder for them to come out as homosexual. Wife at home, two kids and all that. Plus, many hotels in Chile don't let men enter with other men. So they go looking for a *pintada* [lady boy],' Jimena replies.

We talk for an hour or so until the oven bell announces her chicken pie is ready. I leave her to her supper and walk back down the hill. Our encounter leaves me feeling saddened. In Chile, sexual minorities such as Jimena do not exist. When she applies for a job, she gets no response. When she's raped by the police, no one takes her statement. When neo-Nazi thugs mutilate her rectum with a broken bottle, no one investigates.

Jimena is the shameful public face of the nation's sexual peccadilloes. She's also a threat. As a prostitute and a transsexual, the sex-touting she-boy crosses all the boundaries of the 'woman-man happily ever after' model.

Thanks to a small bank loan, Jimena has recently set up a laundry service. The business is run out of her dank bathroom. But if her social banishment on the slopes of the Cerro Baron wasn't already sealed, it is now. Jimena recently discovered that she has full-blown AIDS.

Pencil thin and drawn, Marcela's wasted appearance jars with the standard profile of public celebrities. At a glance, her sunken cheeks and coat-hanger limbs could pass for cocaine chic. But a closer look displays the unmistakable etches of real sickness: the lifelessness of her fair hair, the dilation of her pupils, the wan hue of her translucent skin. Even so, the hotel receptionist has become a regular on Chilean television and radio over the past decade. She owes her fame to two factors: the Human Immunodeficiency Virus and guts.

We meet in her bungalow in Quilpué, a nondescript town inland from the coast. Most of its inhabitants commute every day to the busier cities of Valparaíso or, as in Marcela's case, Viña del Mar. The evening bus is late, and it's after nine o'clock at night when I eventually turn up on her doorstep. Although she's tired from a full day at work, the young mother brushes off my flustered apologies and invites me to have a cup of coffee.

'The girls are with their grandmother tonight, so there's no problem about us talking and keeping them awake,' she says, pointing a finger at a door that I take to be her daughters' shared bedroom.

The bungalow is small and sparsely furnished but meticulously maintained. The tiled floor in the living room shines after a recent mopping. A buff-coloured three-piece suite occupies pride of place in the main room, sparkling with a fake leather finish. In the corner, a gas burner blasts out heat, chasing off the cold evening air as it sneaks in surreptitiously around the windows.

Marcela serves the coffee at her round, glass-topped dining table. She takes a seat opposite me, folding her emaciated legs beneath her in the lotus position. The dining chair dwarfs her.

'I was a virgin on my wedding night,' she starts, her voice wheezy as if she's suffering from a bad bout of bronchitis.

Marcela doesn't mince her words. She shares Blanca's distaste for untruths. Impatience, not ethics, drives her compulsive honesty. Life is too short for hiding, the thirty-six-year-old tells me. Her frankness is refreshing, imbuing her with a vigour that competes mockingly with the frailty of her physique.

Her candid epiphany came with the death of her husband. He had started developing headaches almost immediately after discovering he was HIV positive. It was Marcela who informed him of his illness. In the impassive tone of a presenter reading the evening news, she recalls how she told him after he'd come across her anti-retrovirals in the fridge. She'd been diagnosed six weeks previously.

'He asked me what they were because the labels were all in English. I told him they were vitamins as I was very thin back then too. And then later, over supper, I asked myself how long I had to keep on lying.'

'So you knew that he was HIV positive too, then?' I interject, curious why she hadn't told him immediately.

'Yes, of course,' she replies, repeating the fact that her husband was the only man she'd ever slept with.

'But, in Chile, we women worry about our children first, our children second, our children third and then our husbands fourth.' She pauses. 'It's a bad habit, I know. But we even think about our lovers before ourselves.'

She wasn't worried about herself, she says. Once she'd found out that neither of her daughters had contracted HIV, she knew she had the inner strength to cope. She wasn't so sure about her husband though.

'I knew I'd have to eventually tell him. So very casually I explained that they weren't vitamins but a course of drugs that I was taking.'

He'd asked her if she was ill. Marcela had replied that she was: 'And I have what you have,' she added. Her husband had stared back at her confused. Then she told him straight: 'I have AIDS.'

Speaking ten years on, her expression is as flat as a punctured tyre. I have little doubt that her delivery of the phrase is a precise re-enactment of that fateful supper.

'You can't imagine the look that came over him. He just looked at me and said, "No, this has to be a joke."'

Marcela remembers his reaction perfectly. Her husband didn't say another word. He just got up out of his chair, went outside and sat in his truck. He stayed there all night, until seven o'clock in the morning. His wife knew then and there that he lacked what it took to fight the condition. Long before he died, she lost him to the darkness of depression and self-pity.

Behind the headaches, the doctors diagnosed a malignant tumour. Treatment was incompatible with the antiretrovirals he was taking.

Marcela told her colleagues at work that her husband had cancer. He didn't want anyone to know he was suffering from AIDS.

The day after he died, Marcela decided to set up Fuerza Positiva (Positive Power), an organisation dedicated to helping people with HIV/AIDS. One of her first steps was to inform her in-laws of the real cause of their son's death. The second was to stop lying about her own condition. The hotel where she worked promptly fired her.

'More and more women now are HIV positive. Lots tell me they can't be infected because they're married. What they don't realise is that while they might be faithful, their husbands aren't necessarily the same.'

An attack of coughing suddenly sends her into spasms. She reaches for a glass of water and waits for her breathing to return to normal. Marcela treats her condition pragmatically, much as a ship's captain would a rough sea. It's an unavoidable distraction, to be expected, to be prepared for and to be traversed with as much calm as courage can muster.

'Many married men live double lives, you know?' she says, returning to the same point once her fit has passed.

'Some are secretly bisexual or homosexual. When I give talks, women often come up to me afterwards and admit that they have doubts about their husbands. How many act on their hunch, though, I can't say.'

'And how are your daughters dealing with it?' I ask.

'They know that mum is ill with AIDS, but that it's under control. Constanza, who's fourteen years old, accompanies me to all the public events that I do. The most important thing for Fernanda, my youngest, is that her mummy is on TV.'

The thought of her daughter, who's now primary-school age, brings a smile to Marcela's face.

'"My mum uses condoms," Fernanda tells her classmates. "Condoms are like little hats that men put on their penises."'

With some regularity, Marcela finds her phone ringing and picks up to a distraught mother on the other end. The accusations are usually the same: that she's corrupting their child's innocence; that sex education should wait until they're older. Anyone else would put the phone down. Not Marcela. Honour-bound, she takes the mothers through a full, uncut version of the birds and the bees.

On my last afternoon in Valparaíso, I take a walk down past the unsightly port buildings to San Mateo beach. I am in search of a little piece of gender history.

On the sandy inlet down below, a dad is kicking a football around with his infant son. Two other young boys are digging sandcastles with flimsy plastic spades. Their mum watches them from a safe distance, wrapped in a picnic blanket against the cold. Further up the beach, another young mother sits chatting with a girlfriend, gently rocking a pram. A replica cannon rests on the sea wall, pointing wistfully out to sea. The Chilean flag flaps violently in the wind from the naval barracks on the cliff top behind us. The day is drawing to a close, and, one by one, the beach-goers pack up their belongings.

It's a rotten day for a wedding. A brisk westerly is kicking up off the Pacific, and the dark clouds on the horizon threaten rain. I thrust my hands deep into my jacket pockets and join the twenty or so celebrants already waiting on the beach. We're a misfit bunch: a middle-aged neighbour, a handful of university friends, some volunteer colleagues from the campaign group AccionGay, a friend from the call centre where one of the brides works and a one-legged man armed with a video camera in his right hand and a crutch in his left. Immediate family members are notable by their absence.

While we wait, preparations for the service are made. Someone has brought along two garden torches. Someone else, a glass drinks table. Mauricio, the vice-president of AccionGay, and Pati's godparent for the day, wedges the torches into the sand either side of the improvised altar table. His repeated efforts to light the matrimonial lanterns, however valiant, end in failure. We make do with a nearby street light and the headlamps of passing traffic along the coast road above. The beach is now empty other than four smooching couples on the rocks at the water's edge.

Pati and Ganina, our lesbian lovebirds, eventually arrive just as the sun is setting. The bridal carriage comprises a rust-ridden, four-door Toyota, driven by a student friend of Pati. A white cotton bow flaps in a V-shape across the bonnet. Bringing up the rear of the cortège saunters a television crew. The wedding is due to feature in a one-hour documentary about AccionGay. Hand in hand, the smiling couple walk along the promenade and down the concrete-step aisle onto the beach. We all cheer and clap, and the brides blush shyly in unison.

Formalities are further delayed as we await the master of ceremonies, Inés, the founder of a pro-gay solidarity group for mothers with homosexual children. She's phoned ahead to say she missed her bus. Pati lights a cigarette to calm her nerves. At twenty-two, she's three years older than her teenage girlfriend. She strokes her younger lover's hair with a maternal affection.

After five minutes, Camilo steps up and announces that in Inés' absence he will play the vicar's role. Dressed in a pin-stripe suit jacket and tight jeans, he's certainly the most elegant of our unorthodox bridal party. He's also the most camp, and his self-appointment draws a round of ironic laughter. But our stand-in minister takes to the job with uncharacteristic solemnity and calls all present to gather in. We form a half circle around the glass table and unlit garden torches.

Still holding hands, Pati and Ganina stand next to one another facing Camilo. The effeminate priest gives a brief two-minute address about the joys of love and the importance of mutual commitment. The speech gives rise to more snuffled giggles. He then calls on the couple to exchange rings and invites them to seal their vows with a kiss. Predictably, the cameraman zooms in for a close-up of their lips pressed together. Everyone claps and then, after the newly-weds prise themselves apart, smothers the couple with hugs.

'*Viva la diversidad!*' squeaks Camilo, drawing the ceremony to its official close.

The couple retreat to the Toyota and drive off, the clatter of tin cans announcing Valparaíso's first-ever lesbian nuptials.

There was a freedom between the young couple that had piqued my curiosity. Chilean women weren't generally like this: so open, so tactile, so overt about their sexuality. Their carefree unreservedness put me in mind of Bolívar. Perhaps women in Chile's sexually alternative bracket were the true inheritors of his bedroom licence? Everything else in Chile seems upside down. Why not sex? Could it be that the heterosexual women were living in the closet, not their sisters on the fringes?

Chile's annual gay march was scheduled for a few weekends' time. It struck me as the perfect opportunity to put my theory to the test.

Avenida Libertador General Bernardo O'Higgins, Santiago

To my surprise, I bump into Mauricio, AccionGay's vice-president. He's working as a roadie on the main entertainment float. In the ruckus of hairspray and spandex, it's difficult to envision the Virgin of Carmen walking these same streets just a little while before.

The extravagant pageant has ground to a halt just off Avenida Libertador General Bernardo O'Higgins, the capital's principal avenue. The august stone building of the University of Chile looks down on the mayhem. Beneath the concrete pavement slabs, turning in their grave, lie the interred bones of the country's ginger-haired hero.

Mauricio is standing behind the float on top of a stepladder, trying valiantly to control the flow of people pushing their way onto the makeshift stage. He'd told me that he was going as an angel. On the day, he looks more like a camp Boy Scout in fancy dress. In his flamboyant rainbow neckerchief and figure-hugging vest top, I'm sure his boyfriend thinks him angelic.

Mauricio spots me first and jumps down from the ladder, planting a big gay kiss on my cheek. I compliment him on his costume, and he flaps at me, as if he'd just thrown it on as he ran out of the house. His neatly trimmed beard and eau de toilette give him away though.

'Look who's here!' he squeals to a tall figure in a rainbow cloak on the float above. A technicolored Joseph swivels around: 'Ooooh, Ooo-lii-vér. *Ho-laaaa!*'

From an open palm, a sloppy kiss blows through the air in my direction. It's Marcelo, president of Mauricio's gay-rights group. We'd met briefly in Valparaíso. The flamboyant compère has a jostling crowd of gays, lesbians, bisexuals, transsexuals, hermaphrodites and transvestites shouting up to him. Done with their marching, they are impatient to be entertained.

They don't have to wait long. A technician flips a switch, and electronic dance tracks immediately boom out of the float's four gigantic speakers. An extremely tall transvestite with a short pink bodice and skin-tight hot pants then takes the stage. He descends into an erotic, techno dance routine. He's a popular figure in the local gay clubbing scene, and the offbeat jerks of hips and hands prove a hit with his fans. Marcelo steps up to introduce the next act. Another sphinx-like transvestite takes to the floor. Silver body spray covers every inch of his exposed skin. An explosion of sparks erupts as he jabs the sky with a finger and thrusts his pelvis at the crowd – a move he repeats with heroic tirelessness. Needless to say, the crowd is besotted with him too.

Next up are the stars of the show: four bare-chested, muscle-bound sailor boys. Decked out in preposterously short latex shorts and blue naval bibs, their sinuous figures are doused in bronzing oil and shorn clean of body hair. The waxed icons strut their stuff to a natty pop song and send the male-dominated audience into a collective swoon. Those in the front rows ecstatically snap photos on their mobile phones. Marcelo lets the cheering crowd know that the hunky foursome will be appearing for a longer set at the after-march party at Blondie Discotheque. The news spawns yet more schoolgirl shrieking.

Behind the float, Mauricio is being overrun. The upcoming acts can sense the excitement on stage and want their moment of fame. The authority accrued to him by his Boy Scout uniform is lost in the euphoria. Very soon the trailer is packed to overflowing, with drag queens in leotards, gay men in stockings, transvestites in bridal gowns and two chubby men in wrestlers' masks who are groping everyone within reach. The latter I take to be the anarchist wing of the gay fraternity.

Joining the masked crusaders in creating a rumpus are the militant members of Chile's lesbian wing. They'd decided to stage a march of their own.

'*Nada que celebrar, mucho que protestar!*' ran their killjoy slogan: 'Nothing to celebrate, much to protest!' In contrast to the celebratory mood of Mauricio and his fifteen thousand friends, the hardline lesbians had sulked along at the back of the cavalcade. They'd stopped briefly by a mural of Gabriela Mistral along the Alameda avenue and read out a homily to Chile's 'greatest ever lesbian'.

At the end of the march, they'd settled themselves on a grass verge opposite La Moneda, the solid oblong palace of Chile's presidents. The music from the AccionGay float drowns out their protest ballads. They number around two hundred in total. All are young and kitted out more or less identically: jeans (mostly grey), belts (all studded) and T-shirts or sleeveless tops (uniformly black).

'Love them as we do,' Mauricio had told me previously, 'fashion sense is not our sisters' strong point'. There's also a splattering of men, most of whom are gay activists sympathetic to the lesbians' political cause. Among them is a young man with a boyish face and a megaphone. He's yelling at the top of his voice to passers-by that he's a 'lesbian and proud of it'. I'm not convinced he's helping their cause.

Into the soft earth of the Alameda flowerbeds, the women have wedged a montage of homemade placards. The posters' angry captions are targeted at the presidential seat of power in front. Each of the verbal missiles features the word 'against': against the system, against sexism, against violence, against capitalism, against the 'torture of the establishment', against silicon even.

A friendly girl with a nose-ring and low-slung jeans points out Erika to me. With no make-up and short hair, the journalism graduate conforms to stereotype. I obtained her name through *Breaking the Silence,* Chile's premier lesbian magazine. A serious woman in her late twenties, Erika edits the politically focused publication.

As we speak, I look for signs of Pati and Ganina's happiness. All I find is rage and resentment. Erika regales me with stories of discrimination: the lesbian judge who lost custody of her children when she moved in with a woman; the religious-education teacher who came out as gay and was sacked despite a spotless twenty-five-year record; the ban on lesbians receiving artificial insemination. The list goes on and on.

'But isn't Chile becoming more open to lesbians and sexual minorities?' I interject. I had in mind an anti-discrimination law that had recently been passed by the senate.

Erika chaffs at the idea. Did I know that lesbians in Chile were portrayed as promiscuous, as paedophiles and (for some weird reason I never got to the bottom of) as Europhiles? These typecasts, she's convinced, are put about by homophobes in high society and their poodle press.

'There's a collective plot not to take us seriously.' Opening the gates to pornography forms part of the schemers' strategy. Now every man fantasises about a lesbian threesome. 'They're not interested in who we are, only how we *do it,*' the acerbic editor snaps.

'Aren't things slowly changing though?' I venture. Only that morning, I'd read that mainstream Chilean television was about to broadcast its first-ever lesbian kiss. 'Now surely that's a breakthrough?'

Erika won't allow her black cloud to be broken. Had I noticed that the scene would occur on a show called *Women in Jail*?

'It's as if all lesbians are criminals!' And had I read the actress's comments? How she enjoys challenging roles – Erika pauses, searching her memory for the exact quote – 'like playing a lesbian *or* a psychopath?'

I get her point. Chile's lesbians are forced to live within a social straitjacket.

But don't women have more freedom within the lesbian commu-nity? I tell her about my impressions of the wedding. I also mention the enormous queue of young people I'd seen waiting in line outside Cherry, a gay bar in downtown Valparaíso.

Didn't she think it was positive that the new generation feels at liberty to experiment with their sexuality? Erika takes the editorial theory that good news is no news to the very limit. She welcomes the fact that young girls are testing out their sexuality but worries about the consequences. The tabloids merely leer and publish raunchy photos of teenagers kissing in clubs. The more serious papers write it off as a fad that will pass.

She's also worried about her readers: 'Do you know how full our mailbox is these days?' *Breaking the Silence*'s resident agony aunt is having to work overtime. It seems that silence is not all that's being broken. Die-hard lesbians across Chile are having their hearts snapped by young flighties.

'They fall in love and then the young girls decide they're not les-bians after all.' The editor shakes her head.

I look at the 'against' signs poking up from the lawn. Plucking up courage, I ask Erika a final question: 'Is there anything Chile's les-bians are protesting *for*?' She gives the query some thought.

'For a society in which women don't feel ashamed of saying who they really are,' she finally responds. 'For a Chile with no fears, with nothing to hide.'

Erika is characteristically pessimistic that such a situation will emerge any time soon. Her girlfriend wants them to emigrate to Spain, where attitudes are more liberal. She says the idea tempts her. But she feels her responsibility compels her to stay in Chile and carry on the fight.

Leaving the protest flags and PVC behind me, I wonder if Erika and her female peers will really have to wait that long. Women liv-ing in wartime Europe could not have imagined the fun they'd be having come the Swinging Sixties. The signs of change can already be seen in Chile. Divorce is now legal after a decades-long fight. Female students are outnumbering men on the university campuses.

The Ministry of Health is giving out condoms. And a woman has even taken the presidency.

A silent social and sexual revolution is already brewing in Chile. What was shame-ridden is set to become celebrated. What earned the ire of the establishment is now winning its ear. Desolation is giving way to daring. At long last, gender is being normalised.

My final date in Chile takes place in a castle. Comunidad Mujer, a network of high-flying women, is holding its annual lunch in the Castillo Hidalgo atop Cerro Santa Lucía. A press card was fortunately enough to resolve my status as a single male and snare myself a seat at the all-female event. Despite her pioneering business venture at the bottom of the hill, I note with disappointment that Tatiana hadn't made the invite list. Instead, the great and the good are gathered: doctors, servicewomen, captains of industry, charitable types, politicians, government ministers and one head of state.

On the table beside me, prodding her chicken fillet with a fork, sits Chile's first-ever female president. I reach under the table for my camera. Across South America, Michelle Bachelet has become a living icon for her gender. Here is a woman who had been tortured and forced into exile by the military government, who had lost her father during the turbulent early years of the Pinochet regime, who had brought up three children single-handedly, and yet who had risen to the top of her profession as a physician and who had eventually gone on to take the country's top job.

I move to take the picture just as the silent, mean-faced woman sitting on the right of me touches my arm. We have yet to introduce ourselves.

'Oliver,' I say, '*Encantado*.'

She doesn't offer her name. All I get is her job reference: 'Senora Bachelet's security team.' She eyes my camera.

'Not while *la Presidenta* is eating, please.'

Perhaps your photo instead, then? The charmless bodyguard doesn't appreciate the gesture. She fixes her eyes on her boss, saying nothing more to me for the remainder of the meal.

A sentimentalised reworking of Prince's *Purple Rain* album is playing in the background. The music cuts out as Bachelet takes to the podium. Squeezed into a sensible grey business suit, the sturdy former doctor speaks fluently without notes. Her administration is putting gender rights at the heart of government, she insists. The high-flyers clap.

'As women, we are asking for full rights, nothing more.' A cheer from the back. A long account of policy amendments – earlier pensions, workplace flexibility, crèches, conjugal rights – draws less enthusiasm.

Eventually, the president begins to wrap up. The diners jerk themselves awake. Comunidad Mujer's 'Woman of the Year' is announced. The flat-heeled founder of a women's refuge takes the title. She earns herself a placard and a photo alongside Chile's most powerful woman.

Before making her way back to her dessert, Bachelet impresses on her listeners how far the cause of women has come.

'Little girls used to grow up thinking they'd be mothers or nurses,' she says. 'Now they dream of becoming *presidentas*.' Enthusiastic applause ripples through the room.

Across the *cordillera*, Argentines are geeing themselves up to clap their first elected female president too.

3

MARCH OF THE PENGUINS

Argentina and politics

Like a robust blind man deluded by his sense of power, they [political leaders] march forward as confidently as the most clear-sighted, and bouncing from reef to reef, they are unable to find the way.

SIMÓN BOLÍVAR, 'THE ANGOSTURA ADDRESS', 1819

Buenos Aires

I arrive at City Hall in a fluster. The humidity is intense. It's one of those hot, muggy Buenos Aires afternoons that often descend on the Argentine capital. It was for days like this that the siesta was invented. But this city never stops. Not even for a heatwave. Instead, life becomes air-conditioned. Porteños survive by remaining enveloped in refrigerated, recycled bubbles of the stuff. They travel from their AC car, to their AC office to their AC home.

My journey to microcentro affords me no such comfort. I travel in on the 56 bus, crunched between commuters. All the seats are taken and we standing passengers cling to the dangling straps overhead as the bus lurches through the morning traffic. The trick, I soon learn, is to keep your feet sufficiently apart so as to create a sturdy base and keep from toppling over. The strategy serves me well. Until a taxi suddenly switches lanes without indicating, that is. Then we all bundle forward as the driver slams on his brakes. Readjusting myself, I reach up again for the strap. This time, I edge my shoe against that of my neighbour to better prepare myself for the next emergency stop. I grow conscious that two unsightly sweat marks are appearing under my arms. Damp beads of sweat are also collecting on my brow. One after another they begin slipping into my eye, causing it to sting painfully. I go to rub it. Just as I do so, the bus jerks again. I bump violently into the man beside me.

Profuse apologies. It comes almost as a relief when the bus grinds to a halt.

The road ahead is gridlocked. Avenida 9 de Julio, the carving-knife artery that slices downtown from uptown, is under siege. The *piqueteros*, the country's own-brand protest groups, have come to town. Their makeshift tents line the multiple-lane highway. These are Argentina's Bedouins, their taking up residency temporarily as and when their political demands require it. Today, it's for an increase in *planes sociales*.

The passengers exhale a collective groan at the sight of the urban encampment. Some decide to sit it out, resigning themselves to inch-by-inch progress along a diverted route. Others descend from the bus. I opt to follow them. I'm already late for my meeting at City Hall and decide to cover the final dozen blocks on foot. I step between the picket groups. There are perhaps two hundred in total, not a bad strike force to bring the city centre to a standstill.

I set off down the broad Avenida de Mayo, head bent, too rushed to appreciate the ornate Parisian-style buildings that line the roadside. I drop from the curb onto the road to skip by the other pedestrians. The tarmac is so hot it feels almost squelchy under foot. My shirt is soaked with perspiration by the time I arrive. The smell of body odour mixes with the diesel fumes of the traffic. I take a breather at the steps of City Hall in a vain attempt to compose myself.

Across the road lies the iconic tree-lined Plaza de Mayo. On the far side sits the Casa Rosada, the slightly dumpy *estancia*-styled office of the president. On either side of the plaza stand sturdy, serious-looking government buildings; the Central Bank, the tax office, the economy ministry. These date back half a century to the early days of the Peronist era. Their architectural formidability is intentional, a testimony to the strong hand of the state. Opposite the City Hall stands its colonial predecessor, now a museum. Only half the original structure still stands. The other half was unceremoniously chopped off to make way for a wider avenue. The government of the day aimed to recreate the Place Charles de Gaulle effect in Paris, with diagonal avenues radiating outwards. A similar disregard for the nation's Spanish heritage can be seen in the design of the Cathedral. Inhabiting the far corner of the plaza, its stone columns and pitched roof intentionally mimic a Greco-Roman temple.

The Plaza de Mayo boasts a central role in Argentina's recent political history. It is a place of celebration. It's where crowds gather to celebrate, be it an election victory or a football final. It's where Evita Peron spoke to the masses, in her famous valedictory address from the Casa Rosada's balcony. It's also the scene of darker times. It's where the Argentine Air Force flew over in 1955 and bombed a political rally. Coups and counter-coups have played out within this one-block square. Today, all is more or less quiet. A metal fence armed with police runs as a barrier 100 yards in front of the Casa Rosada. It's a precautionary measure. The only protestors to brave the heat are a dozen Falkland War veterans. They are in pursuit of better pensions. But their presence is more or less a permanent one and they are snoozing in the shade of a tree.

With my breathing more or less back to normal, I walk up the steps of City Hall. Like many public buildings, its impressive façade gives way to a drab interior. Astrid Pikielny is hidden away in a one-room office on the second floor. A rusty air-conditioning unit is doing its best to keep her and her colleagues cool. Her clammy handshake suggests it's failing. It makes me feel better about my own state of dishevelment. Astrid recommends we step out into an adjoining reception area. She points me to a low armchair. I sit down to the noise of creaking springs.

'I haven't always worked for City Hall. It's a temporary appointment. For the bicentenary, you understand,' she tells me.

In her late thirties, Astrid is bubbly and energetic. She trained and worked as a journalist beforehand. When the job came up to help with the City government's bicentenary efforts, she felt she should take it. Though a reluctant civil servant, a sense of civic commitment drove her decision. It's a communications role. Her problem is that there's not much to communicate. With only a few months to go before the Republic officially inaugurates its 200-year celebrations, the City's official agenda is officially empty. But then, forward planning is not Argentina's strong point. Come what may, fireworks will no doubt light up the sky on 25 May, National Independence Day.

In the absence of specifics, our conversation takes a more abstract turn. What purpose does the bicentenary serve? It is an opportunity to reflect on the past, Astrid responds. And to project for the future. 'Buenos Aires was the centre of the revolution of 1810. Its protagonists were predominantly young men, under thirty, with varied education and from different backgrounds. But they united over their vision of the kind of country they could create. Without all the things we have today – running water, a sewage system, proper roads – they were able to unite, to dream of a different future, and propose a path forward.'

Such zeal takes me back. Sluggish bureaucracy has evidently not taken the shine off her political idealism.

She presses on. 'The Revolution grew from values related to liberation and equality. It's as if the revolution is a well of positive values – values that we should never throw away. Ojo, there is no such thing as sacred history or pre-established destinies. As citizens we shouldn't stand on the sidelines. History doesn't happen alone. We all make history, every day, in the roles that we occupy and the decisions we make.'

It's quite the speech. But then, alongside procrastination, the ability to talk politics represents another national speciality. No one does it better than Cristina Fernández de Kirchner, the current president. She set the tone on the night of her election victory. Together with her jubilant campaign staff and a battery of journalists, I'd crammed into the basement of her election HQ, a downtown hotel, to hear her acceptance speech. She'd sounded almost humble. She was the servant of the people. The voice of unity. The President of all Argentines, not just the few. The guarantor of national dignity. Astrid's liberation heroes would have been pleased with her sentiments. Who knows, some television viewers may even have believed her.

Time would belie such fine-sounding rhetoric. Within a few months of taking office, Argentina's first-elected female president had a national strike on her hands. The farmers had downed tools.

They were objecting to a sliding tax on agricultural exports. Their protest lasted four months, leading to shortages on the shelves and billions of dollars in lost revenues. For all her talk of unity, Cristina belongs to the worker-led Peronist party. Shop stewards and blue-collar workers are her natural allies, not 'rural oligarchs'. Run-ins with the church, the army, greedy bankers and other voices of dissent were to follow. City Hall is run by PRO, one of the main opposition parties. That puts Astrid firmly in the 'anti-K' camp as well.

The truth of Argentina's factious political scenario is not absent from Astrid's mind. The more she speaks, the more the trace of realism seeps into her voice. She doesn't want to be naive. 'Here, at the doors of the bicentenary, Argentina is a country of considerable antagonisms. They come in different forms and have different names. But they are there. Everyday there are people in the street calling for work, for health, for education. The inequality between rich and poor causes insecurity. Obviously this isn't the country that the founding fathers dreamed of.'

'So the work of the liberators continues in a sense?' I ask.

'Yes, of course. We want something else. But, hey, from here we've got to work hard to improve things. Apathy is no good. Unfortunately, cynicism is all to common nowadays.'

Not wanting to end our conversation on a low note, I ask her about plans for the Escuela Superior de Mecánica de la Armada. I'd heard that the military base, the scene of terrible atrocities during Argentina's last military dictatorship, was to be turned into a museum. It was due to be opened in time for the bicentenary. Using history this way struck me as an important step.

'Sorry, I don't know anything about it,' the communications officer admits. 'We're the City Bicentenary Committee. The EMSA is a project of the Federal Bicentenary Committee.'

It turns out that the two groups have no interaction whatsoever. Can she put me in touch with someone in the Federal office, I wonder. She looks indecisive, then leads me back to her sweltering office. In a pile of dog-eared business cards, she turns up a name. I note down the contact details. 'Just don't say you got them from us,' Astrid tells me.

I fear her desire to see a unified Argentina still lies some way off.

Simón Bolívar never was a great fan of elections. He judged the 'rustic inhabitants' to be 'so ignorant' as to 'vote mechanically'. Not to mention the 'intriguers in the cities', who he rated 'so ambitious' that they immediately 'turn everything into factions'. Party spirit, he lamented, prevailed in all matters.

In the opinion of the Venezuelan freedom fighter, his homeland had never experienced a 'correct election' during its early years as a sovereign nation. Instead, the government invariably ended up in the hands of 'men who were incompetent, corrupt, or uncommitted to the cause of independence'.

Since Bolívar's day, confidence in the political classes in South America has not greatly improved. Across the continent, politicians are painted as corrupt and self-interested, as money-grabbers and power-seekers. Nothing is beyond their lust for enrichment, their capacity for criminality, their faculty for moral depravity. The politician caught with his hand in the till or his trousers round his ankles is not news here. It's the norm.

On election days, such accusations reach their crescendo. In Venezuela, the post-election press conference where Chávez's (defeated) opponents line up to denounce the vote-taking as rigged has become an established and choreographed part of the whole election process. Argentina is no different. Voting urns mysteriously disappear, critics say. People vote twice. Others are prevented from doing so. Even the dead are said to rise in some voting districts.

Deciding to see for myself, I'd joined my neighbour at the voting station on election morning. It had all looked normal enough. The names of those registered to vote were pasted in long lists up on the wall. Two policemen stood in the street ensuring decorum. Non-partisan volunteers manned the ballot boxes. Votes were cast in secret. Fraud, certainly on a massive scale, seemed unlikely.

Still, Alfonso, my neighbour, had his suspicions of the electoral process all the same. There was something fishy about the president rolling over in bed one morning and anointing his wife successor.

She might be a senator, but it still didn't feel right to him. Nor did all her foreign press trips seem proper during an electoral campaign. Campaign images of the liposuctioned Cristina shopping in New York and fawning with celebrities were uppermost in his mind. As for her husband, he'd left the country more anti-democratic than ever. The courts were no longer respected. Congress just signed the laws he sent it, not vice versa.

'All the power is concentrated in the presidency now. That's never healthy.'

Blessed with a blithe and breezy temperament, Alfonso had been uncharacteristically serious on our way to the voting station that morning. A floating voter, he was putting his money on Ricardo López Murphy. Nicknamed 'Bulldog' by the press on account of his bushy moustache and general grouchiness, the centre-right candidate had less charisma than a damp dishcloth. A serious politician, that's what Alfonso liked about him.

'No show with him; not like the others.'

At least Alfonso is angry about the situation. Many other Argentines couldn't care less.

'No idea,' Alfonso's university-age son told me when I asked him who he planned to vote for. 'They're all the same anyway.' A casual opinion poll among my other friends revealed a similar apathy. Disinterest and disillusion reigned. 'Sleepwalking towards history' was the title one foreign correspondent gave to his election report. Of course, his subeditors doctored it. 'History in the making'. How could Argentines not be tripping over themselves with excitement?

The only person on my block who showed any real political passion was Juan Carlos, the grizzled ex-army veteran who runs the newspaper stall on the street corner. By law, all Argentine citizens are supposed to vote. He was adamant that he wouldn't. None of the candidates deserved his support. Criminals the lot of them. Not voting, the newspaper man insisted, was the only democratic right left to him.

Argentina's recent history certainly makes its citizens more sceptical than most. During the 1990s, the country turned into one huge boot-sale. For the price of a sailing yacht or a flash car, its politicians sold the country from under them. State-run companies were broken up and packaged off. The president drove a Ferrari and built himself an airport. Meanwhile, his underlings sat back, sipped champagne and sold shares on the stock exchange.

Only when the family silver ran out and the creditors came calling did someone think to check the books. The public purse was dry. Not a *peso* of the privatisation windfall remained. The high living and foreign bank accounts of the politicians had swallowed it all up. Naturally, protests followed. Millions took to the streets. Casserole dishes were clanged. Four presidents came and went in a fortnight.

'*Que se vayan todos*,' the people cried: 'Out with the lot of them.' Several government administrations later, the memory of those dark days still lingers. As do many of the grease-palmed politicians.

The pollsters concur with the general state of disillusionment. In the run-up to the election, the Foreign Press Association arranged for a trio of polling experts to hold court at a media breakfast in the illustrious Café Tortoni.

Notebook in hand, I catch the early morning *subte* down to the former hang-out of Jorge Luis Borges and his literary friends. No poets are in evidence this morning, only a few eager German tourists drinking their *cafés con leche* and munching on butter-baked croissants. A bow-tied waiter, his forearm draped with a starched white napkin, politely shepherds me towards a downward flight of stairs. I'm late, and the session has already begun. Sitting at a raised table, the three experts are talking about projections and percentiles. Listening to them is a bleary-eyed group of twenty or so journalists, all of them swigging back strong coffee to contend with the early start.

'According to our interview data,' the one female pollster is saying as I sit down, 'the average voter is most preoccupied with crime rates, inflation and education.'

Her colleagues chip in with data of their own. Economy growing steadily. More jobs. Greater buying power. Low voter interest. A consistent lead for Cristina. News of the first lady's projected victory sends several hands shooting up.

'What about the recent scandals?' asks one journalist, the flakes of a free croissant sprinkled on his shirtsleeves. 'Hasn't that rocked the Cristina vote?'

Muckrakers always have a good time of it before an election. In this case, they hadn't had far to scrape. First there was the environment minister, accused of racking up receipts in luxury hotels and finding jobs for half her family. Then came 'Toiletgate', when over $60,000 in cash was found stashed away in the cabinet of the finance minister's office bathroom.

The best was left for last: 'Suitcasegate', a scandal involving a Venezuelan businessman who'd been caught by airport security with $800,000 in cash hidden amongst his weekend wear. The whole episode stank from the start. The man had been entering in the middle of the night on a private plane chartered with Venezuelan public funds. Photos of the shady businessman with the Argentine president then turned up. The money, the media speculated, was destined for Cristina's campaign. Unfortunately, the man at the centre of the row couldn't be questioned. He'd skipped bail and temporarily disappeared. For a few days, even Interpol couldn't find him.

'No, we've seen no major indent,' the woman's bearded colleague answers. 'The opposition has made some advances in recent weeks, but no more than a few percentage points.'

The flake-sprinkled journalist seems flabbergasted. Around the room, incredulous heads start shaking in agreement with him. The whiff of scandal is enough to topple prospective candidates in the correspondents' home countries. Yet here is the husband-and-wife team sailing through ethical crisis after ethical crisis.

The last of the three panellists obviously feels the need to spell out to his foreign crowd how things work in Argentina. We shouldn't be surprised, for example, if Cristina doesn't grant any interviews. In four years, her husband hadn't held one open press conference. Nor should we be taken aback if none of the candidates discuss their policies in any depth. Argentines vote for individuals today, not ideologies. Finally, we shouldn't lay too much stock in a candidate's party name. Peronism, radicalism, socialism, whatever it may be: as political doctrines, they're all virtually meaningless. People believe the economy is picking up. For most modern-day voters, that's all that really matters.

I left the Café Tortoni not entirely sold on the last pollster's pessimism. Wasn't Argentina the country of General Juan Domingo Perón, after all? Wasn't Cristina fighting under the party banner that bore his name? I'd attended all the leading lady's major rallies. Hadn't the crowds cheered whenever she mentioned Perón and his commitment to the poor and an end to social injustice? Wasn't she supposed to be the 'new Evita', the general's wife who fought so fiercely for the 'shirtless'? Apathy might reign in the streets, but I want to believe that some vestiges of idealism still remain within the party structure.

The fantasy doesn't last long. Reckoning paid-up politicians couldn't be trusted to give me an honest answer, I go in search of some grass-roots activists. My first port of call is the headquarters of the Evita Movement, located beside a McDonald's outlet on a busy stretch of Avenida Callao. Born as a picket group of unemployed labourers, the movement has gravitated into a formal political organisation. Avowed *Kirchneristas*, its followers can be counted on to turn up with their banners whenever Cristina calls.

The wet Friday afternoon that I visit happens to coincide with the annual meeting of the movement's youth wing. Youth, in political terms, means anyone under thirty with student ID. Crowded into a smoke-filled room overlooking the street, the movement's regional representatives are taking it in turns to speak. Each delivers a verbose dialectic on the contemporary political situation of the country: Kirchner is riding a wave; the crisis of hegemony still looms; wealth needs fairer distribution; the proletariat will not stand aside forever.

Sat squashed round a large wooden table, they could be play-acting a sixties' student sit-in. They are certainly dressed the part: the men with scraggly beards and rat's tails; the women all smoking roll-ups and eschewing make-up. The set is perfect too. Copies of a radical left-wing newspaper pass around the table between full ashtrays and catering-sized packets of *yerba maté*. A torn flag hangs across the room's main wall, its rips a telling reminder of the conflicts inherent in *la lucha*, 'the struggle'. When I arrive, the show is entering its sixth consecutive hour, without so much as an interval.

I catch the eye of a curly-haired militant. He excuses himself from the room and comes over to speak with me. Federico is a twenty-eight-year-old political-science student and leader of the movement's Buenos Aires youth branch. He plays with his fluffy beard, subconsciously aggrieved about his boyish complexion.

'Kirchnerism is the politics of transition,' he tells me as he takes a seat beside the computer in the movement's administrative office. 'No one political movement has all the answers.'

A cigar-smoking Che Guevara looks down with approval from a poster on the wall. Beside him glares Cristina, hands pressed to her heart in imitation of Evita. '*Liberación existe*' runs the slogan on the bottom of the campaign notice. 'Liberation exists'.

'Not even the Peronist party, then?' I ask, pointing up at Cristina's campaign propaganda.

'Certainly not. The party's embrace of neo-liberalist policies has destroyed any chance of Peronists really influencing change.' Anyway, the general and his ideas were born in a different age, with political conditions completely at odds with today. Bored by talk of party politics, Federico begins flicking through his emails as he speaks.

'Our hope is to build a vehicle within the political structure.' He presses Send. 'That way we'll build momentum for *el pueblo* to go beyond Peronism.'

Are Argentina's young people with you on this? We both know the apathy statistics. Sure, most people his age aren't interested in politics. He admits that. The youth have been brought up listening to their parents rile against politicians and political parties. That's why the movement is thinking of forming its own party. So young people can have hope in the future.

Later in the week, I catch the bus out to Ciudad Evita. A rough neighbourhood on the road out to the capital's main airport, it's known as a bastion of Peronism. Decrepit blocks of social housing, built in a bygone age as barracks for the general's blue-collar foot soldiers, bear witness to the district's political roots. It's so Peronist, in fact, that the town planners even used Evita's profile to determine the layout of its streets.

I disembark near to the Vallega train station and make my way across a litter-strewn patch of wasteland. Ciudad Evita has not fared well since the general's abrupt exile in 1955. Its brickwork is stained with graffiti and its paving stones caked with dog excrement. Rusted cars splutter down its drab, unloved streets, and spiked guard rails protect its porches. There's not so much as a tattered 'Welcome' sign to greet visitors, not that many pass this way.

With the elections imminent, Ciudad Evita smells of spray paint. The freshly inscribed names of Cristina and her local running mates shout out from wooden fences and concrete sidings. Only occasionally does a rival's name get a look-in. An hour's trudging through puddles and along weed-swamped pavements eventually brings me to what looks like a Peronist party building. On enquiry, the elongated shed with its bust of Evita in the doorway turns out to be the Civil Registry office.

'Try the Social Development Centre,' advises a wormish bookkeeper with thick NHS-like spectacles. 'It acts as a local campaign office in the afternoon.'

At the far end of the shed, I discover a crowd of some two hundred people standing in the mud. Penning them in is a horse and cart laden with old mattresses and bedsteads. A beefy, pugnacious man in a vest-top is leaning out of an open window. Clumps of wiry, black hair sprout from his shoulders and the tops of his arms. He's bawling numbers at a team of dogsbodies in the warehouse behind him. The willing subordinates are dividing up boxes of basic foodstuffs into small piles: rice, flour, oil, sugar, milk.

'Excuse me, is this the Peronist campaign office?' I enquire of the bellowing controller.

'What?' he snaps back irascibly. 'This is the Social Development Centre. Isn't that obvious?'

The man points to the dispirited crowd in the miry forecourt. There was a terrible storm last night.

Can't I see he's busy? Most of these folk have lost the roofs over their heads. A campaign office, really? He couldn't fathom where I got the idea from.

'. . . Andrés! Three mattresses, at the double!' I found myself dismissed.

It takes me an hour to locate a party campaigner who's more forthcoming about his activities. Dante is a paintbrush-carrying Peronist of the first order. I find him in the party's 'sub-commando' centre in the neighbourhood's Los Chalets district. Usually a community hall, the building has been temporarily requisitioned for party needs.

Dante is stationed at the far end of a thirty-foot election banner that's lying across the length of the indoor volleyball pitch. The curly-haired propagandist is adding the final touches to the party's insignia. Tracing the mayor's name onto a second pennant are Jorge and Roberto. All three men work for the municipal government. Conveniently for Cristina, their boss has granted them four weeks of leave in the run-up to polling day. Oswaldo the taxi driver and the story of his vote-collecting lodger spring to mind.

The painting Peronist hands me a brush, and I contribute a letter or two to the campaign cause as we talk. Now fifty-two years old, he joined the Peronist Youth League when he was fourteen. His political education came on twelve-inch LPs. While his contemporaries were listening to Buddy Holly and Elvis, Dante would sit by his parents' 45-rpm record player and listen to crackly speeches given by the exiled Juan Perón.

The man was a prophet, a political genius, a visionary, raves the Peronist militant, his teenager enthusiasm undiminished: 'Other than the general and Eva, no one else was on the side of the workers.'

The comment makes me think about Argentina's last military dictatorship and their staunch anti-unionism. In 1973, to the euphoria of stalwarts such as Dante, General Perón had returned from exile to take up a third term in office. He died within the year. The military government that eventually replaced him detested the left-leaning general and his followers.

'During the dictatorship of 1976 to 1983 . . .?'

'I never once renounced my political convictions,' the dyed-in-the-wool Peronist exclaims, jumping in before I've had time to even formulate a question. 'How could I? True Peronism runs in a man's blood. It's a sentiment, a feeling close to love. It's every Peronist's duty to keep the fire burning.'

I've strayed onto a sensitive subject and quickly change track. After more than twenty-five years of democratic government, the dark days of dictatorship still touch a raw nerve in Argentina. Back then, the country's military-minded politicians hadn't tolerated any opposition voices. Instead, they'd had them 'disappeared'. As many as thirty thousand people were thrown from aeroplanes or buried in mass graves during the junta's murderous regime. Dante counted several activist friends among the number. Did his defensiveness come from not being among them? Was his radicalism a tribute to their memory? It wasn't my place to ask.

'What's Ciudad Evita like today?'

Dante's agitation levels drop: 'It's different now from when I was a lad. Many of the old guard have packed up and gone. People aren't as committed as before.'

The true militants can still be trusted to come out of the woodwork at election time though. Dante serves on the sub-commando's media committee. The banners and spray paint constitute his crude version of press releases.

'Just a few weeks back, a big group of us from here went to Mendoza. For Julio Cobos's launch as the vice-president,' he tells me.

'But that's a fourteen-hour drive?'

'Yeah, but that's no bother. When the party needs us, we go. Besides, our travel and accommodation costs were covered.'

Naturally, his boss down at the town hall gave him paid time off too.

'And what about Cobos's running mate, Cristina? As an old-school Peronist, did he feel she represented him?'

Dante pauses, before responding with an analogy of his own: 'Put it this way. A man goes to the grocer to buy potatoes but finds they're all bad. What's he do? He buys them anyway, because he hates onions.'

It's easier to grasp than Oswald with his ducks, but he clarifies his meaning all the same: 'The Kirchners are cut from a different cloth. As a militant Peronist, no, they don't represent me. In all honesty, I'd prefer someone else. But any Peronist is better than a non-Peronist. The party might be dispersed, but it's the best we have. It's all we have.' That and the general's memory.

Bolívar would have sympathised with Dante's willingness to back a winning horse. In political matters, South America's founding statesman was no head-in-the-clouds romantic. He believed in being pragmatic. When it came to deciding a political system for the new republics, he was content not to strive 'for the best'. The more important criterion for him was 'the most likely of attainment'. Not that Bolívar was a man without principles. Yet he, like Dante, knew that true power lay in unity. The Great Liberator used up his dying breath with a plea for the end of factions. If his death would help the cause of unity, he pledged to 'step peacefully into the grave'.

I could imagine Dante saying something similar about his beloved Peronist party. Yet I doubted he'd step into the grave for Cristina. An evening in the rain was sacrifice enough. Two weeks later, on a stormy night three days before Election Day, we both attended Cristina's closing rally in the working-class district of La Matanza. Arriving separately, the idea had been to meet afterwards. But the free supporters' bus from Ciudad Evita left early. I looked hard for the battle-worn banner of the Evita Movement among the flag-strewn crowd, but I couldn't see it either. Cristina didn't really need the militants anyway. Voter apathy would see her through just fine.

The pollsters proved right. Argentina's parties had mutilated the political process. Voters were tuning out of the traditional party system. Had the nation's political passions simply died? Or had the revolutionary spirit sought out alternative modes of expression? If so, where? They certainly weren't to be found at the top of the political tree. Sensing more potential lay at the bottom, I caught a bus and headed off towards the grass roots.

Gualeguaychú

From the top of Guru's surf-hut on Ñandubaysal beach, the sluggish river Uruguay looks as tranquil as a pot-smoking sadhu at prayer. Its Zen-like waters sidle nonchalantly downstream, easing their way around the wide dog-leg bend before dawdling off towards the sea. As still as a duck pond bereft of ducks, the river's glassy surface bounces back the sun's rays in a perfect, shimmering hypotenuse.

Behind the wooden shack, a pair of rufous-collared sparrows twitter conversationally in an otherwise silent copse of needled pine trees. Below, through a gap in the river's sandy beach, trickles a gentle inlet, its course submerged under leafy bushes and aquatic shrubbery. At its mouth stands a feathery clump of freshwater reeds, swooping into which flies a vanilla-white egret. The motionless setting is set rustling for a second. But almost immediately, the graceful heron bends its jet-black stocking-clad legs and sets off again across the bay. Calm is restored once more.

In spite of the idyllic view, Guru's spirits weigh heavy. He points without enthusiasm to the local landmarks: the upturned boat nodding just above the waterline in midstream, the burnished roofs of Fray Bentos on the opposite shore, the discarded bulk of that town's once-famous meat-packing factory, the river's curving slipstream, the Skorpio beach bar where he and his windsurfing buddies gather after an evening sail.

Being a weekday afternoon out of season, the beach is empty. It's a different story on summer weekends. Then, the road out from nearby Gualeguaychú fills bumper to bumper with trundling Fiats and clapped-out Volkswagens. Out of the tatty train of vehicles and onto the white sand spill the weekenders, with their ball games and freezer boxes, their beach mats and yelling children.

A briefest flicker of a smile crosses Guru's lips as he draws my attention to the line of red-brick barbecues beside the car park. Heaving half a butcher's shop onto the grill is a weekend ritual in Argentina. Guru talks through his approach to salting ('one side,

not too much'), his favourite cuts ('*matambre* every time'), his policy on cooking times ('a few minutes no more . . . a sin to overcook
it'). The hot coals of the *parrilla* obviously hold happy memories for
him: a glass of red wine as the lean meat sizzles, the anticipation of
a juicy steak in a toasted bread roll with a splash of tangy
chimichurri sauce. I'm beginning to savour Guru's feast for myself,
just as the carnivorous connoisseur smacks his lips and snaps us
back to the present.

Across the expansive river estuary lies Uruguay. Can I see the
narrow chimney on the horizon? I strain my eyes, wincing against
the afternoon sun as it lowers in the sky. Upstream, on the other
side of the river, looks like an industrial fortress? I put on my sunglasses and immediately pick out the subject of Guru's descriptions. In terms of sheer size and atrocity, it reminds me of a power
station on the Suffolk coast close to where I grew up; an ugly, concrete, angular monster of a building it was. From the chimney of
the fortress tower seeps a puff of discoloured smoke, like a far-off
distress flare.

'That,' spits out the windsurf fanatic venomously, 'is *Botnia.*'
Such is the horror and hatred in his voice, he makes it sound like a
gruesome plague-perpetuating nerve agent about to be unleashed
on his children. In fact, 'Botnia' refers to a far less frightening entity:
a run-of-the-mill paper company from the tranquil fens of Finland.

Five years earlier, the friendly Finns had announced their plans
for a state-of-the-art pulp factory on Uruguayan soil, right across
from Gualeguaychú. The news was well received in Argentina's
neighbour state, a country of such low population density that it's
said to have three cows to every one inhabitant. The president went
on television to lavish praise on the proposal, the country's 'largest
ever foreign investment'. The World Bank sent its consultants down
to swoon over the blueprints. And money was soon pouring in for
its construction.

Should a doubting Tomás still remain, the Finns promised hundreds of new jobs and the world's cleanest technology. The future,
Uruguayans were assured, was elemental-chlorine free. A pulp

putsch might not have quite the same ring as a gold rush, but hadn't Peru's guano farmers once made millions from selling bird shit as compost? Montevideo was sold.

Across the river, Guru and his windsurfing buddies welcomed the development with distinctly less enthusiasm. My guide for the day had moved to Gualeguaychú for the clean air and lazy outdoor lifestyle. A three-hour drive from the country's chaotic capital, life on the riverside slows as close to standstill as nature permits. Only during carnival month, supposedly second only to Rio de Janeiro's, does the tempo pick up.

Most days, Guru is out of the office and on his surfboard by four o'clock. If there's no breeze, he'll be playing golf with friends or fishing for trout at the cove. Botnia will change that life for ever, he moans. It's as if someone's put a sewage works at the bottom of his garden. No, it's worse. Destroying nature is a moral crime. Like building a whorehouse in front of a cathedral.

Guru might lack the chirpy optimism of the average tour guide, but he's at least dogged in his duties. Did I want to see the mill closer up? We can apparently get a clearer view from the international bridge. Soon we're clambering down from the roof and heading up the coast road through open farmland.

At the wheel, Guru continues his apocalyptic description of the pulp mill and its impending impact. Acid rain. Water pollution. Lymphatic cancer. Mutant fish. On rare occasions, he breaks off his jeremiad to point out the nest of a local bird or the borderline of a native forest. We pass a honey farm owned by a friend of his.

'No flowers, no bees, no honey.'

No end to his pessimism either. Local tourism's for the chop too.

Is it? Of course. What visitors will go to the beach with that monstrosity belching eggy fumes everywhere? The hoteliers and shopkeepers across the shore would see the truth too – if they weren't so brainwashed.

The roadblock comes as a relief to Guru's prophecies. Aside from the doom-sayer's lament, the obstructed highway is the first sign that the folk of Gualeguaychú won't take things lying down. The barricade is well organised. A horizontal cantilever runs across the road, positioned at the height of a car bonnet. The barrier gives the impression of a motorway toll, which in some ways it is. Vehicle users are made to pay, by doubling back and taking the next bridge further up the coast. A volunteer wearing a 'Go Home Botnia' T-shirt written in English operates the metal beam with a piece of string attached to one end.

As the months grow into years, the roadblock has developed into a permanent site. A concrete clubhouse has been rigged up on one side of the road, suggesting that Gualeguaychú is digging its heels in for the long term. The whitewashed multi-space serves as a lounge, a meeting area and, at particularly tense moments, a war chamber. The dormitory and kitchen are located opposite, inside the rusting frame of a conked-out school bus. Portaloos are also installed a hygienic distance away. Enlivening the gypsy settlement are banners and spray paint, all reinforcing the same message as the volunteer's T-shirt. Some wag has erected a signpost directed towards the Uruguayan coast. 'Welcome to the Republic of Botnia', it reads.

Guru pulls over. Half a dozen middle-aged women are sitting on plastic garden chairs beside the verge. Suspicious, they break from their chit-chat and turn as one to inspect the new arrivals. As soon as they see Guru in the driving seat, their chariness gives way to welcoming smiles. Obviously a well-known face at the protest point, the windsurfer alights from the car and moves around the group, pecking each of the ladies on the cheek.

A man with a prodigious beer belly and a curious duckweed hat hears the noise and emerges from the clubhouse. He crosses the road, distractedly scratching his crotch as he walks.

'Che,' he shouts, repeating the catch-all nickname that earned Argentine-born Ernesto Guevara his legendary moniker. The two men also greet one another with a kiss on the cheek. As welcome rituals go, it's a far cry from a good, firm English handshake. But all Guru's kissing pays off, and the barrier is lifted.

The Botnia site lies five kilometres down the empty two-lane highway, immediately across the road bridge that connects the two bickering nations. The afternoon is slipping into early evening as we drive up the humped back of the San Martín bridge. Guru parks inches in front of a white line in the road demarking the international frontier. I skip across it, enjoying the momentary buzz of border-hopping between two sovereign states.

Guru is leaning against the rail on the bridge's edge, his mood too sour to be amused by such frivolities. The sight of the sun's burning orb melting into the river in an iridescent explosion of colour is still not enough to break his churlish mood.

Admittedly, the bucolic scene has an unsightly flaw. Smudged in the corner, throwing the perfect symmetry of setting sun and river delta, lies the staining outline of the Finns' paper-pulping dreams. A thousand artificial lights illuminate the skyscraper towers and twisting cylinders of the industrial metropolis. Spindly metal ladders cloak the buildings in cobwebs of glinting steel. At the water's edge, containers the size of train carriages are laid out in strict military file, all prepped for service. Botniaville is undergoing last-minute checks. The plant's inauguration is due any day. In Gualeguaychú, where the time runs so slow, they are feeling the ticking of the clock.

Proving his sense of humour hasn't entirely deserted him, Guru laughs darkly at a 'No Litter' sign on one of the bridge's suspension cables. A conscientious official in the Municipal Works Department nailed up the weather-beaten injunction long ago. Fizzy-drinks cans and empty crisp packets were no doubt what he'd had in mind. Not several thousand tonnes of concrete. Guru takes my photo by the sign, ensuring the pulp plant is visible in the background, and we return towards the roadblock.

We find the guard of evening gossipers replaced by a nightshift of three men. All in their early sixties, Miguel, Ernesto and José spend their time playing cards, drinking *maté* and chewing over the latest snippets of information about the Botnia plant.

Guru goes off to discuss something with Miguel in the clubhouse. Ernesto is manning the barrier, which leaves me with José, a thin, bony man with a cigarette permanently in his mouth.

You from around here, then? Unlike the other two men, he's not actually from Gualeguaychú, but from Jujuy in the far north of Argentina. Retired early on health grounds, he's been at the road-block for six weeks so far. He sleeps in the bus and washes, if my nose is any judge, with some irregularity. Without family back home, he has every intention of staying until the 'Hitler of the ecosystem' is demolished. Or the Good Lord calls him. Whichever comes first.

And what's his money on? Botnia leaving, obviously. But then he hesitates. He's no spring chicken, mind. An even split, perhaps.

José is more certain about who's to blame for the whole scandal: the Argentine government. It should have responded quicker. The incompetents in Buenos Aires just sat back and let it happen.

But what about the case they're bringing against Uruguay in the World Court? José just laughs. Too late; these bunglers are always too late. He'll be dead first for sure if it's left to the judges to decide. The politicians could sort it out if they wanted to. They don't though because they're all on the make.

How exactly? How should *he* know? He's not one of the political 'mafia'. But someone's pocket somewhere is getting lined. I can quote him on that if I want. Pellegrini, José Manuel. National identity, 80976830. He doesn't see my pen move.

'Go on, write it down.' He repeats the details for a second time, asking for my notebook to double-check.

Wishing José a long life, I clamber back into the car and leave the retirement-age trio at their lonely outpost. On the drive back to Gualeguaychú, Guru chats about the town's now-famous assembly. A newspaper from earlier in the week sits on the dashboard. He turns up the front page. 'Protestors Promise Summer Chaos'. See, the assembly is big news these days. It's one of Argentina's best-known political organisations, despite not having a single elected official or solitary government post. Guru is among its founding members. The fact might persuade him to walk a little taller around town, but it affords him no fringe benefits or extra clout in assembly matters. The citizenry *asamblea*, he insists, is the quintessence of 'popular, participative democracy': one person, one vote. It has no membership lists and no internal hierarchy. Every decision is agreed by common consensus or it doesn't go through. '*No a las papeleras, sí a la vida.*' Participation rests on accordance with that simple creed. 'No to the pulp mills, yes to life.'

Gualeguaychú's early closing hours have emptied the town centre long before dark. We drive through the deserted streets and park around the corner from the town's theatre. With its crumbling tiered balconies and a damp problem, the municipal auditorium is well past its prime. The billboards are bare, and the heavy stage curtain is fighting a losing battle with the year-round humidity. The double-door entrance is still crowded, though, as if an evening performance is about to begin. We push our way past the empty ticket office and into the bowl-shaped hall. Guru spots two free spaces on the far side of the aisle. Apologetically, we shunt along an occupied row of seats to reach them.

The majority of the audience is collected around us, packed into the front half of the dimly lit auditorium. At the back are those with children to put to bed or perhaps secret lovers to meet. Numbers are down, Guru says, scanning the room. With near on four hundred people present, it strikes me as a good turn-out for the small town. A heavy-set balding man is on the mike. The assembly, we're informed, is in session.

Notices first. The Provincial Agrarian Association of Entre Rios requests two assembly delegates to attend its quarterly meeting.

'Any volunteers?' Two men in the front row put their hands up.

'All agree?' A roomful of hands points to the ceiling. Now Juan has a notice. Guru's bee-keeping friend takes the microphone. A delegation from the European Union is due to tour the Botnia site the following month. Juan would like to suggest a demonstration be organised outside their offices in Buenos Aires.

'Isn't Montevideo a better venue?' a voice chirps up from the auditorium. A third, louder voice thinks a demo merits a separate organising committee. Juan agrees and suggests the following Thursday. The motion is passed and the time set.

Finally, a bespectacled man in a blue blazer with shining silver buttons wants to inform everyone about the upcoming prayer night. Anyone who believes in miracles and an all-powerful God is welcome to attend. Food is optional, but he, for one, will be fasting.

The bald coordinator checks his agenda. Emilio has submitted a request.

Emilio? An enthusiastic student walks up to the front of the stage. The young computer whizz is thinking about setting up a web-based environmental mapping programme. Anyone who wants to join him, please let him know immediately afterwards. The reaction is mute.

'Nelly,' the list-holder calls. A well-fed woman dressed in a cowboy poncho stands up. She's been speaking to tourists around town, and she thinks it's a most profitable way of helping 'the seed to grow'. Oh, and before she forgets, she'd like to publicly thank those who hosted the recent delegation from Patagonia. They'd emailed to say they're setting up an assembly of their own. The news prompts a ripple of applause.

One after another, people stand up to make a proposal or to simply enjoy the liberty of speaking. An old lady recounts her invitation to address a church coffee morning in a neighbouring province. The owner of the pizza parlour would like to see more volunteers at the roadblock. Mariano gets up to apologise for an uncalled-for comment he made the previous week. He was worked up and is sorry.

Then Betty steps up. She wants permission to send a letter of support to the anti-obesity campaign in the assembly's name. A skinny man at the back thinks she should read it out. The assembly shouldn't fall into supporting causes willy-nilly. It would dissipate their message. The plump housewife offers a heart-rending account of the battle of the bulge. Uncontrollable cellulite. Cardiac trouble. Finding clothes to fit. Her audience visibly moved, she obtains her 'yes' vote.

A question of protocol arises when a young, cocksure civil servant asks the audience to grant him a vote of confidence.

'For what?' several assembly members inquire. He'd rather not say. Muttered conferences are held along the rows. The local doctor begs a word. Eyes turn to the white-bearded physician, a gentleman of distinguished bearing and the reference point on proper procedure. The young man, in his humble opinion, ought to be more specific if he wants the assembly's blessing. The upstart consents, but only in part. He's planning a protest activity with the assembly's inflatable chimney. That's as much as he's willing to say.

'If it's a pacific act you have in mind, why the need for secrecy?' a taxi driver wants to know. A housewife rebuts him. Time is running out. People should feel at liberty to do whatever they feel necessary.

The discussion over the blow-up chimney bounces back and forth around the audience, highlighting a growing division over the assembly's commitment to peaceful means. A few months ago, an elderly assembly member had rashly told a local reporter that she was ready to die for the cause if necessary. The press immediately dubbed her the 'Granny Suicide Bomber'. Guru is with the moderates. Violence will discredit the assembly's widespread support, he fears. But he admits that the militant wing is gaining ground. Back in the clubhouse, I'd spotted a fake bomb made from cardboard. A handwritten sign was hanging to the fuse. 'Today, it's symbolic,' it said. 'Tomorrow. Who knows?' So far, Guru's camp remains in the ascendancy. The longer Botnia stays, the harder the cause of pacifism will become.

The last item on the agenda is a general picket proposed for the inauguration of the new president. The Bauen Hotel in Buenos Aires has agreed to host an initial meeting between those activist groups who want to participate.

'Is the assembly in favour?' A full show of hands. Delegates are then elected. 'Any other notices?'

It's nearing eleven o'clock, and the coordinator is looking to wrap up. If no one has anything to say, then, the assembly will resume again on Friday. The note-taking secretary closes her ledger, her eyes also on the door. The theatre seats are already emptying when a latecomer rushes down the aisle.

He's sorry to keep everyone. Very quickly. A group of visiting Mapuche Indians will be holding a consecration ritual by the river tomorrow.

'What time?' a youthful voice shouts from the back. Five o'clock in the morning.

'Sure, I'll be there,' the mocker responds. A good wind and Guru might just join him.

Before leaving the next day, I pass by the offices of *El Argentino,* the eight-page daily rag. It's owned by the father of a friend. A lawyer by profession, he inherited the paper from his great uncle, and his editorial interests mostly concentrate on the free lunches the position offers him.

The day-to-day running of *El Argentino* falls to Nahuel, the bearded Mapuche editor. I find the seasoned journalist, pernickety about his appearance, wearing a neckerchief and a tank top in spite of the heat. He's sitting in his customary wooden swivel chair, tapping into his keyboard and smoking his way through a pack of Philip Morris.

We'd met the year before, when I travelled up to the protest town in Entre Rios province to cover a political rally headed by Cristina's husband, the then president. Together we'd listened to Néstor make his promises. The environment from now on would be a 'pillar of state'. Argentina's natural resources were its lifeblood. As a loyal Argentine, he would ensure every effort would be made to evict Botnia. The First World would learn it could no longer dump its dirty technologies on South America. The crowds were left elated. Job done, the Kirchners boarded the presidential helicopter and left the town to continue its fight alone.

Nahuel stifles a yawn.

Had he been to the consecration ceremony? No, he's hopeless at early mornings. He'd meant to go but had slept through his good intentions. A cigarette between his fingers, he taps the computer screen in front of him. The next day's editorial is what's tiring him. Tomorrow is the town's two hundred and twentieth anniversary.

He's chosen Gualeguaychú's history of civic solidarity as his theme: the town's workers' credit union, the public schools and crèches funded by the Society of Cattle Ranchers, the public campaign to have the international bridge built. The civic assembly has deep wells of community to draw upon. Readers, stand firm.

Away from the printed page, Nahuel admits the situation is trickier than it first appears. In the larger scheme, the pulp mill represents a dispute between two sovereign states, meaning that its resolution falls into the sphere of national affairs. Gualeguaychú's regional and municipal authorities carry little sway. There's a strategy problem too. National governments worldwide improvise on a daily basis, never looking further than the next election. Companies such as Botnia, on the other hand, work on fifteen- to twenty-year cycles.

El Argentino's Mapuche editor refuses to become despondent before the big-picture scenario. Gualeguaychú is teaching the world a lesson. Citizen assemblies are spreading not just in Argentina but around South America. The West is always preaching the benefits of 'modern democracy', yet its citizens hardly participate in the political process. Look how low voter turnouts are in Europe. It's because when they do participate, their governments ignore them. In Gualeguaychú, the people are showing the world's citizens how to mobilise, he concludes. Their voice will no longer remain silent.

I leave the riverside town impressed with Nahuel's arguments but weighed down with a heavy dose of Guru's pessimism. For the democratic assembly to find a political voice is one thing. To have themselves heard is another. Botnia likes to say it's listening – just more to its welcoming hosts in Uruguay than to its noisy neighbours across the water. Politicians share this art of selective hearing. The grass roots can scream all they like but, in the world of realpolitik, they'll never be a match for the crisp peel of greenbacks.

Companies dominate the political system in South America, citizens' groups always say. Finnish timber giant versus Guru and his windsurf pals certainly seems an uneven contest. In Gualeguaychú, they plan to keep shouting. In Buenos Aires, a small group of democratic revolutionaries are taking a different path. They've decided to go into business for themselves.

Greater Buenos Aires

It's two years since I was last at the Bauen Hotel. Back then, the one-hundred-and-sixty-room hotel was under threat of being repossessed by the government. Today, the bailiffs are still hovering.

Swamped in debt, the hotel's owners cut and ran during the country's 2001 crisis. One morning in late December, their employees turned up to work as usual and found the doors barred. No forewarning. No back pay. Nothing for them to do but go home and wait. As the banks and lawyers fought over the legalities, not a single guest crossed the Bauen's threshold. More than a year later, the hotel was still derelict.

Fed up with waiting, a small band of ex-employees decided to return to work. They donned their uniforms and stormed the building. The padlocks breached, they gave the rooms a spring clean, changed the sheets and announced the Bauen was open again for business.

Much has changed in the boss's absence. One of the novelties I find at the downtown Buenos Aires hotel is a well-stocked bookshop beside the entrance door. Early for my interview, I take a browse. A glance at the titles gives an idea of the politics now in vogue at the Bauen: *Marx in Argentina, Trotskyism, The Concept of the Other in the Liberation of Latin America*. Postcards of Che rest in a rack beside the counter.

Walking up to the Press Department on the third floor (the three elevators are out of order), I find Marcelo at his desk. Twenty-five years' service under the hotel's former management saw him promoted from bellboy to front-desk manager. At the time of my first visit, he'd been acting president of the workers' cooperative. Occupied with two journalists from a Spanish radio channel, the new media officer points me through to a side office.

Fabio is one of the Bauen's newer recruits. The manager of insti-
tutional relations tells me about his 'lifetime in left-wing activism'.
He could have saved his breath. His appearance says it all: the
unkempt beard, the workman's jeans, the voice croaky from cheap
cigarettes and the weakness for 'anti-isms'. Fabio believes in 'anti-
corporatism', 'anti-neoliberalism', 'anti-fascism', 'anti-individual-
ism'. Even 'anti-Thatcherism' earns a mention. A power cut breaks
his thread.

I comment on Marcelo's job change. It's not a demotion, Fabio is
keen to clarify. Career progression is how capitalists think. The
Bauen is different. It's now a 'worker-led democracy'. Job-hopping
comes with the territory. Anyhow, with their new horizontal management plan in place, job titles are more or less redundant.
Solidarity is what counts. Everyone is paid the same and every decision is made consensually. As with the Gualeguaychú assembly,
nothing happens without first passing though a popular vote. If the
swimming pool needs fixing, the concierge and chambermaid have
as much say as the chief accountant.

And the elevator? That too. They're just waiting for the next
meeting.

In the lobby on the way out, I spot another innovation: a small
stand selling Converse-style trainers. The shoes represent the latest
range from the Cooperativa Unidos por el Calzado, shortened to
'CUC' for branding purposes. An advertising poster is pinned to the
hotel noticeboard. '*Sin Jefes. Sin Empleados. Gente Trabajando*',
runs CUC's slogan: 'Without Bosses. Without Employees. Folk
Working'. I decide to travel out to San Martín, a downtrodden district in the capital's western industrial belt, to meet the politicised
shoemakers.

The Gatic factory used to churn out sneakers for Adidas and
other international sports brands. The gates are shut and the rubber
presses and welding machines switched off when I arrive.
Thankfully, the closure turns out to be only temporary. It is four
years since the bankrupt company was 'recovered', and a half day
has been called to celebrate. The jeers of a party getting under way

can be heard next door in the workers' mess. Cartons of table wine and bottles of fluorescent-green fizzy pop line the tables. The workers are munching greedily on juicy chorizo hotdogs, spilling grease and tomato ketchup in their rush to make room for second helpings.

The factory coordinator has the floor. Never would they forget what it's like to wake in the morning and not have a job to go to. Or the look on their children's faces as they head to school with holes in their shoes. They had every right to be proud of themselves, *compañeros*. Workers should die on their feet, not on their knees.

'Hear, hear, Boss!'

Glasses fill for a toast. But the fight continues. Their victory depends on unity. They need to watch out for individualism weeding its way back into their ranks. He bows out to respectful applause.

Unlike the Bauen Hotel, Gatic folded even before Argentina's spectacular economic meltdown. Round the corner, on the bleak Avenida Puente Perón, the boarded-up factory outlets suggest it didn't run aground by itself. For years, currency meddling by the government had been making domestic manufacturing more expensive. As production costs spiralled, 'Made in Argentina' labels began disappearing from the shelves. Factory jobs vanished in close step behind them.

Hiding behind hand-me-down doctrines from Washington, well-clad politicians would read robotically from pre-prepared scripts. If Argentina was to become 'globally competitive', certain 'contractions' in the labour market couldn't be avoided. Job losses were lamentable but inevitable. As for the queues of unemployed, no, the State couldn't be seen issuing handouts. Had they not heard? Argentina was officially in 'austerity measures'. In San Martín, they stopped listening long before the lectures ended.

Back in the canteen, the first chords of a Chili Fernandez track strike up. Several couples take to the refectory floor and start swinging their hips to the summer's *cumbia* sensation. Jorge, an incorrigible flirt with a beguiling smile and a charmer's turn of phrase, puts down his paper plate and joins them. He works his way through the ladies, joking and laughing. Each one is treated to one of his legendary pelvic thrusts. Wolf-whistles sound out from the back of the room, where the younger men are gathered, boisterous with booze. Their female colleagues look on with exasperated smiles. Even the grandmothers are unable to hide their amusement at the antics of their incorrigible rogue.

Jorge is wheezing heavily when he sits down, but it only takes a moment for the playful vice-president to catch his breath. Soon his cheerful banter and wisecracks are dominating the conversation again. Never has there been such a good party. Certainly not under the stinge-bags who used to run this joint, eh? Back then, they were just wage slaves. Five minutes to go to the toilet. Any more and they docked your wages. Now, they choose what hours to work and how much to pay themselves. How's that for a turnaround?

Not that working without a boss is paradise. Many people are used to being told what to do. That's the hardest thing to break. Four years on, and some still find it hard not taking orders. Gradually that's changing though. Isn't that right, *compañeros*? They're slowly becoming more politically conscious too. At first they were just interested in getting their jobs back. But how can they stay like that now they better understand how labour power influences politics. No bosses. Making decisions for themselves. They're a threat to the capitalist classes. And to the politicians in their pay.

Would he go back to working in a normal company? No, never. It'd mean giving up the freedom they've fought so hard for. What happened here didn't take place from one day to another. It was a long time in coming. The financial crisis just blew the top off the bottle. He uncorks some sparkling wine and sprays the table in fizz. Drunken laughter breaks out. Jorge, always the joker. What's everyone say to a lie-in tomorrow? 'Hear, hear, Boss!'

Marcelo and Jorge may have stumbled on their labour-led revolution almost by accident, but Argentina's fifteen thousand cooperatives have been at it for years.

Diego was so impressed with their efforts that he threw in his job at a bank to 'join the cause'. Initially, he picked up work as a part-time economics lecturer. For the past eight months, the longhaired graduate has also been working at La Base, a non-profit financier of cooperatively minded enterprises. Hotel Bauen paid for its new air-conditioning system thanks to one of its micro-loans. So too some last-minute material costs at CUC.

Now we're heading out along the westbound Ruta 21 in his boss's beaten-up Torino Classic to meet Desde El Pie, another client. As we drive past rows of discount supermarkets and empty lots fenced off with rusting wire, Diego picks up where Jorge left off.

'Cooperatives are preaching democracy within a factory. They decide things consensually, which is revolutionary when you think about it. Capitalists make their money by dividing the workforce into those that manage and those that work. They're the ones that manage, so they're the ones that take the cream of the profits. Imagine what would happen if those on the factory floor started proving them wrong? The whole edifice would come crumbling down.'

Diego doesn't reveal exactly where it is that he lectures, but I have a strong inkling it's not at a business school.

Desde El Pie is located in a one-room factory made from breeze blocks in the La Ferreré neighbourhood of La Matanza. Just up the road is where Cristina's presidential roadshow wound up in the rain. The cooperative takes its name from song lyrics by the Uruguayan singer, Alfredo Zitarosa. 'No hay revoluciones tempranas, crecen desde el pie', runs one of his popular choruses: 'There are no impromptu revolutions, they grow from below.' Little did the singer-songwriter know his words would inspire a production line of steel toecaps.

We pull onto a dirt road by La Ferreré's Eva Perón Health Centre and park the trusty Torino outside the boot factory. Inside, mouldings spill out from narrow metal racks, one for every feasible size and shape of foot. The air in the unventilated room is thick with the smell of glue. A hydraulic machine whirrs in one corner, its operator punching out the outline of feet – left, left, right, right – from sheets of thick rubber. In total, eight of the cooperative's sixteen members are working the afternoon shift. By the door rests a whiteboard. Tasks and corresponding action points fill a basic, two-column table: *mission statement,* 'sent'; *future vision,* 'to email'; *member training,* '09:00–12:00 Sat morning'. I spy the hand of an ex-banker at work.

Through the truck-sized doorway walks José Mario. Dressed in leather sandals and a belly-hugging polo shirt, the spiky-haired father of five is the driving force behind the cooperative. After a quick tour, we cross the road to his house. First to business. What type of pizza do we want? Mozzarella, ham, tomato, palm hearts, olives, the usual.

As we wait for the delivery to arrive, Diego and his client talk through the details of La Base's latest loan. Upcoming orders look good. The industrial boot maker is confident the repayments shouldn't represent a problem. They shake on it, old style.

The pizza boy beeps the horn of his tuk-tuk. In the spirit of solidarity, we split the bill. Ten years ago, José Mario didn't order in. In fact, he hardly ate. As in San Martín, the factories in La Ferreré began to close one after another as production costs shot up. The shoemaker found himself without a job and with little chance of obtaining one. Hungry and frustrated, he joined with his unemployed neighbours to request a basic handout from the mayor. The official said 'no', so they stayed. He and five hundred or so others spent a fortnight camped out on the steps of the Town Hall. Eventually, the mayor backed down. Independence Day beckoned, and it wouldn't do to have a protest camp defiling the official celebrations.

'They were difficult days,' José Mario sighs, a second slice of pizza on the way to his open mouth. 'From protests like these, the *piquetero* movement was born.'

Amorphous groups of dole-seekers, the *piqueteros* used civil disturbances to make themselves heard. They hit their peak in the immediate aftermath of Argentina's financial implosion in 2001.

Suddenly, everyone was a *piquetero*. Even great-grandmothers wore the badge of dissent. In time, the movement's popularity dwindled. The middle classes returned their casserole dishes to the kitchen drawer and went back to work. Stability, not sit-ins, became the desire of every Argentine with a job. Not that this stopped the *piqueteros* staging their marches and blocking the roads. Four in ten working-age adults were still out of work. They were also low on public sympathy.

'The real problem was that the *piqueteros* got bought by political interest groups,' explains José Mario, spitting out a black olive.

The sullying hand of Argentine politics was at it again. Groups that had begun as spontaneous expressions of popular discontent gradually merged into rent-a-mob gangs of professional protestors. If a politician wanted an *escrache,* as the *piquetero*s' staged marches became known, he suddenly knew who to call.

I could well believe José Mario's version of events. Back in 2005, soon after moving to Buenos Aires, I remember listening to the former president on the television news. He was denouncing foreign oil companies for increasing their prices at the pump. This was standard stuff. What surprised me was the reaction. Within an hour, *piquetero* groups were occupying petrol-station forecourts across the capital. Even the emergency services don't move that quickly in Argentina.

José Mario left the *piqueteros* but held onto the lessons he'd learned on those early picket lines. The strength of solidarity. The dignity of work. The dream of a country for all Argentines, not just the big companies. Hadn't Cristina said much the same in her acceptance speech? But what she channelled into the party machine, the toecap revolutionary is funnelling into the cooperative movement.

'Cooperativism shows that this other Argentina is possible,' he says, licking his fingers of pizza topping.

His next plan is to set up a national federation, a sort of centralised hub for all the like-minded cooperatives springing up around the country. He has a name already. 'The Liberation Movement of Cooperatives.'

What do we think? Catchy, eh? Diego signals his approval with a thumbs-up.

There are two pieces of pizza left. They're cold, but edible.

'Che used to talk about the "new man", a person in the full sense of the word,' José Mario continues. 'Working in solidarity, in co-operation with your fellow man, is the fulfilment of that idea in practice . . .'

Diego's attentions have drifted onto the remaining pizza slices. The ex-banker judiciously suggests cutting them into equal portions.

'It's the best solution I've heard so far,' José Mario says, a dreamy look in his eye.

I presume he's still referring to the cooperative movement. As he reaches for a final mouthful of pizza, it might just be the ham and mozzarella he has in mind.

Mendoza

'And for Señor?' the elegantly attired waiter at La Bourgogne is asking.

I'm torn between the mushroom and duck ravioli with baked onions and the chicken breast à jus with garbanzo-bean risotto.

Which would he recommend? Both are excellent, he assures me. The *moso*'s finger runs down the embossed menu to an alternative recommendation: 'However, if Señor likes fish, could I recommend the Andean trout with Dijon mustard in Sauvignon Blanc sauce? It's fresh in today.'

I take him at his word. Trout it is.

The gastronomic marvels of Jean-Paul Bondoux, reputedly the top French chef in South America, weren't the primary reason for my coming to Mendoza. Much as I longed to see Guru or José Mario storming the citadels of power with their revolutionary ideals, Argentina's political elite are a well-fortified breed. Ensconced behind thick buttresses of deals made and favours shared, they remain beyond the immediate grasp of the grass roots.

In the provinces, their position is even more entrenched.

Out of sight and out of mind, Argentina's interior harbours old-style potentates who run their patch much as medieval lords did their fiefdoms. Occasionally, these back-country *caudillos* make it all the way to the capital. Carlos Menem, the fast-car fanatic and president during the 1990s, was twice governor of the cowboy state La Rioja. Néstor Kirchner, on the other hand, governed Santa Cruz province for over a decade – a tenure assisted by his scrapping of the ban on being re-elected. Not that anyone complained too much. With less than two hundred and twenty-five thousand inhabitants, the oil-rich state at the bottom of the world has more penguins than people.

Most provincial potentates prefer sticking to their home turf. In the cattle-raising state of Santiago del Estero, a husband-and-wife team swapped power from one to the other for fifty-four years. Their half-century rule ended in 2004 after police arrested them. The allegations against them ran to embezzling the state pension pot, dabbling in drug-trafficking and murdering a pair of local prostitutes after a group orgy.

Three personalities made me think Mendoza would make an interesting window into this world of feudal politics: Julio Cobos, Cristina's running mate and the province's ex-governor; José de San Martín, Bolívar's former running mate and ex-governor of Cuyo (a wine-growing district just outside Mendoza city); and Graham Greene, who never ran for anything, but who wrote an amusing book about politics in the Argentine backwaters. First published in 1973, *The Honorary Consul* revolves around the misadventures of Charley Fortnum, Her Majesty's part-time representative in an unnamed northern province.

I'd tried Mr Cobos's press attaché first and was politely informed that the new vice-president was 'temporarily unavailable'. General San Martín had been incommunicado since dying in exile in the mid-nineteenth century. Which left me with Greene's fictitious protagonist. A call to the British Embassy turned up a modern-day equivalent: Carlos Pulenta, an Argentine of Italian descent, a winemaker and the consular emissary to Mendoza.

On the drive out to Mr Pulenta's home just outside the provincial capital, I'd understood why Mrs Cobos might be reluctant to leave. Snuggled cosily in the lap of the lower Andes, protected from harsh wintry peaks to the west and flat stifling plains to the east, Mendoza is an Argentine Umbria: picturesque vineyards carpet its silted valley floors; glacial streams babble down its hillsides; leisurely mornings spill into its relaxing afternoons. Clement in temperature and character, it provides a cathartic counterbalance to the hectic, politicised Buenos Aires, like a warm bath and glass of velvety Malbec after a crazy day at work.

Pulling up at the electronic double gates of the multimillion-dollar Vistalba Winery, I'd had to swallow my imaginary hope of meeting Greene's bumbling anti-hero. A flushed-faced sixty-year-old, Charley Fortnum had owned a run-down *maté* farm and driven a barely roadworthy Land Rover. The suntanned Carlos Pulenta presides over one of Argentina's top wineries and speeds around on a top-range BMW motorbike. No, to my regret, the literary consul was definitely not lurking close by.

The security staff had escorted me towards the office of the viniculture mogul. We walked below the gabled outhouse with its luxury guest suites above and through the lawned courtyard of the ranch-style bodega. Their boss was tied up in a business meeting. Sales to Tokyo and the Far East were expanding. I'd have to wait. The departure of two suited executives signalled my moment with the consul.

He was sitting in front of a flat-screen computer with a Blackberry in hand and a signet ring on his finger. A copy of *Meininger's Wine Business International* magazine lay open on his desk. Dressed in brown leather deck shoes and beige chinos, he was wearing a teal-blue cashmere jumper flung casually over his shoulders. He could have been stepping onto the quayside in Saint Tropez – more F. Scott Fitzgerald than Graham Greene.

For the first half-hour, the talk concentrated exclusively on the wine trade. The Pulentas are to grapes what the Santiago del Estero pair were to embezzlement. His premium, high-priced wines are all destined for foreign dining tables. The same is true of his brothers who own a similar high-end winery just down the road. Eventually, the conversation shifted from soil types and grape varieties to his quasi-diplomatic post.

'Most of the job involves promoting links between the United Kingdom and Argentina,' he explained. 'Occasionally, I'm also called on to pick up a hung-over tourist from the lock-up.'

The disputed Falklands Islands, he was glad to say, fell outside his remit. Commercial and cultural ties were more his brief.

And what did this mean in practice? There was a graphic-design competition for students that he'd helped organise. But, from what I could tell, mostly it came down to putting up the British ambassador for long weekends and attending the occasional garden party at Buckingham Palace. The Mendozan schmoozer fulfilled a similar role for the governments of Holland and Finland too.

'Have you read *The Honorary Consul*?' I asked.

Not only had he not read Graham Greene's book, I am surprised to learn he's never even heard of it. I imagined it on the embassy's list of compulsory reading for budding consular staff. On reflection, perhaps that was naive. Charley Fortnum was hardly a role model for the hardball rules of provincial politics. Never as much as a school prefect, the closest he ever came to diplomacy was a wine-soaked picnic with two minor royals. 'Pitiably small beer' was how Greene had the book's British ambassador sum up the inconsequential consul. I promised to send Mr Pulenta a copy all the same.

Today, the Mendozan honorary consul is dealing with some commercial links of his own. Two of Chile's top wine experts are due to arrive for lunch any minute. The debonair winemaker wants their opinion on a premium vintage Malbec he's about to release on the market. If I've no reason to rush off, perhaps I'd care to join them? I make a show of prevaricating, as if juggling important dates around in my afternoon schedule. Not ten metres away lie the crisp white tablecloths of La Bourgogne, recognised by gourmet critics as being among the best dining experiences in the country.

'Yes, I think I've time,' I reply, 'as long as it's just a quick bite.' We cross the corridor for an aperitif.

The meal ends up taking almost three hours. The conversation flows as freely as the wine. Again, much of it is trade talk: international tasting panels, export trends, Old World versus New World. I eat my Andean trout to a heated debate about the oaking process. Strong wood content is 'so yesterday', according to the more effusive of the two Chileans. Grapes should be allowed to 'fully express themselves', his more reflective companion opines. With the cheeses appears the new vintage. Glasses are swirled and aromas inhaled.

'What personality!' the second Chilean exclaims after every sip. The host is content.

'Anyone for dessert?' The waiter returns with the menu, discreetly topping up our glasses before retiring back to the kitchen with our orders.

Cleaning the last crumbs of chocolate dacquoise from my plate, I wonder what Guru or Dante or José Mario would make of all this. Elitist claptrap, I imagine, the fodder of the rich man's table. Not that they'd ever get to taste it. Haute cuisine, like political power, is off limits to the grass roots. The security guards and the politicians see to that.

The long lunch leaves me little time for the second of my appointments in Mendoza.

General José de San Martín might be dead, but the loyal burghers had built him a museum. Squashed into three rooms beside the municipal library, the exhibition shows signs of sorry neglect and underfunding.

I pay my entrance fee and take a stroll around. In the second room, a criminal looking line-up of ex-presidents hangs from the wall. Next to them are suspended the great and the good of the city's history, stiff moustached patriarchs to a man. Flanking them are their piggy-eyed wives and sour-faced mothers, all dolled up in black lace mourning garb. Sabres and rifles occupy the walls of the next room. The museum's attempt at a centrepiece consists of mock-ups from San Martín's domestic life: his study, his private chapel, his garret in exile in Boulogne-sur-Mer.

I stop by the bedroom scene. Considering San Martín's status as the ultimate hero of Argentine history, the display borders on the blasphemous. Seemingly stuck for funds, the curator looks to have struck on a sponsorship deal with the local greengrocer. Lying in bed is Mrs San Martín, her disfigured, papier-mâché face resembling bruised potatoes long past their sell-by date. Rocking in the stumps of her turnip-like hands, uglier than Chucky, rests a suckling baby. The decorated General of the Army of the Andes looks on with paternal affection. Straw pokes out from under his lopsided military hat, and his hips are tied to the bronze bedstead. His back to view, the illustrious champion of Argentine history is lurching to one side like a drunken scarecrow.

My hope had been that San Martín might offer up some insights into the maelstrom of Argentine politics. The museum's cabbage-patch caricatures are regrettably inexplicit on the subject. I'd half anticipated this. Argentines are quick to remember San Martín's heroic feats in battle, particularly his famous march across the Andes to liberate Chile. They're slower off the mark to recall that their national figurehead was really a political conservative. Of all the potential forms of government available to post-colonial South America, the Spanish-trained military man thought a benign monarchy would do best.

At the time, the notion of a puppet king from a second-rate European dynasty wasn't an unreasonable solution. Brazil, after all, pursued a similar plan for the first fifty years of independence. For Bolívar, the idea of a crowned ruler of any kind was anathema, a 'monstrous colossus, whose own weight would bring it down at the least convulsion'.

Constitutionally, the Liberator won out. After a private tête-à-tête between the two titans of South American independence, San Martín resigned his commission and left for France. He never set foot on American soil again. No formal monarchy, however insipid, would ever re-establish itself in Spanish America.

San Martín's political successors would ultimately decide what to do with his hard-won independence. Unfortunately, it took decades of bloody civil war for them to make up their minds. At the grass roots, the debate has reignited.

In a country that has officially given up on political institutions and party politics, such discussions are a breath of fresh air – whether it's the bearded students with their flags and lecture notes, the citizens of Gualeguaychú in their town theatre or the factory workers at their whiteboard.

'We have the governments that we deserve,' runs a popular Argentine adage. The phrase is intended to be self-critical. Almost half the country voted for Cristina. Even her supporters suspected she might fail to fulfil her campaign promises. She hasn't disappointed them. But the other half can't complain as they failed to put up a viable alternative. All sides are at fault.

The longer I stay in Argentina, the more I realise that the phrase reveals something deeper about the national character. The analysts in Café Tortoni were right: people's politics are shaped by individual interests, not those of the wider polity. When José Mario was camping out on the mayor's steps during the 'boom years' of Carlos Menem, the middle classes were out enjoying the bonanza. Only when the good times stopped rolling did they take to the streets and demand a change.

That Argentina's senators and congressmen should devote themselves to climbing the greasy pole of politics comes as no surprise. Voters' self-interest got them there. The politicians' own self-interest then tempts them to stay.

The voices of citizen democracy have yet to carry from the grass roots to the seventeenth floor of the Hotel Continental or to the silver-service tables of La Bourgogne. But, as Bolívar would say, the least convulsion could change that.

Only in the next country on my list do things never seem to change. Paraguay is the antithesis of modern democracy. Famous for being the most corrupt and lawless corner of the continent, its politicians make Argentina's provincial *caudillos* look like playground bullies. As I board the bus to Asunción, I'm reminded of Charley Fortnum. The hapless honorary consul had fallen victim to a bungled kidnap attempt by a group of Paraguayan terrorists. In exchange for his freedom, his captors demanded the release of their imprisoned comrades. Graham Greene paints their homeland as a despotic police state where human rights were regularly trodden underfoot. Carlos Pulenta had proven the novelist wrong about the consular stereotype. I wondered if modern-day Paraguay would also betray Greene's portrait.

4

BRIGANDS AND BANDIDOS

Paraguay and human rights

We have lost all guarantees of individual freedom and security, which were
the very goal for which we had sacrificed our blood.
  SIMÓN BOLÍVAR, 'A GLANCE AT SPANISH AMERICA'

Asunción

Arriving in Asunción after a day on the bus, I check into the run-
down Atlántico Hotel. Located on the corner of Calle México and
Azara, I'd noted the budget hostel down from a South American
guidebook. The options were limited. So divorced is impoverished
Paraguay from the tourist trail that the entire country merited only
twenty pages of the thousand-page tome.

The pallid, cadaverous proprietor shows me a windowless room
off the kitchen with an asthmatic-sounding ventilator and bathroom so small that I need to sit on the lavatory to use the basin.
Neither feature had earned a mention in the cursory write-up. But I
take the room anyway as I'm too exhausted from my bus journey to
look for an alternative. There's hardly any floor space, let alone
cupboards, so I sleep with my bags on the bed. After a short nap, I
get up and go off to find a telephone booth.

I discover a vandalised, coin-operated machine a few blocks away
in Plaza Uruguay, a leafy square backing onto the main train station
of Paraguay's now-defunct railway system. Francisco picks up the
receiver immediately, as though he's sitting by the phone waiting for
it to ring. His daughter Delia is a Paraguayan friend of mine from
Buenos Aires, and she had told me to look her father up when I
arrived. We arrange for me to visit at the weekend, and I wander
back with heavy steps to the Atlántico.

The entrance to the hotel is up a short flight of stairs via a greasy cafeteria. Sitting by himself eating a bowl of soup is a hoary Mennonite. His fair hair is balding and his freckled skin scorched a permanent puce by the sun. In his green dungarees and straw hat, he could pass as an extra in *Huckleberry Finn*. Paraguay enjoys a reputation as a hideaway for elderly Germans. Nazi war criminals flocked here. Among their number was a certain 'José Mengele', better known as Dr Josef Mengele, the psychotic doctor of Auschwitz notoriety. The old man reminds me that it's not just ex-Nazis who find a home in Paraguay. The messianic are made welcome too. Along with their dairy herds, the pacifistic Mennonites occupy the penetrable parts of the Impenetrable Chaco – an area comprising much of the country's western half. Further north, towards the Brazilian border, the Moonies are also biding their time until the 'third Adam' returns.

I have three days to kill until my date with Francisco and decide to take a tour of the city centre. Built on a gradual slope running down to the banks of the river Paraguay, Asunción plays tricks with the eye. From above, it looks to be cloaked in a rich layer of leafy green, like one big cloud forest periodically punctuated by a rooftop or phone mast. Downtown, the impression continues, the arboreal and urban merging together to create an accidental metropolitan arboretum. Not neatly, as with the tree-lined boulevards of Buenos Aires, but arbitrarily, without sense of order. Cedars poke out from behind garage doors. Blossoming *lapachos* spring from children's playgrounds. It's as though city and woodland have grown up together, haphazardly, one on top of the other. Yet, like next-door neighbours in a busy tenement building, they seem almost unaware of each other.

Armed with a tourist map from a craft shop, I set off to check the main sites. In an hour and forty-three minutes, I'm finished. I do a second lap to check I haven't missed anything. The neoclassical cathedral, the marbled Presidential Palace, the dated Old Military College, the crumbling legislative palace, the domed Monument of Heroes – all have a charming, colonial, abandoned feel to them. It's as if the city woke up one day, decided it had all the buildings it needed and resolved not to construct any more. The only notable exception is the curvaceous Congress Building. Funded by the Taiwanese, its glass wall-panelling and postmodern pretensions seem almost improper in a city of peeling paint and soot-stained brickwork.

My time in Asunción is not idle though. Several interview requests with contacts of contacts come good, and I keep myself busy chasing them up. The first is with Patrick, a trim, British-born youth pastor who married the local Anglican bishop's daughter. I run some of the wilder claims I'd heard about the country past him. On most he draws a blank. He isn't sure, for example, if 93 per cent of all electronic goods sold on MercadoLibre, Argentina's eBay, are illegally imported from Paraguay, as an Argentine friend had assured me. Nor could he say if Hezbollah and Al-Qaeda cells really operate in the country or not. One rumour that he is able to quash is that vehicles in Paraguay don't require number plates. On the other hand, the long-term resident points out that second-hand cars are often advertised as having 'full paperwork' – as if legal registration were in the same league as a fuel-injection engine or pneumatic brakes.

My next meeting is also with a man of the cloth, although Fernando Lugo prefers denim to dog collars these days. A former Catholic bishop, he left the priesthood to run for president. His switch of allegiances caused a ruckus in the Vatican, which rejected his resignation and chose to suspend him instead.

I spend the morning seeing what the local papers have to say about him. According to the lead political piece, Lugo is presenting himself as a 'vote for change'. In most democracies, this is standard practice. In Paraguay, it's bordering on revolutionary. The country has had the same Colorado Party in power for more than sixty years, not exempting the thirty-five-year dictatorial regime of Alfredo Stroessner. Lugo is also described as an anti-corruption candidate. It seems a timely theme. Stories of millionaire ex-ministers and dodgy construction contracts dominate the rest of the news pages.

Even members of the Customs Agency's anti-corruption unit are reportedly on the make, falsifying expense claims.

In person, the rebel bishop cuts a more dynamic figure than in newsprint. Silver-haired and bearded, he shares an uncanny resemblance with Brazil's charismatic president, Luiz Inázio Lula da Silva. Sitting in front of a Paraguayan flag, the presidential hopeful ushers me into his campaign office, located in a suburban house near to the city bus station. We speak for an hour. He tells me about the progressive presidential plan that he's currently hawking around the campaign trail. In a pocket diary, the clerical candidate keeps an annotated version of the six-point manifesto. When not checking his notes, he speaks passionately of his plans to break the monopolies of 'a few privileged families', to introduce wide-scale agrarian reform and to provide the poor with emergency aid.

Glimpses of the pulpit occasionally trickle into his political rhetoric.

'It's a scandal,' he says at one point, 'that the few should sit at the great banquet, while the rest are left outside to endure hunger.'

Three months later, he will carry the polls. With the presidential sash over his shoulder, he would be responsible for putting his bullet-point policies into practice.

On Friday, I make my way to another suburban house, also a campaign nerve centre of sorts. Sitting in his modest bungalow on Calle Simón Bolívar, Federico Tatter has his word processor working overtime. Congress is due to rule on whether the disappearance of political opponents under Paraguay's last dictatorship should be formally investigated. Federico is anxious that each member of Congress has a copy of the two-page briefing currently spewing out of his ink-jet printer.

A member of the Group of Families of the Detained, Disappeared and Assassinated, the grey-haired Federico has a personal interest in the matter. His father was one of the five hundred or more Paraguayans who went missing without a trace during General Stroessner's regime. A dissident member of the navy (itself a square peg in a round but landlocked country), the exiled Federico Tatter

Senior was tracked down in Buenos Aires. His son presumes he was then taken back to Paraguay but can't be sure.

'It's possible the Argentines killed him. Back then, the region's military dictators would help catch and kill one another's dissidents.'

The United States even gave them money to do it, the human-rights campaigner continues. During the Cold War, Washington was terrified of its backyard turning Communist.

A page floats down from the printer, and he bends down to pick it up.

'*Dios mío,* if they'd have only come here, they'd have realised Paraguay is the most conservative, pro-US country on the planet.'

Later, as I head back to the hotel along Asunción's lopsided pavements, I spot a traffic policeman controlling a line of non-existent cars at an empty junction. I approach the redundant officer and ask if he knows the whereabouts of the Police Museum. A writer contact of mine had told me about the place. He'd travelled widely in Paraguay and thought it would fit well into my research. I hadn't been able to locate the museum on my freebie map nor could Asunción's main Tourist Information enlighten me.

Intrigued, I'd extended my enquiries to the capital's police force. The search quickly developed into a game between me and Asunción's wider law-enforcement community. I'd mention the museum and then give them marks for helpfulness. Most were frank in admitting they had no idea. Several intimated I had my wires crossed. A few smirked. One tried sending me to the War Museum.

'It's on Cerro Cura Street, just before you get to Brazil Street, close to the police radio station.' At last, maximum points – a policeman who knew about the museum in his honour.

Hidden away in a crumbling terraced house set back from the street, the museum is admittedly easy to miss. I find the door ajar but the lights in the building turned off. The sound of my footsteps on the worm-eaten floorboards causes Olga to appear from a side room. Surprised by the novelty of a visitor, the cheerful administrator invites me to sign my name in her discoloured registry. Mine is the first entry for a fortnight.

The museum is divided into two rooms, and I turn right into the first. Full-length portraits of severe police chiefs with handlebar moustaches and swords at their sides cover one wall. Asunción's first mounted police provide a collage of grainy images on another. A photomontage of ninety or so policemen killed in action provides the exhibition with its centrepiece. A name, rank and date of death appears on a bronze plaque below a mug shot of each deceased officer.

Aside from the wall hangings, the mildew-perfumed room could be mistaken for an office storage depot. Disordered piles of dust-bound ledgers are stacked on a hardwood table. Pushed into one corner are two antiquated RICOH M100 photocopiers and an obsolescent Epson printer. Across from them sits a pre-war German telephone switchboard and several dust-coated radio sets. I'm confused as to why my contact had placed such priority on the place.

The answer lies in the 'Gallery of Criminal Acts' in the room next door. The exhibit provides a window into the ghoulishness of Asunción's underworld. Washed-out photos of the capital's grisliest crimes line three of the four walls: naked bodies lying in pools of blood, a decomposed corpse half-eaten by maggots, a teenage boy hanging from the rafters by a rope, heads with brains blown out, bluish stab-ridden torsos, the bloody anus of a rape victim, a dead baby on a garbage heap. A collection of hatchets, revolvers, hunting knives and other assorted weaponry completes the blood-chilling wall displays.

'Since Cain and Abel, to kill is a constant of man,' an explanatory note reminds visitors.

Around the remainder of the gallery, the macabre curator has scattered some mock-ups of his or her own. The largest comprises a realistic, full-sized dummy slumped at a writing desk. The farewell note of a real-life suicide sits beside his dead, outstretched hand. Next to this fake corpse, the plaster-of-Paris hands of a strangler freeze in time around the neck of an imaginary victim. The most morbid exhibit awaits by the exit door, pickled in formaldehyde.

Looking out from behind the thick glass of a bell jar stares the scrunched foetus of an aborted child. A handwritten label is stuck to the side: 'The most abominable crime of humanity.'

I leave the museum mulling over the curator's final thought, which is plastered onto a poster-sized notice: 'The worst enemy of man is man.' Perhaps my initial faith in Paraguay had been misplaced? Perhaps it really was South America's dungeon state?

With these cheerless thoughts in mind, I head off to see Francisco.

Santa María de Fé, Misiones province

As the afternoon bus rolls into the tranquil village of Santa María de Fé, Delia's father is leaning against his gate. Spotting me walking down the sandy, ochre track, Francisco calls his wife.

Luciana, a motherly woman with a worker's forearms, bustles out of the house. She takes my bags, marches me to the back porch and parks me on an aluminium seat with a square cushion of bare foam – all before I can say a simple *buenas tardes*.

Francisco takes a chair opposite, languidly watching his industrious wife bustle around us. He says something curt in Guaraní – Paraguay's indigenous language and the mother tongue for most of its inhabitants – and she skips back inside the house. In a flash, his well-set spouse is back with a jug of chilled water, a bag of *yerba maté* and a wooden gourd. Leaving her husband with the accoutrements of his afternoon *tereré,* the energetic Luciana rushes towards the gate. Can we excuse her? One of her cows is about to give birth. Then the bovine midwife is off, her short legs carrying her at a scurry up the road and out of sight.

The three litres of cold *maté* give Francisco and I time to get to know each other. Just short of his seventieth birthday, Delia's father has a full head of black hair that's obstinately ignoring the ageing process. Carefully measuring each word as though it were new to him, the taciturn farmer asks about my work and my family and whether it's true about the English sitting down at five o'clock for tea and fruitcake. In turn, he tells me about his own life, which began as the son of a poor farmer from Santa María and has continued in much the same vein. The father of eight is now looking to slow down a little. His project for the year ahead is to install a bathroom inside his modest home.

'Speaking of which, I could do with a pee,' Francisco says, pushing himself up and wandering off to the brick outhouse at the bottom of the garden. 'When I'm back, I'll show you round the village.'

Our tour more or less starts and finishes with Santa María's town square, a neatly ordered forest of native trees. Walking through the tranquil *plaza* in the early evening light, we are serenaded by an orchestra of parrots and spied on from above by a grinning black monkey. Francisco wants to show me the museum. Housed beside the church in a low-lying building with adobe walls and a clay-tiled roof, it dates back to the early eighteenth century when Santa María was a bustling Jesuit mission. We find it locked. Francisco crosses over to a similarly squat house on the other side of the square and returns with the museum's harassed guide.

Irma unlocks the padlocked door and shows us in to a bamboo-roofed room cluttered with the surviving relics of the village's first church: a delicately carved wooden column, one half of the entrance doors and a rough-hewn stone from the original altar. My eye is drawn to a painted wooden map on the wall. It depicts the chain of Jesuit mission towns in the vicinity: Santa María de Fé (1669), Santa Rosa (1698), San Ignacio (1668), Santiago (1669). A cluster of other names, all dated to a similar period, spread to the south and east into what is modern-day Argentina and Brazil. The missions represented an original, New World experiment. The Jesuits would coax the indigenous Guaraní out of the forests, accommodate them in reservations and introduce them to the novelties of agricultural cultivation, communal solidarity and Christian conversion. In no time at all, these religious settlements became models of prosperous, pre-industrial harmony.

'Then, in 1768, the Spanish kicked the Jesuits out, and that was that,' says our perfunctory guide.

As Irma takes us round the exhibits, the murmured chants of a religious procession filter in from the cobbled square outside. We leave the museum just as a Mass for San Roque, the patron saint of dogs and gravediggers, is concluding. Descending from the quaint, whitewashed church into the *plaza* step the town's faithful.

'That's her,' Francisco nudges me, pointing excitedly towards the crowd.

An ex-local mayor, Delia's father prides himself on knowing almost everyone in Santa María. He'd mentioned to me earlier that an English woman had moved to the town. While the two hadn't met, he'd proposed brokering an introduction for me. With red unruly hair, fair freckled skin and an ankle-length denim skirt straight from a seventies' jumble sale, it isn't hard to pick out which is Margaret Hebblethwaite.

'Why hello, welcome to our *pueblo*,' the ebullient Margaret enthuses, breaking off from the departing churchgoers and bouncing over towards us.

'You must be the English journalist?' As in all slow-moving communities, word travels paradoxically fast here in Santa María. 'Come along. We all must have some Cinzano.'

Without another word, she's leading us off to her house, a beautiful Jesuit-style cottage on the opposite corner of the square. Francisco winks at me knowingly, as though the chance meeting was all his own doing.

The act of crossing Margaret's threshold for the first time prompts my friend's father to make a short speech. On behalf of his family and the residents of the town, he would like to profoundly thank her for all that she's contributed to the community. He's thinking in particular of the educational trust that she's set up and the English lessons she offers. Embarrassed by formalities, Margaret says she appreciates his sentiment, assures him it's really nothing and adds some Cinzano to his glass.

'So what brings you to Santa María?' the modest philanthropist asks, turning her attentions to me.

'I know Francisco's daughter back in Buenos Aires.' The answer provokes a raft of secondary questions about my life in Argentina,

Francisco's offspring and my opinions on the 'terrible, terrible' problem of Paraguayan emigration.

'But in Paraguay? What are you doing here?' the eccentric, likeable British expatriate enquires.

I tell her about my interest in Paraguay's nefarious reputation and how this affects everyday people's liberties. It's a long answer to a short question.

'Human rights, you mean.'

'Well, yes, basically.'

'In that case, there is no choice whatsoever. You simply must write about the *Ligas Agrarias*.' It's a command, not a suggestion.

'The *Ligas Agrarias*?'

'Precisely. The Rural Leagues.' Had I heard about the repression of the Jesuits? Yes. 'Well, history repeated itself with the *Ligas Agrarias*.'

Intrigued by his first taste of vermouth, Francisco had sat back to enjoy his aperitif, and Margaret and I had fallen into speaking English. The Spanish term causes him to sit up immediately.

Pulling bundles of essays and photocopied articles from her bookshelves, the fiery-haired Brit assails me with information about the *Ligas* and their fate. As with the Jesuits, they represented an experiment in radical Christian living. Community and solidarity were their watchwords. They resurrected the *minga* and the *jopoi*, two indigenous customs orientated towards loving one's neighbours.

The nearby settlement of Santa Rosa, where the *Ligas* started in the early 1960s, provided the model. There they set up a communal pharmacy, organised a store with discounted food, farmed a shared patch of land and earmarked Saturdays to help repair one another's houses.

Most controversially, the *Ligas* sought to establish an alternative education system. Margaret picks up an anonymously published pamphlet from the time and points to an underlined paragraph: 'Read it.' I do as I'm told. The nameless author describes how the *Ligas*' rural schools aimed to 'set the whole person . . . on the road to development and liberation'. It wasn't long before the authorities came knocking.

During Easter week of 1976, the members of the church-led movement were arrested and dragged off to prison. In total, nearly four hundred people, including women and children, ended up behind bars. Its structure destroyed, the movement died a quick but painful death.

'And is this documented?'

'That's more or less everything there is,' Margaret says, pushing the pile of papers towards me. 'I used to be a journalist too,' she adds, noting my surprise.

Downing the remainder of his Cinzano, Francisco interjects. His good friend Patrón used to be part of the *Ligas* and was among those arrested: 'I can introduce you if you want.'

The Santa María fixer proves good to his word. After lunch the next day, a bird-like man with a hook nose and a raw, leathery face knocks on Francisco's gate. The geriatric farmer is dressed in his Sunday best of black nylon trousers, white cotton shirt and New York Yankees baseball cap.

Over the course of the morning, I'd read through the results of Margaret's investigative research. Amid the materials, I'd been intrigued to discover a transcript of Patrón's confession. The rounded stamp of the Department of Police Investigations is smudged across the top right corner. Written in the clunky script of a Remington typewriter, the three-page document takes me back to the morbid museum in Asunción and its dust-covered office equipment.

The first lines dryly state the date and location of the interview and the name of the interrogator. The second paragraph, equally dry, registers Patrón's personal details:

Full name: Eliodoro Andres Coronel Caballero

Date of birth: 3 July 1937

Occupation: farmer

Alias: 'Patrón.'

After the preliminaries, the pace picks up dramatically. What follows reads more like an espionage novel than a police report: shady meetings at night, secret code words, involvement in a banned political organisation, contact with foreign dissidents. *CLANDESTINA y PELIGROSA.* The typist uses capitals to describe the anti-Stroessner group to which the alleged subversive is linked. UNDERGROUND and DANGEROUS.

Patrón admits to everything. His affiliation to the church is just a sham. Really he and his parish friends are hiding a seditious, military objective beneath their charitable work. Their aim, the document states, is 'to cause the legally constituted government to fall by force and to implant a new regime with a Communist character'. More or less the only accusation that Patrón denies is undertaking weapons training.

On a dotted line at the end of the third page is scrawled an indecipherable signature. Presumably, it belongs to Patrón.

'You want to know about my arrest, is that it?' Francisco's old friend enquires in stilted but intelligible Spanish.

I nod, not mentioning that I'd read a copy of his statement to the police. He takes a deep breath, submerging himself below a wave of torrid memories, and begins.

'The first time I ever met a Communist was in jail. The same was true for all my friends from the *Ligas.*'

'But the Agrarian Leagues had a political edge, no?'

'No, none whatsoever,' he insists, wagging his finger vigorously like a reprimanding schoolteacher.

The *Ligas* were church-based groups focused exclusively on social action for the poor, he continues, before going on to repeat Margaret's earlier description almost verbatim.

'So why did the government want them wiped them out?'

He shrugs his shoulders. He supposes it's because the *Ligas* challenged Stroessner's grip on people. It showed the authorities that rural communities could cope on their own, without them.

And what did the Leagues teach, exactly? Just what it says in Scripture, Patrón answers matter-of-factly: that the riches of the earth are for the good of all men, not just the few. The Leagues might not have had a formal political agenda, but it wasn't hard to see why Paraguay's Communist-obsessed generals thought differently.

The local police came for him on the night of 13 April 1976. He kissed his wife and left silently, not wanting to wake his six young children. He was taken to Abrahán Cué, a barracks turned prison in the nearby town of San Juan Bautista. There he was beaten and tortured for three days continuously.

'First, they hit me with a *tejuruguai* – a sort of thick leather whip with electric cables running along it and a steel ball on the end that ripped your skin right off.'

He makes a circle between his forefinger and his thumb to demonstrate the instrument's inch-wide diameter. His torturers nicknamed the whip 'The Constitution'. 'When one guard got tired striking you, another would step in and take his place,' he explains.

On the fourth day, a police van transferred him to the Department of Investigations in Asunción. Physically broken and mentally numbed, the prison authorities judged him ready to confess.

'And what was the interrogation like?' I ask reluctantly, half wishing I could leave the room and have my tape recorder pick up his answer.

More than thirty years have passed. He remembers little about it, only that it started late in the afternoon and seemed to last for hours. The years have not totally freed him of memories though. He recalls them repeatedly asking him for his 'pseudonym'. Back then, he didn't even understand what the word meant. Another recollection has stuck with him too. At one stage, his interrogators sat him in a chair, placed a metal helmet on his head and attached an electric cable to his finger. One man asked questions while another wound the machine's handle. The faster it was made to spin, the higher the volts that coursed through Patrón's body. The illegible signature suddenly made horrible sense.

His confession signed, Patrón was transferred back to Abrahán Cué, or, to quote him precisely, 'the antechamber of Hell'. He spent three months there, locked in a room with twenty-seven other men.

They had no blankets, and the ground was always bloody from the beatings. Rations consisted of a watery, maggot-infested soup. He suffered constantly from diarrhoea.

'We were made to sleep handcuffed to two other men. They called the handcuffs our 'wives'. You can't believe how difficult it is to sleep like that.'

Not that sleep came easily anyway. At night, tape recordings of prisoners screaming under torture would regularly be pumped via loudspeakers through the cells. In his pocket he has a photocopied photo of the former army barracks. He shows me it, jabbing his finger on the cell block where he was imprisoned. It looks just as it sounded: a concentration camp.

After three months, Patrón was transferred to another prison in his native Misiones province and from there to Emboscada prison in Asunción. Home today to Paraguay's maximum-security inmates, during the Stroessner regime it housed the country's growing population of political prisoners. There too, he faced a continued ordeal of physical and psychological torture. Two years and two months it lasted.

He was arrested a further four times after his release, each time for roughly a month.

What for? 'Whatever. The last time was after they assassinated that Guatemalan dictator Samosa. They said it was a peasant group that organised it.'

You mean the Honduran dictator? 'Honduran, Guatemalan, same difference.' No, Patrón did not have the air of a dangerous political agitator.

The Rural Leagues never revived. The likes of Patrón went back home and kept their heads down and their mouths shut. Today, most of Santa María's youngsters have no knowledge of the terrible events of that Easter. One of Abrahán Cué's torturers was imprisoned, but no investigation has ever been carried out into the remainder. For years after his release, Patrón would regularly bump into the police chief who arrested him. Last year, the elderly victim received a long-overdue compensation package from the

Government. It totalled 1,500 *Guarani*, less than the cost of a local bus ride, for each day of false imprisonment.

I return to the leafy square in the late afternoon. Sitting on a park bench, I ponder the other untold secrets hidden beneath the cobbles of the Jesuit-built town. The bell tolls for Mass. Curiosity draws me up the steps and to an empty pew at the back. The thin voice of a fragile, brittle old lady is reading from the Old Testamnet. A cassocked priest follows with a lesson from the Gospels:

'They will deliver you to synagogues and prisons, and you will be brought before kings and governors, and all on account of my name . . .'

I spot Patrón emerging from the sacristy, a white Eucharistic robe over his clothes.

'You will be betrayed even by parents, brothers, relatives and friends, and they will put some of you to death. All men will hate you because of me . . .'

A short sermon in Guaraní follows. The bread is broken. Supplicants approach the rail in an orderly queue. Into their open palms, Patrón presses the sanctified bread. Each returns to their seat, the Eucharistic minister's gentle whisper still in their ear.

'The body of Christ, given for you.'

Tacumbú prison, Asunción

A patient line of visitors waits in the sun outside the bolted main gate of Tacumbú prison. All, without exception, are women: long-suffering wives, girlfriends, sisters, aunts, grandmothers, mothers. Most have a grocery bag in hand. Few speak. We park on a side street one block away. The smell of fresh vegetables and cooking fat wafts from the food stalls leading down to the prison's entrance portal. Tacumbú's whitewashed perimeter stretches a block in both directions. It's just after 9 a.m. on a cloudless Thursday morning, one of the week's four visiting days.

I'm with Patrick, the Anglican missionary. It transpires that his pastoral duties include a fortnightly visit to Tacumbú, Asunción's

largest prison. I'd been wanting to visit a South American penitentiary for a while. The continent's lock-ups are notorious for over-
crowding, gang-related violence and a general disregard for
prisoners' civil liberties. Nowhere was this truer than in Paraguay.
Obtaining an entrance permit required going through the Ministry
for Work and Prisons. This could take months, I'd been warned.

Which is where Patrick came in. He'd suggested that if an inmate
were to invite me, then I could go along as a day visitor. The friendly churchman offered to make some enquiries on my behalf. A few
days later, he dropped me an email. We were on. Louis Vincent,
Britain's only prisoner in a Paraguayan jail, would be happy to see
me.

At the main gate, an armed guard ushers us through into a pre-
liminary security area, where we're asked for our passports and, in
return, receive a rubber stamp on our forearms. From there, we pass
across an open courtyard, through another security gate and into a
covered antechamber. Across the hallway, six dishevelled prisoners
look out from a bare holding cell. One has his hand upturned
through the bars, his palm cupped open, begging for scraps from
the queue of visitors.

In a side room, two unsmiling guards pat us down and rifle
through the bags of provisions that Patrick has brought with him.
The gruffer of the two takes a metal prong and repeatedly stabs at
a slab of cow fat in the first of the bags. In the second, he finds a pair
of sharp-tipped screwdrivers. The guard raises an eyebrow. Patrick
explains he's going to see Louis. The uniformed oaf shows no reaction.

'The British prisoner,' the pastor prompts. Not a twitch. It's
unclear whether the guard doesn't know Louis, whether he knows
him but isn't sure about him having the screwdrivers, or whether
he's waiting for a bribe before he decides.

'Sure, Louis, I know him. He's clean,' says the second guard,
overhearing the conversation. We're allowed through.

A third gate opens into the main prison compound. On the other
side, dozens of prisoners are pushing up against the bars. Some are

keeping an eye out for visiting relatives. Most are there to scrounge. We're waved through by a beefy official, who unlocks the pad-locked door. Disconcertingly, he remains on the far side, allowing the door to swing shut behind us.

The metallic clang signals our entrance alone and unaccompanied into the prison yard.

'Any change, mister?' The crowd closes in. I feel an arm against my back.

'Hey, gringo, spare me a cigarette?' A hand touches my shoulder. We shuffle forwards through the penitential mêlée, heads down. From the edge of the scrum, Louis steps forward and claims us as his own. We follow him, away from the guards and the exit, deeper into the prison.

Introductions are kept for later. Flanked by two buddies from his cell block, our host in Tacumbú hurries us along a labyrinthine route towards his wing. The prison boasts only a restricted number of single cells, which are reserved for those with the money to pay. The remainder make do with squalid dormitories. Louis ushers us across the threshold of his single-storey sleeping quarters and into the darkness.

It takes a second or two for my eyes to adjust to the lack of light. Once inside, Louis quickens his pace, scurrying forwards with his little entourage in tow. Bunk beds, three high, run lengthways along both walls. A row of single beds occupies the middle of the room. To the right of the entrance door is a small store selling basic essentials: soap, Bic razors, toothpaste, batteries. The room itself is a fraction smaller than a volleyball court. Rushing through behind Louis, it's difficult to estimate exactly how many men live there, but it must be at least sixty. About half that number are occupying the room, most of them lounging on their mattresses. A menacing silence falls as we brush past.

The darkened dormitory narrows into a corridor. A barren kitchenette, no more than a waist-high shelf, rests against its near wall. A man is frying a sausage on an improvised hob. The kitchen's sole cooking instrument consists of two electric filaments soldered to a brick. Turning it on involves hooking two bare wires to the mains electricity cable above. More bunk beds run along the remainder of the corridor, which bends right into a cul-de-sac. There, on the third bunk up, close to the rafters of the single-storey building, is where Louis sleeps. He doesn't stop.

Instead, we carry on through a doorless doorway. I catch a glimpse of the washing area as we pass. The tiles that aren't missing are cracked and stained with mould. A single, dripping showerhead hangs from the cracked roof. The stench of the dormitory lavatory follows us into the final cell. The ten-foot by eight-foot room has three triple bunk beds and just enough standing space for us to worm through to an exit door on the far side.

'Take a seat,' Louis says, pointing to two wobbly wooden benches in the middle of the concreted backyard. Above us, between the corrugated tin roof and damp clothes on a line, is a tapered chink of cloudless, untouchable blue sky.

His two companions leave Patrick's carrier bags on the table and disappear back inside. For a short while, Louis says nothing as he rifles through the bags' contents.

I open my notebook and jot down a short description of my incarcerated compatriot: Medium height. Thin frame. Malnourished? Mid-twenties. Greasy, fair hair, down to chin. Blond, trimmed, pencil beard. Cut-off jeans, shin-length. Baggy, short-sleeved shirt. American football-style. Too big. White trainers, Soviet brand.

'Thanks for the fruit and vegetables. Can't eat the rat food they give you here, man.'

He's grateful for the cow fat too, which he'll melt down to sell as cooking oil to his fellow prisoners. Louis also earns money on the side fixing radios and television sets. A discussion breaks out over an electricity meter that he'd asked Patrick to buy. The odd-job electrician turns the dial.

'Always must show zero.' He turns it half a dozen more times, repeating the same phrase each time he does so. 'Nought point one. Nought point two . . .' Not once did the digital meter read zero.

Agitated, Louis shows the digital reader to his regular visitor: 'You see, Patrick? You see what I'm saying? It's broken, man.'

The missionary apologises and offers to return with a replacement on his next fortnightly visit. Louis grows calmer at the suggestion. He hands the contraption back, gathers everything else up and heads back inside.

Louis is flustered when he returns two or three minutes later. 'Everything's cool. Just got to have someone to watch my stuff,' he says when the pastor asks him if he's OK.

It turns out Louis had been in a punch-up that morning. A fellow inmate had accused him of taking too long in the shower. The more he shouted, Louis explains with stubborn prison logic, the longer he stayed there. Now, he's worried that his locker might be ransacked in retaliation.

'I'm not worried about the guy. He's just some punk. I can smash his head in fine. It's López who's the problem. He could get me kicked out of the wing.'

As narrator of the incident, his version of events naturally has him coming off better. A bruise around his eye and scratches on his neck suggests it may have been closer than he lets on.

'And who's López, Louis?' Patrick enquires, trying to calm him with his best coffee-morning voice. Louis looks exasperated. 'Sorry, I'm just trying to understand,' the pastor apologises. 'Is López a guard?'

'No, he's the *wing captain*.' Bound up in the world of prison life, it's unfathomable to him that Patrick doesn't know who López is.

'The guards put him in charge because he goes around saying how tough he is. But he's not really. He's just a pussy. I could have him. But the thing is he's got lots of money. And with money, you can get anything you want in here.'

'Forgive me, Louis, but then what's López got to do with your fight this morning?'

'The guy hassling me in the shower is his *pitilero*. You know, like his pet. He's probably told López I started it all. They're always giving me grief and making stuff up about me. It's because I'm the only foreigner in this place.'

Patrick had mentioned previously that Louis often gets into scrapes because of his bolshie, don't-mess-with-me attitude. It's painfully evident that no one buys Louis's tough-man image other than Louis himself. A few months ago, someone threw his pet cat over the perimeter wall. Although he'd never admit it openly (Patrick told me), he was inconsolable. The minister counsels him on trying to keep out of trouble, to which Louis nods and says he'll try. It's evidently a regular conversation between them.

So is Louis's dope habit. He claims to have given up when Patrick asks him. 'Roberto came over to my bunk yesterday 'cus he wanted to share a spliff. He's the wing's scrounger – never got any of his own. He was properly pissed off when I told him I'd given up.'

Louis looks pleased with himself, then nervous, as if suddenly afraid his pastoral mentor might think he's lying. Playing the proxy father figure well, Patrick eases the anxiety of his younger charge with a few brief words of encouragement.

'He's twenty-seven,' the youth pastor had said before entering Tacumbú, 'but it feels sometimes as if I'm talking to someone in one of our children's groups.'

It appears entirely natural to both men that Louis should be locked up and yet still have an active drug habit. Later in the visit, I ask Louis how easy it is to get narcotics in prison. He lifts his eyes to the sky, in a way I take to mean 'So easy, you wouldn't believe': 'It's like I said earlier, man. With money, you can get anything in here.'

To prove his point, he gave me a shopping list of prices: one gram of cocaine, 15,000 guaranís; one gram of marijuana, 1,000 guaranís; one desonilem tablet (an amphetamine, he thinks), 3,000 to 5,000 guaranís depending on supply. A quart of Tres Leones whisky, on the other hand, costs about 25,000 guaranís. And if you get caught, what happens? 'Caught' is an arbitrary term, he explains, as the majority of the prison officers are involved in the trade. But usually it's a stint in the Alcatraz, in solitary confinement. Anything from thirty to sixty days.

The length of sentence depends largely on how much the prisoner has for a release fee: 'Could be anywhere between 100,000 and

200,000 *guaranís* to get yourself out early,' Louis states. 'Depending on how much you're *caught* with, of course.'

Arbitrary or ironic, 'caught' describes Louis's situation to a tee. He was detained on a bus in north-western Paraguay while travelling down overland from Ecuador. The plan was to get across to Brazil, where he'd ship the merchandise to South Africa, his native country (his father's British, hence the passport). According to Louis's arrest record, four kilos of uncut cocaine were found in his grip bag. Each kilo carries two years' jail time under Paraguay's weights-and-measures legal system. Louis claims to have actually been carrying seven kilos at the time of his arrest. He allegedly gave the other three to the border guard.

This all happened two years, seven months and four days ago. Louis has been incarcerated in Tacumbú ever since. His case has still to come to court. Two out of three of the country's prison inhabitants are also awaiting their day before a judge. Trapped in the convoluted Paraguayan penal system, Louis is stacking his hopes on making it to the three-year mark before being tried. Thirty-six months is the cut-off period for sentencing. After that, the law allows the prisoner to go free, regardless of their alleged crime. Paraguay's public prosecutors are as aware of the rule as the prisoners. The justice system has an uncanny habit of kicking into acceleration just as an inmate is reaching the obligatory release date.

Louis's lawyer is seeking to avoid this fate for his client. His strategy is straightforward: he books in Louis to see a psychologist, the evaluation is delayed ('they're always delayed'), the trial is pushed back even further and Louis walks out a free man. To me, the plan seems dubious at best. To Louis, it's watertight. In much the same way as López is a total pushover.

'Oh, I almost forgot, I have something else for you,' Patrick says, pulling a letter from the Bible he's carrying with him.

Louis's mother sends short one-pagers via email to Patrick, who prints them out, places them in an envelope and hands them over. This week, the package also includes two printed photos. Louis takes the letters ravenously, skimming quickly across the lines as though surfing channels on satellite TV. He offers up summaries as he reads: his mother's health, his sister's job, the death of his step-grandmother's son ('my step-uncle, I guess, no?'). His voice is a perfect monotone, the information still processing from eye to brain to memory.

He sets the half-read letters back on the table and picks up the two snapshots: 'Hey, a photo of my son. Look Patrick, my little boy.'

Patrick is equally animated, believing that Louis needs family stability if he's to rebuild his life: 'Cute. How old is he?'

'Four.' The photos depict a smiling toddler.

'I guess these must have been taken a while ago, eh?' says Patrick, confused at the discrepancy but trying not to show it. 'What's his name?'

'Jeremiah.' Almost immediately, the imprisoned father changes his mind. 'Jeremy.' Pause. No, what's he saying? 'It's Jayden. Jayden.'

He repeats the name over and again, hoping it will resonate. It doesn't. A panicked, disorientated expression comes over him. He places his delicate hands in his lap, clasping them tight together. Then his shoulders droop forwards, and his body begins rocking slowly back and forth. I try to fathom what it must be like not to remember your own son's name. The visiting pastor isn't sure how to remedy the situation, and an awkward silence follows.

A vivid crimson bruise on Louis's forearm provides them with a way out of the general bewilderment.

'Is that from this morning's fight?' Patrick asks.

Louis nods, holding it up to the light. His bare arm reveals other markings, tattoos that he's had done since being inside and others from his pre-prison 'hip-hop, rap gangster' days. There are half a dozen in total, and Patrick points with interest to the most recent. 'Freedam', it reads, in a diluted blue ink that already looks faded. Louis had a friend write it for him.

'Forgive me for saying this, Louis, but it looks to me as if it might just be misspelled,' says a hesitant Patrick.

'No, I actually got him to write it like that. It's like "free dammit", you see.'

Louis is pleased with his artistry. In fact, if Patrick could only get him a small pot of Chinese paint, he's sure tattooing could make him a killing inside: 'What's a pot worth? 7,000 G, say. A small tattoo costs that in here.' He holds onto the idea, a neat sideline to his electrical repairs and fat-melting enterprises.

Their discussion drifts onto other topics: his health, his need for a haircut, the first time he saw an African dung beetle as a boy in the Transvaal. As though in sympathy, a cockroach scuttles across the floor, resting briefly under the table before sprinting off to the washing area. Louis is serving *tereré* into a stainless-steel mug when he suddenly stops short:

'Benjamin! Benjamin! That's my son's name. Jayden's my sister's baby boy.'

He's happy now, happy to have wrestled back what was his, happy to have defied the mind-dulling torture of Tacumbú.

Visiting time is nearly up, and Patrick suggests Louis might like to show me where he sleeps. 'Sure, man. Follow me.' We leave the backyard and return inside. Eight or nine men are now occupying the final cell, sitting shoulder to shoulder on the edge of the bottom bunks.

'This is where they come to get stoned,' says our host as we pass through, his native English serving as private code.

In Louis's cubicle area, a weary-looking elderly woman is sitting on a crate talking rapidly in Guaraní to a young man. As we enter, she gives her son a quick kiss, bids him farewell and bustles off down the adjoining passageway. Disconsolate at the end of his week's visit, the young man also gets up and wanders off.

'Wanna see my bed then, man?'

Louis steps onto the ladder at the end of the bunk and, with practised efficiency, scrambles up onto his mattress. Peering down from above, his back against the cell wall and his feet dangling off the edge, he repeats the invitation. Gingerly, I haul myself up behind him.

With each separate rung, I'm struck by how strange this will sound in the retelling. When writing the proposal for this book, I hadn't anticipated joining an international drug-trafficker on his Paraguayan prison bed. But as I pull myself up and get comfortable next to Louis, it all feels oddly natural.

An ironed shirt is hanging from a nail on the wall. It's one of the few items of his clothing that hasn't been stolen. The remainder of his wardrobe – another shirt, a pair of trousers and some underwear – is stored in a tatty black rucksack that's suspended from a second nail. A soldering iron is dangling limply from a thin timber strut under the V-shaped roof above us. His wallpaper consists of cut-outs from magazines. One's a full-page ad for Brahma beer. Another is an article torn from *The Economist* with the headline 'Trade, Death and Drugs'. Three poster girls make up the collage. His neighbour on the adjoining bunk has kept with the theme, adding consistency, if somewhat more bare flesh, to the room's decor.

Louis shunts down to the head of the bed and reaches up to unlock his wooden locker. A fraction smaller than a standard bathroom cabinet, it was knocked up for him by a contact of his in the prison's carpentry workshop. He keeps the locker padlocked, but the ward's *viscacheros,* petty thieves, still find a way of breaking in. Once the bolt is removed from the door, it swings open to reveal a toothbrush, several CDs, the screwdrivers Patrick had just given him and a twenty-inch blade, 'for self-defence'.

Reaching into his trousers, Louis then pulls out an MP4 player from his underpants. It's his pride and joy. He hooks the gadget up to a single speaker, which he's lashed to another of the roof beams. As with the other prisoners, he's tied the cut-up remnants of a soiled undersheet between his two bedposts. Pulled to, they act as a curtain. Louis demonstrates by yanking the unlaundered drapes together. Suddenly confined behind the cotton screen, I feel assailed by anxiety. Louis, on the other hand, relaxes. This is where he comes to be alone, his entire world of privacy a mere twenty cubic feet.

As we sit there behind the curtain, I inquire about his cellmates.

It turns out that they're all in for robbery. Except the man in the bottom bunk, who's charged with rape and first-degree murder.

'He says he didn't do it. But he was there when it happened, so he ended up taking the blame.' Louis is one of the few Tacumbú residents who admits upfront to his misdemeanour.

In general, Louis judges his fellow prisoners to have *buena onda,* a 'good vibe'.

Will he go back to South Africa after he gets out? He thinks for a moment and then shakes his head. Probably not, he says. He's worried the police will pick him up if he does. He doesn't clarify exactly why.

'Sometimes I think it might just be easier if I stay here. Things get complicated outside. Here, life's *tranquila.*'

There doesn't seem much more to say after that. Maybe life really is *tranquila,* chilled out, for Louis. Maybe there's reassurance in knowing his valuables are always close to his crotch. Maybe it's relaxing to think his knife's near to hand should anyone attack him in the night.

Thirty-one months in a Paraguayan prison no doubt changes your perspective. Four walls. Terrible food. Constant violence. At least they're constants, I suppose. Even so, I find it hard to believe Louis's claims of tranquillity can be anything but another of his masquerades. What remains unclear is whether it's me or himself that he's trying to kid. Maybe it's both of us. We climb down.

After my visit to Louis, I track down José Luis Simón. A university lecturer in law, he's the bearer of one of Asuncións finest and fluffiest grey beards. We meet for coffee in a café full of students on Calle España.

Now in his sixties, the professor's career has included spates as a sociologist, an academic researcher, a journalist, a prison reformer and, for a brief stint in 2002, the General Director of Paraguay's penitentiary service.

As an insider, I was interested to know if Louis's comments about drugs and corruption at Tacumbú were credible.

'He's only told you a fraction of what goes on,' the former prison chief responds, chortling like a time-honoured cynic.

During his brief tenure at the helm of the prison system, the professor developed what he likes to term his 'pyramid of corruption' theory: 'The system runs something like this. The prison budget comes from the central government and goes first to the Ministry of Work and Justice, then to the Institute of Prisons, and then to the individual prisons themselves. At every stage, the original amount gets smaller and smaller until there's virtually nothing left for the prisoners themselves.'

I ask for some examples. He cites the procurement process. The bulk of the food is pilfered by the prison catering service. The meagre rations that do get through are billed for at ten times their real quantity. Prostitution, as well. Inmates from the women's prison are bussed in under the pretext of conjugal visits. A look at the lists of visiting 'wives' to Asunción's various jails shows the same names cropping up repeatedly. Bigamy or pimping are the only two explanations. And the Guaraní are not ones for wife-swapping.

'You need to understand, Tacumbú is like Paraguay in miniature. It runs according to a whole system of non-visible structures that have nothing whatsoever to do with the formal rules.' Trying to change those rules was what made the director an ex-director.

Sipping at his black coffee, the bearded lecturer recounts his first night in charge: 'I turned up unannounced at the prison gates and requested to be let in. It was just after midnight. Most of the guards were sleeping. Hardly any were at their posts. I asked to be directed to the solitary confinement area. They tried fobbing me off, but I had the prison plans so I found it myself. What I discovered was inhuman – twenty prisoners illegally confined in a single room and unable to lie down because a burst sewage pipe had covered the floor with human faeces. I threatened the prison staff that if they didn't clean it up immediately, I'd lock them in there myself.'

The professor's popularity plummeted further on Day Two when he suggested legalising all the informal payments being made within the prison. By doing so, the huge sums currently lining the prison staff's pockets could be redirected towards improving the prisoners' non-existent services. José Luis hadn't reached the end of his first week before the death threats began arriving.

'Eventually, a riot broke out in Tacumbú, orchestrated jointly by the authorities and the prison mafia. To put it down would have probably led to a massacre. I didn't want those deaths on my hands.' José Luis tendered his resignation, just fifteen days after starting his new job.

What I'd heard from Patrón and what I'd seen in Tacumbú persuaded me never so much as to jaywalk in Paraguay. The idea of spending time under lock and key in the unruliest corner of South America genuinely petrified me. Perhaps that's the theory? Make prison such a lawless, denigrating, terrifying place that it serves as deterrent to the criminally minded? The argument would be stronger if life outside the prison walls was demonstrably different. It's not. All Paraguayans are prisoners to some extent of José Luis's 'non-visible structures'.

Leaving Asunción for the second time, I headed east to the borderlands. If there's anywhere in South America where it's possible to be incarcerated in the open, it's the untamed streets of Ciudad del Este.

Ciudad del Este

Daisy has a broad, soft face, which, while not classically beautiful, is blessed at least with an attractive symmetry. Her russet, medium-length hair is flecked with sun streaks that I suspect come from a bottle but might just be natural. She's tied it back in a bun, leaving the fringe to hang free. The loose hair falls to just under her eye line, not long enough to tuck behind her ear, so she's continually flicking it out of her line of vision.

Her five-foot frame is sat half-slumped in a plastic chair. Bright yellow sandals adorn her feet, which, given how short her legs are, barely touch the floor. She's wearing beach shorts and a cropped T-shirt that reveals two ample rolls of puppy fat. Her smile is wide, and her teeth, though well set, show signs of enamel deficiency.

Under the sleeve of her T-shirt is a faint tattoo with an old boyfriend's name; 'ergio' the lower-case red letters read. The initial S has been crudely rubbed out and replaced with a plaster-sized mark that's a tone or two lighter than the rest of her copper-brown skin. Things, I presume, did not end so well with Sergio. I fail to catch her eye colour, as she never once looks at me directly.

Benigno explains that I just want to ask a few questions. He wants to know if that's OK with her. She nods. They've already spoken about my visit, and Daisy's consented to being interviewed, but Benigno wants to double-check. A neatly dressed man in his late twenties, he's been working as a part-time volunteer with abused children for the past four years. As a lawyer, he's anxious for them to know their rights.

'Are you sure?' Benigno asks again. She doesn't have to if she doesn't want to. Unused to her opinion being solicited, Daisy looks at him with scrunched eyes as though not believing the softly spoken counsellor is for real.

'Sure, fire away,' she responds a second time.

Where to start? She's sitting on her hands, her legs swinging nervously beneath her. Not wanting to startle her, I ask if she can tell me a little about her family. Her voice is initially timid, but audible. Her parents live in San Juan, she says, keeping her gaze fixedly on the glass-topped desk that separates us. It's a settlement eight kilometres out of town on the highway towards Asunción. Her mother is Brazilian and works as a maid. Her *viejo,* her old man, is Paraguayan and originally from O'Leary, a village in the countryside. She's never visited the place and, although her father talks about it often, has no desire to do so. He's unemployed.

Brother or sisters? She's the second of five, she says.

Age? Seventeen in a fortnight. The thought of her birthday provokes an instinctive, childlike smile.

We're sitting in one of the administration rooms of the Centre for Attention for Boys, Girls and Adolescents, a two-storey building full of bunk beds and noisy children. The centre is located on the periphery of Ciudad del Este, formerly known as Puerto Presidente Stroessner. The obvious question to ask is how she ended up here. Unsure how to approach the issue sensitively, I inquire whether she was living at home previously. Daisy rocks on her hands, and her chin drops downwards a few more inches. She left home when she was ten, she says, her voice more muffled than before. Her father had showed her 'a lack of respect'. He beat her and sexually abused her, Benigno later clarified. She went to live in the house of a near-by aunt. At twelve, she moved back home.

Her timing then gets sketchy. What's clear is that, after a brief interval, the problems with her father started up again. She left once more, on this occasion to take up a job as a live-in maid.

How long did she do that for? About nine months.

And what happened then? She met an older girl on the bus one day. The two started talking, and the older girl asked her if she wanted to go out dancing one night. By my calculations, Daisy was either thirteen or fourteen years old by this stage. She jumped at the chance.

Fast forward to Daisy's fifteenth birthday, and she's pregnant, living in the girl's shared apartment, and the two are 'working' together.

The teenager's vocabulary is sprinkled with coy euphemisms. 'Work' could theoretically mean anything. Cooking, cleaning and other domestic chores would be the most probable for a young girl living in one of Ciudad del Este's poor neighbourhoods. Prostitution is also an outside bet. We're in a home for victims of sexual abuse, so it's not difficult to guess on which side the coin landed for Daisy.

Her usual spot was out at Kilometre 7. She knew the area well having grown up just down the road. Benigno offered to take me on a visit a few nights later. We joined up with Nidia, a friendly teacher in her mid-twenties who also helps out as a volunteer. She was carrying a plastic bag with her as we boarded the bus.

'We generally try and bring something useful with us,' she told me. 'It helps break the ice with the girls.' *Useful.* The word played in my mind, and I stared absent-mindedly at the bag. Food, text-books, pens and pencils, money, shampoo, soap? What might a teenage girl need? Nidia noted my curiosity and held the bag open.

'Forty packets of condoms,' she said, as if it was the most obvious gift in the world.

After a fifteen-minute ride, we dismounted beside a truckers' repair store. Mechanics in dirty overalls were changing the tyres of a Brazilian-registered truck. Four others were parked up, waiting their turn. In front, night-time stallholders stood underneath the awnings of their roadside restaurant shacks. Every now and again, they'd turn a chorizo or a hunk of meat on their rusty, barrel-shaped barbecues. There were fifteen stalls in total, lined up one next to the other over a hundred-yard stretch. The traffic along the two-lane highway screeched past ten feet in front. The odd taxi driver pulled into the lay-by for a quick snack before heading out on his night shift, but otherwise business remained slow.

Across the street was a string of cheap bars and nightclubs. Scratched metal tables and fold-up chairs, both stamped with the logo of a beer company, lined the pavement. Only a few were occupied, mostly by men in groups of three or four surrounded by empty two-litre beer bottles. They were all brawny and unshaven and looked like truckers. It was a Thursday night. Despite being the warm-up for the weekend, the well-known nightspot was unusually quiet.

Daisy's former 'work colleagues' were as frustrated at the lack of trade as everyone else. Monday to Wednesday is a washout work-wise, so they rely on the end of the week to get them through. They were waiting on wooden benches outside the food stalls, each paying a small sum to the owner for the privilege. With nothing else to do, they were happy to talk and quick to accept the handouts Nidia had brought.

Most of the conversations would be in Guaraní, so I relied on my two companions to give me brief summaries of what was being said. There were six or seven girls in all, each stationed at a different stall. Most looked to be in their late teens; a few older, a few younger.

One of the older girls was heavily pregnant. Another had the scar of a caesarean running along her exposed belly. All were wearing short skirts and revealing blouses. A modicum of ill-applied make-up covered their eyelids, lips and cheeks. To me, they looked lost and, without meaning to be cruel, mildly clownish. Whatever the case, they were a far cry from the alluring, confident adult women they were trying to imitate.

Nidia would ask after some of the lay-by regulars who weren't there. A couple were off with 'clients', she was told. Others were covering the wheat harvest. The reference was lost on me, and Nidia broke from talking to explain. Many of the girls, it transpired, head off during harvest time to work in brothels in Paraguay's countryside towns.

'All those men away from their families for weeks on end. As you might imagine, there's plenty of work for them.' Never would the laws of supply and demand strike me as less pleasant.

Back in the centre, meanwhile, Daisy is explaining how she'd made friends with a girl two years older than her called Neli. The two worked the same beat at Kilometre 7. Also a prostitute, Neli had recently met a guy who'd told her about a job in Argentina.

'He promised us we'd easily earn at least 300 *Guarani* a night [around £50],' Daisy says, '200 for us, and 100 for the patron of the place.' The girls had discussed the proposal for a while before coming to a decision.

Her version of events momentarily breaks off into silence. She turns her head towards the window and takes a few deep breaths. Benigno reminds her that she's under no obligation to continue if she doesn't want to. No, she wants to carry on, she says. She just needs a few minutes to collect herself. We all sit in silence, Daisy still staring through the window, Benigno sitting patiently, and me flicking back through my notes and wondering what's to come.

She picks up where she left off: 'We figured that the offer was too good to turn down and so let the man know we were in.'

A few days later, she and Neli were taken across the river Paraná into Argentina.

'How did you cross?' I ask.

'A guy in a taxi took us down to Puerto Irala and then an old chap rowed us across the river in a small boat,' she explains.

Before the interview, Benigno had pointed out on a computerised map the main routes used by the border traffickers. Puerto Irala lay about two hours' drive down the coast. Presidente Franco, a satellite town closer to the city, is another frequent crossing point, he'd said. Between the two, the young lawyer had also singled out a private jetty owned by a politician.

'Small boats travel from shore to shore all the time there,' he'd explained, going on to point out at least ten other clandestine routes across the river.

Located at the confluence of two large rivers, Ciudad del Este serves as a gateway to Brazil as well as Argentina. Known as the *Triple Frontera,* the cross-border area is *the* smugglers' paradise of South America. Everything from narcotics and guns to fruit and vegetables finds their way across the porous, ill-policed frontier. Now women and girls have made their way onto the list as well.

Once on the other side, a taxi driver picked them up and drove them the rest of the way. For the next twenty-two days, Daisy was locked up in a brothel called *La Cueva,* The Cave. Not once was she allowed out. She was made to 'service' a minimum of six men a night. On several occasions, it was double that. After three weeks, the owner had given her the grand sum of 10 *Guarani* (£1.65).

Benigno shakes his head as Daisy relates her experience. Working with the centre over the years, he's heard countless versions of the same story.

'Without exception, they all lie. That's point number one,' he'd explained earlier about the traffickers, once we were done with the map.

In Daisy's case, at least she knew it was a brothel she was heading to. Most don't, Benigno had continued: 'They usually say it's a job as a maid or a cleaner. Sometimes, they might say the work is in a restaurant or a bar. Many are recruited by someone they trust: a cousin, an aunt, a neighbour or a family friend. When the girls arrive and realise the truth, it's too late. The brothel owners take their documents from them and threaten to kill them if they ever try and escape.'

'But don't their parents have an inkling of what's happening?'

'Sure, some do. They're often so desperate, though, they prefer to blind themselves to it. Of course, not every offer of an overseas job ends up in a brothel. But they always turn out to be something exploitative, regardless of what it is. As illegal immigrants, they've no rights. Through the centre, we try and advise families of the risks involved. But it's difficult. How do you tell a mother whose child is working fourteen hours a day for an unjust wage that it's not right when she's been doing the same all her life for even worse pay?' It was a fair point, albeit a horrific one.

Daisy begins to talk faster and faster. By the time she gets to the night that Neli located the key to the main door and let them both out, her words are merging into one another. They tumble out with a desire to be heard and dealt with. What is clear is that they fled with a third girl, Nancy, who was sixteen years old and five months pregnant.

Could she tell me where La Cueva was? All she knows is that it was near to the Argentine border town of El Dorado and that they had to walk five hours non-stop to reach the river. They paid one of the illegal ferrymen to row them back across to Paraguay. Then, they had another five-hour walk to the nearest town. Once there, the girls' story won them the ear of a friendly cabby, who drove them the remainder of the way to Ciudad del Este.

My mind flicks to my wife, who, at the time of my visit, is five months pregnant with our first child. Imagining her walking for an hour under the hot, tropical sun isn't easy, let alone ten.

Once home, Daisy soon returned to 'working' at Kilometre 7. She enrolled at the centre only four days ago.

'Why did you decide to enrol?' I ask, aware that Daisy's initial enthusiasm for the interview is now waning fast.

'I want a better life for my son.'

The school term and a hairdressing course are waiting for her if she sticks it out. The statistics are against her. Most older girls end up leaving and returning to the streets. Daisy is determined that won't be her, a stamp of conviction in her voice. She's looking to the door. Benigno taps her on the shoulder to say well done and to thank her for sharing her experience. I concur.

As she opens the door, a final question occurs to me: 'Daisy, one last thing. What happened to Neli and Nancy?'

Half out the door, she turns her head back: 'Neli's gone to Buenos Aires. She got another offer to work in a brothel. An upmarket place, she said. That's the last I heard of her.'

'And Nancy?'

'No idea, I never saw her again.' She closes the door softly behind her.

Alto Paraná

Regina is waiting for me in the middle of a sandstorm. Stepping off the bus at Ciudad del Este's farmers' market, I catch the eye of the wild-haired anthropologist. Then a cloud of stinging grit fires itself into my face, momentarily blinding me. With our heads ducked into the wind and the gale stealing every second word, introductions prove difficult:

REGINA: Did . . . find . . . all right? . . . sometimes . . . a . . . difficult . . . when . . .
ME: What? . . . bad . . . much . . . thanks.
REGINA: . . . long . . . think . . . stay?
ME: It . . . on . . . you . . . planned . . . Perhaps . . . or . . . days
REGINA: . . . many?
ME: . . . or . . . days.

We're saved by a four-wheel-drive jeep, which is waiting with a revving engine on the far side of the vacant market lot. Regina opens the back passenger door and indicates for me to climb up. She has someone she needs to see quickly, she says, disappearing into the warren of the market.

It's late, and most of the stalls are shuttered up. Huddled in the shadows, along a mattress of flapping cardboard, curls a row of sleeping bodies. From beneath a mound of woollen blankets pokes the sleepy head of a young child. He's staring back up the street, into the darkness, puzzling over where so much wind could come from and whether it will ever stop.

Sitting in the driving seat is Meliton, a stocky, pint-sized man with a stubble beard. We sit in silence, listening to the howl of the storm. As soon as Regina comes back, he drops the jeep into gear and speeds off along the town's empty arterial streets. We soon hit a motorway heading north. Storm clouds lurk in the night sky ahead, a wall of impenetrable blackness engulfing the road. Meliton presses his foot to the gas, rushing at the angry, brooding tempest with the crazed bravado of a fairground ghost train.

I turn to look out of the rain-splashed passenger window, convincing myself that all is well and imminent death a mere illusion. I watch the tenebrous profiles of cardboard cut-out trees thrashing from side to side in the maddened wind. The sight does not restore my confidence in our prolonged existence. I close my eyes. If I am to pass from this life to the next, I'd prefer the blindness of the ignorant over the awareness of the fully conscious.

For the first time in twenty minutes, I sense we might be slowing down. I open my eyes cautiously, trying to peek over the front seat to get a glimpse of the speedometer. I can't read the dial, but the needle is no longer feverishly quivering. Out of the rain-soaked fog emerges a large triangular road sign. Dimly illuminated in the jeep's valiant headlights, it signals our approach to the Itaipú dam. Straddling the river Paraná, the concrete behemoth stands with one foot in Brazil and one in Paraguay. Billions of dollars over budget, it's a fitting monument to the country's lawless eastern frontier.

Meliton pulls off the highway shortly after the Itaipú exit, into the docile town of Hernandarias. Torrents of rainwater run along the roadside, submerging the pavements with swirling, liquid murk. Cruising down a non descript residential street, we suddenly grind to a halt.

'Here we are,' says Regina, turning around in the front passenger seat.

Guardedly, I reach for the door handle. Outside, the storm is showing no signs of abating. Leaves are wrenching themselves from branches and lunging at the wind like kite-surfers. A rubbish bin has toppled over and transformed itself into a garbage scattergun. I'm not to worry, she tells me. A reservation's been made for me. They'll be back at 8 a.m. the next morning to pick me up. I disembark, and Meliton revs off into the night.

The surly receptionist passes me a key and points me to one of the tumbledown detached bungalows at the back of the D'Vinci Hotel. A painted plastic gnome, three foot high and with Meliton's smile, greets me at the door. Exhausted, I pull back the frayed sheet on the single bed and try to sleep. A broken shutter swings on its hinges, monotonously knocking against the chalet's flimsy wall. The wind whistles loudly through the slats in the roof. I put the foam pillow over my head, trying to shut out the noise, willing the storm to stop and the bedroom not to be wrenched from its foundations. Eventually I give up on the idea of sleep and try reading my book in the dim light of the room's single forty-watt bulb. Three pages in, the power shorts, and the room is thrown into pitch darkness. In the courtyard, the enraged storm is working itself into a biblical fury. Lying awake for hours on the lumpy bed, I listen to the thunderclaps above and wonder how long it is till morning.

Drifting off to sleep just before dawn, I wake to the sound of my own shouting. A thin ray of morning light is filtering through a hole in the threadbare curtains. An eerie quiet has replaced the angry, canine howling of the night before. My mind grasps around for a bearing, struggling to pull itself up out of the mire of dreams to the world of full consciousness. Until it does, part of me remains stuck in Abrahán Cué, shackled on the floor of a fetid cell, listening to the screams of the torture victims.

The electricity and hot water are still out. After taking a cold shower, I breakfast alone in a dining room the size of a sports hall. Evidently the only guest in the sprawling D'Vinci Hotel, I feel as if

I've stepped into a Haruki Murakami novel. I call Regina and ask her to rescue me from this hard-boiled wonderland.

Over a gourd of *tereré* at the headquarters of the Farmers' Association of Alto Paraná, Regina fills me in on the plan she's formulated since my email inquiry the previous week.

'You want to see the impact the soya boom is having on the lives of *campesinos*, true?'

That's exactly it, I tell her. From my base in Buenos Aires, I'd been watching the miracle crop gradually turning Argentina's traditional grazing lands into a monocultural desert. The same was now happening in Paraguay. In less than a decade, the country had gone from a small-time soya producer to the world's fourth biggest exporter of the 'green gold'. Nearly two and a half million hectares, almost the size of Belgium, is now planted with the humble bean.

To some – namely, the 2 per cent of mega-farmers who own more than four-fifths of the country's land – the soya boom is a gift from on high. To others – the millions of peasant farmers – it threatens the loss of their land and their livelihoods. The soya trail had struck me as a fitting place to finish my journey around lawless Paraguay.

Regina assures me I've come to the right place: 'Roads permitting, you'll go with Meliton and Brigado to Tierra Prometida, the Promised Land. Tomorrow, to San Isidro and Colonia Tavapy. Then on Sunday, if time allows, to Teko Jojá.'

'Great,' I reply, impressed to hear how my simple request for more information had transformed itself into a three-day jaunt around eastern Paraguay.

Our departure is delayed by another downpour. These are the first rains for two months, and everyone in the office is bouncing around ecstatically. Brigado, the association's broad-chested president, is the only one with a glum face. His home lies forty kilometres off the highway along a dirty track. If the deluge continues, it's unlikely he'll get back to see his family.

Looking for a productive use of our time, he picks up a piece of chalk, turns to the conference-room blackboard and commences a two-hour private lecture about soya's relentless expansion. Tired from my sleepless night, I trust my tape recorder to catch the finer details and jot the headline points down in my notebook:

'Large-scale farmers from Brazil, driving expansion. Arrived in 1960s. Little agricultural land in Alto Paraná not owned by Brazilians. Almost all illegal purchases, land originally owned by government. Earmarked for Paraguayan poor farmers, Rural Reform. Late 1990s, huge increase in soya production. Introduction of genetically modified technology. Biofuels. Monsanto agribusiness, Round-up Ready herbicide. Crop-dusters. Contamination, deforestations, skin diseases. Smaller plots, sold up. Local government officials, on the make. Farmers, no choice. Sell up, or stay and suffer.'

Regina breaks up the morning class with a call for lunch. A fried chicken is brought in on a single plate, and the office staff attack the crispy-skinned bird with their fingers. I join the assault. At some stage during Brigado's lecture, the rain lets up. After a conflab with Meliton, it's decided we'll give the dirt road to Tierra Prometida a try.

Brigado sits shotgun, with Meliton at the wheel and me in my customary seat behind. We drive north-west for just over an hour along a barren highway before reaching a dirt-road turn-off. Three farmhands are sitting idly on the kerb. No public transport passes this way. Meliton slows down and allows them to shin up into the back of the jeep. At the bang of a hitchhiker's fist, we set off through the burgundy-red mud of the waterlogged track.

Neither a great conversationalist, Brigado and Meliton are content to pass the journey listening in silence to *cachaça* tunes on the radio. If they do speak, it's in short grunts of Guaraní. Bored, I watch the uninspiring landscape outside the window: rolling, leafy green hills painted with fledgling soya plants; the odd, intermittent farmhouse; thin hedgerows; the occasional lonely copse; bulky metal silos plastered with foreign-sounding names like Cargill, Bunge and Archer Daniels Midland. Add some graveyards, and the landscape could be Normandy.

'Thirty years ago, almost all of this was woodland,' Meliton says, keeping one hand on the driving wheel and waving the other in a broad arc.

As someone accustomed to a countryside sculpted by tractors and crop-sprayers, I hear the anguish in his voice but struggle to place it. To me, Alto Paraná's neatly regulated fields look like how arable farmland ought to look. To forty-six-year-old Meliton, brought up to the sound of bare-throated bellbirds and saffron toucanets in Paraguay's then expansive Interior Atlantic Forest, it must seem like a green desert. My imagination draws a similar blank when, twenty minutes later, Meliton points to the middle of a wide field buttressing the road and says he used to live there.

'Where?' I ask incredulously. Except for a small settlement in a valley further down the hill, there is nothing but soya fields for as far as the eye can see.

'There,' he says, pointing back to the same patch of tilled soil. 'There used to be two thousand families living here. Now there's only thirty, if that.'

As we skid and swerve down the empty backroad, Meliton tells the story of Minga Purá. Owned by an Argentine rancher who fell foul of the authorities, the twelve-thousand-hectare lot was confiscated by the State in the mid-1980s. Somehow, the prime farmland escaped the hands of General Stroessner's cronies. Meliton obtained a plot from the Government's land agency, built himself a basic lean-to and began cultivating fruits and vegetables for his young family. Most of what they grew, they ate themselves. Only the leftovers went to market.

As each harvest season arrived and yet another neighbour sold up, the land around his ten-hectare plot began to fall under the soya knife. Meliton resolved to dig in. Even if he'd wanted to sow soya (which he didn't), he couldn't have afforded the expensive fertilisers and machinery it requires. Producing genetically modified soya only starts becoming economically viable on plots of one thousand hectares or more.

'The nail in the coffin was when my crops began to fail,' a disconsolate Meliton explains.

He put his rotten cassava and putrid legumes down to the tanker-loads of toxic fertilisers used by the new Brazilian arrivals. Concerned the agrochemicals would eventually do him or his family irreparable damage, he threw in the towel. One day, six years ago, he dismantled his house, packed what he could into a friend's lorry and left. The usually taciturn driver falls back into silence. This short speech, it turns out, will be the most I ever hear him say.

The sun is now high in the cloudless sky, and the mud-slush road gradually begins to dry. It's slow going all the same. We stop for a toilet break. With dark humour, Meliton says he wants to mark his territory. Later, we pass a small farmhouse with a rusty tractor in the driveway and two blond-haired boys playing football in the garden.

'Brazilians!' Brigado huffs. A red-faced man in jeans and T-shirt ambles beside the farm's barbed-wire perimeter fence. An air gun rests in the crook of his arm.

When we arrive in Tierra Prometida, nearly two hours past the cheerless remains of Minga Purá, the village feels vaguely familiar. Brigado had sketched a map on the blackboard during his morning lecture: five squiggly lines to resemble the various streams, a woolly cloud to demark the area of conserved native forest, and a fifty-pence coin to signify the 'urban centre' (site of a rustic school building and an overgrown volleyball pitch). I try piecing the chalked plans together as we drive over the fast-flowing brook dividing the village and up to Brigado's house on the other side of the wooded valley.

'Welcome to the Presidential Palace,' Brigado says with a smile, before being mobbed by his two youngest children.

My legs feel painfully cramped as we climb down from the dirt-splashed jeep. We walk past a chicken coop and a well-cared-for vegetable patch towards his simple brick bungalow.

Meliton shares a *maté* with Brigado's wife, leaving the president to march me round his property. Association business has kept him in town for the past week, and the tread of earth under his feet lightens his step. Eagerly he points out the fruit trees and the manioc patch, the sugar-cane field and the pasture that he's grow-ing should, God willing, he buy a dairy cow next year. It's a model of self-sufficient, organic efficiency, right down to the cow urine he uses as pesticide.

With Regina's schedule in mind, Meliton and I bid him farewell and hit the henna-brown road. Cooped up together in the now filthy jeep, we spend the next two days slewing our way across the slip-pery, unpaved tracks of Paraguay's eastern soya belt. Each commu-nity we visit is different, but the story the same: mega-farms expanding, toxins spreading, forests disappearing and peasant farm-ers migrating. In San Isidro, a contaminated stream cost one man his herd of cows. In Colonia Tavapy, a plague of grotesquely bulbous, insecticide-resistant worms is causing havoc. In Teko Jojá, violent clashes with the local Brazilian soya baron have left two freshly dug graves by the roadside. All have the makings of future Minga Purás.

On the verge of losing their land and livelihoods, Alto Paraná's innocent peasant farmers are inmates in a fenceless jail. Sentence has yet to be passed, but the verdict seems already decided.

As with Evo in Bolivia, Fernando Lugo's election signals the deep-felt mood in South America for a change of script. Paraguayans like Meliton are fed up with their rights being trampled on. Among the to-do notes in his pocket diary, the new president had committed to return independence to the justice system and rid the government of corruption. Both pledges will require a miracle.

José Luis Simon, the bearded former head of prisons, faced a riot when he tried to change the rules. President Lugo can expect the same. The Vatican may have given up on the errant bishop, but he'll be hoping that God is still on his side.

On our last night, I stay with Meliton in his new home in the rural community of El Triunfo, The Triumph. The house is a hotch-potch of wood, brick, cement and ceramic tiling, but it's warm and well loved. Situated on the edge of the main highway to Asunción, it's a half-hour drive outside Ciudad del Este. He's lucky, he admits. The city's burgeoning shanty towns are where most other soya refugees end up.

We arrive late, and his wife has two bowls of hot *caldo de carne* waiting for us. Delio, a young student lawyer from down the street, hears the Remírezes are entertaining and pops by. Whether it's the prospect of the watery meat stew or conversation that draws him remains unclear, but he joins us at the table all the same.

Slurping down the steaming *caldo,* he tells me about the victoriously named village. Unlike neighbouring settlements, where plots are divided up between individual families, El Triunfo is jointly owned by all its residents. Adopting a collective front, Delio hopes, will prevent the soya farmers picking them off one by one. Next year, he's also planning to take a special course on the law governing agrotoxic use. 'I'm going to bring forty or fifty cases,' the Paraguayan Erin Brockovich states confidently.

Even with so much enthusiasm, the unqualified attorney admits the chances of success are slim: 'Here, if you have money, you can do whatever you like. You can buy our land illegally, you can buy a judge, you can buy anything.' Regrettably, none of El Triunfo's residents have a dime.

Delio's excited manner puts Meliton in mind of a joke he'd heard the previous week.

'There's a North American businessman, a Japanese tourist, a Brazilian soya farmer and a run-of-the-mill Paraguayan on a plane.' A collective groan goes up round the table.

Undeterred, Meliton presses on: 'The plane's struggling because it's overloaded, and the captain comes out and says they'll have to start throwing things out. He tells them to pick whatever they have in abundance back home.'

'Oh, I know this one,' says Delio, suddenly remembering and starting to laugh. Meliton's wife shushes him, obviously intrigued both by the joke and the fact that it's her reticent husband telling it.

'Well, the Yank immediately pulls out three large suitcases of dollar bills and nonchalantly throws them out the window. Then up the Japanese man gets and throws out seven laptops and a dozen cameras.'

'Next it's the turn of the Brazilian. He's got no soya because he's sold it all, so he throws out some large bags of rice and sugar cane.'

Meliton stops, savouring the silence before the punchline. His wife nags at him to continue.

'Well, as you can imagine, the penniless Paraguayan is sitting there racking his brains as to what he could possibly throw out. The plane is still struggling. He looks around the cabin in desperation.' Another momentary pause. Delio's giggles develop into a fit of muffled laughter.

'And?' exclaims his wife in impatient anticipation.

'Well, then it dawns on him. He goes over to the Brazilian, picks him up and throws him out the emergency door. "Now those, we've got more than enough."'

We all laugh, Meliton more than any of us. It's the second longest I've heard him speak, and by far the funniest.

5

LIFE IN THE SPACE RESERVOIR
Brazil and race

It seems to me madness that a revolution for liberty should try to maintain slavery.

SIMÓN BOLÍVAR, *DECRETOS DEL LIBERTADOR*

São Paulo

Brazil is an island. Agreed, on a map it might not look like one. In addition to Paraguay, the regional colossus has nine countries butting against its borders. Nor is its size that of your typical island. Ireland would fit a hundred times into its ample bulk with room still to spare. As for the wildlife swimming down its rivers and bouncing through its trees, it makes the Galapagos Islands look like a cash-strapped city zoo.

No, its island qualities lie altogether apart from its geography. They have to do with how the country sees itself, its state of mind. History and happenstance have landed it in a continent of strangers. The rites of the Mass and the small print of the Football Association rule book represent the sum of its shared interests with Hispanic America. Everything else is different: how Brazilians talk, how they walk, how they make music, how they dress, how they sing, how they flirt, how they move and how they dance – especially how they dance.

Not that differences don't exist between other South American states. Yet there's an affinity between Spain's old colonies that Brazilians don't share. At continental shindigs, Brazil is the lonely outsider – no one's special enemy, but no one's special friend. Imagine the British delegation at European Union meetings and you have the Brazilians on the South American stage: aloof, apart and funny-sounding. Not that they mind terribly. They quite like it that way.

But there's another stark peculiarity about Brazil. For the continent's Hispanics, skin tone matters. Brazil, by contrast, is officially colour-blind. There's no tune to which the samba nation won't dance, or so they say.

I take a room on Rua Dom Jose de Barros just off Praça da República. Located in the heart of downtown São Paulo. The hotel came recommended. The area did not.

Feeling filthy and exhausted after the night bus from Paraguay, I take a quick shower and flick on the television. Without satellite, the choice is limited: a lottery game show, a couple of *telenovelas* and a dubbed cop movie. I switch the set off and instead listen to the hushed chatter of early risers eating breakfast on the floor below. Within seconds, I'm asleep. Waking an hour later, I feel fresher and ready to check out the neighbourhood. Down to my last set of clean clothes, I pack a week's worth of washing into a bin liner and go in search of a launderette.

Life outside has grown busier since I checked in. A maze of market stalls now winds along the pedestrianised street on the hotel doorstep. Between the racks of cheap Bermuda shorts and denim jeans squeeze stalls of sunglasses and pirated DVDs. Half a block to the right lies the Rua Barão de Itapetininga, a street of low-budget clothing stores already buzzing with window-shoppers and people heading to work. I turn left.

The temporary market stretches to the corner and peters out. Looming above the ground-floor shops runs a row of featureless tenement blocks. They obstruct the morning's slanting sun, throwing the whole quadrant into gloomy shadow. I take a right down a confining corridor of darkened doorways and broken rubbish bags. The blanketed bodies of the city's homeless fill the empty alleyways. Some are just beginning to rustle. Around the next bend, a tawdry, four-storey shopping centre presents itself. Reckoning it might have a launderette, I venture inside. I'm not in luck. There are shoe-repair shops and hairdressers and tattoo parlours and key-cutters and heavy-metal music stores, but no launderette.

The tacky, low-budget mall exits onto the other side of the block, bringing me out into Largo de Paiçandú. A cement-clad square squashed in between ugly office buildings and yet more unloved high-rises, Paiçandú houses a plain but attractive chapel. Built by black Brazilians at the turn of the twentieth century, the church's wide triangular spire marks the only patch of its custard yellow exterior that has escaped the graffiti artists.

Aerosol cans contend with urine as the dominating feature of downtown São Paulo. The urine, I reckon, has the edge. Carried on the stagnant, humid air, its sickly stench overrides even the smoggiest of traffic fumes. Feeling as if I'm trapped in an odorous underground car park, I flee up the traffic-choked Avenida São João and away from the Paiçandú square.

My flight leads me to the corner of the car-clogged Avenida Ipiranga. I am standing, my tourist map informs me, on immortalised ground. The unexceptional metropolitan intersection is referred to in the song, 'Sampa', a quintessential classic about São Paulo. Looking up the lyrics later, I'm disappointed to discover that the hit brushes over Habbib's fast-food store and the twenty-four-hour triple-X cinema. Perhaps it didn't fit with his rhyming scheme, but the omission strikes me as an unfortunate oversight, especially the cinema. Compared to the ornate but empty Municipal Theatre four blocks away, the República's thriving adults-only movie halls look to be meccas of popular culture. Tatiana's sex shop might be a novelty in Santiago, but São Paulo's old town has Buttmans, Butt Sellers and other similar erotic (mostly rear-end related) emporia on every other corner.

Crossing the three-lane Avenida Ipiranga, I pass into Praça da República. At weekends, the tree-shaded square fills with a hippy market of ethnic jewellers and handicraft vendors. During the week, though, it's the realm of down-and-outs, drunks and drug pushers. Brightening the day for the park's habitués is a four-man indigenous

ensemble. They are led by a pot-bellied recorder player in a feathered headdress. The Brasil Inkas are playing hits from their cos-
mologically inspired woodwind album, *Magic Mountain*. The
audience listen with polite attention, tapping their feet to the
rhythm and emitting the odd drunken burp in encouragement. A
barefoot mulatta then takes to the floor and engages in a hip-
shaking two-step with her carton of wine.

I walk on, through to the far side of the park towards a group of
tall, African-looking men wearing colourful kaftans that float down
to their shins. The five friends are sitting on a bench by one of the
park's stagnant emerald ponds, arguing in a coarse Portuguese. A
Chinese woman rushes past. Spilling from her hands are two
Styrofoam burger boxes of steaming noodles, freshly ladled from
her portable food cart. Beyond them, in a second pond, two dark-
skinned boys splash noisily, indifferent to the scum-green sludge
floating to the surface.

Leaving the park, I head up Rua do Arouche, stopping briefly at
a kiosk stocked high with women's magazines and the day's newspapers. To move on requires sidestepping a butch female bouncer
patrolling the entrance to a busy pavement café. I swerve round her
and take the next right. The turning opens onto the quieter Rua
Aurora. A dim, litter-strewn street, it leads me past a series of open
yet unmarked doorways. Each gives way to a steep staircase
manned by a bored sentry sitting on a stool. Heavy curtains drape
across the windows on the floors above, an oddity in the morning's
stifling humidity. The shady Aurora is empty of other pedestrians,
substantiating my growing suspicion that its usual clientele might
be of a more nocturnal disposition. A few streets down and the
names of cheap hotels begin appearing above the same threadbare
staircases. I walk by a restaurant with a sign claiming to have the
'Best Brazilian Italian Food in São Paulo'.

Reckoning that so many flophouses must have a launderette in
the vicinity, I begin scanning the side streets with a more avid eye.
Three buildings down Rua Guaianzes, I eventually spot the word
lavanderia above an open-fronted store. Leaving the plastic bag

with the friendly, fair-haired laundry woman, I agree to pick it up the next day.

Resolving that República's rough-edged reputation is well earned, I cut my sightseeing short and head back.

Of São Paulo's nineteen million inhabitants, I have one good friend. Back in the hotel, I waste no time in telephoning her. I first met Gisele when she was a poor university graduate studying English in London. Seven years later, she's still a poor university graduate, only now she spends her days thinking about shoots for an ad agency rather than irregular verb forms.

It is good to hear her voice again, although its shrillness at the news that I'm staying downtown is mildly disconcerting. Convinced I'm going to get mugged, stabbed or otherwise assaulted as soon as I step outside, she orders me to remain barricaded in my room until the next day. Tomorrow she has some time off work, she says, and can chaperone me around the city.

Fear of crime is a guiding sentiment among most Brazilians. São Paulo's municipal government seriously discussed changing the traffic laws a few years ago to protect motorists from being robbed at traffic lights. Drivers, it was proposed, would not only be allowed to run a red light after dark, they would be encouraged to do so. However bad the crime rates, the idea of petite Gisele – barely taller than a prepubescent twelve-year-old – acting as anyone's personal security is as cutely preposterous as it is kindly proposed. I promise to take care and make arrangements to meet the next day.

Before our date, there's one sight I particularly want to check out: the Hospedaria dos Imigrantes. From the middle of the nineteenth century onwards, thousands of poor migrants – most of them European – boarded ships and headed to the New World. Many set off with one-way tickets to São Paulo, Brazil's largest city and its industrial capital.

As the city grew more prosperous, it became the natural jumping-off point for the growing flood of foreign fortune-seekers. Not that the new arrivals managed to jump too far. As soon as they stepped foot on the quay, most were corralled onto a steam train and whisked off to the Hospedaria. A mega-boarding house of sorts, the service was bankrolled by large landowners in need of cheap manual labour. In exchange for a health check-up and a roof over their heads, the new immigrants were presented with an ink pen, a work contract and a line on which to sign. For the majority, it was then off to the coffee fields.

More than two and a half million people passed through the Hospedaria's doors between 1886 and 1915. Not all new immigrants came to São Paulo. A large population of Germans settled in the south, while hordes of Dutchmen headed north. Even so, the ledger of the immigrant hotel contains surnames from more than seventy different nationalities. Some escaped their backbreaking contracts and realised their dream of becoming rich. Most did not. Rich or poor, though, nearly all got on with one job in common: procreation. It's that genetic melting pot that today adds so many different layers to South America's rainbow nation.

Bearing Gisele's words of caution in mind, I empty my pockets of valuables and head with a confident stride to República metro station. In spite of her predictions, I survive the five-stop journey to Bresser without assault or battery. Disembarking at the overground station, I follow the train tracks back along a quiet suburban street until I reach a huge two-storey barracks. Spotting two tour coaches parked up against the kerb, I take it to be the Hospedaria. Paying my entrance fee, I cross a well-kept lawn towards the building's arched portico. Men with brilliantined hair pasted flat against their scalps stare out from a grainy photo on the wall of the entrance corridor. Beside it are other images taken by the hostel's turn-of-the-century cameraman: a doctor holding a stethoscope to the back of a bare-chested labourer, three women sitting on a bunk bed in a starched dormitory, children eating bread and soup at long wooden benches in the Dickensian refectory.

Along the front runs a shaded colonnade. Tucked underneath it on the ground floor, I come across a small visitors' bookshop. Browsing the shelves gives a feeling for Brazil's diverse gene pool.

Beside the accounts of Bulgarian and Belarusian migrants is nestled a dictionary of Japanese names and a book of Arabic sayings. The next shelf carries the memoirs of an English exile, a survey of Spanish coffee farmers and tales from Jewish colonists. The first floor spells out the same in more graphic terms. The ledger's surnames have transformed themselves into life-sized dolls with eyes as big as saucepans and comic-book lips. Trussed up in the costumes of their native lands, the flag-waving crowd starts with an Orthodox Jewish couple in Russian felt hats and finishes with two doe-eyed Arabs wearing white headdresses.

Leading away from the multicultural exhibition are the former starched dormitories of the photos. One contains a theatre set depicting São Paulo at the turn of the twentieth century. Downtown, I conclude, could do with winding back a century: the mock pharmacist has the lab coat of a true professional, the tramway boasts an air of efficiency, and Café Girondino is free of scary doorwomen.

Another exhibition space in the second dormitory traces the story of the coffee boom. I stroll slowly around the exhibits until a reproduction painting draws me up short. It depicts a corpulent plantation owner dressed in a three-piece linen suit. Sporting a carefully lacquered moustache, the Portuguese potentate is sitting in a wicker chair on the veranda of his grand estate. Between his chubby pink mitts, he's grasping a delicate china cup of freshly roasted coffee. Beside him is a severe-looking white woman in a buttoned-up dress and two silent children in similarly stifling attire.

What catches my eye is not the painting's main subjects but a forgotten figure in the corner. Looking on at the family scene, with her back straight and a tray in her hands, stands a diminutive black maid. She too is immaculately dressed, in a pressed pinafore and braided bonnet. Yet the indentured servant girl hails from a different world.

Brazil's history of slavery barely gets a mention in the Hospedaria's exhibits. Admittedly, the museum is dedicated to the memory of the hostel's migrant residents. But Brazil saw two major influxes of foreigners, one voluntary, the other not. No refectories or dormitories awaited the latter.

Shackled together in the holds of slave ships, over three million Africans made the month-long journey across the Atlantic. A cruel life on the plantations of sugar and coffee barons awaited most. Not until 1888, on the eve of the Republic, did this sad chapter in Brazil's history eventually close – more than six decades after Bolívar ordered freedom for the slaves of Gran Colombia.

Brazil's immigration patterns are given a fuller airing in the metro than the museum. On the ride back from the Hospedaria, I pull out my notebook and make a note of my fellow passengers.

Sitting next to me is an elderly black man with white, closely cropped hair and the wizened, knotted face of a mahogany sculpture. On the seat in front of us sits a teenager, also of African descent, but several shades darker. He has a voluminous Afro and is wearing a chunky silver chain around his neck, long basketball shorts and a black vest with 'Hip Hop' written on the back. He could be from Brooklyn. Sharing his bench is a thin white girl with straight, marmalade-tinged hair and sunburned shoulders. Her eyes are hazel and her skin freckly.

Across to my left stands a pensioner, with shallow cheeks, bony pianist's fingers and an olive face shadowed by half a day's stubble. Beside him is perched a thin, middle-aged woman with sparrow eyes and the skin of a wrinkled walnut. Bulging across from the next-door seat, an overweight twenty-something girl in a clinging T-shirt is speaking with a companion. The two could be twins, both pasty white, both light-eyed and both crowned with tresses of mouse-brown hair.

República metro stop is called, curtailing my crude exercise in phenotypic documentation. Every other South American country feels racially monochrome all of a sudden. With more time, I'm confident I could have worked my way through a paint store of skin colours.

Official figures use blunter language, but their message is the same. According to the Institute of Geography and Statistics, around half of Brazilians classify themselves as 'white'. Another two-fifths tick the 'brown' category when asked. A mere one in sixteen (6 per cent) consider themselves 'black', while fewer than 1 per cent reckon themselves to be 'yellow' (to borrow the institute's terminology) or 'indigenous'.

Not all bureaucratic investigations are so imaginatively restrictive. A brainstorming session at the census office once came up with one hundred and thirty-five separate descriptions for Brazilians' pigmentation. Among the options to choose from were *alva-rosada* (white with pink highlights), *branca-sardenta* (white with brown spots), *morena-canelada* (cinnamon-like brunette) and *tostada* (toasted). Such poetry is rare in today's politically correct circles. Today, Brazil's African descendants have just two categories to choose between: *preto* (black) or *pardo* (mixed race). Most identify themselves with the second.

I'd like to see an immigrant neighbourhood, I tell Gisele when we meet the next day.

'A *what?*' she says, a frown of confusion creasing her forehead.

Does she know what the English word 'ghetto' is? Yes, she thinks she does.

Well, does São Paulo have any migrant ghettos? In such a large, diverse city, I imagined there must be a Chinatown or a Little Italy or a Jewish Quarter. Her brow still puckered, she says I may be able to see some Orthodox Jews if I go out to Luz district on a Saturday afternoon. It's Wednesday.

Does she have any other ideas? Another option might be Rua José Paulino, a street of clothes stores in Bom Retiro. She thinks it's run by Koreans. People say Italians used to live in Bela Vista, but, other than perhaps having a few more pizza restaurants than elsewhere, she doesn't think that is still the case.

Our best bet, she reckons, is Liberdade. She's never been but knows it to be very Japanese. Within walking distance of República, it doesn't take us long to find our way to the congested canton.

More frying wok than melting pot, oriental shops line the bustling thoroughfare.

We pop into a dress store called Minikomo. Gisele holds up a kimono to test the fit, while her boyfriend, Ale, eyes up a pair of 'ninja slippers'. In the Marukai supermarket next door, we find everything from Kani sticks and Ajitaka fish paste to samurai swords and chopsticks. We settle on a lucky-cat fridge magnet.

Later on, over ice cream, I ask Gisele if she can fill me in on Brazil's race-related slang. While not taboo, talking about race head-on runs against good manners. In a racial democracy, the subject of skin colour is officially a non-issue. Brazilians are indoctrinated to be race-indifferent in public. White, brown or black, it doesn't matter. Bringing the theme up, therefore, is as likely to brand you a bore as it is a bigot.

Gisele's brow wrinkled in furrows at my question. Reading her discomfort for confusion, I set out to clarify my meaning.

'You must have names for people of different races. What do you call those of Japanese descent, for example?'

'*Japonese*,' she says without humour, as if answering a vocabulary test.

I'm not after words that I'll find in a dictionary, an objective I sense she understands but is shrinking back from. Running the risk of appearing both boring *and* bigoted, I ignore the hint and press on.

'No, what's their nickname? They must have a nickname. In England, for example, we might call them "Japs".'

'But isn't "Japs" rude?' she asks, the eternal English student.

'Yes, you're right. "Jap" is generally considered pejorative. And while I wouldn't use it, others might.'

Comforting herself that I'm no closet racist, she warms a fraction to the theme of my questioning.

'Well, we also use *China*,' she admits, her cheeks reddening and her voice dropping so those around us won't hear. 'But that's for anyone from Asia. It's not meant in a bad way, but the Japanese don't really like it.'

'So *China*'s the strongest you've got?'

'Umm. People might use *Bruce Lee* sometimes.' Her embarrassment seems to lessen. 'Or *Jaspion*, which is the name of a Japanese cartoon character, although that's not polite at all.'

'And *negros*?' I enquire, careful to shorten the first syllable [*né-gro*] as in the Portuguese for 'black', and not to lengthen it [*knee-grow*] as in the Ku Klux Klan for 'lynching material'.

'*Negros* are *negros*,' Gisele says straightforwardly. 'There's a movement now to call them *afro-descendentes* as well, but most just use *negro*.'

'And what do blacks call each other?'

'*Negro* too. Although there are lots of other derivatives too, like *nego*, *neguinho*, *negão*, *negraço*.'

'And do white people use them too, or is that taken to be racist?'

'Maybe not *negraço*, but the rest, sure. Why not? They're seen as terms of endearment. Of course, it depends on how you say it. If you say, "Watch your bag, there are lots of *negros* in this area," then sure it's racist. But generally, no, *negro* is just the term we use for "black".'

'But there are outright racist terms, right?' I can't believe Brazil is so racially harmonious that stronger prejudices don't exist.

Gisele hesitates before answering and then asks for a pen and paper. Never having vocalised the terms before, she refuses to start now. She writes down half a dozen words with their English translation in brackets: *tissão* (very black), *macaco* (black monkey), *Pelé* (black, as in the famous Brazilian footballer), *meia-noite* (midnight) and, lastly, *escravo* (slave).

She's insistent that I never, ever consider using any of them: 'We have very strong anti-racism laws here. If you don't get beaten up first, then you stand a very real chance of getting locked up by the police.' Again, I find myself promising her that I'll be attentive.

'And whites? Is there a pejorative term for them?' The question occurs to me just as we're finishing our cornets.

'No, they're just *brancos*,' she replies, 'Unless they're foreigners, of course.'

'And in that case?'

'What, like you? We call you *gringo*. It doesn't matter where you're from. If you're white and foreign, you're a *gringo*.'

Later in the week, I catch a local bus down to the prestigious University of São Paulo. The traffic is so bumper-to-bumper that the logjam streets would make a dodgem track seem roomy. After almost an hour, the bus pulls up outside the social-sciences faculty and I climb down with the longhaired students.

Along a corridor of metallic doors, I find a door with Professor María Ligia Coelho Prado's name badge nailed to it. Visiting the professor came at the recommendation of a student friend of Gisele's, one of the professor's ex-pupils. I knock, and a well-dressed white woman with a sensible haircut and the air of an academic invites me in.

Wearing my new status on my sleeve, I explain my *gringo* fascination with Brazil's apparent interracial harmony. I was hoping that, as a historian, she could spare me a few minutes to explain how the phenomenon came about. The professor is only too happy to help, but I've caught her between lectures. I'm to forgive her if she's a little brief. She'll cut to the chase.

The easiest way for a foreigner to understand the country's racial democracy is to consider what Brazil is not. It is not, in short, the USA. Slaves in Brazil, for example, were able to buy their freedom. Even before the formal end of slavery, therefore, a black man walking the street could feasibly be either slave or free. That's very different from how the situation was in the USA.

Brazil's colonisers were also more pragmatic than the Puritans. To exploit the natural wealth of their New World discovery, the Portuguese required a workforce. As the royal accountants pointed out, begetting one was a good deal more practical than buying one. So from the outset, the Portuguese crown consented to its subjects siring children whenever and with whomsoever they could. Having sex with their slaves or indigenous servants became nothing short of a patriotic duty.

Another difference with the USA: after emancipation, Brazil never had any segregation laws and, therefore, no ghetto-mentality. Tough anti-racism legislation in the past two or three decades has strengthened the notion that everyone is equal, regardless of colour.

She checks her watch. The lecture hall beckons.

'How long are you here for?' A month or so, I tell her. Have a look around, she encourages me.

'You'll see that being black doesn't mean just having black friends. Society is more mixed here. It makes life easier, more pleasant.'

She places her lecture notes in a satchel. 'Don't let me mislead you. All this doesn't mean Brazil is *truly* a racial democracy.' She's heading for the door. 'We might be different from the United States, but silent discrimination is still deep-rooted here. Five minutes in a *favela* will show you that.'

Before taking my leave of São Paulo, Gisele and Ale take me to the upmarket Iguatemi shopping centre on Avenida Faria Lima. My friend is adamant that the dinginess of downtown not be my lasting impression of her home city.

She parks her ten-year-old Fiat between two newly licensed station wagons and we ride the car park lift down to the ground floor. It's the beginning of December, and the main entrance area has been converted into a lavish Santa's grotto. Manicured mothers push three-wheeled prams through the children's fantasy, stopping occasionally to let their little darlings admire the miniature train and fairground games.

We turn to a map of the mall in an attempt to orientate ourselves. Every other store, it would seem, houses a luxury brand: Tiffany & Co., Versace, Salvatore Ferragamo, Prada, Christian Dior. Wandering round, we discover an embroidered leather shoulder bag for US $3,265 in Louis Vuitton, a US $645 Leóville-Las-Cases 1994 Bordeaux in Expand Wine Store and a three-kilo, thick glass chalice of Belgian truffles in Chocolat du Jour priced at an astronomical US $1,537. The closest item to our price range is a pair of Armani briefs. A snip at US$250.

'For that price, I'd wear them outside my trousers,' says Ale, who earns roughly that amount per month working as an assistant in a film studio.

Leaving the window-shopping aside, we head to the food court to grab a bite to eat. The restaurant selection reflects the cosmopolitan tastes of São Paulo's moneyed classes. Gisele chooses some falafel from Arabian Express, Ale a spaghetti dish from Spazio Pasta and I a beef stroganoff from Bon Grillé.

The parting words of the professor are occupying my thoughts, and I ask my two dining companions if they too think Brazil is silently discriminatory. Ale, who's of mixed-race ancestry, looks up from his spaghetti and slowly casts his eye around the room: 'What do *you* think?'

I follow his eye. Other than the tan-skinned Ale and a young black man with a shaven head eating at Sushi Dai, all the diners in Iguatemi are white. Those who are darker-skinned are either holding a dishcloth or an order form. It sounds crass. But that's the way it is.

Rio de Janeiro

There exist several ways of seeing a *favela*. The easiest and by far the most common is to pull out your Speedos, take yourself down to Copacabana beach, hire a deckchair, turn it away from the water and look up at the hills.

Nowhere is South America's wealth gap more evident than in Rio de Janeiro. Five-star hotels and penthouse apartment suites wrestle over every inch of Brazil's iconic beachfront. Above them, in contrast, clutching precariously to the hillsides, are the homes of the have-nots.

Slum-dwelling is not new to Rio. In a downtown bookshop, I pick up a copy of Aluísio Azevedo's late-nineteenth-century classic, O Cortiço (*The Slum*). The story plays out in the choking confines of the fictitious São Romão *favela,* a heaving slum created by a Portuguese tavern-owner, João Romão, 'who never wore a jacket and slept and ate with a Negress'. Stealing planks and bricks and sacks of lime from his neighbours, the avaricious immigrant and his black lover-housekeeper throw up one rental shack after another. Soon, a bustling community is born.

The slum's impoverished residents provide Azevedo with his colourful cast: Leandra, the washerwoman with 'haunches like a draught animal'; the half indigenous, half crazy Leocádia; Florinda, the black teenager with lustful eyes who 'stubbornly preserved her virginity'; Rita, the sensual Bahian mulatta who wears vanilla flowers in her hair and smells of clover; the steadfast Jerônimo, who played sad *faros* and yearned for home until he 'became a Brazilian'; plus a roll-call of quarry workers, prostitutes, shop owners, policemen and peddlers, as you'd imagine in a turn-of-the-century slum.

More than a hundred years later, it's Azevedo's creation that I picture when I look up from the sandy beach to the hillside shacks: the archetypal *favela* from whose 'sultry humidity, a living world, a human community, began to wriggle, to seethe, to grow spontaneously in that quagmire, multiplying like larvae in a dung heap'.

Azevedo and beach binoculars can only reveal so much about the realities of contemporary *favela* life. I resolve to take a closer look. Packing up my deckchair, I head off and book myself onto a 'slum tour'. I do so reluctantly. The prospect of ogling at other people's poverty with a group of camera-touting tourists makes me feel distinctly uncomfortable. But so too does going it alone. Gun battles with police result in over one thousand deaths a year in Rio's seven hundred or more *favelas*. The tourist option, I decide, represents the better of the two evils.

At two o'clock the next afternoon, an unlicensed taxi picks me up at my hotel and bunny-hops southwards through Rio's afternoon traffic. In the front seat is an Irish backpacker who's 'along for the craic'. Squashed into the back with me, meanwhile, are Bob and Brenda, a retired Chinese-Canadian couple of unrelenting enthusiasm.

Leaving the palm trees of the Ipanema seafront, we drive past the Jockey Club and the Flamengo football stadium and finally through the Dois Irmãos road tunnel. Emerging on the other side of the mountain, we pull up beside a minivan of other tourists and are collectively ushered out towards a row of waiting motorbikes. Within seconds, we're dodging oncoming traffic and breaking into hairpin bends as the taxi-bikes speed full throttle to the top of the Rocinha *favela*.

Our guide is called Daniel, a handsome thirty-something Brazilian with an Americanised accent and a word for all the women that we pass. He's been in the job ten months and appears to be a popular face in the *favela*. He groups us together, counts us off and launches into his spiel.

Rocinha has an estimated two hundred thousand inhabitants and is reckoned to be the largest of Rio's *favelas*. The settlement's origins date back to the 1920s, when poor farmers from the north-east started flocking to Rio in search of work. Almost 50 per cent of the *favela*'s children are not in school. Family incomes are around 400 *reals* per month, less than half the average for Rio. Rents range between 150 and 700 *reals* (roughly £45 and £200) per month, with the cheaper housing found on the hill's lower reaches where the sewage and garbage tend to collect. Two health centres serve the entire population. Only those living on the main street that we drove up pay for water and electricity. Everyone else steals from the grid.

That's as far as he gets before the heavens open and a monsoonal deluge tips down. Cutting off his speech, he beckons us to follow him. Shoving my rain-drenched notebook into my back pocket, I tag onto the line now filing towards a tapered passageway leading off the hillside's principal street.

At first, it's difficult to determine who is observing whom most keenly. Rocinha's residents are accustomed to tour groups, but the sight of eleven foreigners splashing through the mud in flip-flops, wetter than a litter of drowned kittens, is entertaining enough for them to drop what they're doing and stare.

Our *gringo* grouping, on the other hand, shuffles forward with heads down, like prisoners in a chain gang. I feel awkwardly self-conscious, as if heading out to a fancy-dress party in the middle of the day. How much my fellow tour-goers share my discomfort is difficult to tell. Perhaps they're looking down to avoid losing their step on the uneven path. Only Bob and Brenda appear entirely unperturbed. They stroll along waving eagerly at the children and issuing a loud 'How ya doing?' at their mystified parents.

Once off the main street, I feel less conspicuous. Most people are inside their homes waiting out the rainstorm. Those caught by the downpour rush along under cheap umbrellas, not stopping to talk. Only a straggle of young boys and girls are outside, splashing in puddles and playing games with empty plastic bottles in the rainwater.

Within minutes, a rushing torrent several inches deep is cascading down Rua 1, the tapered alleyway along which we're descending. The zigzagging path carves its way down the mountainside, slicing a passage through the warren of Rocinha. So closely pressed together are the houses that Rua 1's residents can reach out of their top windows and exchange things with their neighbours across the street. The only public infrastructure is the occasional telegraph pole, every one of which is weighed down with a disordered jumble of illegally rigged cables.

Every few hundred yards, we stop under an overhanging doorway to shelter briefly from the rain and to allow people to regroup. On one such break, a skinny man strolls by. Oblivious to the rain, he's wearing surf shorts and a soaking vest. Hanging by a strap over his shoulder swings an American-made AR-15 machine gun. He acknowledges Daniel with a nod of the head and continues on his way up the hill. Open-mouthed, we watch him pass and disappear around a bend in the path.

A day-care centre for toddlers and small children further down the hill provides us with our next stop. It's funded by Daniel's tour agency, and he's anxious we all know what a wonderful job they're doing to provide for its upkeep. We listen patiently, but it's not long before someone asks about the man with the machine gun.

'Oh, him. He's just patrolling the neighbourhood,' Daniel explains casually. 'Rocinha, like almost all Rio's *favelas,* is policed by the drugs gangs.'

The Pure Third Command currently rules the roost in Rocinha. The gang is an offshoot of the Third Command, which itself is an offshoot of the Red Command. The three together control the majority of Rio's slums. Our visit to the *favela* is conditional on the gang's prior approval. The day-care centre, I have no doubt, contributes towards our entrance ticket.

Two hours later, waterlogged and weary, we arrive back at the bottom of the hill. We hail two taxis, and Rocinha's rickety residences are soon fading behind us. Within minutes they've disappeared entirely, obliterated by the tunnelled outcrop that conveniently keeps Rocinha out of sight and out of mind for Rio's richer residents.

'Ever noticed what great feng shui Rio has?' pipes Bob's perky voice from the back as we emerge out from the tunnel. The storm has eventually let up, and the sun is shimmering across the glass-topped bay.

'It hadn't occurred to me, dear, but now you mention it,' responds Brenda, her capacity for cheerfulness not in the least abated by our rain-saturated excursion. 'It's just like Yosemite.'

As the taxi weaves along the coast road, their conversation moves seamlessly from the city's harmonious symmetry to its yin and yang: the ocean and the mountains, the beauty and the beastliness, the sea-view suites and the sordid slums.

Tuning out, I think back to the professor's comment about silent discrimination. Very few of the faces I saw in Rocinha were white.

It's not necessary to go all the way to a *favela* to appreciate Brazil's unspoken apartheid. A trip to the government's public databases would suffice just as well. In a dingy cybercafé later that evening, I search out some statistics online.

The headline facts are indisputable. Seven in ten of very poor Brazilians, for example, turn out to be non-white. In contrast, nearly nine out of ten (86.8 per cent) of Brazil's richest 1 per cent are white-skinned. If you're born black and poor in Brazil, not only are you more likely to remain poor than a non-black, you're also more likely to suffer ill-health and die younger.

I click through to the Ministry of Education website, figuring that access to schooling might explain some of these incongruities. Typically, the child of a mixed-race or black couple receives two years less education than their white peers. At university, the difference becomes even more marked. Over a third (37.3 per cent) of whites between eighteen and twenty-four years of age are enrolled in university or an equivalent institution. That number drops to one in twenty (4.9 per cent) for Brazil's black population. Little wonder that Afro-Brazilians are more than twice as likely to be illiterate as their white contemporaries, and have half the earning power.

Driving back from Rocinha, though, it is Rio's social ladder that captures my attention. Its rungs are unmistakably inverted. To move up requires climbing down. From the bottom rung on the highest hilltop to the top rung on the beachfront, the journey spans decades of discrimination.

The bad-tempered taxi driver grows progressively more irritated as we ascend Rua Tavares Bastos. 'What's the exact address, son?' he barks back at me as we turn yet another corner up the steep incline.

I recheck the scribbled details in my notebook and ask again that he take me to the end of the street. Not believing that a foreigner would be heading off into the night with such vague directions, he asks to see the notebook for himself.

Annoyed by his incredulity and general gruffness, but reluctant to lose my ride, I hand over the information. He reads my scrawled handwriting.

'Tavares Bastos, to top. The Maze, ask. Tel: 2558 5547.' Muttering something about 'bloody *gringos*,' he turns the next bend and finally blows his top.

'It's a frigging *favela*. Are you crazy? I'm out of here. Go on, get out.'

He slams on the brakes, hurls open the door and practically shoves me onto the kerbside. Throwing me a two-*real* note in change, he crunches his gear stick into reverse and speeds off blindly down the hill.

I'm left standing there, alone, in the dark, my rucksack and laptop bag lying in a heap on the road. Momentarily, I ponder if a four-night break in Rio's premier *favela* hotel was such a good idea after all.

Forcing the thought aside, I continue with the instructions. Scanning the dead end for someone as unlike a gangster as possible, I catch sight of an elderly lady manning a kiosk.

'Could you direct me towards "The Maze"?' She can, and points to the entrance of the *favela,* indicating for me to follow it up the hill. 'You should find it no problem. If not, just ask.' I thank her and step into the cramped quarters of the Tavares Bastos slum.

It's late, and I pass no one as I venture up the pinched, shadow-strewn passageway. It's as threadlike as Rua 1, but better paved and not as steep. The houses are similarly constructed, one on top of the other with no concern for plastering or building regulations.

With each step deeper into the *favela*, the nagging doubts begin to reassert themselves. I feel ready to bolt back down the alley just as I stumble across seven large concrete letters fixed against the wall of a house. 'The Maze', the blocks read. Relieved, I dart through the open door and off the street.

'Ah, so you made it then. Good show,' booms an old-school London accent across the room.

The imposing, white-haired figure of Bob Nadkarni strides towards me. The place is extraordinary. Large oil canvasses cover the walls of the multi-level lounge area. Off each of these angled walls, rooms sprout like false leads in a labyrinth: cubbyholes, bathrooms, a bar, door-less gaps, storage spaces, a kitchen. Stout pillars of reinforced concrete and beams of demolition wood keep the chaos from collapsing. A carved quote from Oscar Wilde reminds revellers that work is the curse of the drinking classes.

Bob takes me to my room, which is located up two flights of winding stairs, across a courtyard paved with broken multicoloured tiles, under a curved archway and through a small, gabled doorway. The bed is made from recycled plastic bottles covered by a thin layer of concrete. The tiled bathroom is hyperbolically misshaped and has a window in the form of a human eye. Two French doors give way to an outdoor corridor, which leads through to a spacious rooftop terrace. Behind, up the hill, is the dense foliage of an urban rainforest. All that remains is for Gaudí himself to float down through the skylight.

'Not having to ask for building permission has its advantages,' Bob remarks, luxuriating in his architecturally eclectic dream house. 'Imagine trying to do all this with some bureaucratic twerp around.'

I'd heard about the unconventional hotel through a local journalist friend a few days before. It's been almost three decades in the making. Bob laid the first brick after walking his sick maid home one sunny afternoon. Dropping her off at her wooden hut, he turned to see the picture-postcard view of Rio that she enjoyed from her front door. He's not stopped building since.

A British-born documentary-maker and one-time BBC cameraman, Bob is now onto his eighth floor. It's soon to be nine once the twisting turrets on the rooftop are completed. I'd figured sleeping in a *favela* would be an altogether more authentic experience than the tour bus.

I quickly settle into a routine. In the early mornings, I watch people locking the doors of their self-built homes and setting off to low-paid jobs in the city below. I eat breakfast looking out at the cable cars shuttling tourists up Sugarloaf Mountain. When Bob pops out to run some errands, I tag along. I discover that the teenage assistant in the fruit shop is writing a film script and learn from the hairdresser in the barber shack that my hair needs cutting. Lunch is a concoction of rice and ribs at the local café. The afternoons I spend on the terrace staring down at the yachts in Rio's sky-blue bay and waving at the bikini-clad neighbours on their roofs. Come night-time, I chat with Bob and listen to *favela* funk bellowing up from Bilo's Bar below.

The authenticity of Tabares Bastos has its limits though. It looks like a *favela*. It smells like a *favela*. Its residents are predominantly non-whites like in other *favelas*. But it's no Rocinha. There is no drug-dealing and no gang presence here. That means no gun-touting patrol men, no armed police raids, no drug-related executions and no lying under your bed in fear of being hit by a stray bullet. Only once do I wake to the sound of gunshots. Then, when they start up again moments later, I realise they're really just the builder hammering at the turrets above.

The reason for Tabares Bastos's tranquillity lies in the abandoned casino hotel located on the hill beside The Maze. In 2000, a ruthless, highly trained division of the Rio police moved four hundred men into the hotel's empty rooms. Bob claims it was all his doing. During a televised press conference, the bolshie Brit suggested that the then governor use the redundant building as a police garrison. A few months later, the police squad arrived, leaving Bob to take the credit with the locals. The crack squad's reputation for shooting first and asking questions later persuaded the drug-dealers to pack up and seek out safer territory.

Today, Tabares Bastos is so safe that film crews come to 'shoot without being shot at', as Bob likes to say. A few months before my visit, he'd rented out his house for the filming of the Hollywood blockbuster, *Hulk II*. One local boy even landed a minor role, travelling back to Canada with the film crew.

'Imagine it,' Bob said, recounting the story with a belly-shaking laugh one morning, 'his first job outside the *favela* and he had to thwack Edward Norton on the nose.'

Life hasn't always been as sedate in Bob's backyard. Soon after he moved in, gang members from a nearby slum entered the *favela* and shot a small-time drug-dealer. The victim's family went in search of the perpetrators. On finding them, they made them dig their own graves and buried them alive. Now, with the police marksmen looking down from the casino's balconies, Bob feels comfortable enough to invite his friends over for live jazz nights. House prices are also rocketing now the views can be enjoyed without gunfire.

'You know what people call it now?' my reporter friend joked. '*Favela* chic!'

The phrase is apt, even if the taxi-driving community doesn't yet believe it.

Taxis won't take you into Vigario Geral either. A huge slum on the northern outskirts of Rio, it's sometimes referred to as 'Rio's Gaza Strip'. It used to be the hub of the Red Command, Eve Belanger explains to me as we head out on a municipal bus.

I'd met Eve the previous day at AfroReggae's headquarters, located in a staid government building by Rio's domestic airport. AfroReggae is a non-profit, black-inspired arts project working in the *favelas*. Its dull surroundings do the organisation a disservice. AfroReggae is about as hip and happening as it gets when it comes to inner-city youth work. Eve, in contrast, is a blonde, blue-eyed thirty-something from a middle-class suburb of Montreal. Somehow, the two gel perfectly. To show she belongs, they even call her *neguinha*, 'Little Darkie'.

We sit in the office of Junior, the appropriately named director of Rio's most successful youth programme. The obligatory poster of Alberto Korda's Che Guevara adorns the wall. Framed next to it is the blown-up release cover of *Favela Rising*, an award-winning documentary about AfroReggae's work in the slums. Wedged between the two hangs a photo of a grinning Mick Jagger. The ageing rockstar had popped in to see Junior and his crew when the Rolling Stones were last on tour in Brazil.

'Lots of musicians and singers have supported AfroReggae over the years,' Eve says. 'They like the idea that through music and arts these kids can escape a life of crime and do something worthwhile with their lives.'

Public recognition came later though. AfroReggae began back in the early 1990s with just a handful of dedicated volunteers. With their drums tucked under their arms, they ventured into the no-go lands of Vigario Geral and started making music. Soon they were running workshops for the *favela* children. As novices, the youngsters proved fast learners. From those early percussion classes, AfroReggae has given birth to ten separate bands, one of which –

Banda de Reggae – has a record contract and tours the world. Youth dance groups, theatre companies and circus acts also add to its creative mix.

'If they weren't involved in AfroReggae, most admit that they'd be in jail or dead,' says Eve in her French-accented English.

It sounds a little alarmist. That's until she tells me about a video documentary AfroReggae produced shortly after starting out. Of the twelve boys featured, only one is still alive today. It's a lucky drug-dealer that sees it to his twenty-fifth birthday, she says. Many don't even reach adulthood.

Aged twenty-six, Rosalí Nunes has so far made it through in one piece. She's more than made it through, in fact. Earlier this year, she became the first of AfroReggae's two thousand participants to obtain a university degree. The municipal bus, now almost empty as it nears the end of the line, drops us opposite her house.

Rosalí lives in a three-roomed rented house with her parents and two of her five brothers and sisters. There is little room to sit, let alone study. Yet we find her lying on her bunk bed with her nose in a book. She is swotting up for an entrance exam with the state energy company, Petrobras. Down from her bed she jumps and sends off her brother to buy bread, cheese and Coca-Cola.

Strictly speaking, the economics graduate no longer lives in the Vigario Geral *favela*. The family moved out two years ago after her mother had a minor heart attack during a gun battle. They made it three blocks, setting up their new home within sight of the high brick wall that surrounds the slum.

A rival gang took over the *favela* in May, Rosalí explains, making the situation inside Vigario Geral extremely tense. We phone ahead to see if it's possible to visit but are told we're not welcome. Outsiders are more or less banned for now. Only AfroReggae still gets in.

Eve and I sit on the worn sofa in the middle room of the house, while Rosalí parks herself on the floor. A member of one of AfroReggae's theatre troupes, she speaks fluidly and confidently. Instinctively, she uses her hands to express the full sense of what she wants to say, pausing only to laugh – something she does with regular, deep-throated alacrity.

Just staying in school is hard enough in the *favela,* she starts, when I ask about her school life. The education in the private system is obviously much better, but, with her father selling plumbing parts on the street and her mother a cleaner, her parents didn't have enough money to send her. The teachers in the public schools are either under-qualified or off sick with psychological traumas. Excessive pupil numbers is also a problem. Pressure for spaces is so high that mothers often camp out overnight before enrolment day for the new term.

Most students last until they are about thirteen or fourteen before dropping out. I ask why. The girls often get pregnant, and the boys start with the gangs.

It's as basic as that? Unfortunately, yes. Being a mother means girls can have something of their own, someone to love them exclusively. Being a gang member, on the other hand, means the boys can have all the clothes and all the women they want.

'They can eat all the things they dreamed of eating as young kids,' she says, 'like yoghurts and hamburgers.' Bling and burgers seem poor compensation for an education. To a teenager from the *favela,* though, gang life pays handsomely. Going straight, Rosalí points out, means spending your days shining shoes or selling chewing gum on the street. Most prefer the bling.

How did she stick at school then? She has her parents to thank for that. They feel like they're nobodies because they didn't go to school: 'That is why they make us study – so that my four siblings and I might have a better future.'

And AfroReggae, did they help too? Sure, she admits. Her older brothers got involved first. Then later she joined a theatre troupe. She thinks being an actress is probably the profession that gives a person the opportunity to be whoever they want: one day she can be rich, the next poor; one day a beggar on the street, and the next a lady. Acting, she says, has taught her to open her mind to possibilities outside the *favela.*

Junior and his colleagues also have a broader education agenda.

'They don't just give workshops. They teach us what being a citizen is as well.' Rosalí's a top-grade student in the subject. 'Being a citizen signifies that we have rights – rights we have to go after because the State doesn't teach us what they are.' She starts enumerating them on the fingers of her hand.

The first on her list is access to education. A part-time job, several bursaries and what her parents contributed from their meagre salaries meant she could pay to go to a private university. Under a new law, federal universities are now obligated to take in a percentage of black students every year. All the same, for most of her peers in the *favela*, university remains a pipe dream.

Funding her university studies turned out to be just the first of several hurdles though. Next came the prejudices.

'You live in a *favela*, you're black, that makes you a hick,' Rio-based writer Patricia Melo has one of her gangster characters say in her novel, *Inferno*. In a class of sixty, Rosalí was only one of six non-whites. Just one other student came from a slum. The wealthy students presumed the drug-dealers were covering her fees. She had to prove to them that she wasn't involved in drug-peddling or prostitution to pay her way.

And why did she opt for economics? Wouldn't acting be more fulfilling for her? Brazil has few economists, she answers, and so the job opportunities are better. It's the sensible answer and the one that concentrated her mind during six years of lectures. But she confesses to a secondary impetus too: the stylish women from the soap operas. Growing up in her *favela* shack, she'd watched them on the television wearing their power suits and high heels and leaving every day for a job in an office. She dreamed of being like them: 'I could have chosen to become a doctor, I guess, but to be able to wear those nice suits I preferred to study economics.'

From a chipped wooden sideboard, she pulls out a black-and-white family photograph of a muddy street. Children are playing in the puddles between two rows of half-built wooden huts. Plastic sheeting is flapping in the wind. Rosalí has yet to find a job. But she's already chosen the picture for her office wall.

Back at Bob's, the ragtime tunes are playing. The one-time lead singer for the Crouch End All Stars is on the mike. Two German brothers who squat somewhere in The Maze's muddled floors are paying their rent on the sax and clarinet. Other practised musicians drift in and out.

After midnight, the jazz gives way to a faster, livelier samba. Couples take to the dance floor. The lime caipirinhas are flowing. Neighbours sit out on their rooftops to listen. The night is cool, still young. The *favela* is breathing quietly.

Sitting on the low brick wall of the terrace, I gaze out at the circuit board of Rio's twinkling lights below. Angela, a black tour guide whose husband is friends with Bob, is also admiring the view. We fall into conversation.

She's one of only a handful of black guides working in Rio. She used to be a model in Argentina. There were hardly any blacks there, so she had plenty of work.

Is Brazil racist? Yes, no doubt. Direct prejudice is not common though. It's hidden, more subtle. She has suffered a little. Her mother suffered more. And her kids, she hopes, will suffer less. But what are we doing talking? The samba is calling.

Pernambuco

'Black is Culture.' The phrase appears on T-shirts and banners across Brazil. The country's Afro-Brazilian population might be kept out of the law courts and the universities, but they've made the cultural space their own. No carnival float is more eagerly anticipated than the Blocos Afros. No footballer is more highly vaunted than the 'next Pelé'.

I take a flight to Pernambuco to test the phrase for myself. Jutting into the Atlantic Ocean along Brazil's north-eastern shore, the coastal state is holding a month-long cultural festival. Having survived for centuries on its slave-driven sugar trade, Pernambuco's African roots run deep.

I spend my first afternoon wandering around the flint-paved streets of bohemian Olinda, drinking in the weather-beaten colours of the town's crumbling colonial façades. The best view is to be had from the sixteenth-century Igreja de Sé, stationed resolutely on top of Olinda's highest hill. Worming their way down from the cathedral parapet, the town's spiral streets twist towards the sapphire-blue sea. Draped over the houses lies a blanket of earth-stained terracotta tiles and tropical green palm fronds. Punctuating the fired clay mantle, the spires and bell-towers of the town's ecclesiastic trinity poke up: convent, church and monastery. On a clear day, the tower blocks of neighbouring Recife can be seen down the coast. They shiver in the haze of the afternoon heat, apparitions awaiting an Atlantic gale to carry them off.

According to the cultural festival's flyer, carnival practice is scheduled for the next evening in Recife's old town. Arriving in good time, I'm primed for the sight of colourfully dressed percussion bands and seven-foot-tall dancing busts. It's not to be.

An unnerving quietness surrounds Rua da Moeda and its parallel streets, the supposed venue for the practice. I enquire with a lady in a grease-stained apron grilling chicken kebabs at a pavement stall. She tells me there's normally a small carnival band about this time, but she's not seen any sign of them so far. Perhaps they changed the date, she proffers, unhelpfully. Disappointed, I hang around for another half-hour and make my way back towards the bus stop.

As I stroll through the old town's backstreets, all boarded up for the weekend, I hear someone testing a sound system. 'Uno, dois, uno, dois.' It's coming from somewhere off to my right, and I make a detour to investigate. The noise brings me out into an expansive, handsome square, separated from the ocean by a man-made breakwater. Backing onto the water's edge, final touches are being added to a concert stage. I approach the technical engineer, who's fiddling with various knobs on his soundboard as his assistant counts to two on a microphone. I ask if there's going to be a show tonight.

'What?' He takes off his earphones and comes over towards me.

A show? Tonight? He's a smiling Afro-Brazilian in his late twenties.

'Sure. Eight o'clock. *Forró.* Come along.'

I'd read about *forró,* but never heard it. Along with *frevo, marakatú, coco, maculele, afoxé, ciranda, seresta, caboclinhos* and *cavalo marinho,* it's one of the many distinctive Afro-Brazilian genres associated with Pernambuco. I thank the sound engineer and assure him I'll be back to check it out.

Walking off, I throw the programme in the first bin I pass. Brazilian culture is tremendously vibrant and expressive but spontaneity, not forward planning, is its forte. Guide-less and map-less, I decide to continue following my ear and see where it leads me. I've not walked fifty yards from the stage in the Praça do Marco Zero before I'm stopped short by the unexpected, but unmistakable, sound of carol-singing.

Waking to bright sunshine every morning, I'd almost forgotten that Christmas was approaching. I push open the glass door to the floodlit Banco Real cultural institute and take a seat. For an enjoyable hour, I listen to winter classics such as 'Gloria in Excelsis Deo' and 'Jingle Bells' being sung in Portuguese by black gospel choirs.

Back outside, I breathe in the ocean air and look around for what to do next. There seems to be some activity at the end of the adjacent Rua do Bom Jesus and I amble in that direction. The road runs to a stop just where two open-air cafés, crowded with evening drinkers at plastic tables, spill into a cobbled square. Positioned beside an open-air excavation of the city's original foundations, a quintet is playing *charinho,* yet another Penambuco invention. A few of the audience are swaying their hips to the gentle, guitar-led ensemble. I order a beer and listen a while.

My drink finished, I set off again in search of more distinctive Pernambuco creations. Half a block away, in the courtyard of an observatory tower, I discover a costumed troupe performing a traditional samba. Unlike its contemporary equivalent, this has a more hard-edged, backcountry feel to it. A white-haired black man wearing a cloth hat and playing a fiddle heads the musical accompaniment. Joining him are a tambourine player and man with two maracas shaped like rolls of wallpaper. A fourth man is playing an *agogo,* a conical iron instrument connected by a U-bend and struck with a metal baton.

In between their musical interludes, two clowns dressed in tinsel wigs and polka-dot trousers keep the audience amused. Joining them is another comic duo in rough-hewn jackets and trousers tied up with twine. A slapstick game of cat and mouse around the stage plays out between the foursome, during which the clowns thump their counterparts with balloon-shaped containers. Each hit inspires guffaws from the crowd. One by one, the samba's main act takes the stage, and soon there are seven or eight dancers twirling and jumping across the small courtyard. Over the next hour, a loosely knit story based around plantation life unfolds. The full sense is lost on me, but it involves more indiscriminate hitting by the clowns and a dancer dressed as a horse. I wait until the perplexing spectacle draws to a close and make my way back to the main square, figuring the *forró* show must be well under way by now.

An hour late, the main act has just turned up and is beginning his set. A fusion of traditional, percussion-heavy, accordion-led rhythms overlaid with splices of rock, jazz and heavy electronics, the aesthetic appeal of the eclectic Recife beat is hard to pinpoint. But the crowd love it. The elderly lead singer, wearing dark glasses and resembling an old Ray Charles, has no problems coaxing his audience onto the open-air dance floor. Not that Brazilians need much persuading. Old or young, fat or thin, rich or poor, everyone is soon up and shaking their stuff.

Never is the country more equal or more united than when it's bumping and grinding on the dance floor. Only the beach and the football pitch compare as spaces of genuine democracy. Mid-dance, Brazilians of every creed and colour exude a joyful, bubbly, almost spiritual aura. Even the most inexpert appear free of the awkward self-awareness that inhibits other mortals.

I stand with my back against the stage and watch in awe at the sight of so many rhythmic bodies hypnotised by the *forró* beat. Closest to me, a late-middle-aged couple is lost in a feverish, hip-shaking embrace. The woman's thin, blue slip is stained with sweat, revealing a bulky pair of underpants and generous rolls of fat underneath. Her short, slim-built husband couldn't care less. The transforming power of the music has made a spellbinding temptress of his humdrum wife. Beside them dances a thin-hipped man with a jaunty cap. He too is under his partner's magic. A huge black lady with buttocks the size of water balloons and a bosom to match, she presses up close against him. The man is contentedly subsumed, his tiny frame completely enveloped but for two tiny feet kicking happily below.

Not far from them, a mixed-race couple is dancing. This time, it's the man who's setting the pace, his waist, hips and legs all writhing in different directions simultaneously, enticing his girlfriend to follow. Across from them is a beautiful *mulatta* with light-tan skin and a svelte, sexy figure hidden seductively beneath a low-cut dress. Thigh to thigh, she gyrates up against her partner. One arm around her waist, the other touching her leg, he smothers her thin neck with soft kisses and whispers sweet seductions in her ear.

Commanding the dance floor, though, is a stout black grandmother. She is boogieing by herself, agile as a teenager. Skipping from foot to foot, she holds out her arms as if embracing a lover of long ago. Round and round she spins, never pausing, never breaking stride, only her and the beat of the *forró* band.

Neither the music nor the dancers show any signs of letting up. If I'm to catch the last bus back, I need to pull myself away. Not that Olinda has put itself to bed either. Near the Praça de Aboliçao, Abolition Square, just by the bus stop, I come across a carnival band practising a percussion sequence. Ten Afro-Brazilian teenagers are laying into hide-bound tambours with a tribal enthusiasm. Recife's old town, I discover, has saturated my senses, and I pass on by.

Climbing with tired legs up the hill to my hotel, my path is blocked by a procession of clapping merrymakers. I walk behind, watching as the strumming guitars of a *serestra* medley drive them along like sheep before a sheepdog. Reaching the crest of the hill, the musicians steer their dancing flock back to the town, their romantic ballads and midnight cheer growing fainter and fainter as they dance away into the night.

I lie in bed, the windows open, kept awake by the stereos from neighbouring bars. Just as the collective drone grows quiet, the sound of a child practising a clarinet strikes up from the next-door house. To the sound of a tuneless B-flat scale, I finally fall asleep.

At dusk the following day, I head out to take some photos of Olinda's postcard colonial houses in the changing light. While I'm sizing up the monastery in my viewfinder, the sound of drumming curls up from somewhere further down the hill. I put away my camera and head towards it. Fifteen minutes later, I find myself opposite the Fernando Santa Cruz theatre, a warehouse-shaped building at the insalubrious end of town. Obedient to the call of the drumbeat, I go inside.

Annexed to the back of the theatre, I discover a sizeable dance hall. Inside is a small stage and what looks like a drum-pounding mob of Congolese warriors. A poster on the far wall announces the eighteenth anniversary of the Nação Pernambuco Carnival Group. To celebrate their coming of age, they are performing a *marakatú*, the longest-standing and most Afro-Brazilian of all the region's cultural traditions.

There is no one at the door, and I sneak in without any questions. The room is stiflingly hot. Packed around two dozen tables, drinking rum and beer and eating off paper plates, sit friends and family. I spot a spare seat at the back and head for it as inconspicuously as possible. It's like the Iguatemi shopping centre, but in reverse: now all the faces are black but mine.

Curious eyes watch me to my seat, and I fix my gaze on the backing singers, pretending to be absorbed by their vocals. Behind them, relegated to the back corner of the stage, hide the Old World concessions: a saxophonist, guitarist and trombonist. Any residual interest in who the *gringo* gatecrasher might be is soon overtaken by an explosion of sound from the stage.

Leaping from the wings at the climax of a manic drum roll bounds a flamboyant company of barefoot athletic dancers. The tasselled troupe is adorned with pointed golden headbands and lustrous chest plates of loose-hanging necklaces. Guiding them is a princely figure decked in a gilded crown and golden armbands. A black bantam belt stretches across his taut stomach, holding up a pleated regal skirt of heavy, cerise cloth. Prowling up and down the stage, microphone in hand, his melodious voice beguiles the spellbound audience, wooing them to join his homesick song in a journey across the oceans.

A glittering coronation scene concludes the gala. The singing prince beckons forth a sword-carrying king and his elegant queen. Surrounded by courtiers and the sounding of trumpets, the regal procession laps the stage in one last marching dance. The king is crowned, the dancers retire, the backing singers slip off, and only then, when the stage is empty, do the drums cease their pounding. Ecstatic, the audience clap and whistle and head off to fill their glasses with more rum.

First thing the next morning, I determine to find someone to teach me *marakatú*. Renato, I'm told by the hotel receptionist, is the man to speak to. I knock on the door of his house, located just down from the hilltop cathedral, and an imposing black man more than double my body weight comes to the door. I inquire about the possibility of a lesson, but it seems I've caught Renato on a bad day. His wife is due back from a trip, and he's behind on the domestic chores he'd promised to do. He gives me the number of another instructor and wishes me well.

As I turn to go, I notice he's wearing a T-shirt advertising an equal-opportunities conference. I ask him about the event and discover that Renato is Olinda's representative for Unegro, a black rights movement. Breaking from his household tasks for a moment, he pops inside and reappears with a map he bought in Rio. It depicts the location of Brazil's *quilombos,* the settlements established by escaped slaves. Most are located along the north-east coast, where the sugar plantations were once most concentrated.

Renato takes the map with him to the *marakatú* workshops he runs for the town's young people.

'Like the music, it reminds us of our history as Afro-Brazilians – or Brazilian-Afros.'

What's his message to the children? That as black Brazilians, they are not descendants of slaves. That they are the descendants of Africans.

'Here we were enslaved. There we were free. Some of us were even kings and princes.' The coronation scene suddenly makes sense.

Later the same day, I meet Carlos, the alternative instructor, in an airy practice room of the Henrique Días music syndicate along Veira de Melo street. We kick off on the wrong foot, arguing about the cost of the ninety-minute session. He is asking more than I am willing to pay. Feigning affront to his honour, he tells me that he respects my profession as a journalist. I, in turn, should respect his as a dance instructor. So rare is it to hear the words 'respect' and 'journalist' in close conjunction that I immediately quit my bartering and cough up.

Carlos suggests we begin with a relaxed warm-up. As I gently stretch, my new teacher busies himself tying his waist-length dreadlocks into a knot at the back of his head. His hair in order, we are ready to start. The CD player's 'on' button is pressed and a traditional, percussion-led *marakatú* booms out. Carlos turns the volume down, but not before the noise has drawn several onlookers to the open window. I ask if we can close the shutters, but my teacher gives me a scathing look, ordering me to stop fretting and to take up position opposite him.

'We'll kick off with the Queen's dance, OK?' The Queen's dance? This is not what I had in mind. He's going to have me in a skirt. The onlookers are going to be in hysterics.

'Relax, the Queen is an easy one. She just walks up and down. Like this.'

Carlos takes two steps forward, stops, brings his lagging leg square with the other, and then repeats the motion backwards. No skirts. No swirls. This I can do. Falling into step with the beat and keeping my knees high, as Carlos instructs, I soon get the hang of it. I feel my body relax.

'Think fluid.' Fluid it is.

Now for the top half. Contemporary *marakatú* has a range of flourishing arm movements, he explains, but it's perhaps best we stick to the old-fashioned version.

'It's simpler.'

I thank him. Holding his thumbs to his chest, as if gripping hold of a pair of braces, Carlos thrusts one elbow sharply upwards. With each step, he alternates arms: right leg, left arm; left leg, right arm; and so on. He encourages me to copy. It takes me a few steps to pick it up, but I master it without too much trouble. My confidence swells.

A polite clap comes from the window. I look up to see an unshaven man with a beer can in his hand and a sarcastic smirk on his face. I follow Carlos's lead and just ignore him. It feels liberating not to care what the stranger thinks.

The next step also belongs to a female part.

'This is the *Bahiana*,' Carlos says, shifting into a slow sidestep. 'She forms part of the royal cortège and dances before the King.'

As well as a change of direction, the new step also requires a new arm movement. No longer punching the air with my elbows, I cross the room back and forth, sculpting the imaginary shape of a narrow-necked Chinese vase.

Ridiculous though I must look, the simple, repetitive motion exerts a pull on me that's hard to explain. The same, hypnotic drum rhythm plays on and on:

> *Leão Coroado*
> *With his strong arm*
> *Who was born in the north,*
> *With his drum,*
> *Who beats his drum wherever,*
> *When he meets another nation,*
> *With its cortège,*
> *Our Dona Isabel.*

An hour has flown by. Our onlookers have grown bored with their *gringo* entertainment and have moved on elsewhere. The *dama de paso* concludes the class. We're back to the same flapping-chicken motion with our elbows, but now Carlos is skipping between the heel of one foot and the tiptoes of the other. To complicate matters further, he adds a pelvic thrust into the mix, ramming forwards with one step and pushing his bottom back with the next.

The multipart choreography is beyond me. I'm either skipping or thrusting, but never in sync as the dance demands. As for my elbows, they're flailing like a frightened battery hen on a slaughterhouse conveyor. Carlos claps in time with the music and makes the rattling *chhh chhh chhh* sound of the maracas to get me back on track, but the *Leão Coroado* has abandoned me. Carlos thinks it best we finish the session perfecting the Queen and Bahian woman. I agree readily.

Before leaving Pernambuco, I travel back to Recife. Once a week, different bands gather to perform African-influenced music in the quaint colonial square of São Pedro. I'm hoping 'Black Tuesday' will provide the opportunity for me to give my new dance moves a public airing.

Regrettably, *marakatú* isn't on the programme the week I visit. I wait out a rock band and a reggae group, until an *afoxé* singer takes the stage. The beat is much faster, more rave than royal coronation. Young, hip and almost all black, the crowd throws itself trance-like onto the dance floor. I see no sign of braces or Chinese vases, only jiving hips and vibrating buttocks. There was nothing else for it; the *dama de paso* it would have to be.

Salvador

Africa's cultural traditions were not all that Brazil's slaves brought with them on their tortuous passage across the Atlantic. The continent's gods came too: the ancestral spirits of the Bantos, the divinities of the Inquices and the voodoo lords of the Yorubá. The slavers' frigates were not just prison ships; they were floating pantheons.

I took a night-bus down to Salvador, the capital of Bahía and initial centre of this expatriated spirit world.

Unleashed onto Brazilian soil, the African gods mingled and mixed, creating hybrid forms of worship for their slave devotees. Of all these syncretistic creations, Candomblé is the Afro-Brazilian religion that has won widest appeal. Spreading out from the overwhelmingly black province of Bahía, the voodoo-influenced belief system now counts tens of thousands of followers across Brazil. There are even groups in Lisbon.

Yet it's the Catholics who are celebrating when I arrive in the Bahian capital. The toll of Salvador's cathedral bells is calling the faithful to Christmas Mass. In the cobbled Terreiro de Jesus square, carol singers compete with capoeira performers for the tourists' attention. Broad-hipped Bahian dames in voluminous skirts pose coquettishly on the corners of Pelourinho. Down in Barra, the lighthouse is resting out the festive season, ceding its tasks to the fireworks department. Everywhere, the smell of spicy seafood stews and bean fritters doused in *dendê* oil carries on the air.

The Candomblé places of worship lie far from Salvador's historic centre and the hubbub of Pelourinho's pastel walkways. Hidden down the alleys of the city's working-class districts, their *terreiros,* or meeting halls, have no bell towers or noticeboards. Through the National Federation of Afro-Brazilian Culture, I locate a gathering place in the poor northern neighbourhood of Vasco da Gama.

Before I pay a visit, though, there are two black-rights activists I've been waiting to meet.

Silvio Humberto is caught up in a staff meeting at the Steve Biko Institute when I climb up the wooden stairs, past the Dutch Consulate, to his second-storey office.

I sit by an open window facing the ocean and wait for him to finish. Fishing vessels bob at anchor in the bay below. A pink trim licks the wispy clouds that still linger in the late afternoon sky. The last shuttle boat of the day sets off for its final run to Itaparica Island across the rippled water.

From the classroom across the hallway, the sound of scraping chairs and young people's chatter wakes me from my reverie. The institute doubles as a crammer, providing black high-school students with tuition towards their university entrance exams. The group of satchel-bearing students, now heading down the stairs and talking about the weekend ahead, are the future of Brazil's black-rights movement. At least, that's Silvio Humberto's hope.

Done with his meeting, the institute's young director invites me over to sit with him. A black academic with a doctorate in economics, he asks me how I am enjoying Salvador. Loving it, I tell him, enthusiastically recounting my trip that morning to the Afro-Brazilian Museum.

The dreadlocked director is pleased. This is his home city. What can he help me with exactly? I fill him in on my recent trip to Pernambuco. The news of my *marakatú* class also seems to gratify him. We talk briefly about AfroReggae. He too thinks they're doing a superb job of using culture creatively. The conversation then turns to the *favelas* and so to the bottom-rung status of many Afro-Brazilians.

'And your question?'

'Yes, sorry, my question.' I open my notebook to the page where I'd scribbled it down earlier: 'How is culture helping Brazil's black population break the social and economic barriers that they face?'

It sounds like an exam question when I read it aloud, but Silvio chuckles: 'It's not just *your* question. It's *everyone's* question!'

He sets to answering it: '"Culture is black," that we all know. Naturally, black music, art and religion remind the country's Afro-Brazilians who we are and where we came from. In this sense, culture is a vital tool in self-identity.'

The cultural director then cites another saying in Brazil, one he says isn't printed on T-shirts: 'We love black culture. It's the black people we can't stand.'

Like a good exam student, he clarifies his meaning: 'They say there are no ghettos here, yeah? Well, culture is the black person's ghetto. It's like a jail without bars. Sure, they let us sing and dance and party during carnival. But let a black person try stepping out of the culture space and into the business world or into the political arena or into the lecture theatre. Then you'll see the fiction of Brazil's racial democracy. Culture is a space reservoir for blacks here. It hems them in.'

Space reservoir. I like it. As a concept, it zings off the page. My examiner's pen hovers over the page, keenly awaiting the conclusion. It arrives with verve and attack:

'Yes, culture is the base. Yes, it's essential to the black-rights movement. But no, it won't break the barriers of prejudice. Only politics can do that. Slavery might have disappeared more than a century ago, but slavers continue to run things. In Salvador, Brazil's blackest state, there are only three non-white representatives in the State Assembly. Three out of sixty-three! Affirmative action is what's required.' Pens down. Silvio finally draws breath. It's an A+ performance.

I glance out of the window. The boats are still bobbing, but the world outside no longer looks so idyllic. There's an ugly, unseen element to the scene, as if the shuttle boat had sunk silently beneath the waves or an invisible oil slick were spreading across the bay.

The director shares a quote with me as he shows me to the door. It's from Steve Biko, the late South African anti-apartheid activist after whom the institute takes its name.

'Black consciousness is not just for blacks. It's for whites too.' The words loll heavily on his tongue like a boiled sweet he doesn't want to finish. 'It frees them from their superiority, you see? It gives them back their humanity.'

My one question multiplies into many others as I head across town to meet Vilma Reis, a sociologist at the Centre for Afro-Oriental Studies.

It's the Christmas holidays, and the faculty building is empty of students. It's also empty of Vilma. I wait outside in the sun, on a bench in the Largo Dois de Julho square. From my bag, I pull out a copy of *Dona Flor and Her Two Husbands.* I'm a third of the way through Jorge Amado's Bahian masterpiece and still on husband number one.

I open it at the bookmarked page and re-read how Amado's madcap hero fell lifeless one tragic Lenten Sunday during carnival. He'd keeled over amidst a 'samba group of drag queens and masqueraders'. As coincidence would have it, the tragic event occurred in the same square where I'm sitting. Dona Flor's first spouse had been in the embrace of a heavily rouged Romanian at the time. Times have changed, or my luck's out. Half an hour waiting, and the only rouge I see is the sunburned flesh of a potbellied American couple from the cruise ship in the bay.

When Vilma eventually turns up, the Afro-Brazilian academic leads me into her office and presents me with some questions of her own.

'How were race relations perceived outside Brazil?'

'Excellently,' I tell her. Racial democracy. The antithesis of the USA. The model state.

My upbeat answer meets with a frostier reception this time round: 'Thirty years of activism, and the old myth still holds true. How persistent are the white man's lies.' From the start, racial democracy was a 'FARCE'. She writes the words in capitals on a blank piece of paper in front of her.

'Brazilians are all equal, they say. Because we're all equal, if a white man succeeds and a black man doesn't, they say it's the black man's problem. He's too stupid or too lazy or too fond of fiestas. In Brazil's racial democracy, racism could never be the cause. Oh no, NOT RACISM.' More capitalised scribbles.

Discrimination in Brazil is very sophisticated. The national censuses are a perfect example. Did I know the categories they use in the census? Yes, I'd heard about them. Whites have only the *branco* box to tick. Blacks are divided between *pretos* and *pardos*. There's no *negro* option. WHITES come in at around 46 per cent. BLACKS amount to 49.3 per cent.

'If you lump the *pretos* and *pardos* together, that is. Of course, the authorities never do. So, whites remain the official majority. All the state policies are therefore orientated towards them. The rest remain INVISIBLE.' She underlines the word until the ink begins to blot through the page.

White academics are finally accepting that Brazil is not as racially harmonious as they'd once maintained. Vilma reckons this is a major step forward. But they deny that affirmative action is the right solution: 'Reparations and specific pro-black policies will create divisions in the country, they say. It's ironic. The white elite finally recognises the problem, but rejects the obvious answer. Brazil needs EQUITY, not equality. Equity for blacks in the health service, in the education system. Across the board.'

Her comments take me back once again to the professor's study in São Paulo. Brazil never imposed segregation laws as in the USA. As Vilma is speaking, I wonder if that is why Brazil has never had a powerful civil-rights movement? No Brazilian has ever been banned from a restaurant because of the colour of his or her skin. Explicit racism therefore cannot explain why a food court in a posh shopping mall should remain a whites-only zone.

Official segregation gave Afro-Americans in the USA something tangible to fight against. In Brazil, black-rights activists are flailing against a shapeless, secret phantom. Affirmative action will certainly help their cause, but not unless the myth of the country's colour-blindness is shown for what it is.

Vilma gets up to take a phone call. The pile of books balancing unsteadily on her desk suggests she's been doing some reading of her own. I scan the spines. All are by left-leaning academics or black authors. Balanced above a paperback edition of Toni Morrison's *The Bluest Eye,* the top volume has a marker pen wedged in the centrefold. It's a collection of lectures on race by the French philosopher Michel Foucault, entitled *Society Must Be Defended.*

In the middle of the circle, an outstretched black woman lies flat on the ground, convulsing epileptically. Her nose is knocking hard against the concrete floor. Her arms pushed out far in front of her, quivering, as though tied to a torturer's rack. Every part of her is shaking: her knees, her toes, her legs, her chest, her head. From some primordial corner of her being, animal-sounding grunts rise to the surface. She rolls over onto her side, her fists and feet suddenly lashing out. An agonising wail erupts from her lips. Then, as if struck by a stun gun, she falls totally motionless.

The fit lasts a full five minutes. The Candomblé devotees continue dancing around her, ignoring the juddering body, now deathly still. All are dressed in free-flowing garments of white cotton, men and women alike. They accompany the beat of the drums with the low-pitched murmuring of an ancient African tongue. Round and round they dance, dizzying even the icons that line the shelves of the whitewashed room.

Into the circle steps the Babalaxé. High priest and master of ceremonies, the cotton-clad celebrant is wearing a fawn-coloured leather hat and smoking a sausage-sized cigar. In one hand, he holds a bottle of Nova Schin beer. In the other, he grasps a grey-painted wooden trident three feet in length. A young female novice drops to her knees and rolls up his trousers until they're just below the knee.

I watch from a bench at the edge of the ceremony as the barefoot Babalaxé strides towards a dancer in the circle. He hits her softly on the shoulder with his devilish grey fork, discharging some invisible current that sends her toppling back towards me. I budge up the bench just as the hypnotised black woman collapses beside my shifting foot. An Orixá god from the temple of Candomblé's divinities immediately pounces on the stricken victim, infusing her prone body with violent body jerks and trembling. Soon the inculcated spirit has her barking like a dog and frothing at the mouth. When her lathered spittle begins gathering in a pool on the floor, I judge that I've seen enough.

Standing in the yard outside, the smell of cigar smoke clinging to my clothes, I wonder what Silvio and Vilma would have made of the ceremony. Were the prostrated dancers juddering and thrashing in a space reservoir? Was the Neptune-like Babalaxé perpetuating un-EQUAL power structures?

The next morning, I climb the steep wooden stairs to the first-floor office of the National Federation of Afro-Brazilian Culture. Located down the hill from Pelourinho square, it's close enough to the cathedral for the sound of church bells to carry on the breeze through the open window.

Antoniel Alaide Bispo, the Federation's elderly and elegant secretary, ushers me towards his desk. Dressed in white right down to his goatee beard, the Condomblé priest explains the various stages of the purity ritual from the previous night.

'And the cigar and trident?'

'These are the symbols of Exú. Every Babalaxé has their own Orixá. His will have been Exú.'

'And who's Exú?'

Antoniel smiles: 'Why, Exú is the first son of Iemanjá and Oxalá. He's associated with sorcery and mischief. You Christians know him by another name: the Devil.'

I gulp involuntarily, thinking back to my night of devil worship in Vasco da Gama.

'These are just labels that the early missionaries used though,' the federation secretary assures me. 'Candomblé wasn't legalised in Bahía until 1989. So, before then, we'd link our gods with the Christian saints. As a cover-up, sort of.'

He runs through some of the better-known examples: Xango, the god of justice, is compared to Saint Jerome; Iansâ, the god of wind and storms, to Saint Barbara; Omulú, the god of health, to Saint Lorenzo.

'And who's Jesus Christ?' I butt in.

'Oxalá, our god of creation.'

Now Candomblé is legal, it's not necessary to hide behind the white man's religion, Antoniel continues. But the tradition has stuck. Ironically, it's the Catholics who now encourage the association. The saints' days give the Church an excuse to encourage Candomblé followers to come to Mass: 'I don't see the need to go but many others still attend.'

For the Catholics, there are bigger battles to fight. Across South America, church pews are emptying as the faithful migrate to new brands of worship. The Reformation has arrived, and it plays guitar. In the Universal Church of the Kingdom of God, Brazil boasts the largest and most lucrative of these ecclesiastical upstarts.

Candomblé finds itself in the firing line, Antoniel maintains: 'On their television channels and in their pulpits, the leaders of the Universal Church are always denouncing us as Satanic and our religion as black magic.'

As a Babalaxé himself, the cotton-clad secretary claims not to be overly concerned. His African Orixá is a match for any white man's god: 'Ogum, the god of war, will come to our aid.'

In the square above, the bells toll the hour. Meanwhile, across the mighty Amazon, high in the plateaus of the Andes, the gods of the Incas are stirring too.

6

HOLY DISORDERS
Peru and religion

God has destined man to be free; he protects him so that he can exercise the
divine faculty of free will.

SIMÓN BOLÍVAR, BOLIVIAN CONSTITUTION

Ayaviri, Altiplano

In Ayaviri, a drab town of greys and browns, the locals think Dante
and I are Mormons. The mix-up is understandable. My companion
is six foot three and I am a white-skinned European. Both features
mark us out in this remote Andean settlement of short-legged Incan
descendants.

Spending the day door-knocking only compounds the confusion.
Unlike the pavement-pounding preachers from Salt Lake City, our
mission is not to proselytise. At least, not overtly so. Instead, it's
fallen to us to help map Ayaviri's religious profile. Dante is one of
thirteen seminary students drafted in by the local parish for census
duties. Originally from Arequipa, Peru's second city, he's accustomed to the highlanders eyeing him suspiciously. Before I joined
him, people mistook him for a travelling salesman.

Setting off on our afternoon rounds, Dante charts a finger along
a photocopied map. Ticks in orange highlighter pen mark off the
houses that he's already covered. On the first block, it's just the
tailor's shop that still requires surveying. Clipboard in hand, Dante
strides down the unswept, sun-baked street towards the outfitter's
one-room workshop.

'*Buenos días.* Could we possibly bother you for a couple of minutes? We're from the parish. Just a couple of questions.'

The lanky trainee priest has an endearing, almost puppy-like demeanour that makes him difficult to turn down. Besides, two strides of his long legs and he's already under the garment-maker's nose.

'Sure, I guess so,' the tailor replies, slightly overwhelmed by the giant interrogator blocking the light in front of him.

Pulling a sharpened pencil from his shirt pocket, Dante fires off the personal data questions at the top of his sheet.

Name? Rodrigo Pérez.

Age? Thirty-eight.

Birthday? August.

Dante doesn't push him to be more specific. Five weeks into his census duties and he's learned that many Ayavirans don't concern themselves about dates of birth. Celebrating means buying presents, and buying presents means having money. Living on the breadline, many of the townsfolk in this altiplano outpost find it easier to forget about birthdays.

Marital status? Single.

Since we walked in, Rodrigo has been absent-mindedly spinning a pair of scissors around on his thumb. At the marriage question, he drops the sharpened blades and begins conscientiously examining a stretch of fabric on his workbench.

The clerical student moves on to the religious part of the questionnaire. It starts with all the subtlety of the Inquisition: 'Is the house Catholic?'

No matter how many times I hear the question asked, its directness never fails to unsettle me. Growing up in a multicultural world of all faiths and none, the query sounds awkward and invasive. The multiple-choice approach to religion obviously doesn't extend to Peru. Nor does the element of personal choice. 'Terraced', 'semi-detached', 'two bedroomed'. These are terms I grew up associating with houses. Not religious affiliation. In Peru as in the remainder of South America, Roman Catholicism seeps into the very brickwork of life. People don't choose the one true faith. It chooses them. Stamped on with a baby's entrance into the world, it works much the same as a religious birthmark. More than eight out of ten

Peruvians carry the seal of Rome. Neither the blessed water of the baptismal font nor the fires of the funeral home can remove it.

'Oh yes, we're all good Catholics here,' Rodrigo answers robotically.

As with the initial question, I've heard the same answer many times. On the first few occasions, I interrupted Dante to ask the respondents what they meant by being a 'good Catholic'. Their flustered reactions dissuaded me from continuing the line of inquiry. Some became defensive, as if my interjection contained a veiled criticism. Others appeared to have given the term little thought. These initial responses were enough to give me a general picture. Ayaviri's 'good Catholics' religiously go to Mass every Christmas and Easter, wear a cross around their necks, keep a Virgin about the house, try to do their best by their neighbours, refrain from stealing and, as one old lady assured me, kiss a photo of the Pope before going to sleep.

Dante puts a tidy, pencilled tick in the 'Catholic' box and continues with his questions. The parish administrators had obviously presumed an affirmative answer first off, as the remainder of the questionnaire deals with the interviewee's church credentials.

First off, the sacraments.

Is he baptised? 'Of course.'

Is he confirmed? 'Yes, that too.'

Has he received his first communion? 'Yes.'

When he marries, will he do so in church? 'Probably.'

'Probably? Why only probably, if you don't mind me asking?' says the gentle-spoken Dante, breaking from his script for the first time.

The tailor lays the outline of a pair of suit trousers over the fabric and begins tacking the cloth with pins: 'Well, you know how it is, these things are expensive.'

Spain's early missionaries did much to tweak the culture of the Incas to the mores of the Church, but Catholic marriage rites have always proved a difficult sell. Lifelong monogamy didn't suit Peru's indigenous nations. Men were accustomed to giving their women a trial run. If the girl were found to fit, they'd marry. If not, he'd move on to the next. Then, as now, weddings were communal affairs as much as contractual. No self-respecting groom could leave the altar without a three-day knees-up for his guests.

'We're saving up for it though,' Rodrigo clarifies, hoping his good intentions might earn him at least half marks on Dante's score sheet.

Shifting topic, the gawky seminary student turns to his final set of questions about religious practice. Rodrigo's marks drop rapidly when it comes to church attendance. 'Occasionally' is the most he can muster without staining his conscience. Oddly, Mass doesn't seem to feature on the 'good Catholic' requirement list. Fewer than two hundred worshippers regularly attend the Sunday service in Ayaviri's seventeenth-century baroque cathedral. A poor turn-out considering the twenty-five thousand 'faithful souls' in the parish registry. Dante skips the last question about the proposed introduction of a regular weekday service at 6 a.m.

The novice thanks Rodrigo for taking the time to answer the questionnaire. He puts away his clipboard, signalling the end of his official investigation. From his bag, he takes a plastic rosary and hands it over. The better-funded Mormons probably pave a more lucrative line in promotional materials, but Rodrigo seems genuinely appreciative: 'The missus will love it.' The parting gift comes with an instruction leaflet containing some basic prayers.

Oh, and here's a sticker too. He wouldn't mind putting it up, would he? The outfitter is trapped by his earlier answers. He accepts the 'This house is Catholic' adhesive label, promising to put it up later.

'Are your children baptised by the way?' Dante drops in, as if the thought had just occurred to him. 'Because if not, the parish is running a pre-baptism class. Perhaps you'd like to send them along?'

While discussing his plans for a church wedding, the unmarried tailor had let it slip that he had two sons with his common-law wife. The eldest was six years old, suggesting his wedding savings account had been ticking along for some time. Either Rodrigo's suit sales were going slowly or he was saving for Ayaviri's most extravagant nuptial party yet.

'Maybe. I'll have to talk to the missus about it,' Rodrigo replies. He moves out of Dante's shadow and sits down at his sewing machine. Half turning his back to us, there's an unambiguous 'Are we done now?' attitude to the movement.

Dante has the material about the baptism class on him as it happens. He'll leave it just here, on the counter, so the tailor can look over it at his leisure. The course runs every Thursday, for six weeks. Rodrigo nods distractedly, his attentions apparently absorbed by the humming Singer machine.

We thank him again and head for the door. The canny trainee isn't quite done trying though: 'About the wedding. If you decide on the kids' baptism, I can talk to the bishop. I'm sure we could sort out a two-for-one deal. Think about it.'

That evening, after helping Dante mark off two more blocks on his photocopied map, I make my way across the withered grass lawns of the central square to the town prelature. Built with Ayaviri's bias towards insulation over aesthetics, the bishop's nondescript home is notable only for the cheese shop at one corner. Greenish slabs of fetid-smelling goat's cheese line the store's counter. The malodorous repository is the sale point for a church-led dairy project and the closest thing the Altiplano town has to a delicatessen.

Inside the Bishop's residence, half a dozen clergymen are sitting down at a wooden table to a Spartan supper of homemade bread and the parish cheese. Dominating proceedings is Monsignor Kay Martin Schmalhausen, Ayaviri's recently appointed bishop. Surrounded by his disciples, the cardigan-wearing cleric looks like a plumper version of Jesus, only with a trimmer beard and a more sensible side parting.

There is only one woman in attendance, a superannuated cook, who scuttles between kitchen and dining table with her head bent and lips sewn shut.

In his early forties, Rome's representative in Ayaviri is one of the youngest appointees to the fifty-six-member Peruvian bishopric. Youthful, dynamic and archly conservative, he fits the Vatican's model as snugly as an embroidered pontifical glove. Traditionally minded Church leaders first started moving up the ecclesiastical ranks under Pope Juan Pablo II. Cardinal Cipriani, for example, the Archbishop of Lima, owes his allegiance to the hardline Opus Dei movement. Under Pope Benedict XVI, the trend in the clerical corridors of power continues unabated.

The census was the bishop's idea. It is Step One in an extensive campaign. Step Two is to teach his parishioners the basic tenets of Christianity. Dante has a place in the advance guard. Recently dispatched into the mountains on foot, the long-limbed postulant spent a fortnight teaching the ABCs of the catechism to an unschooled flock of illiterate villagers.

Bishop Schmalhausen invites me to join them at the table. The clergymen shift down a space to make room. The conversation continues uninterrupted by my arrival. Preoccupying the prelates are the town's recent festivities. Ayaviri's faithful might have problems remembering their own dates of birth, but the holy days of their patron saints are immutably engraved in the town's calendar. The Virgen de Candelaria's recent annual shindig lasted three days. In September, Ayavirans brush off their traditional dress and dancing shoes once more in honour of the Virgin of Alta, another divine benefactress. The bishop and his team worry that culture and creed are perhaps falling out of sync.

Their discussion touches on a question that had been bothering me since my chat with Antoniel in Salvador. The Candomblé authority had mentioned how, with a subtle sleight of hand, his fellow Afro-Brazilian religionists had hidden their gods by hitching them to the Catholic pantheon. Wasn't that essentially what the early Christian missionaries did with the Incas, only in reverse? Hadn't they taken the earth-maker Pacha Camac, the sun-deity Inti, the god-of-all-things Viracocha and merged them with their own panoply of biblical saints?

My conviction had been strengthened the previous week during a short visit to Cuzco. Unfortunately, my sightseeing plans around the idyllic mountain capital of the Incas were cut short by an innocent-looking bowl of unwashed lettuce. The fiendish leaves kicked in just as my train was leaving for Machu Picchu. The majority of the twisting, three-hour journey I spent in the toilet, alternating turns at the flusher with an altitude-sick Swede. In like manner, my appreciation of the Incas' magical hideaway citadel concentrated primarily on the lavatory facilities at the entrance café.

On my fourth and final day in Cuzco, I finally felt well enough to hit some of the city sights. My truncated tour took me to the museum of religious art at the Santa Catalina convent. Scores of gloriously painted Virgin Marys, Madonnas with Child and taffeta-skirted archangels peered down from the walls of the seventeenth-century nunnery.

The techniques I recognised from art-history lessons on Flemish and Italian masters: oil on fabric, gold gilt to imitate embroidery, lack of perspective. The subjects also draw on the same coterie of biblical figures: saints, angels, virgins, baby Jesuses. Yet the Cuzqueño paintings somehow maintained a style altogether their own, a distinctive subtlety that shone forth through the similarities.

I turned to the museum's one-page information leaflet in pursuit of an answer. I found it in the first paragraph: it was not the colonial artists but their indigenous apprentices who created the convent's magical artwork. Native Peruvian painters had dipped into the palette of their own cultural cosmos – its colours, its characters, its creation myths – and mixed what they found with what their European instructors had taught them. The result was the syncretic masterpieces of the so-called Cuzco School.

What the leaflet hadn't made clear was whether the indigenous painters were hiding their own beliefs behind those of their colonial masters. That would fit with the camouflage tactics of Candomblé. Or were they genuine Christian converts, adapting what they knew for the glorification of their new god? It seemed important to me. One implied centuries of heroic resistance to religious imperialism. The other suggested the victory of the cross as well as the sword.

I try and think of a subtle way of asking if the Catholicism in Ayaviri is anything more than Inca beliefs dressed up in Christian clothes: 'Could it be that many Catholics here in the Andes are still privately clinging to their old beliefs and customs?'

My attempts at diplomacy miss the mark, a fact confirmed by the silence that falls over the room. Knives are deliberately placed back on plates, and a dozen eyes slowly turn to the crass foreigner at the table.

Sensing further clarification is being asked of me, I nervously venture an example: 'I mean, could it be possible that in the minds of some, not all of course by any means, that a . . .' – I search around for an alternative to 'cover-up' – 'confusion exists between, say, the Virgin Mary and the earth goddess Pachamama?'

The diners' attention shifts to the head of the table, where the bishop is sitting with his elbows planted firmly on the table and his hands clasped together in a gesture of prayer. He's shaking his head from side to side, slowly, as though my question wearied rather than annoyed him.

'It's a common mistake among foreigners,' he responds, his manner that of someone accustomed to being listened to when he speaks. 'From the outside, I understand how it may seem like a crude sort of syncretism. I, on the other hand, prefer the term "synthesis".'

From the bishop's perspective, the issue is more than simple ecclesiastical pedantry. 'Syncretism' hints at a merger of equals, a supposition he vehemently rejects when comparing the one, true religion with the primitive beliefs of the Andes. 'Synthesis', on the other hand, captures the 'historic reality': Catholic truth joining with local culture to produce an authentic expression of faith. For the defender of orthodoxy, Christianity is where the European and indigenous meet, the highest expression of South America's hybrid, *mestizo* character.

The ecclesiastical governor sits back in his chair and watches me process his argument. His semantic distinctions satisfy those at the table, who pick up their knives and return to their cheese and biscuits.

'Why else would Santa Rosa de Lima, Peru's first saint, be a South American-born woman of Spanish descent?' he asks assertively, as if his whole argument could be deduced from the rhetorical question.

Syncretism or synthesis? The two still seem more or less inter-changeable to me. I doubt Ayaviri's 'good Catholics' could distin-guish between the two either.

The next day, I take a shuttle bus out to Santa Rosa, a neighbouring hamlet some forty minutes from Ayaviri. Bishop Schmalhausen's outreach team hasn't reached here yet. Nor had his theological tech-nicalities.

In an adobe house along the main street, I find Shiny Kurian, a Kerala-born nun. An affiliate of the Sisters of the Cross of Chavanod, the headstrong Indian missionary has been in Santa Rosa for five years. She's supervising mealtime at the soup kitchen for the village elderly.

We'd met briefly in Mass earlier the same day. As in Ayaviri, turnout was low. Sunday is the village market day, Shiny explains, as she ladles rice onto a plate. Sitting on benches against the wall, two geriatric ladies are munching at saturated clods of coca with toothless gums.

'Do they pray to Pachamama or to the Catholic saints?' I ask, pointing towards the old ladies.

'Does it really matter?' the charitable nun replies. 'They find God in everything. What is most important is that they *feel* they are Christians. I can't complain if they aren't practising in the way we would like.'

This is the sort of liberalism that the prelature wants to stamp out. Faith, not feelings, is what interests the bishop. He just needs his parishioners to see the light.

Lima

Mario Vargas Llosa keeps me company on the flight down from the mountains to Peru's desert coast. In his book, *Aunt Julia and the Scriptwriter,* the acclaimed Peruvian writer describes the antics of a Bolivian genius whose radio serials have taken Lima by storm.

At twenty thousand feet above the Andes, Vargas Llosa introduces me to Father Leyva, the protagonist of one of the scriptwriter's chronicles. The invented priest works in La Victoria, an insalubrious neighbourhood in the Peruvian capital.

Gifted with a brilliant mind, the unorthodox churchman is continually in trouble with the ecclesiastical authorities. His first run-in occurs over his student thesis, a scandalous work on 'The Solitary Vice as the Citadel of Ecclesiastical Chastity'. But the unorthodox ways of the clerical renegade meet with success. As a young curate, he doubles attendance at morning Mass by beating the local witch-doctor in a bare-knuckle fight. His approach to youth work is similarly original, hiring the local brothel-keeper to run classes on the 'female arts'. The authoritarian bishop predictably disapproves, rebuking the parish priest for creating an 'academy for prostitutes'. La Victoria's permissive *padre* replies with discerning logic: the district's girls are going to be 'forced to take up that profession' anyway, so they may as well be talented in it.

Vargas Llosa's colourful imagination naturally lends itself towards exaggeration, but there's a grain of truth in the Father Leyva saga. The liberal and conservative wings of the Church have been at one another's throats for years. Tensions between the Shinys and the Schmalhausens are clearly nothing new.

The scriptwriter points to a far more serious problem brewing. An equally unconventional personality has been added to the La Victoria scenario. Depleting the father's Sunday services is a youthful, energetic evangelical pastor from out of town. The now elderly *padre* sticks to his trusted tactics and challenges the newcomer to a fight. Weakened by the sin of Onan, the liberal Leyva is no match for his upstart contender and ends up flat on his back.

The plane is taxiing down the runway. I look out at the sprawling urban jungle of Lima and wonder how Peru's new brand of Christianity is faring.

We've been standing for almost an hour, and my feet are beginning to tire. The band shows no sign of letting up, rolling out one belting hit after another. Through a dozen industrial-sized speakers, the energetic rhythm of an electric guitar invigorates the already exhilarated crowd. Drums beat, backing-singers weep, and the stage lights beam down from the ceiling.

Around the room, people are jumping on the spot and twisting to the music. The spectators are drenched in the show's exuberant, non-stop energy. Thousands of hands clap out a rhythm as the lead singer holds his arms aloft and keeps time. We join in with the chorus, played over and over on permanent encore. Hands go up, palms pressing skywards. Eyes shut, staring upwards, searching out Heaven. Hypnotic, rapturous, the singing continues. Every face has a smile. There's no sadness here.

This is no pop concert. Even though Martin Luther might not recognise it, this is Protestantism – South American style. Every Sunday, the Agua Viva church in downtown Lima spills over with worshippers from dawn till dusk. Satisfying demand requires six services, each two hours long. And there's no question: this is a supply–demand game. People come to be entertained, to feel the love, to soothe their souls.

Agua Viva, the Living Water, does not disappoint. The worship session is just the warm-up dish, something to get the blood pumping. The Word, the Word is the main course, brothers and sisters. The Scriptures flow to overflowing with the wonders of God.

Step up pastor, in immaculate suit and businessman's tie. 'You are conquerors. Repeat after me: I am a conqueror. *Amén!*'

'We are different. Unique, each one of you, children of God. Who says *Amén?*'

'Boy, has God prepared victories for you! Victories in your homes, victories in your family, victories in your workplace.'

'Praise Him, King of Kings, Lord of Lords.'

'Believe your dreams. Trust in the blessings Jesus has in store for you, blessings waiting to be found along the path of your life.'

'An applause for Jesus, eh? A big applause for our Rock and our Redeemer.'

'People are looking for leaders. You are winners. *Amén.*'

'Liberate the call of Jesus of Nazareth for your life. Praise Him.'

'Remember, brothers and sisters, he who gives much receives much. No? *Amén.*'

It's from the haphazard school of preaching: a Bible verse here, a point of doctrine there, all mixed in with a heavy dose of self-help, emotionalism and religious cliché.

Then it's on to dessert, a generous helping of extemporary prayer.

'Let's pray.'

'For the children, Father God, for the children. That they might study hard; that they might be obedient; that they might grow in Jesus.'

'All those here for the first time, come up to the front.'

'What's your name? Arturo. Praise God for Arturo. Holy Spirit, strengthen him, keep him, guide him.'

'Protect our sister. Anoint our brother, Spirit of Fire.'

'Everyone, now, join with me. Let us pray. Jesus, I receive your death. Your resurrection has given me life.'

'I make a new pact with you today to serve you all the days of my life. Thank you, King Jesus, Lord of Salvation, that you have chosen me to be your child, to become a new person.'

As soon as the two-hour show is over, I make a beeline for the door. After being cooped up in the converted cinema with several thousand Spirit-filled worshippers, I feel a desperate need for fresh air. I hit the street almost at a run.

Outside, groups of friends are mingling on the pavement, leather-cased Bibles under their arms. Stretching along the church wall, like early-morning bargain hunters before a sale, queues the next batch of eager congregants.

On the corner with Avenida Javier Prado, a boy is hawking T-shirts. I ask which sells best. He holds up a crimson-red T-shirt with a Superman logo in the centre. 'Comes in five other colours,' he assures me, pointing to a lurid pile beside him. All carry the same slogan, 'Christ is my superhero'.

Before heading off, I pay a visit to the church bookshop, located in an annex of the Agua Viva complex. Its three rooms are crammed to the brim with Christian merchandise. The first is dedicated to music, the next to books and the last to what can be best described as religious tat.

I head straight for the tat. The shelves resemble a Christian version of Woolworth's. Religious tracts, wood-engraved Bible verses, posters of ethereal meadows, 'What would Jesus Do?' bracelets, bookmarks, key rings, china sheep, plastic doves and furry angels fill the room. At £3 a pop, it's even possible to pick up a personalised vial of 'Light of Jerusalem' anointing oil. This is Mammon gone mad.

With my shopping basket still empty, I wander into the book section. The titles are divided into categories. Christian life is stacked beside prayer, marriage beside family, women beside men and children, and leadership beside the workplace. Almost without exception, the authors sound Anglo-Saxon: Mary Baxter, John Maxwell, Joyce Meyer, Benny Hinn – names unpronounceable for most Peruvians.

Their preoccupations also display a North, rather than South, American flavour. Motivational titles such as *The Power of the Positive Mother* and *More Over the Summit* promise lives of victory and achievement. A whole segment of the Christian-life category is devoted to building your own business. Where are the books on struggling with poverty? Or dealing with unemployment?

I go looking for matters of a less material nature. These are to be found in the spiritual-warfare section. For Peru's Pentecostals, nothing escapes the Devil and his handiwork. One book is chillingly entitled, *Satan: My Children Are Not Yours*.

Health appears to represent a particularly fraught battleground in the spiritual realms. Fortunately, Agua Viva's members can read up on *The Diet of the Creator* or learn 52 *Ways to Protect Yourself from Cancer*. For those unsure whether raw *quinoa* salad or lime-marinated *ceviche* have the Saviour's blessing, then help is at hand in the Christian nutrition guide, *What Would Jesus Eat?*

Despite my own Christian convictions, a lifetime in the Anglican Church has not prepared me for the Agua Viva experience. I genuinely try to accustom myself to Peruvian Pentecostalism, but the more songs I sing and the more sermons I sit through, the more alien it all seems. I am left feeling cold and cynical. In the world of cinematic church services, this puts me in the minority.

As in the remainder of the continent, Pentecostal churches have multiplied exponentially in Peru over the past two decades. According to the country's National Evangelical Council, three in twenty Peruvians now swear allegiance to Peru's non-Catholic churches. It might not sound like much, but compared to a handful just fifty years ago, it's a veritable explosion. The vast majority are found in the charismatic Pentecostal wing of the church. In Lima alone, there are at least half a dozen mega-churches in a similar mould to Agua Viva, all with memberships in excess of three thousand people. Many members are middle-class professionals with sensible jobs and university degrees. But these are the flag-bearers, not the foot soldiers, of the movement. Most Pentecostal churches in South America remain small, tin-shack affairs, more likely to be located in the shanties than the city centres. Membership is generally in double figures, if not single. Multiply many times over, though, and you have yourself a religious revival.

I spend a week in Lima trawling around evangelical mission agencies, church halls and seminaries in search of an explanation. All start with the same proviso: man is but a tool in God's work. The Evangelical Church is growing thanks to a bountiful outpouring of the Holy Spirit. Most concede a role, albeit minor, to human intervention. The evangelicals' success has to do with involving lay people, the head of a mission agency tells me. It comes down to demonstrating God's love in action, the Anglican bishop thinks. The opportunity for upward social mobility, a church historian argues. Charismatic leadership, the rector of a theological college opines. Aggressive evangelism, one pastor insists. In Brazil, the evangelicals put it more bluntly: the Catholics might have opted for the poor, but the poor opted for us.

Catholics, the losers in all this, are perhaps best placed to bring some objectivity to the debate. A Peruvian friend of mine from university days gives me a book on the subject by José Luis Pérez

Guadalupe, a Peruvian Jesuit cleric. The author's explanation is threefold. First and foremost, he credits evangelicals with offering a personal encounter with Jesus Christ, 'a religious experience so profound and intense, which they had never before come across in the Catholic Church'. In a single stroke, evangelicals have succeeded in 'lowering God from the clouds', as he puts it.

In second place, the Jesuit academic cites the experience of community. Join an evangelical church and the convert gains himself not just a personal saviour, but a new family to boot. In contrast to the Mass, where the congregant enters and leaves unnoticed, evangelical churches station a grinning welcome committee on the door. In that warm embrace, the theory goes, urban migrants especially find the sense of belonging that they lost on moving to the city. Doctrinal training is Pérez Guadalupe's final point. As was clear in Ayaviri, most nominal Catholics do well to pick up the basics of the catechesis. New converts to evangelicalism, on the other hand, are given a Bible and told to get reading.

Not all Catholics are as generous. My friend passed me another book as well, this time by Javier Gutiérrez. An ordained theologian, he criticises evangelicals for taking advantage of the physically sick and emotionally vulnerable. Where that doesn't work, then talk of the battle of Armageddon does. 'No option remains but to enrol yourself in one or other of these [evangelical] *armies,* where salvation is assured.' The very title of the book, *Those who came after ...,* sums up the impostor, second-rate status that Gutiérrez and many Catholics feel towards the evangelical 'sects'. It's the thesis Father Leyva would have written were he not so preoccupied guarding his clerical chastity.

My head awash with so much theory, I put in a call to another friend of mine. I was hoping Enrique might offer me a more personal perspective. We'd met three years ago while I was working on a volunteer building project in his neighbourhood. Enrique had acted as our construction adviser, bodyguard and general chaperone.

We arrange to meet for *chifa,* Chinese, in Lima's relatively upmarket Miraflores district. Despite the growing reputation of the nation's spicy cuisine, Peruvians can't seem to get enough of fried rice with glutinous meat and fluorescent goo. Enrique munches down his meal, washing it down with a half-litre bottle of Inca Cola, a bright-yellow fizzy drink that looks and tastes like radio-active waste.

Enrique hasn't changed much since the last time I'd seen him. He still dresses much like a teenager, in tracksuit bottoms, a hooded sweatshirt and an immovable baseball cap. In his mid-thirties, he has a job at a prestigious university. He cleans the toilets. Every day, he travels an hour by bus from his earthen-floor home in El Agustino, a rough area near to one of the capital's main cemeteries. He lives with his invalid mother, his stepfather and his drug-addict younger brother. His bedroom is a room on the top of the house. It has no door and no roof. On his meagre earnings, he maintains his son, aged ten, who lives with his maternal grandmother. The boy's mother died years before in a fire at the market where she worked.

In spite of these hardships, I've never known my friend to complain. '*Hay que seguir para adelante*,' runs his favourite saying: 'You've got to keep moving forward.' Six years ago, Enrique became a born-again Christian. I ask him why.

He takes me back to his childhood, to experiences he's never shared with me before: to his father who left when he was a baby, to his stepfather who used to beat him and to his adolescence living rough on the streets. When he was nineteen, he went to look for his father, who lived in the mountains and had a new family. Initially, they hit it off, but later they started to argue and he threw Enrique out. When he turned twenty-one, his mother took him back to confront his father. She said that he'd never paid a penny towards Enrique's upkeep and thought it was time he gave him some sort of lump sum.

My friend begins to cry, making no attempt to cover up his tears as they flow into his wonton soup: 'Do you know what my father's response was? He pointed into his back garden, at the oranges that had fallen off the tree. "He can have those," he told my mum. That's all I was worth to my father: a pile of rotten oranges.'

The waiter looks over to us with mild alarm. Wiping his streaming eyes, Enrique composes himself just enough to finish his story: 'One day, a guy from my football team invited me to his church. People treated me kindly. When the pastor started speaking, it was as if he was talking directly to me. He said I had a Father in Heaven who loved me, loved me so much that he sent his own Son, Jesus, to die in my place. I wanted to know that love, to know the God-Father that the pastor talked about. I asked if they would teach me.'

Once his tears have finally dried up, I pay the bill and we step out onto the congested evening street.

Over the coming days, I reflect on my conversation with Enrique. My experience at Agua Viva had left me feeling sceptical about Peru's new churches. To me, the atmosphere felt hysterical and people's reactions contrived. But how many had testimonies like Enrique's? How many could now cope with life's distresses thanks to a personal encounter with the 'God from the clouds'? Perhaps I'd been too quick to judge? Could it be that the evangelicals were indeed offering a spiritual form of liberation?

It is a Wednesday night and among the shacks on a chalky, parched street in Lima's California district singing can be heard. 'You give peace, you give love, you give happiness,' a dozen voices chant discordantly.

This is the mid-week Bible study. The neighbours meet together in Antonia's house, because it's the largest and because she was first to offer. Built from breeze blocks and concrete, her front room is sparsely decorated with mismatched furniture. While the group's size fluctuates, it's guaranteed that the women will always outnumber the men.

Tonight, the ratio is ten to two. The age range runs from a girl of eighteen to a wrinkled widow of eighty. What they don't share in years, they share in poverty. California, an ex-*invasión,* as Lima's residents call their shanties, has only just had running water and electricity installed. Most houses still lack a working toilet. The group sits in a circle on chairs borrowed from the church. A single energy-saving light dangling from the ceiling is all there is to read by.

All are relative newcomers to the *barrio*. Just as doctors never want for sick people, Margaret the church-planter never lacks new migrants. The 1980s were boom years for Peruvian urbanisation. With the terrorist group Shining Path at its bloodthirsty height, tens of thousands of *campesinos* fled to the cities. Most headed to Lima. Rural poverty still keeps them coming.

Margaret kicks us off with a prayer and invites one of the women to read the evening's Bible passage. In her late fifties, this tireless English missionary has been working in the capital's slums for nearly three decades. She's at the quieter end of the evangelical spectrum, her faith more considered and rational than the wilder Pentecostals.

California is the fourth church Margaret has helped establish. The first was in Villa Salvador, now an established shanty town. When she first arrived in Peru, the neighbourhood was literally a patch of desert on the city limits. She came to know of it through Palmeira, a single mum with whom the veteran missionary had become friends at another church. Palmeira had moved to Villa Salvador after the mayor in her previous shanty booted her out. All those without a permanent job or a permanent spouse had been given six sheets of bamboo matting and told to construct themselves a house in this inhospitable desert scrub. Margaret's friend fitted both categories so set herself to building.

The two women worked through a course on Christian basics with the seemingly inappropriate title of 'Abundant Life'. Then they started a kids' club, the mustard seed of what was to become Margaret's first church. Today, the fledgling congregation counts over sixty registered members. The services are led by Palmeira's eldest son, the youth club's very first graduate.

Back in California, pages are rustling as the group searches through their Bibles for the Gospel of John. Once the turning stops and everyone has found their place, Margaret assigns one of the women to read. The text is taken from Chapter 8 and deals with the failure of the Jewish authorities to recognise Jesus as the Messiah.

'My disciples will know the truth,' the woman reads, 'and the truth will set you free.'

'What does Jesus mean by being free in the truth?' Margaret asks.

'Freedom from sin,' Antonia responds, shooting up her hand, the keenest student in the class.

'Very good,' Margaret affirms. 'We all sin and therefore we need to accept Jesus and have him change us and sort out our problems of sin.'

Sin is vitally important for South America's evangelicals. They even jibe at the Catholics, despite their confessionals, for playing it down. For without sin, people will never know just how far they have fallen, and, by extension, just how much Jesus has rescued them. Inspiring gratitude is the end goal.

As a result, wrongdoing represents one of the few areas where evangelicals are uncharacteristically liberal. Sin knows no bounds. The Ten Commandments – do not murder, do not steal, do not lie, et cetera – serve as a foundational base. Add to these the Catholic list of moral vices: greed, jealously, anger and so on. Slap drugs, abortion, hard liquor, smoking, pre-marital sex and homosexuality on top and the essential remit of sin is broadly covered. For the more traditional denominations, there's also the sin of 'worldliness' to consider. Out, then, with dancing, shopping on Sunday and wearing lipstick.

Of course, the Agua Vivas package wrongdoing differently. Peru's contemporary pastors prefer not to talk about rules or religion. Today, the vogue is all directed towards 'relationships'. No longer is God the Almighty the distant killjoy with a correction stick poised to strike. He is God the Abba Father, God the Soulmate Son, and God the Help-at-Hand Holy Spirit. It's the Holy Trinity remarketed as a buy-one-get-two-free best buddy.

The doctrine neatly reinvents sin. Gone is the long list of dos and don'ts. Instead of fire and brimstone, talk of feelings now fills the pulpit. Listen to rap music, the faithful learn, and you 'grieve' the Holy Spirit. Covet your neighbour's Oakleys and you are 'rebelling' against the Father. Suddenly, a penniless *campesino* has a hand in affecting God's mood. It's a compelling case for Peru's prodigals.

'Remember what we talked about last week?' Margaret adds. 'God hates the sin, but loves the sinner.'

In California, the room has gone quiet. A general feeling pervades that having Jesus sort out their problems of sin must be a good thing.

The Bible-study leader is not done: 'What else might this verse about truth setting us free refer to?'

Blank faces all round. There's a saying in Sunday-school circles that if you don't know an answer, you should plump for 'Jesus'. As a general catch-all, it can almost always be made to fit. Few in the California study group completed school, let alone the Sunday variety, and so the easy answer goes unsaid.

Margaret breaks the studious silence with a suggestion of her own: 'What about self-confidence?'

Being a Christian means not having to concern oneself about what others may think, the Bible teacher explains. More important is how God views you. The idea presents the listeners with yet another novelty. They mull it over, and our study leader receives a few nods in assent.

Margaret clearly has a few more freedoms on her list, but the evening study group has fallen silent again.

'Freedom from anger?' she prompts suggestively, probing for a response.

This time, the notion resonates more directly with her listeners. They all know what it means to feel maddened. Again, it's Antonia who responds with the greatest enthusiasm. The evening's host confesses to having beaten her teenage daughter with a stick the previous week:

'I prayed about it and felt God was calling me to apologise. So I did, and now I don't feel any anger at all.'

Her daughter, who didn't speak to her for four days, obviously saw things slightly differently.

'Thank you, Antonia. You are right; with prayer, hatred goes away. I know that many of you feel you have been maltreated. That can bring rage and a desire for revenge. But that rage is like a prisoner. It keeps you trapped and means you can't be free.' The Bible study is beginning to feel closer to group counselling than a theology class.

Freedom from fear – of death, illness, unemployment, unpaid gas bills – appears last on Margaret's list. Again, this elicits a round of head-nodding and even an '*Amén, hermana*' from one emboldened lady.

Eleanora, a heavy-set middle-aged woman with a grubby child hanging by her ankles, plucks up the courage to voice her opinion: 'Could it mean being free from difficulties?'

It is a tentative stab and Margaret is keen to encourage her: 'Good, can you elaborate a little, Eleanora?'

'It's just that when I gave my life to Jesus, I experienced an incredible sense of peace and joy, even in the midst of my problems. I felt free from my worries.'

As with Enrique, this kind of personal story is a hallmark of almost all the born-again Christians I meet in Peru. Forget chit-chat. They want to share the darkest secrets of their past: lives of drug abuse, decades of alcoholism, prison time for wife-battering, addictions to internet pornography. The more impious, the better. Again, it serves as an approbation of God's generous grace.

'Yes, sister, very good.' Everything about Margaret exudes genuine warmth. You feel she might just get up out of her seat any minute and come and hug you.

Even the way she qualifies Eleanora's enthusiastic response is typically generous and heartfelt: 'Yes, it is true that Jesus helps us in our troubles. Like us, he too suffered and so he can also understand us when we suffer. Becoming a Christian doesn't mean we will no longer face difficulties. But, as Christians we can be confident that Jesus will always be there with us, walking beside us, holding our hand.'

The image of a divine assistant ever at her side brings out a beaming smile on Eleanora's face: '*Amén, sister, Amén!*'

It is around 9.30, and the group is growing tired. Margaret is anxious that we take away one more lesson before we close in prayer.

'What is it that sets us free?' Eyes return to the open Bible in their laps.

'The truth,' several say in unison, repeating the passage.

'And where do we find the truth?'

There is nothing existential in Margaret's questioning. They have the truth right there in their hands. This miraculous fact seems to escape her pupils. Another lengthy silence ensues.

It's the ever-attentive Antonia who saves our missionary instructor from pedagogic despair: 'In the Bible?'

'Yes, yes, Antonia, very good, excellent. We find the truth in the Bible. Brothers, sisters, that is why we need to continue to study God's word and learn what he wants for us.'

We're encouraged to continue attending the weekly group. There's also an invitation for the non-regulars among our number to come to church. The Devil is happy when we don't go to church because that's where we learn more about the truth, about Jesus.

'And who would we rather make happy? The Devil or Jesus?'

'Jesus!' the group responds, the first emphatic answer of the night.

'Exactly right. *Amén.*'

We finish with a prayer and a song. The sound of singing stirs the old woman beside me, her eyelids heavy from the late hour. Margaret wishes us *bendiciones,* blessings, for the remainder of the week.

'Sunday, 7.30, see you all there.'

Margaret has never had to go looking for converts exactly. Her offer of friendship and freedom draws people in. Others take a more extreme approach. The final injunction of Jesus, they point out, was to 'go and make disciples of all nations'. People of every tribe and every tongue must hear the Good News. That means a visit to the jungle.

Iquitos

In one of the many internet cafés around the spacious Plaza de Armas in Iquitos, I meet Gary and Zack. They come from a small town in the Midwest of the USA. Their T-shirts proclaim the love of Jesus in big, bold letters. I surmise they might belong to one of the fifty missionary agencies operating out of this jungle town and introduce myself.

I catch them at the end of a two-week evangelistic trip into the *selva*, the bush. Located in the Amazon rainforest close to the Brazilian border, Iquitos is the world's biggest city without road access. If its million or so citizens want out, they must either fly or take a boat five days downstream. Most never leave.

There's nothing stopping the missionaries getting in and out though. Gary and Zack are affiliate members of an independent group called the Ambassadors for Christ Worldwide. Zack, who runs his own DIY shop back home, has a badly sunburnt nose and a peeling forehead. In his early forties, the tall, blue-eyed shop-keeper does most of the talking. God had blessed them richly it would seem. In the village of Santa Isabel, six people renounced Catholicism and gave their lives to Jesus.

'Catholicism cannot convert the soul of man because it is inundated with idolatry,' Zack tells me over a coffee at their hotel. 'God cannot bless a false religion that operates outside the Scriptures.'

'We simply explained to them that there is only one way to God, through the God-man Jesus,' the avid evangelist continues.

Isn't that a little close-minded? Apparently, not at all. The opportunity is there for everyone to accept Jesus. The son of God is not exclusive. A short sermon, replete with Bible verses, follows.

'Jesus died for sins, once, for all, the righteous for the unrighteous, to bring me to God: 1 Peter, chapter 3, verse 18.'

It occurs to me that Zack is possibly more interested in converting me than answering my questions.

Gary, an ex-Vietnam veteran, chips in briefly about other mission trips they've made around the Americas. The love of God constrains them to go and tell the message. After an hour listening to them, I am feeling the constraining power of a full bladder and a bent ear. I thank them for their time and take my leave.

Two days later, I bump into Zack in the street. He greets me warmly. It turns out that God was still being mighty generous in his blessings. The do-it-yourself preacher had spoken in a local church the previous evening. Three more convicted souls won for Jesus. He would be returning to his home-improvements store a contented man.

Another happy man in Iquitos is Pastor Luis Davila. The sound of singing and laughing alerts me to his church, located just half a block from my hotel. Situated on an otherwise nondescript street, the box-shaped building stands out for its bright yellow exterior. Celestial blue lettering above the open door reveals it to be the Salt and Light Missionary Centre. I walk in.

A group of young people are acting out a sketch in front of a thick velvet blue curtain at the front of the church. Two huge speakers dominate the improvised stage area. 'Rock system' the logo on the amplification system reads. The amateur dramatics turn out to be part of the closing ceremony of a two-month Bible school. The training initiative is put on for pastors and enthusiastic youngsters from villages up and down the region's widespread river network.

Despite being dressed casually, Pastor Davila has an air of affluence about him. His short-sleeved shirt is embossed with a Lacoste logo, and his gleaming white sports shoes look fresh from the shelf. He comes over and strikes up a conversation.

Born and bred in Iquitos, the church's founder claims to have spent thirty-one of his forty-eight years working as a missionary to indigenous groups. His ministry has taken him as far afield as Bolivia, Chile, Ecuador, Argentina and Brazil. He returned to his home town a decade ago. Now the religious enthusiast concentrates his efforts on what he calls *campos blancos* – untouched areas far upriver. To help him in his expansion endeavours, he's founded his own ambitiously entitled missionary society, the 'Far-Flung Places World Mission'.

The pastor has also managed to squeeze in time to build a small business empire. He owns six petrol stations dotted around the city and a handful of sawmills. The profits support fifty-five pastors, one for each church that he has set up along the Amazon tributaries. With the leftovers, the entrepreneur churchman has also bought himself a speedboat. What used to be a fifteen-day trip by barge to his *campos blancos* now takes him a mere forty-eight hours. He's recently extended his house as well. He invites me to pay him a visit. 'You'll find it easily enough; it's the only three-storey building on the street.'

I'm intrigued to know the secret of Pastor Davila's church-planting success and ask if he can fill me in. As with the Church leaders back in Lima, he credits his advances in far-flung evangelism to the out-working of the Holy Spirit, God's omnipotent secret agent on Earth and the Church's stellar recruitment specialist.

From a human perspective, he admits the springboard is often the conversion of one or two key people in the local community: 'We visit them regularly and continue to teach them. They are our contact point.'

Margaret had said much the same. In her case, the breakthrough came when she arranged an outing to the beach with Palmeira, Palmeira's neighbours and a busload of their offspring. When the children were off making sandcastles, Margaret took the mothers through a Bible passage. Astutely, she chose a parable about house-building. The wise man constructed his house on rock and the foolish on sand. For women living in a shanty surrounded by treeless desert, the lesson hit home. From that moment on, Margaret had her key contacts.

Aside from allies in the community, Pastor Davila points to a second, much more effective hook with which to fish: miracles. There is nothing like a drop of the divine to win people to Christ, he enthuses.

Could he give me an example?

He throws up his hands as if not knowing which manifestation of Almighty power to choose from. The Pentecostal pioneer plumps for the most recent. Two months ago, he was preaching in a village deep in the Amazon when a young man with a mental illness and a disfigured face was brought before him. His parents requested prayer for their disabled son. The pastor duly laid hands on the boy and evoked Jesus's healing hand to do its work. The next day, the teenager awoke with a lucid mind and a regular face. The villagers, naturally, were in awe. The doctors, as is always the case, were baffled.

Stories of miracles abound in South America's evangelical churches, particularly those of a charismatic, Pentecostal variety. Wheelchair-users get up and walk. Tumours disappear overnight. AIDS victims are cured.

In the Mivia Pentecostal church in Iquitos, miracles happen on Wednesdays. After a few songs and a short Bible reading, Pastor José Arce Vásquez invites those in need of divine intervention to step forward. The stage fills with the needy and desperate. Mivia is situated on the riverbank in a swamp-ridden shanty below the bustling Belén market. Its congregants are the poorest of Iquitos' poor. Their wooden shacks rest precariously on the city's main flood plain. Every year, the river breaks its banks with almost spiteful regularity.

The church is located just off Calle Venecia, a cluttered thoroughfare full of banana-sellers during the day and merchants of vice at night. After dark, even the locals refuse to enter Lower Belén's cramped, seething passageways. Standing on stilts thirty feet off the ground, the church building itself is reached via a thin pathway made from slippery wooden boards. Foul-smelling sludge squeezes through gaps in the planks and onto my shoes.

Given the gruelling circumstances in which the shanty's residents live, it's understandable that the church is better attended mid-week than on Sundays. Wednesday is earmarked for the 'service of power' meeting. I ask the pastor if he himself has experienced a miracle. The answer goes without saying. Of course he has. The Lord delivered him from the bottle.

'I went to a witch doctor for help, but after a month I started drinking again. From the first day I accepted the Lord Jesus Christ, however, I have never touched another drop.'

'How about those who come forward but don't experience such deliverance?'

Pastor Arce is in no doubt. They lack faith. What could be clearer? Does the Bible not teach that those with sufficient faith can move mountains? We tell them that they need to pray for more belief. Then they'll be healed.

For those outside the fold, the miracle-on-tap formula provokes everything from mild mockery to virulent denouncement. Into the second camp fall many churchgoing Catholics.

Heading back after my tour of Belén, I pass by the local parish church of Our Lady of Rosario of Fatima. Located on a busy corner of Calle Próspero, its bulky stone edifice dominates a fair portion of the block. I decide to pop in. The church is empty except for two wizened old ladies bent over in prayer. From the market across the street, the bartering of the fishmongers and grocers intermingles with their whispered petitions.

A senescent priest is in attendance in the church office. Short, plump and good-humoured, Father Nicolás invites me to take a seat. His accent still carries the lisp of his native Spain, whose shores he left as a young man for a life in the Peruvian jungle. I explain my interest in Iquitos' non-Catholic churches. Far from the hostile response I was expecting, his pale Iberian eyes light up at the topic. Compared to the saintly tasks of hearing confession and preparing the Eucharist, some wholesome sect-bashing appears to be manna for his soul.

'The thing with these sects is that everything has to be all shouting and miracles,' Father Nicolás starts out. Still sitting in his chair, he begins flailing his arms in the air and warbling nonsense in imitation.

I get the idea, I tell him, but he is enjoying himself too much to cease the impersonation immediately.

'People feel threatened into giving money. They fear that if they don't give, then they won't be healed or saved.' There's a slight wheeze in his voice after his acting exertions.

I ask if he can give me an example.

'Let me think. Ah, yes. Take the old widow who lives across the way. Not so long ago she fell and bruised her hip. It was so bad she could hardly walk. Some friends took her to one of these Pentecostal churches in Belén to ask for healing. The pastor came and explained that she would have to give an offering if God was to hear her. She only had 50 *soles* [about £9] and handed it all over. The man then did his thing, but nothing happened. She didn't get any better.

So a few days later, the religious charlatan pays her a visit. Again he said an offering would be necessary. She no longer had any money. All she had was a cockerel, so he took that instead. He prayed for her, but she still wasn't healed. Now she has lost her 50 *soles* and her cockerel, and her hip remains as bad as ever.'

I suspect the version that reached the ears of this parish cleric was slightly one-sided, but he enjoyed retelling it, and it served to confirm his conviction that all the non-Catholic churches were really just money-making mercenaries in religious clothing.

Not, of course, that the Catholic Church wasn't above a bit of miracle mongering itself. What, after all, was the panoply of gilded saints all about if not to intercede on behalf of the faithful? Our Lady of Rosario of Fatima, for one, was kept plenty busy by Belén's praying public: intercessions for good health, a safe home, a prosperous market stall. What were these if not requests for divine intervention?

Stories of miracles abound in the history of the Catholic Church in Peru. San Martín de Porres, a black saint born in the sixteenth century and the patron saint of hair stylists, is credited with curing the mortally ill, communicating with animals and being on hand to encourage early missionaries in China and Japan – all without ever leaving his convent cell in Lima. The difference, Catholic tradition teaches, is that such miracles result from an individual's saintliness and not, as in the case of the 'sects', thanks to a sizeable sound system and group hysteria.

Another complaint targeted at South America's missionary groups is that of cultural destruction. The loudest critics are generally liberal-minded Westerners who rile about ethno-cultural rights and ethnological purity. Christian missionaries, they argue, are nothing short of modern-day cultural imperialists.

William Powers, a North American environmentalist who worked to protect the Chuiquitanos people in neighbouring Bolivia, typifies the opprobrium many feel towards Christian proselytisers. In a book recounting his experience, he frets about highlanders moving to the jungle. The Chuiquitano culture, as well as their land, was being slashed and burned. Then 'Jesus spotted them.' This, the author infers, was not a positive development. He pictures a future of Jesus freaks 'polishing' the native's brown skin until 'the holy shine gleams forth'.

There's some truth in such fears. The early history of Spanish America certainly provides some ugly precedents. The conquistadores famously invaded the continent with the cross *and* the sword. Which came first remains hotly debated. According to Spanish custom, native peoples were cordially invited to accept Christianity. Should they 'maliciously make delay', the colonists were within their rights to butcher them as savages. It took almost half a century before the Spanish could determine if South America's indigenous population even had a soul.

The *encomienda* system grew out of just such a worldview. Under the arrangement, Spanish colonists were granted substantial plots of land in the New World, together with the right to exploit the natives for labour. In return, the new arrivals were supposed to instruct the Amerindians under their charge in the essentials of the Christian faith. The settlers kept to the first part to the letter. History fails to record such enthusiasm for the second half of the bargain.

Relics of these old days can still be seen in some missionary quarters. In Iquitos, I came across one fundamentalist missionary who maintained that human cultures meant nothing 'because the cultures of men are insignificant to the ways of God'. Another North

American preacher was adamant that Amazonian Peru was '100 per cent heathen'. As soon as the native people get ill, he assured me, they run to the resident shaman and start praying to the snake god. Or perhaps it was the tree god? The messenger of the good news wasn't exactly sure. His ignorance about local customs didn't surprise me. He lived in a walled compound paid for by his church back in the Bible Belt and employed a guard to keep local Peruvians out.

Such blinkered thinking is, thankfully, the exception among today's mission societies. Most are at pains to point out the priority they now put on preserving indigenous culture.

That is certainly the message from the Lima-based Summer Institute of Linguistics, the Peruvian branch of Wycliffe Bible Translators and one of the country's longest-standing missionary agencies. Peru boasts ninety-three different living languages. The Institute has so far studied seventy-four of these, helping create alphabets and translating works of 'high moral value'. It even receives a contract from the national government to do so.

Before leaving Lima, I'd gone to speak with the institute's Abe Koop. An amiable Canadian Mennonite with a ginger beard, he has worked with South American indigenous groups for over two decades. The sun was high in the sky on the day of my visit, but a hazy grey mist kept it from frazzling the city below. *Limeños* fondly call this daily smog the 'donkey's underbelly'. It is precisely these sorts of local idioms that Abe and the institute's team of sixty translators dedicate themselves to understanding and conserving.

I'd started by asking him what his motivation was for dedicating his life to translating these languages. 'We love the Lord, and we love his Word' came his response. That much I'd expected.

Language translation was not just a back door for publishing the Bible, Abe continued, anticipating the most frequent criticism directed at the institute. The linguistic experts have produced more than three thousand three hundred publications in Peru's indigenous languages. Grammar books, dictionaries and other materials geared towards promoting literacy constitute the majority of its output. Its backlist also includes manuals on agriculture and basic health primers, as well as thirty-two different translations of the 'Universal Declaration of Human Rights'.

'For me, it is a privilege to see people become proud of their language,' the long-term missioner had explained.

He went on to recount how as a child he'd been made to feel ashamed for speaking *Plattditsch*, his mother tongue. The pastors in church would only permit the Bible to be read in High German or English. Reading in *Plattditsch*, they used to say, was an insult to God.

Then he'd shown me a battered copy of the first book that the institute ever produced in Peru. It was dedicated to improving literacy among the Aymara population, the country's largest native linguistic group. The text was written in the Roman alphabet. I'd asked Abe why.

'We normally use the national alphabet because our experience is that people will eventually want to learn the national language as well.'

'But won't that end up causing them to stop using their native language?' I enquired, wondering if the institute wasn't in fact shooting itself in the foot.

'Learning both languages helps strengthen people's cultural identities. If their education is truly intercultural, it doesn't stop them from wanting to see their native language blossom and grow.'

I knew what the Mr Powers of this world would say to that. Even if the Spanish language didn't undermine their cultures, then the Bible would. I put the question to Abe.

He batted it off with practised aplomb: 'No, not necessarily. Christianity can actually strengthen the good in indigenous cultures.'

Not all see it that way, he'd been frank enough to admit. He'd told me about a run-in he'd once had with a member of the Tikuna tribe. The woman had accused the institute of 'bringing division' to her home community:

'"At one end of the village, people got drunk and the children were always dirty," she said. "At the other end of the village, where the Christians lived, they all dressed well and enjoyed good relations with one another. You, you've brought that division." Those were her words exactly.'

Abe saw no need to apologise, neither now nor then.

Iquitos' latest generation of neo-Pentecostal missionaries are quick to stress their cultural sensitivity too. Their motive has less to do with political correctness and more to do with results. Pastor Davila is one such convert to a more softly-softly strategy.

'Every village has their own customs and religions. We try to work within their culture,' the pastor to far-flung places had told me.

In practice, his culturalisation translates as going easy on the initial hard sell. Instead, he and his messengers first endeavour to get to know people and win their trust. To do that, they start by giving out medicines, clothes and other material assistance. He's not the only one to use aid distribution as a door into indigenous communities. Two former British navy supply ships regularly trawl up and down Iquitos' tributary rivers delivering medical aid and dental care. They sail under the flag of the Unión Bíblica del Perú, a foreign-sponsored evangelical group.

Only once the local community invites them in does Pastor Davila start his door-knocking and his preaching of the saving truth of Jesus.

But how does he tackle customs that are, to use his own words, 'pagan'? For the jungle missioner, who preaches with the aid of a top-of-the-range laptop, the answer is not clear-cut.

On the one hand, Christians must show an openness to cultural assimilation. He cites the example of the Yakumama, the god of the river: 'Every day, the region's fishermen ask the river god for a good catch before heading out in their boats. We basically tell them that if the Yakumama exists, then he is a creature of God. The logic is that they should worship the creator, not the things he has created.'

On the other hand, the motorboat missionary judges some indigenous customs off limits. Polygamy represents one obvious no-

no. It is the habit of *curacas,* the village chiefs, to take several teenage brides. This, according to Pastor Davila, 'clearly contradicts the Bible'. So too does drunkenness. Many Amazonian tribes are accustomed to drinking *masato,* an alcoholic beverage made from fermented yucca. It staves off hunger but leaves the villagers semi-sozzled. This is not God's will, the pastor clarified.

'We don't change their culture,' he'd concluded. 'We merely remove the parts that contradict the Bible.'

As a semantic argument, I could see it appealing to Bishop Schmalhausen. But I suspect a Western-trained anthropologist would have problems with it. So I go in search of a second opinion.

I hail the first moto-taxi that passes: 'The Remnant of God International Church, *por favor.*'

In Iquitos, these three-wheeled monsters cram the one-way streets like a biblical plague. Half motorbike, half hooded Roman chariot, they offer cheap transport in a city where few people own cars.

'Sure, hop in.'

'How much?' Payment, I've discovered, is better agreed upfront.

'Three *soles,*' the driver fires back.

Overcharging is obligatory among Peru's taxi-driving population. I'm not sure how far the journey is, but I know it's almost certainly worth less.

Is that the fair price or the 'gringo *price'?* The question always gets a laugh and helps in the compulsory bartering process that comes with the moto-taxi ritual. We settle for 2 *soles* and 50 *centavos* and race off into the afternoon traffic. Ten minutes later, Iquitos' answer to Michael Schumacher deposits me outside a multi-storey warehouse. I take it we've arrived.

An assistant at the door shows me through to the plush office of Bishop Elías Valles Win. A gigantic map of Peru's Amazon basin stretches across one wall. Coloured pins depict villages where the Remnant Church has a presence. I count forty-eight in total, spreading out in concentric circles from Iquitos city centre.

Twisting his bulky bishop's ring between his thumb and fore-finger, the oval-faced church leader points to a small settlement on the map called Lagunas, lying several hundred kilometres west along the Ucayali river:

'That is where I grew up. My father worked as an evangelist along that whole stretch of river. He used to speak Cocamilla.'

He chuckles to himself: 'The only problem was that Cocamilla has two entirely different forms: one for the women and one for the men. And my father was taught by his grandmother. So when he went to preach in Cocamilla communities, everyone would be in hysterics because he spoke just like a woman.'

His father overcame his communication problems and laid the groundwork for his son's current ministry.

Bishop Elías' grounding in the communities of the Amazon gives him a head start on foreign missionaries and even his fellow Peruvians.

'I speak their *language*,' he tells me, emphasising the final word to stress its broadest sense, not simply a shared linguistic affinity but an empathy with their worldview.

I mention the American missionary and his private fortress. The Bishop shakes his head sadly: 'It's hard enough for foreigners to integrate into our culture as it is. When they adopt a bunker mentality like that, it's simply impossible.'

The Remnant's missionaries adopt a more integrated approach: 'We eat what the villagers eat and live how they live. If they serve up monkey for dinner, then we eat it with them.'

'But what about your preaching activities?' I ask, thinking back to the Chuiquitanos and their holy shine. 'There are many who'd say you're undermining these very cultures that you hold so dear?'

The affable bishop takes no offence at my question. As with Abe Koop, I suspect it's not the first time he's been called on to defend himself against the charge of cultural destruction.

He believes the Gospel is the only alternative for his beloved Amazon: 'Much witchcraft and alcoholism goes on here in the jungle. Both have been responsible for some atrocious things. But we see a radical change in Christian villages. There, the people are freed from oppression and exploitation.'

If true, it backs up Margaret and her message of spiritual liberation.

I leave the Remnant church wanting to believe the bishop's version of events. Cultures aren't static. They change, develop, mutate, depending on external influences. Need the evangelicals' message necessarily ruin cultures? Could it not refine them, even improve them?

I catch another moto-taxi, this time to the offices of the Inter-Ethnic Association for the Development of the Peruvian Jungle. If anyone in Iquitos was going to excoriate the evangelicals for their incursions into tribal life, I figured it would be this group of indigenous-rights activists.

I find Manuel Ramírez, the association's vice-president, surprisingly positive. He readily acknowledges the contribution of the mission agencies in terms of medicines and education.

Peru's far-flung places are no pushover though. Every community makes a careful calculation of the pros and cons of the white man's religion before deciding whether to accept or reject it.

'We might live in the jungle, but we're not half-wits,' Manuel says. 'If they tried to impose their culture on top of their religion, we wouldn't accept them. It's as simple as that.'

An urgent text message on his mobile phone cuts our conversation short.

On my last evening in Iquitos, an email from Zack pops up in my inbox. He wants to pass on the contact details of one of his worldwide ambassadorial contacts. Brother Sears, he thinks, would be useful for my research. The missionary adventurer is heading off to find a lost tribe on the Peru–Ecuador border. The government is planning to turn the area into a national park, and Brother Sears feels called to locate the tribe and convert them before access is cut off. It is a race against time, the email informs me.

Zack signs off with characteristic religious fervour: 'I pray to God that you will live soberly and righteously for Jesus Christ in all holiness with fear and trembling as the coming of Jesus draws near. Be ready, Oliver!'

At the time, I'm readying myself more for an evening meal of fresh grilled fish in a quiet riverside restaurant. I want to watch the sun set over the silent, broody Amazon one last time before heading back to Lima on the morning flight. Finding a pavement eatery down on the promenade, I disregard Zack's caution about sober living and order a cold beer.

The outdoor table is perfectly positioned for people-watching. It's a Saturday night, and the Ramblas is bustling with strolling families and enamoured couples, both young and old. A cool breeze blows off the river. Hawkers go from table to table selling chewing gum and cigarettes, their wares laid out in a wooden tray attached around their necks. They remind me of the ice-cream sellers who used to appear during the interval in small-town cinemas.

Across from my table, a girl with a short straw skirt and tribal markings across her face pouts for photographs. Her friend is working the same beat, swapping the face paint for a fangless cobra that's coiled around her shoulders. Further down the riverfront, a street performer is attracting a crowd of curious bystanders.

My beer almost finished, I'm weighing up whether to order another when I spot an attractive, fresh-faced woman sitting on a bench opposite. She too is watching the passers-by, although with a distant gaze in her eye, her mind evidently elsewhere.

It's not her looks that catch my eye, but her clothes. Hardly out of her teens, she's decked out like an elderly spinster. A long, shapeless, navy-blue dress reaches down to her ankles. Above it, she's wearing a granny's wool cardigan in the same colour. A cotton head covering, similar to a nun's habit but longer at the back, obscures her long hair.

The oddly attired girl catches me staring at her. Embarrassed, I look away, but it's too late. She begins gathering her things together, presumably discomforted by my intrusive gawking. Instead of moving off down the promenade, though, she sets a course directly for my table. Stopping beside my chair, she reaches out her hand. Much as I pretend to be studying the small print on the empty beer bottle, there's no escaping her hovering presence. I look up.

'Hello, my name is Queen Sánchez, and I am an Israelite of the New Universal Pact. I was wondering if you might like some literature?'

Now it's my turn to be discomforted. 'Thank you,' I mumble, taking the folded tract from her. 'That's very kind.'

But she doesn't go. Instead, she has a second question.

'Have you heard of the Israelites of the New Universal Pact?' Her gentle voice is barely above a whisper.

'No, I must confess, I haven't.'

When Peruvians began breaking with Rome, it wasn't just the Protestants that entered the fray. The Mormons, Seventh-Day Adventists and a shopping cart of other quasi-Christian groups began popping up too.

Old-school Catholics such as Father Nicolás write them all off as 'sects'. Even the mainstream Protestant denominations try to draw the line somewhere. The Brazil-based, tithe-taking Universal Church of the Kingdom of God is one of those that falls into the heretical category. In Peru, where it trades under the Pare de Sufrir (Stop with Suffering) label, its money-for-miracles formula makes it unwelcome in the official Christian community.

One man's sect is another man's salvation. I've tried to keep this adage in mind during my journey around Peru. But Queen Sánchez's explanation pushes this to the limit.

According to the pretty Old Testament acolyte, the Israelites of the New Universal Pact owe their origins to a direct encounter with the divine. In 1968, Yahweh appeared to Ezequiel Ataucusi Gamonal with a message. The unschooled cobbler was to establish God's chosen people on earth. The Almighty was done with the sinful sons of Abraham.

Obedient to the call, the Quechua-speaking Gamonal set off to find the Promised Land in the Peruvian jungle. His followers live together in communes, dress as the Israelites of old and observe the commands of Mosaic Law, right down to butchering animals as atonement sacrifices. Their services run from Friday at six o'clock in the evening until the same time the following day.

As Queen Sánchez speaks, I begin looking over the tract she's given me. It seems Zack is not the only one worried about impending judgement. Every two thousand years, God will come to wreak his vengeance, I read. And the time was nigh. Since 1978, the Sun has apparently been encroaching on the Earth at a rate of two and a half leagues every year. Mankind will be fried to death, all to the glory of their God.

'Can I be saved?' I ask, thoughts of the blistering Armageddon beginning to occupy my imagination.

'Why, of course. Just leave your current life of degenerate sin and join us on the path of truth that Maestro Ezequiel has prepared.' Her voice is still soft and delicate, as though she were letting me in on an amorous secret.

We continue talking about the coming apocalypse and my options for avoiding it when a man with a wispy beard joins the table. Dressed in similar long robes to Queen Sánchez, he introduces himself as Brother Jesús. Unlike his angelic companion, his manner is rough and pushy. He fleshes out the gory details of the scorching Last Days with prophetic precision.

I catch the waiter's eye just as Jesús is calling on me to repent. The aggressive proselytiser has brought a dark and menacing atmosphere to the conversation. Every minute that passes, I feel increasingly uneasy. I pay the bill as soon as it comes and make my excuses.

Bolting into the night, I imagine the smile on Zack's face. His prayer for fear and trembling is unfolding quicker than even he could have imagined.

Cajamarca

The parish church of Father Arana is located a dozen blocks south of Cajamarca's main square. Of all Peru's purveyors of religion, I imagine Bolívar favouring this protester priest.

As is still the case with most contemporary Peruvians, the Liberator conformed to the rites and rituals of the Church. He was baptised into its codes and buried by them too. Under the standards of Ayaviri, he'd even qualify as a 'good Catholic'. He went to church more or less regularly, respected the authority of the Pope and protected the 'Catholic, Apostolic, Roman' creed as the state religion. But Bolívar was primarily a secular-minded man. He spoke ill of royalist clerics because they stirred the people up against the cause of Independence. Religious fanatics worried him for their impact on civic cohesion. In essence, people's freedom in the here and now mattered more to him than their fate in the ever after.

Father Arana shares that spirit. I catch him at the end of a busy week. He's tired after travelling back from meetings with activist colleagues in Lima. A German film crew is packing up their equipment as I pass through into his modest office. The *padre* is much in demand ever since winning Peru's top human-rights prize a few years ago.

'Christ didn't announce God's good news within four walls,' he says, when I enquire about his religious philosophy. 'He preached out in the fields serving the people.'

This smacks of classic liberation theology. Developed during the rebel years of the 1960s, the Marxist-influenced doctrine inspired radical Catholics across the continent to put their faith into action. Their message was a simple one. The God of the Bible desired to redeem his people in *this* world, not just the next. Poverty, they argued, concerned the Almighty as much as purgatory. Some priests were so convinced that they swapped their cassocks for Kalashnikovs. Peru's own Shining Path revolutionaries counted men of the cloth among its early leaders.

In his mid-fifties, Father Arana left seminary school before liberation theology went into decline. The Vatican gradually grew concerned that the theory – developed in large part by the Peruvian Dominican priest, Gustavo Gutiérrez – was politicising the Church. Bishops were ordered to stamp it out. The 'preferential option for the poor,' much vaunted by the Church during the 1970s, was filed away on the canonical shelf. But vestiges can still be found, as the Cajamarca clergyman bears out.

'I joined the Church to become a priest, not a protestor,' Father

Arana says. 'But I found that I couldn't preach justice in the pulpit and then sit back while abuses happen.'

Soon after taking over a rural parish close to the colonial city of Cajamarca, in northern Peru, a newcomer joined his flock. Newmont, the Colorado-based extractive company, had come in search of treasure. Within a flash, South America's largest gold mine was operating on the parish lawn.

Complaints at the prelature door began as a trickle. When the mine's construction started dislodging people from their homes and a mercury spill contaminated their drinking water, the grievances turned into a flood. Taking up his parishioners' cause, the politicised *padre* set up an environmental activist group to lobby against the mining company.

'I came to see that many of these injustices require not only a pastoral and spiritual response but also a political and technical response,' he explains.

When he's not travelling by bus to and from Lima, he's jetting off to Colorado to harangue shareholders. The fact he spends more time on the picket line than in the pulpit doesn't appear to bother him or his parishioners. The dog-collar demonstrator maintains that fighting side by side with his congregants provokes a spiritual response: 'When I help the people, they feel closer to God.'

Father Arana might be comfortable in the vestments of theological activism, but back at the bishopric they're less sure. If nothing else, Newmont provides a tidy annual sum to the local seminary school. When the rebel churchman first started sounding off against the mine, his superiors shuffled him off to Rome for a two-year sabbatical. When he came back, they found a low-profile post for him in the university. Their strategy didn't work. The *padre* began mobilising the student population.

The Church authorities have repeatedly tried to censure him, but so far to no effect. He admits it would be easier to keep quiet: 'If I just announced God in heaven, I wouldn't have any problems. Only when you preach the love of God in this world do you face opposition.'

His fifteen-year fight has also been a thorn in the flesh for the mining company. A few weeks before our interview, Father Arana began noticing a conspicuous man following him. The stalker turned out to be an employee of the security firm hired by Newmont.

When police raided the firm's offices, they unearthed hundreds of photos of the priest and his campaign colleagues. The inept espionage agents had come up with an equally clumsy code for their spying operation, 'Operation Devil'.

Prayers can move mountains, the Bible teaches. So far, the invocatory approach hasn't worked for Father Arana. The miners continue boring deeper and deeper into the Earth, their appetite for bullion insatiable. He has no plans to stop petitioning his God on high though – nor to quit hassling the powers below.

Father Arana is closer to Peru's outcrop of new churches than either group would accept. Both are in the business of promising liberation through religion. In the supermarkets of faith, their packaging may be different. The God of the Cajamarca cleric is the Almighty One who smites the wicked and delivers justice to the poor. Peru's eclectic Protestant wing prefer the suffering Jesus who saves and the Holy Spirit who drums up miracles. But both are tapping into the human longing for spiritual succour.

Reflecting on the right to religious freedom, Bolívar's instinct was to allow individuals the free will to decide. Choosing the true religion is harder than inheriting it, especially with today's panoply of denominations to wade through. But Peruvians seem hungry for the search. The prize, they believe, is worth it. 'For the truth will set you free.'

Cajamarca is my exit point from Peru. Almost half a millennium ago, it served the same function for Atahualpa, king of the Incas.

The indigenous emperor had the misfortune of falling into the hands of the conquistador Francisco Pizarro and his band of Spanish adventurers. Even by the fabulous standards of Vargas Llosa's scriptwriter, Atahualpa's capture beggars belief. The Inca chief had just emerged victorious from a particularly sanguinary civil war. His battle-tested troops numbered eighty thousand. Under his control lay almost the entire Andean region, from Quito in the north to modern-day Chile in the south.

Pizarro, in contrast, had precisely one hundred and sixty men and not so much as a knighthood to his name. His nearest reinforcements were two thousand miles away in Panama. But he did have musket and shot, something the Inca warriors had never experienced before. The same was true for the Spaniards' cavalry. Tricking him into a tête-à-tête in the cloistered courtyard of the town's main square, the daredevil conquistadors succeeded in overcoming the Inca emperor and his royal bodyguard.

On that mid-November day in 1532, the Spanish reputedly hacked to death a staggering two thousand men. With the massacre in full swing, Pizarro led a separate swat team to seize Atahualpa. In exchange for the king's freedom, the conquistador negotiated a healthy ransom in gold – then, as now, the invader's metal of choice. Several months later, when the gold bullion was almost counted, the buccaneer Spaniard reneged on his word. Atahualpa was subjected to a mock trial and sentenced to death.

The court papers recorded the dastardly felony of idolatry. As legend tells it and custom had it, the native emperor was given an initial opportunity to convert. Already at their battle stations in the courtyard, Pizarro sent out a friar with a Bible to meet with Atahualpa.

Spanish chroniclers record the Inca king listening attentively. But the *padre*'s sermon fell on rocky ground. Atahaulpa wasn't impressed with a Christ that died. His gods, the sun and moon, never die. Nor did the Good Book convince him. Jeering that God's Word didn't speak, he threw the Bible on the ground. And so the key of history turned. From that moment on, it was war, Holy War.

I contemplate the story from the balcony of my hotel, looking out onto the two magnificent colonial churches that surround the city's main square. It was here that Atahualpa's story ended. Threatened with the stake, the king converted to Christianity at the very last moment. His sentence was commuted. They garrotted him instead.

Ahead of me lies Ecuador, once home to the Incas' northern king-dom. The relationship between South America's native peoples and the outside world started badly. Heading back into the Amazon, I want to see what has changed.

7

HIP CORDS AND FEDORAS

Ecuador and native peoples

Equality is incompatible with the personal service that has been imposed on native peoples, and equally incompatible with the hardships they have endured due to the miserable conditions in which they live.

SIMÓN BOLÍVAR, QUITO 1825

El Oriente

The jungle day starts early. When the night bus rolls into Coca at 6.30 a.m., the port town has its bed sheets kicked off and coffee on the boil. Day labourers sit huddled in twos and threes at the food stalls along the main street. Shoulder to shoulder along rickety wooden benches, they hunch their heads like flu victims over bowls of steaming soup. They eat in silence.

Across the street, restaurant diners are tucking into fried plantain and rice. A noisy, grime-layered television set rests on brackets above them, nailed fast to the wall against theft and earth tremors. From the flickering screen, the weather presenter trundles out his day's projections. Hazy start to the day, giving way to high temperatures. Humidity, saturating. No change there then. They tune back in for news of a grisly murder in Guayaquil, an Ecuadorian city so far away and so different from Coca that it may as well be in the steppes of Central Asia.

Back along the main strip, a newspaper vendor has taken up his position under a solitary traffic light. He looks mournfully down the road, waving day-old copies of *El Comercio* at drivers as they pass. The cattle-grid sound of shutters opening adds a metallic trill to the morning chorus as shopkeepers ready their stores. They station themselves on stools in their doorways, get comfortable and wait to wind the shutters down for the afternoon siesta hours.

The traffic in this Amazonian frontier town is still light. What has made it onto the roads wheezes and splutters lethargically down the sleepy high street. Recently woken, the vehicles stagger forward with the heavy, plodding steps of an overweight smoker making his way from bed to bathroom. For authenticity's sake, some even hack up black clods of diesel phlegm from breathless exhausts.

Our transport down the unpaved road into the jungle keeps to form. A beaten-up truck with tattered seats borrowed from an old bus, the suspension-less *ranchero* is built with durability, not comfort, in mind. As the pot-holed road crosses the Napo river and winds its way eastwards, the surrounding jungle grows thicker and more verdant. I watch the passing trees, their trunks as stout as ship masts, their tops leafy and luxuriant.

Soon my eyes begin to cloud, and the passing foliage merges into one long blur of arboreal greens. Only the occasional wayside settlement breaks the spell, sudden specks of colour carved into the forest screen. These wooden shacks play home to Ecuador's poor immigrants. The road has brought them. Well, to be more precise, what lies at the end of the road: oil – copious, sticky, oceanic reservoirs of the stuff.

A fat, rusty pipeline testifies to the black gold that lies under this remote patch of the Ecuadorian Amazon. The pipe's obdurate bulk snakes along the curves and crevices of the roadside, a bulging metal eyesore that scars a path from here to the Pacific coast. Thousands of gallons of oil travel along its crude-clotted arteries every day. Its high-temperature contents make it the perfect place to hang out wet washing on a sunless afternoon.

An hour out of Coca, we pass a pumping station and clamp our ears at the thunderous sound of the generators. Fuelled by the same million-year-old sludge so recently extracted from below the forest floor, the hulking pumps push the pipeline's cargo along on its undulating journey to the sea. Residual gas left over from the compression process burns off in molten red flares. Three columns of fire blaze above the jungle canopy, the incandescent flames fighting and flickering in the fresh morning breeze like giant garden torches at a summer barbecue.

Pendulous trucks carrying bulky maintenance equipment rattle past us in the opposite direction. Oil-company workers bump along behind them in their grey Chevrolet jeeps, talking into two-way radios as they drive. They wear tight-fit jeans and denim shirts, the petroleum cowboys of Ecuador's Oriente.

Brothels and bars have sprung up for the off-shift hours, mingling with the mission huts and company-sponsored schools that also dot the highway. This is the infamous Vía Auca, the gateway to the Amazon – and arguably the harbinger of its demise.

Río Tigüino

Our three-hour journey ends abruptly at an iron bridge. The fast, coffee-liqueur waters of the River Tigüino cascade below it.

Thirty years ago, this area was virgin forest; now, the ugly steel cylinders and squat portacabins of an oil depot line the river's banks. Across the road lie the single-storey barracks of the Ecuadorian Army. A bored soldier stands guard by the perimeter fence swatting at mosquitoes. Today, all is quiet on the western Amazonian front. It's not always so. Rarely does a week go past without a roadblock that requires clearing or an oil spillage in need of sorting.

Two tall metal signposts stand like silent sentries at the bridge. One informs us that we have arrived at the Manpawe tourist project, the object of which appears to be a thatched, oval dining area down to our left. The sign leans at an angle and is on the point of toppling over.

On the second signpost, a large 'Y' is painted in white. To the right lies an oil facility, which, according to the lettering, takes the name of 'Petrobell'. My imagination briefly toys with the name, recasting it as an oil version of Tinkerbell, a lovable fairy at the bottom of the garden. The reality, as always, is far cruder. The nine-letter moniker refers to the less than lovable Canadian company that runs the plant.

Off to the left stretches the genuine article, an authentic children's book fairyland. The Huaorani Territory. Ordnance Survey's cartographers never made it this far. There are no distance charts, no maps, no grid coordinates, and no phone numbers for emergency services.

We hang a left.

After a quick lunch of chicken and rice, we are gliding eastwards in a motorised steel canoe, Huaorani-bound. Behind us, we leave the Vía Auca and the invasive hand of modern man. It will be a week before we see a bridge or road again.

Among Ecuador's eleven indigenous nationalities and their various sub-divisions, the Huaorani remain among the most untouched. They have only become 'civilised' within the past two generations. Before that, they lived for hundreds of years as Amazonian nomads.

Traditionally, their territory stretched over two million hectares, covering what map-makers today demark as Ecuador's Orellana, Pastaza and Napo provinces. Huao, their native tongue, shows no linguistic connection to other indigenous languages in the region. Nor does it include words for modern contraptions such as the personal computer, the combustion engine or chewing gum.

Their first contact with the outside world came at the end of the nineteenth century, when Brazilian farmers arrived in search of rubber. Sustained contact would have to wait for the arrival of Protestant missionaries half a century later. Only then did the Huaorani give up their nomadic ways and build themselves semi-permanent settlements alongside the jungle's rivers. With the introduction of hoes and basic husbandry, they set about cultivating garden plots of yucca and plantain. They also learned to swim.

The incursion of outsiders brought with it a raft of undeniably negative consequences too. Disease topped the list. Within two decades, the total Huaorani population had dropped to as few as eight hundred people thanks to the flu and other everyday Western illnesses. Internecine conflict also took its toll on the tribal demographic. The Huaorani like a good family fist fight. Their alternative name, Auca, comes from the Quichua for 'savage'.

All foreigners – that is to say, all non-Huaorani – represent potential targets of the tribe's warring ways, especially if they threaten their traditional territory. Huaorani culture historically holds outsiders to be cannibals. Legend had it that *cohouri,* white men, would one day come and eat them. When five North American missionaries floated down the river in canoes half a century ago, they presumed that day had arrived. Taking no chances, the tribesmen finished off the visitors with an avalanche of spears.

Father Alejandro Labaca, a Spanish missionary priest, shared a similar fate in 1987. A friend of the Huaorani, he was flown in by an oil-exploration company to negotiate with the neighbouring Tagaeri tribe. The sixty-seven-year-old priest had first begun visiting the communities along the river Cononaco a decade beforehand. His journals record the Huaorani as 'totally friendly, open [and] happy'. When the chopper returned a few days later, the pilot found the missionary mediator in exactly the same spot. Only now, seventeen spears pierced his spreadeagled body. The autopsy revealed eighty-nine individual stab wounds. Oil workers venturing into Huaorani territory have since met with similar treatment. Nowadays, with the wisdom of hindsight, they generally choose to keep away.

Today, Huaorani aggression tends to focus more on the timber trade. Several reports of illegal loggers found slumped over their chainsaws have circulated in the national press over recent years. Tourists, I am assured, have so far remained off limits. We have over one hundred and fifty miles of winding Amazonian tributary to reconnoitre before that salient fact is put to the test.

The trip takes us the best part of two days. During that time, we float lazily downriver and watch the wildlife on the bank. Halfway through the first afternoon, the river broadens as it merges with the honey-brown river Cononaco. I rely on Gulío, our eagle-eyed guide, to point out what my urban eyesight would otherwise miss: river turtles basking in the afternoon sun, caimans brooding in the shallows, capybara rodents rummaging for roots, monkeys playing in the tree tops, tapirs taking an afternoon bath.

Up above is where the real action is taking place. Scientists estimate that over six hundred bird species inhabit this corner of the Upper Amazon, more than four times the number found on Ecuador's Galapagos Islands. Soaring high on thermal currents, perched on a ceiba tree, diving for fish, skimming for bugs on the river surface – it's avian heaven.

Gulío helps me identify the most common of our two-winged travelling companions. The shape of a tail feather or bend of the bill is enough for him to distinguish one sub-species of egret, eagle or toucan from another. I'm a confident birder in a British country garden. But the first time a cobalt-winged parakeet flies overhead, the inadequacy of my tropical ornithological training becomes apparent. Together with the macaws, these raucous plumes of colour provide us with a constant escort during our journey downstream. By the end of the first day, my bird-spotting list has expanded to many-banded araçals, green Amazon kingfishers, orange-faced caracaras, white-banded swallows, black vultures, yellow-legged tiger herons and blue-headed parrots. Our boat driver, known as Casi Guapo, Almost Handsome, mimics the birds' guttural squawks as he navigates.

Armies of butterflies add further texture to the jungle canvas. We make playful attempts to catch blue morphs as they flutter by the canoe. Their flapping wings, painted jet black below and phosphorescent blue above, resemble the flash of a police siren. Butterfly collectors pay hundreds of dollars for these dazzling gems. They skip easily through our lunging grasps, leaving us doubly empty-handed.

The meandering canoe trip also allows me time to get to know my fellow cannibals. Our tour comprises four *cohouri:* a trio of fifty-something North Americans and me.

Kevin and Rick are schoolboy buddies from Seattle. There exists an endearing, childhood chumminess between them, born from fishing the same streams and chasing the same girls while growing up. As well as lifelong friends, they are also work colleagues. Kevin is a general contractor, and, as of last year, the semi-retired Rick his stooge. Sitting side by side in the bow of the slim canoe, they natter away continually like a pair of old women. Both men are keen naturalists, and they are soon competing with Gulío as the boat's top spotters. They chat about termite nests, birds' migratory patterns and the building merits of tropical hardwoods.

Suzan also likes to talk, although chiefly about herself. Her knowledge of wildlife doesn't even cover a back garden. She thinks a caiman is a Caribbean Island and wonders if flying monkeys have wings. Yet on Suzan's specialist topic – namely, Suzan – she is a world specialist. With the boys engrossed in the passing flora and fauna, it falls to me to sit next to her and listen to her life story, a two-day epic that leaves me tossing up between jumping ship or blood-letting mutiny.

Suzan has found herself an agent and is in the process of writing up her transition from Los Angeles-based music executive to hippy globetrotter. She shoots me a pitying look when I start scribbling down one of Gulío's explanations about the jungle's monkey species (there are nine in total, including the howling, spider, *capuchino* and squirrel monkeys).

'I am not a fact-based writer so much. I'm more, like, an observationalist,' she informs me.

Her point made, she closes her eyes and promptly dozes off.

A blissful moment of rare silence follows. The sun is dropping in the sky, the late-afternoon rays playing the alchemist, converting the river surface into a sea of shimmering silver. The canoe rocks gently from side to side. I too nod off. It is late on the second day, and we are all tired. I dream, fitfully, of land beneath my feet and mud between my toes.

Bameno

I wake with a start to Gulío shouting: 'Bameno, round the next bend.'

Blurry-headed, our imminent arrival among the Huaorani suddenly feels far too soon. Casi Guapo is steering us around the final bend. A thatched house comes into view. My heart jumps to my mouth, while an intravenous shot of terror mixed with curiosity pumps through my bloodstream.

An elegant, elderly man is standing high on the bank at the entrance to the village, watching. He is wearing nothing but a thin jockstrap. A spindly, bare-breasted woman stands behind him. Higher up the bank is a gaggle of children. They are all staring at the river-weary *cohouri* with blank expressions. And then our canoe is ramming the muddy bank. We have come to the end of the left-hand fork.

A short man with broad shoulders and the beginnings of a paunch boards the front of the boat. He has long flowing hair down to the middle of his back. Across his left breast runs the blue-ink tattoo of a harpy eagle. A smaller, second tattoo covers the triceps of his left arm. 'Comando', the faint lettering spells out. He is wearing a pair of cut-off jeans and black wellington boots. Gulío appears to know him, and the two exchange greetings in Huao. He turns to smile at us, and we all respond with what we hope are ingratiating grins. Then he shoves a booted foot against the bank and the canoe is heading back across stream.

The butterscotch River Cononaco is fuller now, stretching perhaps two hundred feet from side to side. Its far bank consists of a muddy slope as high as an articulated lorry. An old woman, all bones and elbows, is cleaning pots and pans on a log platform at the river's edge. Silt water circles around her knees. She is wearing what look like men's underpants and no top. A garland of plastic necklaces falls conspicuously between her flat breasts. Above her, looking down from the bank, stands the remainder of our welcome committee: three women, all similarly attired. A little girl is holding her mother's hand. The infant is the only one with a T-shirt on. She is also the only one smiling.

Gulío forms us into a chain gang up the slippery bank, and we begin the arduous task of unloading: tents, food, tarpaulin, cooking utensils, toilet paper, drinking water, fizzy drinks, gas cylinders. The Huaorani women look on, seemingly bemused by the excess of the *cohouris'* trappings. As we busy ourselves making camp, the three women increase to eight.

Gulío takes the lead in brokering an introduction. Like kinder-garten pupils at the school gate, we hang back a few yards until he signals for us to come forward. At the centre of the group is the eld-erly lady we'd seen previously. She welcomes us with a delicate handshake and a wide, toothless grin. A scraggly yellow T-shirt now covers her scrawny frame. She wears the dirty extra-large top as a dress. It carries the image of one of the presidential candidates in the last elections. I wonder if she knows that the man with the broad grin and spotless coiffure is now her president. Would it make any difference to her if she did?

She appears highly animated and engages in a rolling, candescent commentary about our individual appearance. My glasses, Kevin's camera and Rick's handlebar moustache all garner her attention. But it is not until Suzan steps forward that her interest truly peaks. The jungle matriarch examines her jewellery, her clothes, her hair, her skin, pressing and prodding all the while. She traces the tattoo on her shin, saying something unintelligible in Huao that has the other women laughing hysterically.

Suzan is loving it and tells us later over dinner about the 'deep spiritual bond' she feels she has established with the Huaorani women. In reality, the old lady seems more intent on relieving Suzan of her large silver ring than on honing their spiritual connection. They enter into a playful tug-of-war, a tight-lipped determination belying the grandmother's good-natured teasing. Just as it looks as if she might wrench Suzan's index finger from its socket, a wooden canoe carrying a party of fellow villagers arrives on the bank below.

Awa, as we later learn the elderly lady is called, takes the occasion to break out into song. From her wrinkled body arises a beautiful, primordial chant. Her voice sounds as old as the forest, her lyrics borrowed from the wind and the rain. The Huaorani love to sing. They welcome the sun with song and likewise bid it farewell. We stand in a small circle, watching, listening, mesmerised by the tune's rhythmic force and Awa's trance-like rapture. On the edge of the group, a woman is stripping down a pile of palm leaves to extract the string inside. Working with factory-line efficiency, a high-pitched whoop temporarily throws her rhythm. Awa's song has finished.

Almost imperceptibly, night has crept up on us. Pitch darkness obscures the far bank. There is no street lighting in Bameno, only candles. Gulío ushers us towards the largest of the four wooden huts on the bank. It houses a single, bare room. Empty spaces in the walls serve as windows. Cobwebs hang from the rafters, and the earthen floor is sodden with rainwater that's leaked through the palm-leaf roof.

As we wait for supper, Kevin and Rick make a friend of an inquisitive oval-shaped bird perched on the window frame. It allows them to stroke its velvet black neck. Crooning with pleasure, their feathered friend lets out a deep-throated gurgle, a perfect mimicry of the canoe's outboard motor. Its throbbing cry excites the jealousy of its mate, who is carefully guarding her chick on the ground below. Ruffling her ash-grey feathers, she leaps onto the windowsill and pecks at her flirtatious husband. The childhood buddies are quickly left without their new plaything as he jumps back down and dutifully rejoins his dependants.

For the duration of our stay in the village, this curious little family of great-winged trumpeteers is never more than a few yards away – pecking one another, cleaning themselves and, in the case of the two parents, endlessly squabbling. We spot other domesticated wildlife living in Bameno: macaws, an infant squirrel monkey, a pair of turtles, an adult anaconda and even a full-grown harpy eagle caught as a baby. Perhaps because of their hilarious matrimonial tiffs, the trumpeteer family are the only ones treated with the true affection of pets. The remainder live on a leash or in a cage, used as tourist curiosities in the good times and lunch in the bad.

The soup has reached the boil, and the aroma of cooked vegetables wafts across the room. A gnawing appetite awakens inside me. Food has preoccupied me ever since we left the bridge. As soon as one meal finishes, I find myself thinking about the next. For the Huaorani, food also represents an all-consuming issue. Big game is scarcely seen around Bameno these days. For the richer hunting grounds, they must travel a day or two by canoe. The provision of vegetables and fruits depends on the forest's generosity.

After the meal, Rick pulls out cigarettes for a post-prandial smoke. Three Huaorani men immediately cadge some off him. They puff at them contentedly, none of them inhaling. Meanwhile, Suzan is at the other end of the table doing her best to communicate with a group of three or four women. 'India,' she says in her loud, laboured New Yorker accent, as they yet again point at her ring. 'Me buy in In-di-a.' She cackles with laughter. Her audience look bemused. She persists with the approach as they touch the other accessories attached to various parts of her body. 'Chi-na.' 'Vi-et-nam.' 'Guat-e-ma-la.' 'Palm Sp-rin-gs.' With every new place, her giggles intensify. The women look at the strange, walking shopping centre with even greater curiosity.

Awa approaches the group, and they shift down the bench to make room for her. As the eldest, the right to speak falls to her. She begins an elaborate tale about a trip to Cuenca that she'd made with her husband and son a few years ago. Their travel and lodging had been paid for by the Central Bank of Ecuador, who wanted to use the indigenous trio for an advertisement highlighting the country's diversity. Awa starts throwing her frail sparrow body up and down on the bench. The next moment, she is wrapping her arms around herself as if shivering to the core, all the time jabbering away in rapid-fire Huao.

'She says the journey by bus was long and cold,' translates the youngest woman in the group, seemingly the only one with any command of Spanish.

Awa is now tripping. She barely stops to breathe. Like a mime artist on amphetamines, she acts out her first experience of travelling by elevator. She jumps from the bench, crouches down on her haunches and then stretches herself up until she is standing on tip-toe, all five feet of her straining to the stars. Then comes the downward leg: pangs of terror, knees shaking, prayers to Heaven, joy at landing. She describes the houses and roads and cars and churches, oblivious to the fact that we understand not a word. Her flailing body actions are enough for everyone to get the gist, and she carries on unimpeded, at one stage even dropping into song again. After fifteen minutes, she is spent and retires to the far end of the bench.

'She went to the city. She never thought she would before she died. She enjoyed it,' says the laconic translator.

'But she prefers the jungle, no?' Rick interjects.

Awa barks something curt and rude-sounding back at him. 'Of course not!' the translator replies, blank-faced.

At the other end of the table, Kevin and I are struggling to communicate with two Huaorani men. One is the tattooed gentleman who boarded our canoe earlier. The other is a younger man, with gap-teeth, a large, flat nose and shoulder-length hair.

After some basic interrogation, we learn that they are called Guinto and Caminga respectively. They've been hired by Gulío to act as our 'native guides'. Their constant company over the coming days proves an education. We learn that Guinto can imitate almost any bird or animal in the forest. He can also weave a palm-leaf basket strong enough to carry five kilos of berries in six minutes flat. Caminga, on the other hand, can shin up a bark-less tree with bare feet. He is also capable of determining the size, weight and probable location of a peccary from a muddy footprint. The skill set of both these jungle men also stretches to carving out canoes from a single tree trunk, building houses from scratch, skinning a tapir and, naturally, killing things.

I try to broach the subject of the Huaorani's murderous reputation several times with Guinto but find him reticent on the matter. The breakthrough comes during a walk through the jungle on our third day in Bameno. He's talking about the best way to kill a pig and makes a throat-cutting motion with the forefinger of his right hand.

'*Petroleros?*' I ask. 'You, kill?' I copy his hand gesture, drawing a straight line under my chin.

'*Sí,*' he replies, grinning. 'Now, no problem in Bameno.'

He begins a convoluted story about a raiding party with Kempery, the village chief, back when oil prospectors first moved into the area in the 1970s.

'One dead,' he says, repeating the slicing gesture. 'Others . . .'

He throws his hand out, palm flat, and flicks his fingers forwards and upwards. The sense of the action is obvious. The remainder had, very wisely, fled for their lives.

Downriver

For all the talk of bloodletting, the only life I saw snuffed out was that of a twenty-five-pound spider monkey.

It happened on a scheduled hunting trip with our two Huaorani guides. The previous day, we had travelled four hours downstream from the village and set up camp on a sandy beach.

The area was teeming with wildlife. At nightfall, we had taken the canoe and our flashlights and gone spying for caiman on the riverbank, their red, pinball eyes glinting back at us from the shallows like the infrared sighting on a sniper's rifle. In the morning, I awoke to the crazed, whooping laughter of a band of howler monkeys in the forest behind.

I pushed my head out of the tent. A thin mist hung over the river. Guinto and Caminga were already up and impatient to get going. Usually the Huaorani hunt from first light to early afternoon. With the *cohouri* in tow, our hunting posse left after a leisurely breakfast, thereby breaking custom by the late hour and our full bellies. Rick decided to stay behind, preferring to spend the morning fishing for piranha. Suzan, on the other hand, was on hunger strike and was refusing to come out of her tent.

'I'll totally, like, freak if I see a dead animal,' she had announced the previous evening over dinner.

Guinto leads the way. Like Kevin and I, he is still wearing his pair of standard-issue wellingtons. Above, he wears a T-shirt and shorts. The *Comando* swishes and swipes at the undergrowth ahead of us, carving out a path with his machete. Caminga brings up the rear. Unlike Guinto, he prefers to go barefoot in the jungle. His feet looked like paddles, thin at the ankle before widening out into a pair of splayed waders. So much tree-climbing has made his big toes distended, like two dislocated thumbs pointing outwards.

Caminga also wears shorts and a shirt, although he discards the latter after only a few minutes, making it into a bandana and tying it round his head. It falls to him to carry the blowgun. He holds the two-and-a-half-metre instrument flat on his shoulder. The method enables him to duck under branches and swerve through the foliage without a snag.

We walk fifty yards, stop and listen. We wait perhaps two or three minutes. Then Guinto signals us forward, pointing his hand forward like a platoon leader on night patrol. Fifty yards later, we halt again. Ears pricked. This start-stop process continues for the best part of an hour.

'You hear the rushing wind? Monkeys ahead,' Guinto says.

I can hear nothing, only the usual orchestra of insects and the pumping of my own heart. Caminga has dropped back and is also listening intently. None of us utters a sound. The two Huao huntsmen begin making signs to one another and point into the bush off to our right. Guinto cups his hand to his mouth. From the back of his throat springs forth the guttural cry of a monkey. The noise reminds me of the sharp yap of a terrier pup.

We wait. No reply. He repeats the performance, this time lowering the pitch. The sound is harsher, more violent, close to the croaking cry of the macaw. Still nothing, but their body language shows a shift in gear. Their movements are quicker, their eyes and ears alert. I presume we are growing closer to our prey.

We continue onwards at a half jog. Trees and branches brush by. Brambles scratch at my legs. Guinto and Caminga run looking upwards, necks angled towards the treetops and lunch. We, the *cohouri* reserve unit, sweat and pant behind them, eyes down, navigating the roots and fallen branches on the forest floor. Then Caminga, who has taken the lead, stops abruptly and throws up his arm. In a wheezing bundle, Kevin and I crash into him from behind. We are standing in a gully, at the bottom of which trickles an emerald-green stream.

'Up there. See?' I follow the line of Caminga's outstretched finger, but can't make out a thing. Only leaves and more leaves.

Then Kevin spots some movement in the canopy overhead and guides me where to look. My eye settles on the subject of our hour-long chase: a full-size howler monkey sitting high on an out-stretched branch. He's watching us through the leafy camouflage with angry suspicion. Rattled by our presence, the perturbed primate grabs at a nearby bough and starts thrashing at it and barking down at us. I feel pumped, my whole body coursing with adrenalin. Our Huaorani guides, by contrast, seem downbeat.

'Howler. Not very tasty. We wait for spider monkeys. Spider monkeys very tasty,' Guinto explains, licking his lips and patting his rounded belly.

I look around for a makeshift seat and park myself on the moss-covered tree stump. Flies buzz around us. Soon everyone is sitting down, all of us slapping at our arms and legs and necks. Guinto points to a pile of half-chewed fruits by the trunk of an ungurahua palm, evidence that a group of monkeys has recently been through this way. We'll hunker down here and wait for them to regroup, he advises.

Caminga sees the break in proceedings as a good opportunity to fart. His sudden flatulence has all four of us giggling. Civilised or otherwise, it pleases me to know that lavatory humour is shared by men of all cultures.

As we sit there on the jungle floor in the middle of the Amazon, I wonder what other universal, transcendent themes we as men could have in common. Football, I surmise, might be one. A few days before, I'd spent an enjoyable but exhausting hour kicking a ball about with Guinto and Caminga's two boys on Bameno's water-logged pitch. The fact that puddles came up to our knees in places only added to the fun.

Drinking? Huao men are certainly not averse to the occasional tipple. Every Huaorani household has a pot of *chicha* at the ready in case a friend or family member should pop by. Created from the fermented offshoot of masticated yucca, Huaorani 'beer' has a striking resemblance to homebrew cider gone awry – viscerally sour, vomit yellow and prone to solid lumps of indecipherable origin.

Guinto resolves my question by broaching the one unanimous subject of male interest: women. He does so with remarkable candour. His confession breaks our waiting silence and hangs there, briefly, trapped in the humid jungle air:

'Last night, I went to Suzan's tent.'

As it happens, his secret revelation is not news. The whole campsite was aware of his midnight escapade. It was impossible not to be, so shrill and piercing were Suzan's screams on seeing Guinto leering into her tent. Our late-night Romeo had got no further than unzipping the flysheet. He did not seem to have taken the rejection badly. If his cheeky smile meant anything, then he actually seemed to consider the whole incident rather entertaining.

'No, No!' he squeals, imitating the petrified cries of his Amazon Queen.

Guinto's impression of Suzan earns him a fraternal laugh from all of us. Kevin commiserates with our longhaired guide, assuring him that what looks like a rebuff is really a lucky escape.

When Caminga gets up to go, I follow. He climbs out of the gully and heads into the surrounding foliage. I trot along behind. Sweating, panting, flies, brambles; it soon turns into a standard afternoon jog in the jungle. Five minutes in, Caminga picks up pace. Our hunters had been right: the monkeys had calmed down and regrouped a short way ahead of us. Caminga is shaking his hands up and down like an overexcited flight controller. I've no clue as to the meaning of his desperate sign language. Fortunately, Guinto understands well enough. He branches off left, Kevin on his heels.

We are running at full pace now, crashing through the bushes with no concern for keeping quiet. The chase is back on.

Up ahead, the monkeys are engaged in their own frenetic, pendulous race through the treetops. Deftly they navigate the forest ceiling, swinging from looping branch to looping branch. We race below, louder and with less grace, but catching up on them with every step. A stream obstructs our path, although Caminga doesn't break stride. Over he goes with the consummate grace of a leaping gazelle. My long-jump effort ends less spectacularly, with one foot lodged in the muddy bank and another slipping back into the water. With one foot now sloshing around in my wellington, I pull myself up and stumble onwards.

My hands and knees are now caked in earthy red slime. Caminga is charging forwards with not so much as a glance behind him. Nimbly sidestepping tree trunks – to the left, to the right, to the right again – he could be mistaken for an ace college quarterback. I drop off the pace; down a ditch, up a bank, over a log, through a bush I go. For a second, I lose the fleet-footed Caminga. *Where is he?* I swivel round. He's gone, vamoose, enveloped by the jungle. I look around in a mild panic for Guinto and Kevin.

With relief, I hear snapping twigs and rushing footsteps off to my left, at perhaps thirty metres distance. They are running like hurdlers, bent double, beating a trail through the undergrowth. A rather feeble relay partner, I tag along.

Fifty yards more and we catch sight of Caminga again. This time he's standing stock still, his heels dug into the ground, planted a few feet apart. The blowpipe is pressed to his lips and pointing upwards, stiff and straight like a flagpole on a parade ground. His left hand holds the bamboo weapon tight to his mouth. His right he uses to bring balance and to give direction to his aim.

A rapid gulp of air inflates his checks. The veins in his neck bulge. He rocks his head back an inch and then unleashes an Exocet blow. His whole body whiplashes forward. The dart bursts soundlessly from the end of the bamboo pipe, slicing the air with aerodynamic efficiency. It's a miss.

Quickly and with no sign of consternation, he reloads. He removes a second dart from the sheath hanging around his neck. Dangling from the same string is a set of piranha jaws. He takes the homemade fish scissors and etches a groove around the dart about an inch from the tip. He then reaches into the third and final element of his homemade arsenal – a hardened fruit shell – and pulls out a bud of fluffy cotton. This he rolls between his thumb and forefinger, wraps it around the dart's base and shoves the now-armed arrow into the blowgun. Again he takes aim and fires. Again he misses. Immediately he sets to preparing a third dart. Even a good hunter needs four or five shots to hit their target.

The process of reloading takes no more than fifteen seconds. It is time enough for me to try to catch a glimpse of what he is aiming at. I look up and spot the object in his sights at the first time of trying. It is an adult spider monkey. I can just make out its colouring: the back, black; the chest, a speckled white.

Sitting motionless on its haunches, the monkey is resting on a sturdy branch directly above us. It doesn't appear to be looking our way, although it must be alert to our presence. The shot is a clear one thanks to a gap in the trees. The monkey is preposterously high up, at least one hundred and twenty feet from where we are standing.

The chances of Caminga hitting it strike me as highly remote. If I were a betting man, I'd give him a ten-to-one chance. It is lucky I'm not. With the third dart, his aim is truer. The arrow plugs into the monkey's thigh.

'Woooo!! You're the man!'

I'm jumping up on the spot like a football fan celebrating a last-minute goal. I hold up my palm to high-five the hero of the moment. The gesture confuses Caminga, but he grips my hand anyway and crunches my fingers in a celebratory handshake. I carry on whooping like an idiot.

Caminga, by contrast, is intent on acting cool and professional. Even so, he can't help the corners of his mouth curling upwards with involuntary pride. Meanwhile, on the branch above, the monkey is looking understandably agitated. It is scratching at the arrow with its padded fingers. The dart snaps, leaving the top two inches above the piranha serration lodged in its upper leg.

Now Guinto steps up. He takes the blowpipe from Caminga and also raises it to his mouth. It takes him three attempts to strike home as well. He catches the monkey in the chest. With the second blow, the embattled primate finally loses its balance. Instead of falling off its perch, it hangs there, suspended by its tail which is latched fast to the branch. Dangling below it, its hands and feet punch the air – one two, one two – just as a boxer might in a pre-fight warm-up.

Minutes pass. Down below, Guinto is clapping and shouting, provoking the animal to continue its fight. The two darts are tipped with a powerful anaesthetic. What the monkey doesn't know is that with every punch its heart is pumping the poisonous bark extract through its bloodstream. Gradually, it grows drowsy, its punches now more like the sluggish jabs of a boxer on the ropes. At last, it falls still.

Guinto stops with his shouting. For a few seconds, the scene is motionless. No one and nothing stirs. And then, as we are standing there looking up, our necks straining, the quivering shape of an infant monkey runs along the branch and approaches its inert parent. A few feet away, the baby stops. It looks down, bewildered, and then scuttles back to its hiding place. It is the briefest and saddest of farewells.

Seconds later, the body of the immobilised monkey is hurtling through the trees towards the ground. It lands with a thump. Straight away, Caminga is on top of it. He takes the tail in one hand, bends it over the monkey's back and then ties it in a loop around its neck. We watch from a couple of paces away as he fashions a shoulder bag from the stricken animal.

Despite its fall, the monkey is still breathing. Its rib cage rises up and down with short, shallow breaths, and its nostrils flare ever so slightly. Yellow mucus dribbles from its mouth and digested fruits from its backside. Two black, terrified eyes stare up at us.

It makes for a sorry sight, but the men are thinking about supper and don't seem to notice. Then the monkey's eyes cloud over, its breathing stops and the life spills out of it. The hunt is over.

Caminga indicates for me to pick up the dead creature. I do so with hesitation. The body is still warm. Its fingers are black and rubbery, the wrinkled hands of a grandmother wearing thick washing-up gloves. I slip my arm through the improvised shoulder strap and haul up the corpse. It is heavier than I imagined. Caminga nods his approval.

For the first time, I feel part of the hunting party, albeit as the poor monkey's hearse.

Months later, when I am back in Buenos Aires, I pull out a photo that Kevin had taken of Caminga and me together.

Standing there next to a half-naked tribesman with a spider monkey around my shoulder, I struggle to recognise myself. In my wellington boots and a white Adidas T-shirt, I cut an incongruous figure.

Caminga, in contrast, appears entirely in his element. His face is serious for the camera. His thick fringe falls down over one eye. He holds his blowpipe firmly in his right hand, planting it into the ground just as an African warrior would his spear. There is something almost regal about him, in his unblinking stare, in his puffed-out chest, in his powerful shoulders.

The more I look at the photo, the more it strikes me that there, in that corner of the jungle, at that moment in time, he and Guinto are the undisputed lords of the forest.

It sets me pondering how long their reign can last. The question sticks with me for the days and weeks to come. Every day, the outside world encroaches ever closer, bumping down the Vía Auca, infringing inch by inch into the world of the Huaorani. It comes innocuously: in the shape of battery-powered torches, polyester shirts, plastic hairclips and penknives. After the recent visit of a foreign film crew, one Bameno household now even boasts a diesel generator, a fridge freezer and a dozen empty vodka bottles lined up on the windowsill.

The hand of the *cohouri* is not always so innocuous, as the pipelines and oil spills go to prove. Bameno itself is the product of the oil boom. Four decades ago, Kempery and his clan were living deep within the jungle without contact or care for the outside world. Their 'discovery' came in 1970. It's not a date they commemorate.

Three years later, the tribe were being carted off to make room for the intruding oil companies. They eventually resettled in Bameno, home to a disused airstrip built by a French prospecting firm. The Huao chieftain built his house at the end of the grassy runway. Small tourist-laden aircraft still land in his backyard from time to time.

The Huaorani are by no means the only Ecuadorian tribe affected by the world's insatiable thirst for fossil fuels. The Cofan, Secoya, Huarani, Siuna and Quichua tribes know only too well what oil exploration can bring. In the mid-1960s, the US company Chevron-Texaco won a concession not far to the north of Bameno. Over the next two and a half decades, the company dumped millions of gallons of crude and drilling wastewater into waterways and unlined open pits. The contamination spread over fifteen hundred square miles of once spotless rainforest. Today, levels of skin disease, cancer and reproductive disorders among the indigenous groups in the area are off the charts. They've been waiting since 1991 for the courts to grant them compensation. The trial remains ongoing.

Along with constant fights over territory, another battleground has formed in the classroom. Ecuador's indigenous people, who represent around a quarter of the total population, had to wait until the 1980s to win the right of a bilingual education for their children. Up until then, Spanish was the universal language of learning and Western Christianity its dominating ethic.

Bameno remains a rarity for having a Huao teacher who instructs his pupils in his maternal tongue. In most indigenous communities, native dialects are relegated to the foreign-language class, much like French or German in an English-speaking school. Indigenous children learn that their language is second-class from the moment they can speak.

If the rest of Ecuador is anything to go by, then the clock is ticking for the Huaorani. The country's once rich patchwork of native cultures is fraying, and fraying fast.

La Sierra

Two in every three Ecuadorians consider themselves *mestizo,* the generic term for those of mixed indigenous–Hispanic blood. Homogenised and proud of it, their wardrobes are full of jackets and jeans, not ponchos and pleated skirts. They shop in malls and watch *Latin American Idol* on television.

The fortresses of *mestizo* culture are the metropolises. In big cities such as Quito and Guayaquil, modern office blocks and fast-food restaurants play to the needs of this dominant demographic.

As urban imprints go, Ecuador's indigenous are hard to spot. They mark the cityscape as street vendors and the occasional token statue. In the coastal regions, their impact is equally peripheral. Around five millennia before the Spanish arrival, Ecuador's Pacific coastline was home to the Valdivians, a culture almost as ancient as Mexico's Mayas. On the pristine beaches where they had once gazed out at the ocean and worked wonders at their potter's wheels, foreign sunbathers now lounge and *cholo* fishermen put out to sea.

Outside the depths of Ecuadorian rainforests, it requires a trip to the Andean highlands to scout out the remaining boltholes of *indígenismo*. For a fortnight, I wandered through the hills of Ecuador's central sierra on just such a search.

In the shadows of the snow-crested Tungurahua and Cotopaxi volcanoes, I find traces: remote rural communities, lost in the clouds, hidden down mule tracks, where adobe houses predominate and Quichua dialects prevail. Living off the land, these descendants of the Inca wars today survive by growing vegetables, rearing livestock and keeping themselves to themselves. Life isn't easy; the summers are cold, and the winters freezing. Clean drinking water and electricity remain the exception. Unsurprisingly, people are leaving in droves, heading down the hills in their thick blanket shawls and calf-length trousers to build a future for themselves in the towns and cities.

Saquisilí, a market town forty-seven miles south of Quito, is facing just such an exodus. Its population of over twenty thousand people is split roughly two to one between indigenous and *mestizos*. Thursday is market day and a good time to gauge the town's mood.

If Segundo Monta is any judge, it's not good. He runs a hat stall in one of Saquisilí's eight markets. He has been in the job thirty years. Segundo's felt hats only come in one shape, a thin-brimmed oval fedora typical to the region's indigenous population. As a concession to customer taste, he varies the colour. Shoppers can choose between blue, black, green and brown. He recently introduced a smaller version in red for children. But the locals aren't buying.

'Business is bad these days,' Segundo moans. 'Folk just don't wear sombreros as much as they used to. Before, people round here would replace their hats every six months or so. Now they come perhaps once a year, if they come at all. I'm at a loss as to what to do. Hats are all I know.'

A brief survey of Saquisilí's clothes offering shows just how fast tastes are changing. In the case of native fashions, fluorescent is currently all the rage. Luminous knee-length stockings and blinding lime ponchos jump out like neon lights from several stalls. But indigenous garb, however spruced up, is on the wane.

Mass-produced Western clothes are what people want. The stalls, like the shoppers, are bedecked with tracksuits, sweatshirts and US-style baseball caps. If they have a foreign brand name, whether fake or not (they are always fake), so much the better. Everything is brought from the capital Quito, where it is produced in clandestine factories or, more likely since dollarisation pushed up production costs, imported from Asia. 'Made in Korea', reads the English label on one $14 coat: 'B.D. BangWei, The choice of the Excellent Wear.'

At the vegetable market, the feel is much the same. Over-production has sent the price of potatoes, the region's staple food, through the floor. A coal-sack of spuds now retails at around $3. At that price, it is hardly worth the impoverished indigenous farmers bringing them to market. Whether from habit or necessity, they do so all the same.

The mood is at least a little sunnier at the shoe market. The traditional, slip-on *alpargatas* sandals piled up high on Marlena Ribiera's stall continue to sell well. She lets me in on a trade secret though. Turning a pair over, she taps the bottom. It's made of rubber.

'They used to be rope-soled,' she says, turning her nose up ever so slightly. 'The manufacturers now use rubber to keep prices down.'

The material is not the only incongruous feature of the Spanish-style shoe. The logo of the car manufacturer Land Rover is moulded to the base.

From shoe wear, our conversation shifts to society. As it does, Marlena's good humour cools. With dour foreboding, she describes the exodus of the town's young people in search of work.

'Once they are in the cities and away from the countryside, their character changes. They become violent and get drunk. Here in Saquisilí, life remains quiet. But the children are still modernising all the same, and their parents just leave them to it. We're losing our customs as a result.'

A teenager with an earring and hair gelled into a spike walks by. She follows him with her gaze, raising her eyebrows in a 'See what I mean?' gesture. I raise mine in return. She sees that I see and looks pleadingly to the skies in a 'Heaven help us' fashion. I inflect my shoulders with a sympathetic 'What can you do?' She nods back resignedly, 'Nothing, I suppose.' Why our conversation has suddenly slipped into silent-movie mode, I'm not sure. Perhaps we've said all there is to say? I wave goodbye. 'Goodbye,' she waves back, without a word.

Change, however unspeakable some may find it, is afoot in every indigenous village. Opinions differ on how best to respond.

For many, the answer is political. In Saquisilí, the Town Hall is in the hands of an indigenous party. I knock on the door and am shown up a winding staircase to the second floor. A huge montage of indigenous figures and symbols, set in bronze, hangs over the atrium. Belisario Cholocinga, the fedora-wearing vice-president, greets me in his boss's office with a firm handshake. It's straight down to business.

'We grew tired of the politics of the big oligarchies who governed not for the people but for their own interests. When the *mestizos* controlled things, it was almost impossible for us indigenous to get as much as a hearing.'

Almost a decade ago, that all changed. Thousands of indigenous men and women from Saquisilí and other towns in the Cotopaxi province took to the road and marched on Quito.

Mr Cholocinga and an army of hoe-carrying *indígenos* had wanted to tell the president directly what they thought. Conquered by the Incas, marginalised by the Spanish, oppressed under the Republic, they were sick of feudal servitude. As far back as 1825, Bolívar had written an edict from Quito ordering employers to pay the 'native peoples' in cash 'without forcing them to accept other forms of pay against their will and at levels below that commonly paid for such work'.

Abuses continued all the same. Well into the second half of the twentieth century, Ecuador's indigenous tenant farmers were still working half-day Saturdays in their patron's house for no pay. Even their traditional ponchos, bought by unwitting tourists for their pretty colours, are little more than cattle branding. An indentured tartan, each separate design corresponds to the hacienda to which individual labourers once belonged.

To the chants of the indigenous civil code, '*Ama sua, ama llulla, ama kjella*,' thousands of Mr Cholocingas had stormed the palace. 'No thievery, no lying, no laziness.' Temporarily, they even occupied Congress. Jamil Mahaud, the Harvard-educated president, got the message and quit his post. The moment marked the zenith of an indigenous political movement that had been bubbling up for four decades.

Since then, indigenous politics have followed a rockier path. With Mahaud gone, the native leaders immediately chummied up with a gaggle of disgruntled generals who staged a coup. The collusion proved a grave mistake. Their three-man junta swiftly collapsed. So too did most public sympathy for the indigenous cause.

To their credit, they have not given up. Under the banner of the Pachacutik Party, indigenous representatives can be found scattered sparsely on the benches of Congress, their fedora hats and long hair a stark contrast to the smart suits of the other legislators. Today their fight is focused primarily on increasing government support for agriculture. The agenda makes sense. Ecuador's native peoples are mostly *campesino* farmers, which generally categorises them as indigent as well as indigenous.

'We used to live in an abundance of natural resources,' Miguel Karanki, a representative of the national indigenous confederation, told me during an interview in Quito. 'But the Government just sees our land as a space for generating dollars. If that continues, we'll soon be living in a desert.' I ask how many congressmen they have to make their case. 'Six,' he says, throwing up his hands in dismay. 'Alone, they can't really do anything.' He is pinning his hopes on the current constitutional assembly to reset the balance.

At the grass-roots level, people display less optimism in the formal political system. Voting and law-making, they feel, has let them down.

Moisés Tixilema, an ex-local politician from Simiatug, a poor rural community in Bolívar province, epitomises such disillusion. I bump into him by accident in the village's only hostel. Over an evening meal of warm chicken broth, we get talking about the mass indigenous mobilisations of yesteryear. His eyes shine at the memory. But as with many of his fellow militants, he eventually resolved to quit protesting and enter the formal political process.

'We thought it would bring improvements for our village.' It didn't, he laments. 'As *indios,* we lost power because we thought that the electoral process would help us make a change. Those in Quito still believe it will. Here, in the countryside, we can see that's rubbish. The democratic system only sidelines us and makes us weaker.'

Moisés wants me to meet someone, someone from the new generation of indigenous politics. He bustles me into the back of his work jeep (Moisés has some ill-defined job with an agricultural agency that earns him his own vehicle) and drives me into Simiatug's pitch-dark central square. Evening Mass is just finishing, and drabs of loyal parishioners are dribbling out of the church and into the night's shadows.

Moisés swings his car around a sharp bend and pulls up beside a crumbling terraced house. He jumps down and raps on the door. No one answers, so he knocks again, harder this time. Eventually, a tired-looking Lucas Chimbo opens up. He is just in from milking his small herd of cows and was obviously hoping for the chance to put his feet up. The two talk in brisk Quichua, and Moisés persuades him to join us for a brief chat. He puts on his boots, still caked with wet mud, and joins us on the porch.

In his early thirties, Lucas wears a baseball cap and a scarlet puffa jacket. I ask him what it means for him to be *indígeno*. 'It's about speaking our language and using our traditional dress,' he responds, speaking in Spanish and fiddling with the peak of his cap. I repeat Moisés's point about the indigenous movement being short-changed by the political process. Does he agree? As an acting member of Simiatug's political committee, he is more optimistic than his veteran companion.

He's not oblivious to the problems that exist though: 'We support the policies of Pachacutik. What happens though is that those who lead the party get distracted by elections and political infighting. They put personal and family interests first, and that ends up dividing us.'

White and *mestizo* politicians always used to be the self-serving vermin of Ecuadorian democracy. Now the indigenous are lumped in too. Power is colour-blind. Moisés and Lucas cite cases of indigenous leaders owning shares in oil companies with exploration activities in the Amazon. The 'indigenous mafia', they claim, robbed state funds earmarked for Ecuadorian ethnic minorities. Divided ideologically among themselves, the indigenous candidates flopped at the last election. Pachacutik's presidential hopeful posted a dismal 2 per cent at the polls – less than one in ten of the indigenous vote. The two friends stay chatting on the doorstep and strategising about the future. I stumble back uphill in the dark and towards my bed.

In the ferment of political power play, attention rarely stoops to dreary matters such as local public transport. If I am ever to leave

Simiatug, I have to be on the village's only bus the next morning. At 5 a.m.

In Río Colorado, a village of some twenty families nestled below the mighty Chimborazo volcano, they are taking a different approach. Blackboards, they say, not ballot boxes, are what indigenous communities need.

I happen to be passing through on the same day as a public meeting. It is a bright, chilly Saturday, and everyone has downed tools for the big *asemblea*. On the agenda are plans for a new school. The whole village is sitting outside the existing one-room schoolhouse, where they chat and laugh and generally enjoy the rare luxury of some time off. They invite me to join them for fresh rabbit stew. As I eat, I watch a group of boys playing football on a bumpy patch of land nearby. They are all dressed alike: black or red ponchos, wellington boots and black fedora hats, which they never take off other than to head the ball. Our plates empty, and people begin to drift towards the schoolroom.

Seating is arranged by seniority, the older men occupying the benches, the women and younger men taking the children's chairs, and everyone else sitting on the concrete floor or standing. An architect from Quito has agreed to help them with their project on a *pro bono* basis. Today is his first visit, and he asks the purpose of the new school.

'We want to keep our children here in the community,' comes the straightforward response from a moustached man in late middle age.

Everyone nods their agreement.

'At the moment, the village school only caters for the children up to eleven years old. After that, people tend to leave for the nearby towns so that their children can continue their education.'

The architect wants to know how many pupils they have in mind. A quick conflab ensues among the older men.

'Five hundred should do it.'

The architect visibly gulps: 'And how many pupils do you have at present?'

'Nineteen,' pipes up the interim teacher, a bearded volunteer from the southernmost tip of Argentina. 'At least, that's the number registered. Only sixteen actually attend regularly.'

The question of numbers takes an hour to resolve. When the meeting finally adjourns, the architect has committed to drawing up designs for a school of fifty students, with capacity for more as and when the need arises. The boys scuttle back to the football field and the fathers to the beer bottles.

Driving away from Río Colorado, I turn around in my seat for one last look at the village, nestled in the flat belly of a sweeping valley. The clouds briefly part, providing a rare glimpse of Chimborazo's magnificent icy peak.

Almost two centuries earlier, the sight of these same 'eternal crystals' had inspired a fit of poetry in Bolívar. In the most lyrical of all his letters, he recalls his climb up 'the ice-white hair of this giant of the earth', his arrival at 'the threshold of the abyss' and, spent by the effort, his nap atop this 'immense diamond'. The experience also inspired a fit of madness, what he himself describes as 'a spiritual tremor . . . a kind of divine frenzy'. In his delirium, a vision of Time as an old man appeared to him. Bent over, scythe in hand, the 'ancient figure' addressed the Liberator:

'I am the father of the centuries, the Arcanum of fame and secret knowledge. My mother was Eternity. Infinity sets the limits of my empire. There is no tomb for me, because I am more powerful than death.'

Time might be Bolívar's friend, but it is not Río Colorado's. Poverty, not infinity, currently sets the community's limits. And if there is any secret knowledge to be had, it is not to be found in the schoolroom's one-shelf library. Learning might expand their horizons, but a college education is a stepping stone not the bridge to Mother Eternity.

Bolívar secretly knew this. Towards the end of his life, he decreed that the *indios* be allotted farm land and afforded full property rights. The Great Liberator understood that freedom for South America's indigenous would only come when they had sufficient territory to provide for themselves. The landowners and administrators of his day resolutely ignored the order.

It required a young Italian priest to arrive in Ecuador for the Liberator's decree to achieve its long-awaited trial run. Father Antonio Polo came to Salinas three and a half decades ago. Back then, this forgotten village in the rugged mountains west of Guaranda, the capital city of Bolívar province, constituted the private fiefdom of the Cordovez family. Originally from Colombia, they ran the salt mines from which the town took its name. Through a combination of low wages and overpriced company stores, they had succeeded in keeping the inhabitants in debt and under the thumb.

Despite their thievery, making the salt mines pay became an increasingly uphill battle. The Colombian salt barons took the arrival of the charismatic priest as a divine sign. They sold up and departed to their homeland. Into their place stepped Father Antonio, brandishing an economic action plan of his own.

Under their new benevolent patron, the folk of Salinas have since transformed the Andean parish into a veritable business hub. The sound of whirring machinery from the balloon factory, the chocolate-makers and the town's other sixteen micro-enterprises reverberates along the village's sloping lanes. From a two-storey building down a shadowy side street wafts the smell of cheese. Marketed under the 'El Salinerito' brand, the town's mozzarella, camembert and gruyère today sell in supermarkets across the country.

The cheese factory, Father Antonio likes to think, represents an 'example of solidarity in action'. Others might just call it a great business concept. Ideology aside, one thing is undeniable: cheese is changing the lives of the district's indigenous inhabitants. Every morning, dairy farmers can be seen guiding their cows towards the two dozen milking stations now scattered around the hunchbacked hills and valleys of Salinas.

'We get a set price and a stable market for our milk these days,' says Amable, a young farmer who sells the milk from his five cows in the nearby parish hamlet of Pambabuela. 'There's not much migration any more. Now it's only the lazy who leave.'

The message is the same wherever indigenous communities have hit on a successful money-spinner. The best ideas tend to draw on existing local skills or on Ecuador's natural beauty. Textiles, handicrafts and tourism come in high on the list.

In the Hostería Indi Wasi, the Patuloma family are engaged in all three. The hostel-cum-ethnic emporium is to be found on Salasaka's main street. The Patulomas enjoy a healthy passing trade thanks to their location on the trunk road to Baños, a resort town in eastern Ecuador popular for its hot springs.

I walk in one sunny lunchtime and find Juan, the owner's twenty-two-year-old son, busy at a wooden, Victorian-age spinning wheel. He is pedaling frantically but stops when I come in and welcomes me with a beaming smile. We get talking and, as often happens in rural corners of South America, he invites me to his house. Normally, their homes are just down the road. In Juan's case, the family homestead lies six kilometres away in the neighbouring valley. We set off on foot. Fortunately, we don't have to trudge too far before a pick-up truck stops and gives us a lift.

The Patulomas are certainly an enterprising gang. Their house, like their Hostería, has rooms for guests and a workshop for weaving. César and Leonardo, Juan's younger brother and cousin, are both sitting working at two imposing looms when we arrive. All the family wear their hair long and speak in Quichua. Their talk is of the recent Capitán festival, an annual knees-up where the Salasakans dress as Spanish soldiers and re-enact the oppression of their forefathers. I ask them if they wouldn't like the opportunity to go to discos or to the cinema like their contemporaries in the city. My question meets with a friendly, but firm, reproach.

'Our parents and our leaders teach us that we don't have to think like the city or the *mestizo*,' says Juan, who switches between Quichua and Spanish with absent-minded ease. 'Anyway, we've never been to a modern cinema or a disco, so, no, it's not something we're too bothered about.'

The longhaired Juan has been to Quito twice in his life, both times for cultural festivals. Unlike most indigenous migrants, who remove their traditional costume to enter the city gates, he hit the town in his smartest black poncho and white, pressed linen trousers.

The Otavaleños wear their traditional garb with similar pride. The country's most commercially minded indigenous community, they were making money trading between the coast and the highlands even before the Incas arrived. They are still raking it in today. Their crafts and clothing sell around the world, from the streets of Seville to the market stalls of Vancouver.

The pony-tailed Otavaleños have turned their ethnicity into a brand. It's what sets them apart. Juan, who has never eaten pizza let alone read a marketing textbook, instinctively understands the value in being different: 'For me, being indigenous is something to be proud of. We're unique. We're not a mix of anything.'

We exchange addresses on a piece of paper torn out of an exercise book. When I look at it on the bus later on, I see that he's scribbled a short note in Quichua beside his phone number. '*Cashna mi ganchi, nucanchi causay. Alli, alli.*' He's added the same phrase in Spanish below. 'This is us, our life. It's the best.' I pin it to the photo of Caminga, confident my Huaorani friends would agree.

The jaguar, not Time, is the all-knowing being for the Huaorani. His wisdom is for the shaman to divine. But culture, like the current of the Cononaco, keeps moving. A mountain-top séance isn't necessary to see that. Unlike their elders, the ear lobes of the Huaorani children are free of balsa-wood piercings. Nor do the boys or young adult men follow Kempery in wearing the string hip-cord. Like Adam and Eve they prefer to cover their nakedness and instead choose to don grubby Bermuda shorts and branded T-shirts. Were it not for our presence, I suspect Guinto and Caminga would have taken their rifles into the forest rather than the blowgun.

Is cultural change and adaptation necessarily a bad thing? Will the world be any worse if naked tribesmen stop appearing on the pages of *National Geographic*? Is it fair for me to enjoy the comforts of modernity yet insist that 'natives' keep living in the Dark Ages?

Shortly after my arrival in Ecuador, I had put these questions to Francisca, a Swiss guide who has been visiting the Huaorani for almost a decade. She had had little patience for the anthropological purists who cry ethnocide at the first hint of modernisation. 'The Huaorani are not a museum,' she kept repeating. After all, we in the non-jungle world preserve the right to adapt and develop. There was no public outcry, she pointed out, when the iPod replaced the Walkman, or the Walkman the stereo, or the stereo the gramophone, or the gramophone the evening singalong around the piano. We just learn to change in step with our environment. But our essence – our appreciation for music, in the case of Francisca's analogy – remains the same.

Initially, I had found her argument a compelling one. Yet, as we chatted in a vegetarian restaurant along Quito's Amazonas Avenue, it dawned on me that something lay behind her carefully crafted reasoning, a powerful, compelling, overwhelming force – the need for an apology.

Our discussion owed its origin to the fact that we, the outsiders, had encroached into the Huaorani world. Without that, there would be no discussion. Even more so in the case of Francisca, whose regular encroachments with camera-snapping tour groups like mine serve to pay her rent. On reflection, I wonder if it is really true that material goods do not change a culture's essence. Can the Huaorani stay Huaorani if they live in brick houses or use mobile phones, as some already do?

Driving into Coca at the end of our trip, I caught sight of a Huaorani man standing on the high street. He was looking up at a traffic light, deciding whether to cross the road or not. Unresolved, he stood motionless, simply staring at the light. He was wearing shorts and a telltale pair of wellington boots. His long flowing hair was partly covered by a baseball cap. Pedestrians brushed by him. He neither moved nor shifted his gaze from the light.

This was not his world, and he was certainly not the lord of it. At best, he was just another pedestrian; at worst, a disorientated foreigner in his own country. As I watched him, I realised that there would be no undoing of what had already been done. Good or bad, the world was already on the Huaorani's doorstep. And soon it would be kicking down the door. Tourists and television are already pushing at the hinges. Now contracts are being signed to develop a massive oil field on the edge of Guinto and Caminga's territory.

The Huaorani have no sense of apocalypse, it has been said. That is fortunate. If they had, their spears would be out once more and the Coronoco red with blood.

In neighbouring Colombia, things are different. The End Times have already arrived. The bloodletting has begun.

8

INTO THE HANDS OF TYRANTS
Colombia and violence

Let the monsters who have infested Colombian soil, covering it with blood, vanish forever.
SIMÓN BOLÍVAR, DECREE OF WAR TO THE DEATH, 1813

Bogotá

As my plane taxied to a stop in Bogotá's international airport, Guillermo Pascuas received a .45-calibre bullet in the middle of his forehead. He died instantly, his body crumpling to the muddy floor of his uncle's farmyard.

The murder went unmentioned by the newspapers. No police report was filed. No coroner was alerted. It would be weeks before even his mother found out.

I only hear about the killing because I happen to bump into his uncle. Three days after the event, Álvaro is sitting on the steps of a Mennonite church in downtown Bogotá. He's staring listlessly at the belching traffic as it inches down the congested Avenue 19. His shoulders are hunched and his gaze blank. Álvaro is a man in shock.

The unschooled farmer is dressed in the same work clothes that he wore on the morning of the murder: a pair of mud-stained jeans, a black T-shirt imprinted with the insignia of a heavy-metal band and a scuffed pair of trainers with a hole in one of the toes. A charitable stranger had since donated a winter coat to his meagre wardrobe. The garment is too big, and its long sleeves droop down over his hands. He keeps trying to roll them up, but they insist on falling down again. The oversized jacket has the effect of shrinking Álvaro's slim frame even further.

On the step beside him lies a small bag of lemons, a gift from the same unknown Samaritan. The fruit is overripe, and Álvaro's initial attempts at street hawking have so far met with failure. He has no money, no friends, no identity papers and is fast running low on hope.

I sit down on the step next to him and pull out my tourist map from my backpack. The Colombian capital is new to me, as it is to Álvaro.

I'd spent my first day in Colombia walking the cramped, colonial streets of La Candelaria, Bogotá's delightfully dishevelled old town. I'd breakfasted on corn-dough *arepas,* paid a visit to the military museum and hunted down the cloistered hacienda where Simón Bolívar once lived.

The following day, I'd ventured by tram to the city's new districts in the plusher northern suburbs. Compared to the old quarter, the hustle and bustle had surprised me. Everything was movement and glinting glass. Suited executives were running in and out of metallic skyscrapers. Office workers were gulping down morning shots of strong black coffee. Businessmen were gabbling into mobiles. Colombia felt and looked like a country on the up.

My initial interviews confirmed this rosy picture. Stellar growth figures, a booming stock market, foreign companies clambering to invest. Apparently, it all had to do with something mysterious called *confianza,* 'confidence'. According to the cover story in that week's *Business Week* magazine, Colombians were high on the stuff. With crime statistics at their lowest for years, Colombia Inc. was back in business. Let the good times roll.

Álvaro could be excused for seeing things differently.

'*Tiene la hora?*' he asks in a timid voice, tapping his finger on his thin, bare wrist.

'*La una y media.*'

He asks if I'm from round here. Everything about me – my dress, my accent, my map – must indicate I'm not. I suppose he is looking to start up a conversation.

'No, actually, I'm from Britain,' I reply.

The out-of-towner looks briefly nonplussed, realises it must be a long way from Bogotá and concludes we have an important factor in common.

'I'm also from far away. The province of Meta to be exact, further south from here,' he says. 'My name's Álvaro, by the way.'

'Oliver,' I reply in kind.

My new acquaintance then tells me that he knows no one in the city. By the look of his ruffled hair and unkempt appearance, I guess he could be sleeping rough.

'What made you leave home, if you don't mind me asking?'

He doesn't answer immediately, just looks at me with vacant, bewildered eyes and then turns away, sniffing quietly.

'It's a long story,' he replies eventually, more to the church's granite step than to me.

I'm conscious that my city map and foreign face make me a prime target for confidence tricksters. But Álvaro doesn't come across as a conman. His distress seems genuine. I take a punt on his story being so too:

'Perhaps you'd like to tell me over some food?' I suggest, pointing to a lunch bar across the street.

One bowl of lumpy potato soup and two heaped portions of beef stew later, Álvaro is ready to talk. Placing his knife and fork side by side on the empty plate, he explains how he and his sister's son had grown close over the years. Álvaro's wife had upped and left four years ago, taking his two children with her. In spite of being fifteen years younger than him, Guillermo became more like a brother than a nephew.

He shifts forwards to the more immediate past and the morning of the murder: 'I was sitting with my nephew on the low stone wall at the front of the farmstead.'

The two men had both risen early, as they always did. It was a Wednesday, and the week's list of jobs still stretched out before them. The priority for the day was to buy some medicine for an ailing heifer. That required a trip to La Macarena, the local town, a twenty-minute car journey away. But Álvaro had no car – never had done. On foot, the journey was closer to two hours. Neither man fancied the trek. They had just resolved to flip for it when four armed men appeared around the corner of the wall. The toss was never called.

'Guillermo was sitting with his back to them. It was me that spotted them,' Álvaro says, his mind's eye seemingly flitting back to that fateful morning three days ago.

Although he'd never seen any of the men before, the farmer identified them immediately. In their frayed green fatigues and rubber boots, the gun-toting foursome bore the unmistakable appearance of the Revolutionary Armed Forces of Colombia or the FARC as they're more commonly known.

Established in the mid-1960s, when the Cold War was just getting hot, the FARC had taken to the hills to strike a blow for socialism. Other left-wing guerrilla groups had joined the call. Somewhere along the line their ideology gave way to banditry.

'I guess the fear at seeing them must have shown on my face because Guillermo swivelled round immediately.' Álvaro reaches for his Coca-Cola.

It wasn't the first time the FARC had come to the farm. They were regular visitors. Álvaro's land lay in the middle of one of Colombia's guerrilla-controlled 'red zones'. Each month, someone would come calling for his *vacuna* – literally, his 'vaccine'. This regular protection fee is calculated according to head of cattle. With thirty cows in his herd, Álvaro's monthly antidote came in at 150,000 *pesos*. An additional sales tax of 30,000 *pesos* was tacked on for every cow that he sold.

'The FARC say the money goes towards their ongoing struggle for the *pueblo*,' he explains, virtually spitting out the Spanish word for 'the people'.

Fail to pay, and the *pueblo*'s alleged defenders turn very nasty, very quickly. Álvaro recalls an occasion when a buyer had landed him with a bad debt for two prize heifers. Bean-counting FARC style doesn't allow for such discrepancies. The soldiers stripped him naked and tied him to a *viga linda* tree. Then a member of the accountancy unit dealt a few sharp, well-aimed blows at the bark with a machete.

Out of the tree and onto Álvaro's naked body scuttled a small army of electric ants. The FARC heavies kept him there for five minutes. He had heard of men being tied up for nearly an hour. Even so, it would be a fortnight before the painful welts began to subside.

In the case of the FARC, their frequent visits did not breed familiarity. They only served to augment fear. And on this occasion, Álvaro had good reason to be afraid.

'It all started at the beginning of the year when a foreign photographer appeared at the door of my farmhouse,' he says, his storytelling inching forwards and backwards as he struggles to fit all the pieces together.

From Álvaro's description, his forty-hectare plot in the midst of Colombia's central *cordillera* sounds truly idyllic: fields of ripe plantain and banana trees stretching out like rows of feather dusters, miles of thick forest cover tracing the rolling-pin curves of the hills, a stream coursing down the mountainside, fat with the winter rains.

'I told him to go ahead. I guessed it was for a calendar or something. To tell you the truth, I quite like the idea of some *gringo* admiring the view that I wake up to every morning.' He checks himself. 'Used to wake up to.'

Álvaro forward winds two months, to a second unannounced visit. This time his guests came with AK-47s rather than Nikon digitals. The Colombian army had decided Álvaro's farm would make a strategic spot from which to attack the FARC. There was no 'please' or 'thank you' on this occasion. It was Álvaro's patriotic duty to do as he was told. The army were fighting for the *pueblo* after all.

'Another Coke?' I ask as Álvaro taps the empty base of his glass with a plastic straw.

'Sure, thanks.'

He watches the waiter pour a refill and waits for the bubbles to settle before taking a slurp. His thirst temporarily quenched, he picks up his thread.

The army platoon ended up staying three weeks. Uncle and nephew remained holed up inside the farmhouse throughout. The pair spent their days listening to the rattle of machine-gun fire in the nearby hills and the sound of heavy artillery rockets overhead.

The government conscripts suffered eight fatalities in total. Their corpses were piled unceremoniously in body bags on Álvaro's back porch. Four times as many guerrilla members died, or so the army claimed.

Thinking back to those days cooped up, a prisoner in his own home, he claims the fighting itself didn't scare him. Death or survival lay out of his hands, he resolved. What kept him awake at night were the repercussions. Having government forces camped on his lawn, whether willingly or not, singled him out as a collaborator. And, as every Colombian knows, collaborators come to an ugly end.

To Álvaro's surprise, the expected reprisal didn't materialise when the army unit decamped. For four weeks they waited, and nothing. But just as he and Guillermo thought life was returning to normal, the government soldiers returned.

'When was that?' I ask, trying to bring some sort of chronology to the pattern of events Álvaro is describing.

'Let me think. What are we today? Sunday, no? It would have been two weeks ago to the day then.'

These were no garden-variety recruits. Army headquarters had ordered in Colombia's crack mountain battalion for the second assault. Trained and equipped with the help of USA Special Forces, they're specialised in locating and eliminating guerrilla insurgents. Their offensive lasted six days. No body bags appeared on the back porch this time round.

The four FARC soldiers comprised the long-awaited payback committee. The leader was in his mid-twenties and prematurely balding. According to Álvaro, he was the only one who spoke. The remainder stood guard, each brandishing a large machine gun. None of the lackeys were out of their teens.

There were no introductions; the FARC spokesman only dealt in questions and curses. 'He wanted to know why they had not been informed about the photographer,' Álvaro recalls.

Tears begin welling up in the corners of his eyes as he plays back the incident. 'They cared more about the *gringo* than the army. The soldiers they could kill, but the *gringo* they could kidnap. They wanted to know why I hadn't reported his visit.'

Three days, and it's the first time he's recounted aloud the events that have been constantly swimming around in his head.

The bald-headed leader said that they had already overlooked his 'discrepancies'. First, the photographer. Then, the army. Their patience would only stretch so far, he'd said. By entertaining the enemy a second time, Álvaro had overstepped the mark.

'He demanded I leave the farm right then and there. I said I would but asked if he could give me some time – just a few hours – to sell some things. I hadn't a single *peso*, you see.'

The previous days of pent-up emotion suddenly overwhelm him. Asphyxiating, discordant sobs rack his shaking body. He lifts his trembling hands to his face, tears rolling down his cheeks, wetting his fingers.

'He swore at me again.' The sentence is barely audible, engulfed by despairing, grief-stricken sobs.

'"You–"'

He chokes on the phrase as if it were a physical entity, an obstruction trapping his windpipe, making him gag and splutter for air.

The restaurant's customers are down to just us and a slovenly dressed office worker across the room. Álvaro's outburst causes him to break from his newspaper crossword. He stares over at us, his expression a mix of curiosity and annoyance at having his concentration disturbed.

'"You obviously don't understand the word 'now'," the leader screamed back.'

My dining companion remains oblivious to the office worker's stare, shouting the word 'now' in imitation.

With that, the FARC commander pulled a pistol from his holster, turned to Guillermo and shot him at point blank range in the head.

'It was so quick and casual . . .' Abruptly, his crying stops, his tear ducts momentarily checked by the atrocious vividness of the scene in rewind. 'Like putting down a dog.'

He falls silent. I order us both a coffee. Neither of us speaks for the five minutes it takes for the order to arrive. When he returns to his story, his voice is muffled and his eyes dazed and blurred. The trauma of the past few days seems to have caught up with him.

'The man then raised his gun at me. "Now do you understand 'now'? Get out of here or the next bullet's for you."'

Álvaro turned and fled, dashing through the gate, leaping over the stream and tearing down the hillside as fast as his legs would carry him. He hit the main road in little over half an hour. Wheezing madly and still blind with fear, he flagged down the first bus that passed. He jumped on without inquiring where it was heading. Noting his distraught state, the driver waived the fare and dropped the empty-handed farmer at the end of his route three hours to the north.

Álvaro isn't sure what the town was called. He just remembers sitting for hours in a busy bus terminal, his mind dulled by grief and panic, his ability to rationalise temporarily immobilised. After what felt like hours, a kindly woman approached him. He was huddled on a bench, shivering in his T-shirt, more from shock than cold. They spoke briefly, he forgets what about exactly. But it transpired that the lady had a truck. She was travelling to Bogotá that night and offered him a lift.

Álvaro took the ride. And so it was that he went from sitting outside his farm one sunny morning to standing at a busy intersection in Bogotá the next.

Two days later, and Álvaro was still at a total loss as to what to do. The man who gave him the lemons had suggested he go to the Abasto fruit market and buy some papaya. He could then sell it in the street and make some money that way.

'But how can I buy papaya when I don't even have a *peso*?'

Above all, Álvaro wants a paid job, any job. With a small wage, he hopes he can restart his life. He could save some money and eventually move back to the countryside.

'I've asked in restaurants and on building sites, but no one will give me the time of day. They only care about having work for themselves. Here people are so proud. They could see someone dying on the floor and they'd just step over them. I almost wish they'd killed me too, rather than arriving here and being rejected and humiliated. You're displaced, and then in the city they kill you slowly.'

His desperation becomes almost unbearable at night.

'Sitting there in the dark, I think to myself, "This isn't fair." I had land, land I bought. And now I have nothing.'

And then, come morning, it starts again. Where to go? What to do? Yesterday, he toyed with the idea of hitching north and joining the *auto-defensas,* the illegal paramilitary groups set up to fight back against the FARC and the rebel groups like them. But he's decided that he's had his fill of violence.

The waiter starts flicking channels on the television. He settles on the afternoon news. A reporter's voice breaks into our conversation. We both turn to watch. The headline bulletin features the capture of six FARC members in an army raid. Álvaro looks away.

'If you live where I do, you know all the news is a lie,' he says despondently. 'They keep what is really happening a secret. The government says it is winning the war, but no one is winning the war. It just keeps going on. There are only losers. Personally, I don't think either side is really interested in winning. There are too many people with something to lose if it stops. It'll never end.'

At that moment, a uniformed soldier walked in. He sits across the room, next to the scowling office worker, and orders a coffee and a sandwich.

Álvaro clams up immediately. Visibly shrinking into his donated jacket, he begins playing nervously with his empty coffee cup. I put my notebook away and ask for the bill. We walk back to the Mennonite church. It was next to my tram stop, and, reluctantly, I tell him that I'd better get going. Does he know what he's going to do?

He'd heard the church ran programmes for *desplazados,* 'displaced people'. He's hoping they might be able to help.

I wish him the best, and we share an awkward farewell. Before I go, I give him what's in my wallet. He offers me his lemons in return. I tell him to keep them: 'Buy yourself some papaya instead. But make sure they're ripe.'

We laugh. It's the first time I've seen him smile. We shake hands a final time, and then he sits back down on the church steps, waiting for help to arrive. As I turn to go, he mutters a final thought, whether to himself, to me or the granite stair, I can't tell:

'The worst is that I don't know what they did with Guillermo. I don't know whether they buried him or threw him in the brook or just left him there. I just don't know. What am I to tell his mother?'

Before arriving in Colombia, I'd never heard the word *desplazado*. Until recently, it hadn't been a regular part of Álvaro's vocabulary either. Three days on, and he's still getting used to the term.

Before touching down in Colombia, I'd read a few books on its history. Writ large on every page is the same dominating theme: violence – raw, barbaric, blood-curdling, teeth-chattering, brain-twisting, heart-wrenching, mind-wincing violence.

The country's reputation for brutality dates back at least to the times of the Liberators. The War of Independence is reckoned to have cost a third of Colombia's adult population. The Liberators contributed their part to the carnage.

Bolívar notoriously declared *Guerra a Muerte* against his colonial adversaries. The edict was unequivocal. War to the Death. No royalist would be spared and no prisoners taken. 'Even if you profess neutrality, know that you will die,' Spaniards on South American soil were warned. He kept to his word. In 1814, a few months after this fatal declaration, he gave the order for thirteen hundred imprisoned royalist soldiers to be executed. It was not the Liberator's finest hour.

Even for the bellicose standards of his day, Bolívar's order represented a clear violation of martial etiquette and wartime norms. His apologists spare no time in lumping the blame on Spain's murderous battle tactics. The royalist soldiers were certainly no angels. Most had no compunction about raping and pillaging. As a strategy of colonial dominion, the ruthless techniques were supposed to deter people from sympathising with the patriot rebels. In reality, such rough treatment only drove them more towards the anti-Spanish cause.

The colonists had their sadists too. Peeling the skin from prisoners' feet and making them walk on hot coals emerged as a particular favourite during the revolutionary wars. So did tying captives up in hammocks and burning them alive.

The most notorious psychopath of them all was an Asturian-born bandit who'd originally come to South America with Spain's merchant navy. José Tomás Boves's idea of entertainment was to kill pregnant women and have their stomachs cut open. He enjoyed watching the spasms of their unborn children. On one especially gory escapade, the deranged Spaniard entered the Venezuelan town of Cumana and ordered every last male killed. That much was standard. But then, as night fell, he corralled their women and forced them to dance. The jig over, his soldiers raped them and then executed them. The musicians got the chop too.

Not that the patriots were innocent either. The Liberator once had to severely censure a senior member of the patriot forces for issuing promotions according to Spanish scalps. Thirty and a cadet made it to lieutenant. Fifty and he was bumped up to captain. Bolívar sent message that the brutish system must be stopped immediately. He received two heads by return of post.

The Liberator later annulled the War to the Death, but the damage was done. The citizens of Gran Colombia had already acquired a taste for bloodshed. Before Bolívar's body was even interred, rival political factions would be bumping one another off in search of the spoils. In the second half of the nineteenth century alone, the independent Republic of Colombia would suffer thirteen blood-splattered coups.

If Colombians hoped the new century would bring a let-up in the terror, they were sadly mistaken. In fact, from the late 1940s to the early 1960s, levels of savagery became so bad that historians simply refer to the period as *La Violencia,* The Violence.

Those bloodstained decades proved a marker post in Colombian butchery. From armed men killing other armed men, civilians were dragged into the fray. A contemporary eyewitness report describes how federal soldiers sacked a rural village: 'They murdered [the inhabitants] and carved them up, little by little; they cut them into small pieces and the pieces jumped. When the sun rose there were bodies everywhere. They took a little child from a pregnant woman and they put one of its limbs in her mouth.'

Boves's perverted diversions evidently survived the generations.

Grotesque massacres such as these turned out to be a warm-up for what was to come. Summary executions, disappearances, disembowelment, systematic rape, torture and group assassinations became the hallmarks of a civil war that had since torn Colombia apart. Over the past four decades, the country's bloody domestic conflict is estimated to have cost at least thirty thousand lives. With mass graves still turning up, the figure could well be more. As a rule, the left-wing rebel groups and their paramilitary enemies contented themselves with terrorising the countryside. That left the cities to the drug cartels.

In the days of Pablo Escobar, Colombia's most notorious *narco* and one-time member of *Forbes* rich list, the per-capita murder rates in Medellín and Cali were the highest in the world. Even the morgues of Somalia, which was swimming in blood courtesy of its own monstrous civil war, couldn't compete.

'The thing about men like Escobar is that they would kill so casually. It was just an everyday part of doing business,' a veteran reporter in Medellín told me one night over a beer. 'Many in fact are charming. When you speak with them, you have to remind yourself they are cold-blooded murderers who would as soon slit open your granny with a carving knife as look at her.'

If the official statistics are to be believed, then Colombia is at last getting safer. The drug cartels are no more (or no longer so evident); the paramilitaries have supposedly handed in their guns; and the rebel groups are allegedly on the run. Today, you're only twice as likely to get killed on the streets of Cali as those of Beirut.

If being killed is the most obvious way in which violence impinges on your personal liberties, then being kidnapped comes in second.

For much of the past decade, kidnap rates in Colombia have run at around three thousand victims a year. After cocaine-smuggling, hostage-taking counts as the next most lucrative industry for the country's armed groups. The left-wing National Liberation Army historically set the standard in the art of abduction. The guerrilla group once stormed a church in Cali during Sunday Mass and frog-marched all one hundred and fifty congregants into waiting trucks.

Less professional means are also used. Setting up a roadblock and nabbing passing motorists represents one of the old-time tricks. 'Miraculous fishing', the strategy was nicknamed, after Jesus's injunction that his disciples 'go and fish for men'.

More popular nowadays are targeted kidnappings. Compared to random motorists, wealthy businessmen constitute a far more lucrative catch. Children are also popular. Kidnappers find that parents tend to find the cash quickly. Another strategy for a fast pay-out is to send ears, fingers and other body parts in the post.

Less common are political hostages. Until recently, the FARC held around fifty such unfortunates. Most were public figures or members of the security services. They were worth more to the guerrillas as bargaining chips than bank notes. The most famous was ex-congresswoman Íngrid Betancourt. Daughter of a former Miss Colombia, the mother of two was seized in 2002 during a visit to a demilitarised zone in central Colombia. At the time, she was running for president. Her husband pledged to continue her campaign, but the public guessed they wouldn't be seeing her for a while. She ended up garnering less than 1 per cent of the vote.

My visit to Colombia brought fresh news of Íngrid through John Frank Pinchao. The emaciated policeman had been a guest of the FARC for eight years, six months and fifteen days. He'd given his guards the slip and spent the previous fortnight or more beating a path out of the jungle. He emerged with twenty worms under his skin. He also had with him reliable information about Íngrid. She was alive. At least, she was the last time he'd seen her several months beforehand. Her relatives at last had reason to hope. The international campaign for her release picked up pace.

Then, a little over a year later, the remarkable happened. Íngrid was rescued. She and fourteen of her fellow captives had been travelling by helicopter from one rebel-controlled zone to another. The trip turned out to be an elaborate ruse. The pilots, dressed as international mediators, were really undercover army soldiers. Once in the air, they quickly disarmed the two FARC guards and pronounced the surprised hostages free. For a week, the daring rescue captured world headlines.

There's another means by which violence in Colombia deprives people of their liberties. Displacement may be less newsworthy than massacres and kidnappings, but it's far more commonplace. War-ravaged Sudan is the only country in the world that boasts more internal refugees than Colombia. Álvaro is just one of more than two million people who have been forced from their homes over the past two decades.

Lack of combat training and kidnap insurance dissuade me from hunting down the perpetrators of Colombia's violence. Instead, I decide to go in search of their victims, the *desplazados*, the silent collateral of Colombian savagery.

Medellín

From her back porch in Altos de Oriente, María Moreno has one of the best views in Medellín. She also has a plague of termites and rats that scuttle noisily across the floor at night.

She and her six children moved into the one-room house about a month ago. Their clothes are neatly parcelled on the three shelves of a tall, thin wardrobe. Black plastic sheeting lines the walls of her wooden framed house. It is supposed to keep out the wind, but it is only partially effective. Her neighbour tells her that sheets of newspaper would be better, but María has not had time to redecorate.

The roof, like the door, is made from corrugated tin. A handful of basic kitchen utensils are piled up on a low wooden bench beside a rust-stained oven. Two beds are shoved up against one wall – one a single, the other a bunk. Both are metal-rimmed and resting on wooden blocks to prevent them sinking into the muddy orange floor.

Leo, her three-month-old baby boy, is lying on the bottom bunk kicking his legs in the air. There is no cot for him to sleep in nor a bath in which to wash him. Nor does the house show any signs of a chair, a mirror, a television, a photo on the wall, a book or even a shelf to put one on.

The cupboard-sized porch has a seat-less toilet at one end and a washing-up bowl at the other. A rubber pipe drips discoloured water into a red plastic bucket. The majestic view reveals itself through the cracks in the wooden plank wall. Damp children's clothes hang wherever space allows.

This is María's new home, six months after having to escape her old one.

A buxom black woman of thirty-three, María had been a witness at her husband's murder. Daniel, her eldest son, had seen it too. Apparently, her spouse of almost a decade had been mixed up with an armed group. María didn't know which one nor did the men who shot him deign to tell her. None the less, when they told her to clear out of town, she took them at their word.

The young mother caught the overnight bus with her children to Medellín. Arriving at the bus terminal, she approached a policeman, who advised her to go to the Centre for Attention and Orientation for Displaced People. The official-sounding building was located across town, and the family took a bus. The watchman was used to the sight of whole families arriving empty-handed at the entrance and ushered them through.

The centre reminded María of school, with its classroom blocks, high fences and sloping basketball court. She was directed to the main building, where she presented herself at the front desk. The attendant told her to go up the stairs to the second floor and wait. She sat in line for two hours as the children grew increasingly fidgety. They were hungry and frightened too. So was María.

Her name was eventually called, and she went through to the adjoining office. The room was divided into eight cubicles, each with a small desk and a computer screen. She sat at the one free desk, and a friendly woman on the other side took her through some questions. The woman typed while María answered what was asked of her. The questions were a government requirement, the lady explained. They would take a look over her case, and, all being well, she would be granted displacement status in the very near future.

'When?' María wanted to know.

'Oh, it shouldn't take long,' the administrator responded.

María's mind then turned to more immediate matters: 'Is there somewhere my children and I can spend the night?'

The woman's questions hadn't covered the issue of accommodation: 'You mean, you don't have any family or friends here?'

María knew no one. The lady then excused herself and went out to make some phone calls. She returned five minutes later. María was in luck. A family had just moved out of the state-run boarding house. She and her children could stay there. It was back across town.

According to the official regulations, the halfway house is only supposed to accommodate people for twenty-three days. With newly displaced people arriving in the city every day, the pressure on beds is extreme. A month is reckoned to be time enough for residents to find alternative lodging. But there had been a bureaucratic hiccup with María's neatly typed papers. As a result, her status and subsequent benefits were left hanging in administrative limbo. Added to that, she was seven months pregnant. In the end, they let her and her family stay five months.

Before visiting María, I'd paid a visit to the boarding house. Located on the corner of Calle Argentina and Calle 42, the building fronts onto a busy street full of traffic and pedestrians. A small gaggle of schoolteachers were staging a sit-down protest at one end of the block. Uniformed pupils were milling around as well, although they looked more interested in smoking than demonstrating their solidarity. The noise of roadworks and car horns generated a steady, unremitting din.

The entrance to the boarding house was through a passageway of peeling paint, which gave out to an open patio at the back. The red and yellow tiled floor brought a splash of much-needed colour to the otherwise drab decor. A canvas awning stretched overhead to keep out the rain. What it failed to catch was collected in buckets at strategic spots around the room.

The hostel was overrun with yelling children, screaming toddlers and mothers struggling vainly to exert control. Many of the men were out, searching for housing or a job. In most cases, it's both they were after.

Two bedrooms ran directly off the patio, with more down the corridor and others on a second floor above. There were ten in total, with space enough for seventy-five residents. Each room was furnished with only the bare essentials, but for the most part they were clean and free of damp.

A staff member brought out milk and bread from the kitchen and for a minute or two the children fell silent, their attention absorbed by the morning snack. I used the break in the mayhem to ask the adults milling around if they might answer a few questions. The women stuck with the kids, but four men shuffled forward. Together we sat down at a round table in the corner of the patio; I with my notebook, and they with their stories of lives turned upside down.

Each of them had arrived in the city within the past month, and all bar one were from Antioquia province, of which Medellín is the capital. Unlike María, they had eschewed the bus and instead hitched by truck.

Twenty-two-year-old Edison had had the longest journey. He hailed from a small village in Boyacá province, north of Bogotá. It was there, in 1819, that Bolívar's army had defeated the Spanish and won independence for Colombia. The trip to Medellín had taken Edison three days, the same length of time it took the Liberator to march from the battlefield to a hero's welcome in the capital.

Edison had taken flight to avoid joining the paramilitaries. Every Tuesday and Thursday, the right-wing militia would come through the village recruiting. The wage wasn't bad – 500,000 *pesos* a month – with home leave once a fortnight. For someone without a job like Edison, the money must have been tempting. But the thin, spotty young man was no warrior, and he repeatedly turned them down. The paramilitaries took his snub badly.

A month ago, rumours reached Edison that they planned to recruit him anyway, by force if necessary. So he took off. He'd not been able to tell his parents where he was for fear that his pursuers might come and find him. He missed his mum.

Twenty-eight-year-old Juan had a similar story. Retired from the army after seven years' service, he had moved back to his father's farm in Chigorodo, a small town in northern Antioquia. His credentials as a trained soldier earned him the attentions of both the paramilitary and the guerrilla recruiters. As with Edison, he declined their offers.

Then, one morning, a folded bulletin was shoved under the door of his house. It looked at first like junk mail. Juan opened it to find a neatly typed death threat. It was addressed to him and his extended family: either they left town immediately or their lives would be taken, one by one. The killers would start with the youngest, the unsigned letter threatened. Juan and his relatives escaped to Medellín the next day, all thirteen of them crammed into a pick-up truck.

Javier and Carlos also fled from the province's northern badlands. It was Javier's second experience of eviction in as many months. Two days before Christmas, he and his wife had been working at their sewing machines on the outskirts of the city. They had expanded their family-run textile business a few years beforehand, constructing a small workshop at the back of the house. Since investing in the extra capacity, orders had increased and business was going well.

The improvement in trade had not been missed by the local paramilitary group. Their money-collector, a gruff overweight man, well-known in the neighbourhood, came knocking at the door. Normally, the monthly cut was 200,000 *pesos*. From now on, the sum would be triple that, the plump extortionist informed Javier.

'Market forces,' the local mafioso had said. 'Think of it as a Christmas bonus.'

Javier didn't have that kind of money, and soon the threats started coming. He and his wife decided to pack up and return with their six kids to the town of Apartadó, where Javier had once lived and where he still had some friends.

As he was talking, his wife wandered up and put her arms around his neck. She rested her head on his shoulder, and Javier took her hand in his. She was petite and, in her off-white school overall, looked barely out of school.

Soon after the family's relocation, two FARC members came to the house where they were staying. They told Javier they wanted to buy his ten-year-old son – so he could 'grow up to become a good guerrilla'. They said they'd pay, offering a one-off fee of 1.5 million *pesos,* roughly the cost of a second-hand moped.

Javier was desperate, but not that desperate. It fell to the family to pack their bags again and return as refugees to Medellín.

As for Carlos, a roasted-peanut-seller in his former life, it wasn't the armed groups that sought to recruit him. It was the police. They wanted him as a witness to a murder. Five months previously, he'd seen a man stabbed to death in an alleyway near his house. The police called him in for questioning, but he'd been unable to identify the perpetrator. Last month, his neighbour had been killed. Again, the police hauled him in to testify, and again he had nothing to give them.

The criminals were less convinced of his silence. At 3 a.m., eight armed men surrounded his house. He was given five minutes to pack a bag of clothes for his two daughters before being thrown out on the street. They told him never to come back. He wasn't planning to.

As I returned to my hostel in Parque Bolívar, I was hit by the senseless cruelty of it all. It took me a full day to pack for my trip.

There was the extra memory card to buy, the jeans to pick up from the laundry and the piles of clothes to whittle down. These people had a matter of hours, often only minutes, in which to collect together all their worldly belongings.

Worse still, most weren't even the principal protagonist in the drama, just uninvolved relatives or incumbent children. Sometimes they didn't even know *who* exactly it was they were running from. But they knew *what* it was: it was the thought of a stranger hanging around the school gate waiting for their child; it was the heavy breathing down the phone line; it was the midnight knock on the door; it was the gnawing fear that at any time, anywhere, *they* could get you.

Nor are the *desplazados* necessarily safe once on the run. Back in Bogotá, I'd met a female community leader who was still receiving threats two years after escaping her guerrilla-controlled town. In the past twelve months, she'd been forced to move twenty times to different locations around the capital. I'd also spoken with a man under the government witness-protection programme who had sought refuge in Chile. Even there, his persecutors had tracked him down.

Fortunately for María, she has suffered no such repercussions. But the nightmares have not left her. Every night, the image of her husband's killers comes back to haunt her. The stress of the past six months has also brought on stomach cramps and blinding headaches. At the boarding house, she'd been to see a psychologist. He had given her some tranquillisers but advised that the best thing to do was talk openly about her experience. She had done her best to do so.

All my questions, she said, were helping her: 'It's like therapy.'

Her comment reminds me of a sign I'd seen back at the centre. 'Silence increases pain – talk.' A helpline was given below. Daniel won't be ringing it. At fifteen years old, María's introverted son had suddenly found himself the man of the household. The once out-going youth now spends most of his days in the cramped, one-room house. He helps his mother with the younger children and the household chores. Once they're settled in, she hopes he'll find a job.

María frets about how taciturn and insular he's become. Dropping out of school hasn't helped, she admits. His new responsibilities no longer allow for regular classes, and he goes to an adult-education centre on Saturdays. The opportunity to find new friends is slim. Everyone else is at least twice his age. What Daniel needs is interaction with other teenage boys, friends with whom he can play football or hang out in the park. What displacement has left him is precisely the reverse. Anyway, Altos de Oriente has no park.

I ask what María does for food, and she points to a cardboard box beneath the kitchen utensils. It's stamped with the logo of the United Nations-backed World Food Programme. Under Colombian law, all newly displaced people are entitled to emergency relief for three months.

Back in the displacement centre, a large warehouse is given over to storing boxes like María's. A chart on the wall lists off what a family of six should receive per month. The bulk of it consists of rice (10 kilos), beans (4 kilos), maize (5 kilos) and tuna (seven tins). Into the box also go packets of powdered milk, pasta, salt, coffee, sugar, noodles and sardines. Not the most inspiring diet, nor the most protein-rich.

With several children under ten years old, María is eligible for a three-month extension to the emergency rations. Even so, with seven hungry mouths to feed, the rations don't go far, and María is often left relying on leftovers from neighbours. But she is not one to grumble. The displacement centre had also provided her with bedding, pots and pans, toiletries and clothing.

All these handouts were part of her legitimate rights, the centre's administrators had informed her. Soon after her displacement, she'd attended an orientation session to learn more about these purported rights of hers. She had left with a nine-point sheet and a healthy dose of scepticism. Her doubts were not misplaced.

A few years ago, Colombia's highest court ruled that the Government wasn't meeting its constitutional obligations towards its displaced citizens. Since then, more money has been earmarked for the problem. But it still falls woefully short. By the government's own admission, only around one in three displaced children has access to adequate health and education services.

María is by no means alone. Four out of five families in Altos de Oriente are victims of forced displacement. They are among the ninety-five thousand internal refugees who have flocked to Medellín over the past decade. Situated in a mountainous bowl, the city has nowhere to expand but upwards. Hence the proliferation of shanty-town communities on the highest ridges of this heavily urbanised valley. As with María's new home, most are ramshackle, precarious affairs.

On the night before my visit, heavy rains washed away several houses in the hills west of the city. Seven people died in the mud-slide, five of them children. María constantly worries about something similar happening to her and her family. As it is, the children all have colds and the baby is suffering from a wheezing cough.

'They want to know when we are going home to our own house. What am I supposed to tell them?'

I had no answer for María. She'd had longer than Álvaro to adjust to being a *desplazada,* but adapting to her new status wasn't proving easy. I travelled north to learn about the road ahead of her.

North Antioquia

In Mutatá, the slum at the bottom of the town is called El Progreso, or Progress, an optimistic name given the circumstances.

Roughly eight hundred families live in the ten-block neighbourhood. All have been displaced from surrounding provinces. For water, they rely on a communal pumping station. It functions for four hours in the morning and two in the afternoon. The water is only good for washing. Drinking water needs to be bought by the bottle. Electricity supplies are erratic and sanitation services abysmal.

The cramped single-storey houses become so hot during the day that people spend much of their time sitting outside. Unemployed men gather together at the three or four kiosks that operate in the neighbourhood. Run out of the residents' own homes, the stores are little more than large front windows looking out onto the street. Usually the proprietors put out a few plastic chairs for their customers.

For want of a better alternative, the shops act as popular meeting places for El Progreso's army of bored and unoccupied men. They plonk themselves in the seats and lounge there idly. Some order beer. Most buy nothing. Permission to hang out is not provisional on purchase. Occasionally, someone pulls out a deck of cards and they play a round or two of *arancon*, a popular game in these parts. In general, though, they spend their time chatting and exchanging friendly insults between one another. Their objective is to while away time, to see yet another day through from start to finish.

While I am wandering around El Progreso's damp, unsanitary streets, Carlos Alberto sidles up to me. He introduces himself as a member of the neighbourhood committee and offers to show me around. A jovial, moustached man who I guess to be in his late forties but could be older, Carlos proves to be a popular man. As we walk, he waves at people on their doorsteps and ruffles children's hair. There is no one whose name he doesn't know, a familiarity that even extends to their pets. Then that's not so surprising. Living in such close quarters to one another, everyone in El Progreso knows everyone. Privacy comes at a premium here.

Carlos fills me in a little about the shanty town's history. Most of the residents moved to the town ten years ago. They came en masse, fleeing a spate of 'disappearances' and massacres unleashed by the paramilitaries. At first, they'd lived in tents. Carlos has been slightly better off than most. He'd disassembled his old house in the countryside and managed to salvage enough materials to build himself a rudimentary shack.

'From that start, anything is progress. Hence the name.' He laughs. It must be a well-worn joke.

Now the houses are made from wood, and all have concrete foundations. The number of jobless is also going down. At the beginning, more than nine out of ten people couldn't find work. Now it's half that figure.

Despite the improvements, I ask Carlos if he would prefer to go home. Since the paramilitaries handed in their weapons, reports of forced evictions and arbitrary killings are down considerably. He says he would but that it's impossible. He used to work as a peon on a sizeable estate. As part of the deal, the landowner gave him a plot of land of his own.

'It was just a casual agreement, you see. There were no papers or anything like that.'

He still gets on well with his ex-employer and not so long ago went back to discuss the possibility of returning. The problem is the house. Since Carlos' dismantling job, there isn't one. His former boss says he doesn't have the money to build him a replacement. And Carlos definitely doesn't. His weekend job at a transport yard barely provides him with enough to get by, let alone to construct a new home from scratch.

Many other displaced Colombians find themselves in a similar situation. As former farm hands or migrant *colonos,* they lack official title deeds to the land where they used to live. Under Colombian settlement legislation, land ownership should technically pass to new colonisers after five years of productive occupation. The law underpins the frontier feeling in much of rural Colombia. Every year, migrant farmers push further and further into the country's vast uninhabited interior. But to enact their legal entitlement requires all sorts of paperwork – paperwork that most never get round to doing.

María Cervantes, a forty-one-year-old grandmother and permanent resident of El Progreso, has a different problem. She and her husband sold their land. Rocking in a chair on her doorstep with her grandson in her lap, she says she still rues the decision. But at the time, she had felt backed into a corner. She and her family had abandoned their two-hundred-and-fifty-hectare farm after the deaths of half a dozen neighbours at the hands of the paramilitaries.

'Soon afterwards, men started turning up in the refugee camp in

Mutatá. They said they were representing people interested in buying up our land. We had fled with almost nothing, so we ended up selling. I so wish we hadn't.'

María obtained a fifth of what her property was really worth. Added to that, the middlemen took a 20 per cent commission. Now her land is covered in African palm, the boom crop in this tropical corner of north-western Colombia. Others didn't even get to negotiate.

'In many cases, the paramilitaries would just turn up, accuse you of collaborating with the guerrillas and order you to sell your land to them,' Carlos chips in. 'Deal with us today,' they used to say, 'or tomorrow we'll be dealing with your widow.'

Despite such threats, a handful of brave souls still attempt to return. Many are simply displaced a second time. Others are dispatched more permanently. Yolanda Izquierdo is a case in point. A virulent campaigner for the resettlement of *desplazados*, the mother of five was recently gunned down on the patio of her home. The assassination occurred in Montería, three hundred miles north of Bogotá and the birthplace of the paramilitaries.

Only a few days before her death, Yolanda had testified against Salvatore Mancuso, a paramilitary hard man wanted for all manner of atrocities. A 'death foretold' is how one human-rights representative put it. Her slaying came several weeks after the murders of two other notable land activists. All three deaths are attributed to the paramilitaries. As part of a general plea bargain struck with the government, demobilised paramilitary members are being promised lighter sentences in exchange for confessing their crimes and returning the property they have appropriated. Many don't much care for the second clause.

Luis Olvidio will not be deterred though. He was once the proud owner of one hundred and seventy hectares of prime arable land outside Mutatá. A decade previously, paramilitaries had killed his father-in-law, prompting him to leave. Seven months ago, he decided to move back.

I'd heard about Olvidio through a human-rights worker back in

Bogotá and, over a crackly phone line, arranged a visit. His house lies a two-hour drive from the town down a bumpy country road. No buses travel the route, so I hire a rusty jeep to take me.

We trundle out of town, across the swollen river Sucio and through fields of fruit-laden banana plants. After an hour, we hit the first army checkpoint. Two soldiers, both in their early twenties and dressed in battle fatigues, step out from behind a wall of sandbags. Since the paramilitaries' demobilisation, control over this blood-soaked region has passed over to the Colombian armed forces. The armed privates order me out of the jeep, check my passport and enquire after the purpose of my visit. They don't buy my story about 'seeing the countryside', but they can't find anything illegal about it and so let me pass.

After a second checkpoint twenty minutes up the road, the palm plantation starts. For five kilometres, the view from the road is reduced to the stumpy fat trunks and arching, vertiginous fronds of African palm. The trees look like huge sprouting pine cones, row after row after row. Olvidio's farm lies down an overgrown track at the plantation's perimeter. The view from his front door is the same.

Olvidio is standing on his porch when the jeep pulls up. He's a giant of a man with a barrel chest and, as I couldn't help noticing, an unusually extended belly button. Wearing no shirt and with a towel thrown over his shoulder, he's just returned from his morning wash in a nearby stream. He greets me warmly and shouts out back for some breakfast.

Busying herself in the open-air kitchen at the rear of the house, Olvidio's wife soon appears with a bowl of steaming fish soup and fried yucca. She's dressed in a ragged T-shirt and a long skirt hitched above her bulging stomach. Her hair is specked with white and face etched with the wear and tear of a gruelling life. Their two young girls are also at work, mucking out the pigsty.

On a bench in the kitchen, silently darning a pair of frayed socks, sits Olvidio's widowed mother-in-law. The old woman's snow-white Afro is tied into two pigtails that hang limply from the side of her head. They remind me of the floppy ears of a Dobermann.

The house itself is a two-storey wooden structure. It looks basic, but sturdy. I ask Olvidio when he'd built it. He didn't, he says. A local Colombian palm company constructed it in his absence. That firm had since sold his land to a larger palm-oil producer.

Staring out at the lines of mature African palm, the imposing Afro-Colombian is bemused by all that has happened: 'This latest company says it has legal papers for the land, but I don't know how that can be as I have titles dating back twenty years.'

From Olvidio's original farm, only a space as large as a football pitch escaped the palm invasion. On his return, the industrious homesteader set about clearing. It took him and his two teenage sons months of back-breaking work to complete. He was planning to grow plantain, maize and yucca, just as he'd always done. But the company beat him to it. They ordered in their workers and planted over Olvidio's freshly prepared plot with palm. It was a sending-off offence, but the gormless soldiers at the checkpoint were the only referees present. Olvidio didn't bother appealing.

Later, I would put a call in to the National Federation of Palm Oil Producers to see if Olvidio's experience was common practice. I was patched through to the trade body's general director, who was at the organisation's national conference in Cali. He'd sounded mildly frantic. Numbers were through the roof for this year's meeting thanks to a government proposal to use palm oil for biodiesel. Suddenly everyone wanted a slice of the windfall.

Biofuels already have a bad reputation in much of South America. Land once devoted to growing crops and raising livestock is being supplanted by soya, palm and the other vegetable ingredients for modern agro-fuel alternatives. Food is scarcer and prices higher as a consequence, the critics argue. Now biofuels have displacement to add to their rap sheet too.

The director would go on to admit that the palm boom had indeed attracted its rogues. Illegal land expropriations were, he confessed, 'lamentable'. In his defence, he'd suggested that Colombia's banana and sugar industries had been doing the same for decades. Still, I was interested to know who these palm companies might be.

The director said he'd rather not name names but insisted that they were most definitely not members of his prestigious federation.

Olvidio is only too happy to pass on the company's details. He just sees little point in doing so. An international human-rights group has taken up his cause, but he's not confident they'll meet with success. For every one hundred cases of forced displacement, on average, one reaches court. Far fewer obtain a guilty verdict. In the mean time, Olvidio is reduced to taking his rowing boat up the nearby river and chopping down trees in the forest. He sells the timber to local builders. He knows it's illegal, but he says he'll take his chances: 'It's not as if the law has much of a presence around here.'

Lawlessness is a common complaint in rural Colombia. Whole regions such as Olvidio's have been left for decades without sight or sound of a policeman, let alone a judge. Armed rebels have historically been the only reference point. They hold the weapons, so they make the laws. 'Arms will make you free, but laws will bring you liberty,' Francisco de Paula Santander, the post-independence president of Colombia, had once said. The law of the gun turns that early ideal on its head.

Not all legal custodians opt for the law's heavier hand. Olvidio and others like him have an inspirational role model in the Nasa. One of the more numerous of Colombia's eighty-five native people groups, the Nasa have staged one of the most remarkable resettlements in recent Colombian history.

I first heard their story through an excited Peace Corps volunteer, who thought them the perfect model for Colombia's path to post-conflict reconstruction. Spread across the foothills of North Cauca, two hours south of Cali, the Nasa have been the victims of one land grab after another. Eventually, they decided enough was enough. As a collective group, they marched down the mountains and seized back part of their traditional territories. At the beginning of the 1990s, their exercise in mass squatting obtained legal sanction. Under a new national constitution, parcels of tribal land were earmarked for indigenous reservations.

Earlier in my Colombia trip, I'd taken the bus from Cali to see how the experiment was working out. I was dropped off in the quiet town of Santander de Quilichao and from there caught a truck up into the mountains to Canoas. Home to around six thousand people, the indigenous settlement commands a spectacular view across a lush, forested valley. The reservation consists of isolated wooden houses stationed sporadically over the hillside.

Gernán Valencia showed me round. A well-built man with a crew cut, he is head of the Nasa's non-violent community guard. He was sporting a long fawn poncho and carrying a wooden staff decorated with green and red ribbons.

'The staff is a sign of authority in our community. Whoever holds it must be listened to,' he'd told me, deadly serious. I wasn't about to argue.

The guard boasts four thousand representatives. Without their permission, no one can enter or leave the Nasa communities. They also provide shelter for Nasa's *desplazados,* preventing the victims of violence from fleeing to the cities. Gernán shows me round Canoas' communal safe house. It's located in a sprawling hacienda with multiple bedrooms, a flourishing vegetable patch and a balconied veranda looking out across the valley. The house used to be the holiday home of a Cali drug baron until Gernán and his guards peacefully reappropriated it. Due to a lull in guerrilla attacks, the displacement centre has been converted into a temporary correction centre for the community's criminals. It must be the only prison in South America with no guards, no bars and an outdoor swimming pool.

To win back the remainder of its ancestral lands, the Nasa of North Cauca have mapped out a plan. It goes under the rubric of 'Project Life'.

'The large landowners have a "Project of Death" designed to destroy us,' Gernán explained, 'so this is our response.'

Protest marches, campaign letters and legal action are their weapons. For the Nasa, the fight is more than just a battle for ownership. It's a struggle to liberate the Earth. Mother Earth cannot be free, the Nasa teach, while private interests exploit her for personal gain.

'While she who gives us life is kept enslaved, then we, her children, who respect her and live with her, also remain slaves,' the local figurehead had said, pounding the ground powerfully with his staff. The Nasa have spoken.

El Progreso. Project of Life. These are optimistic names indeed.

Cartagena

I headed up to Cartagena de Indias on the northern Caribbean coast conscious that my time in Colombia was drawing to a close. I had been told the country was on the road to peace. Parts of it, I suppose, were. If I'd stuck to the salsa clubs of Cali or the shopping malls of Medellín, perhaps I could have persuaded myself it *all* was? But behind the bright lights and talk of business buoyancy, there is no hiding the ravages wrought by four decades of interminable conflict. Families are torn apart, lives are lived in fear, and hundreds of thousands have lost their homes.

I had little confidence that this colonial port town, the old stomping ground of Nobel Prize-winning writer Gabriel García Márquez, would change my perspective. When Bolívar visited in 1830, the Liberator had bemoaned the abundance of beggars on the streets. 'What good has this damn independence done anyway?' he supposedly inquired of the city's governor. In a matter of weeks, Bolívar would be dead, going to his grave with Cartagena's vagrants in the forefront of his mind.

The homeless are still there, loitering around the Mercado de Bazurto and sleeping rough in the Parque Centenario. I take a room in the tatty Getsémani district of the Old Town. Bolívar's list has since expanded to include prostitutes, drunks and crack-dealers. That's not to demean the charms of Colombia's UNESCO World Heritage Site. Even with its army of down-and-outs, Cartagena well deserves its status as one of the colonial jewels of South America. I follow the guidebook's instructions and spend two days losing myself in the winding historic streets of the walled city. I visit the baroque domed cathedral, people-watch from charming pavement cafés and hunt out Parque Bolívar for a photo of the Liberator's statue.

Done with sightseeing, I telephone Patricia Guerrero. Her name had been given to me by a local journalist working in Bogotá. 'Go and meet her,' was all she'd said on learning about my interest in the *desplazados.* And so it is that, early on a Monday morning, I find myself knocking at an unmarked door down one of Getsémani's labyrinthine side streets.

A young man with a goatee beard answers and shows me into the spacious headquarters of the League for Displaced Women. Conference flyers and international awards litter the walls. He directs me up a narrow staircase to the office of *la doctora,* the doctor. She sounds frightening but couldn't be less so.

An attractive woman in late middle age, she's sitting at a large desk by an open window. The breeze is ruffling her papers, which are piled unsteadily like pillars of Jenga bricks across the table. She apologises. She's just adding the final touches to a new research report. The league is lobbying for the demobilised paramilitaries to be made to confess their crimes against women.

'How many of the women who were murdered or displaced were raped first? Nobody knows. The State doesn't care, and the paramilitaries aren't interested in telling us.'

Before I have a chance to ask a question, she starts reading the headline facts from the report in front of her: incidences of verbal abuse, torched homes, beatings, mock executions, forced sex, unwanted pregnancies. It's all quite harrowing for a Monday morning.

'Isn't there any good news?' I finally get to ask.

'Good news? Yes, of course, just go visit the City of Women.'

An hour later, a bus from the city limits drops me off at the front door of Eidanys Lamadrid's home. Her house is located on scrubland off the main highway, eleven kilometres south of Cartagena proper. From the outside, it's unremarkable: a rectangular-shaped bungalow built from floor to low-hanging ceiling from ugly, concrete blocks. The seventy-eight-square-metre floor plan – divvied up between two bedrooms, a kitchen/living room and one small bathroom – is identical to that of her ninety-six neighbours. The City of Women looks and feels like a soldiers' barracks. There is no church, no supermarket, no park and, as yet, there are no street names.

But it is the first permanent home that Eidanys has had for almost a decade, and she is rightfully proud of it. Inside, there is little room to move, what with the three-piece suite and bulky dining table. Her two daughters are sitting with friends watching a DVD on the new television set. Everything down to the liquidiser is bought on credit.

She makes no apologies for splurging. In Colombia, there's a popular saying, she tells me: 'He with no house is very poor. He with a house is very rich.' Despite not having a *peso* in the bank, Eidanys is, in her mind at least, suddenly very rich.

Eidanys even likes the breeze blocks. She should do because she helped make them. Working from morning till night at the community kiln, she and her women companions produced twelve hundred bricks a day. After six months, they had enough to start building their new homes.

Since moving in a year ago, several of the women have established micro-enterprises around the City. One lady rents out her washing machine by the load. Others run small stores from their homes or make handicrafts to sell to Cartagena's tourists. The kiln is also still operational, making bricks for sale to the local construction market. Eidanys's mother has even opened a small restaurant.

Thirty-four-year-old Eidanys credits Patricia Guerrero for much of the miracle. The *doctora* badgered local officials and buttered up foreign donors to raise the money for the housing project. More importantly still, she pushed the women to start believing in themselves.

Eidanys is the first to testify to the change in her own self-perception.

'Years ago, some of my neighbours and I tried forming a committee of displaced women. But we didn't know our rights nor what organisations should be helping us. The authorities just ignored us and pretended we didn't exist. Then Patricia came, and we entered the league. That's when we started getting training about our rights and about how to empower ourselves. Now when we go to the government offices, we know what we are entitled to, and we won't take no for an answer. They don't try and fob us off any more like they used to.'

I am reminded of her shift in mindset later in our conversation. We're chatting in her kitchen when my eye settles on a handwritten card above the sink. It exhorts the reader to forget the mistakes of the past and fight for great achievements in the future.

The league gave similar notes to all the new house-owners, Eidanys explains. She agrees with the general sentiment, although she doesn't like the word 'mistake'.

'Being displaced is never the victim's "mistake". It can never be. It can never be our fault!'

For many of her new neighbours, the journey towards self-belief has been harder. Displacement is the common theme that links all ninety-seven households in the City of Women. Many still carry the trauma of having witnessed family members killed or their worldly possessions set on fire. A large number of the City's residents have been widowed by violence. Others have separated from their menfolk during the tough years following their displacement.

As we stroll around the freshly laid streets, Eidanys points to various houses and the abuses that their owners have suffered. The cases sound much the same as those from the *doctora*'s list earlier that morning. Several are survivors of the El Salado massacre.

She fills me in on the details as we continue our walk. The incident takes its name from a village in Bolívar province. Salvatore Mancuso and his men invaded the supposedly FARC-friendly hamlet eight years ago. The paramilitary brigade stayed three days. They had with them a man in a hood. The disguised snitch went from house to house identifying alleged guerrilla sympathisers. Anyone he pointed to was shot on the spot. Mancuso's men had rigged up a sound system by the town football pitch. With the sound of every bullet, they turned up the volume and danced.

Thirty-nine people were slaughtered in total. Everyone else was forced to flee. It was José Tomás Boves all over again.

Eidanys' running commentary also suggests that violence against women does not end with displacement. Life in the urban slums often brings with it domestic and sexual abuse. At least half a dozen of the City of Women's residents have been raped since leaving the security of their homes. Others have seen their children turn to drugs, petty crime or prostitution.

I put down my notebook, my writing hand growing sore with so many stories. Eidanys notices me tiring and suggests we go and meet a friend of hers. In her late forties, Julia carries a permanent worry line between her eyes. We chat for a little while about her new house but soon the subject turns back to the hardships of displacement. It was the culture shock that she found most traumatic at first. I ask if she can elaborate.

'It's simple,' she responds. 'In the countryside, a woman's role is carefully mapped out between housework, motherhood and a little agricultural work near the house. Generally we have nothing to do with money matters, political involvement or other things touching on the world outside the home. That's the men's business.'

When Julia came to the city, she found work in a restaurant washing the dishes. Employment, albeit in menial domestic jobs, is easier to find for a woman than it is for a man. Generally illiterate or sub-literate, the curriculum of a displaced farmer isn't going to feature the education or experience that a company is looking for. Odd jobs and day labouring is often the best they can find. Many men end up withdrawing into themselves, Julia says. Over time, the responsibility for the emotional and economic welfare of the family shifts to the womenfolk.

Eidanys is a rare exception in the City of Women in being both married and having a husband with a job. It's not much, she says, just as a caretaker for a firm in town, but it pays for their bills and monthly hire-purchase quotas.

He even supports her taking part in the league. 'Not that he ever thought they would achieve anything,' Eidanys snorts. 'He always used to tell me that my job was to stay at home and look after the kids.'

The feisty *mulatta* had made her spouse eat his words. Now, she says, the men feel excluded because their names don't appear on any of the City's documents. To help their husbands through their feelings of disenfranchisement, the women have contracted a male counsellor to run a monthly 'masculinity' workshop.

'As *campesinas,* our role was never recognised,' Eidanys remarks. 'Now, at last, we are realising our rights.' And don't their menfolk know it.

Not everyone goes to the workshops. Resentment among the male-dominated local elite remains fierce. The mayor in the nearby municipality of Turbaco has yet to visit them.

'If you resist instead of submitting as everyone else does, then you're a threat to the powers that be,' Eidanys states matter-of-factly.

The league has formally denounced the Town Hall for corruption. Public funds for the *desplazados,* they claim, have disappeared into the mayor's pockets and those of his cronies. The women now have the mayor up on an incompetence charge. Twice they wrote to him asking for greater police protection after various incidences of intimidation. He told them they were exaggerating. Several months later, a 'freak' fire burned down the City's community centre.

'They tried to say it was caused by an electric fault. But that's impossible. The electric cables had been stolen the previous month!'

The fire is the last in a series of attacks, dating back to the assassination of Julio Miguel Pérez two years previously. A victim of three separate displacements, the father of six was planning to move to the City of Women with his wife. To show his solidarity, he offered to guard the brick factory at night. His daughter had found him lying dead in the street when she came to bring him his morning coffee. He'd been killed with a machete. There has been no arrest nor, as far as his widow knows, any investigation into his murder.

I ask the women why Colombia is so prone to such terrible, repeated violence. They both shrug their shoulders. No one else I've spoken with in my travels around the country seems to have a convincing answer either. Some blame violent segments in society: the guerrilla, the paramilitaries, the Army, the drug-dealers. Others find fault in the system: poverty, poor education, police corruption, inflexible social structures, legal impunity.

Bolívar, in contrast, blamed the Spanish. The colonists' barbarity had to be met with greater barbarity. Is Colombia today at the bottom of a self-perpetuated downward spiral? Is this where an eye for an eye leads? A country accustomed to the horrific, blind to peaceful means? It seems far-fetched. Yet so does killing a man because his wife and her friends are building a home for themselves.

We leave Julia's house, and Eidanys walks me to the bus stop. As I wait for my ride back to town, the City of Women's indomitable resident tells me about the upcoming public assembly. She and her female companions have decided it's time to name their streets. They're thinking of naming the main avenue after Julio Miguel, in memory of their murdered companion. Eidanys knows what she wants to call her own street: Calle Dr Patricia Guerrero.

In the heroines of Cartagena, Bolívar finally had an unexpected answer to what his damned independence had achieved.

Santa Marta

The Liberator was in no mood for being inspired in the days before he died. By the time he arrived up the coast from Cartagena in Santa Marta, he only had a month to live. His outlook for Colombia was grim: 'This country will fall inevitably into the hands of the unrestrained multitudes and then into the hands of tyrants.' The FARC and their foes have proved it a prescient prediction.

Bolívar had left Bogotá seven months earlier, resigning the presidency of the country and committing himself to a life in exile. The journey from the capital took him up the river Magdalena towards the Caribbean Sea. They were months of growing anguish. He stood by in the sidelines as new leaders arose and fought among themselves for their corner of the liberated continent. The last leg of his trip saw him taken by horse and cart to the hacienda of Joaquín de Mier, a pro-republican Spaniard who lived just outside Santa Marta. The intention was to recover his failing health before setting sail to Europe.

In *The General in his Labyrinth,* Gabriel García Márquez's fictional account of the Liberator's final few months, it's a disillusioned Bolívar weighed down by 'lugubrious thoughts' who arrives at the outlying ranch in the village of San Pedro Alejandrino. Factions are prising apart his vision of a united South America. Attempts are being made on his life. Tuberculosis is eating away at his lungs. Lying in his borrowed bed, with the clairvoyance of impending death, García Márquez imagines him 'shaken by the overwhelming revelation that the headlong race between his misfortunes and his dreams was at that moment reaching the finishing line'.

As I walk around de Mier's former estate, I too try and conjure up an image of the Liberator in his last days, drugging himself with herbal palliatives, arranging his personal effects, giving instructions to his loyal servant José Palacios, writing a last letter to his beloved Manuela and dwelling at length on his legacy.

Bolívar, more than anyone, knew what it was like to belong to a place, and then not to. He understood what it meant to invest in building something, only to see it snatched away. He died homeless and almost penniless, outside his country of birth and heading into exile. Yes, I think Bolívar could have empathised with the likes of Álvaro, María, Carlos, Luis Olvidio and Eidanys.

Yet, Bolívar's last thoughts were not focused on individuals but on the countries he'd liberated. Aware death was only hours away, he longed to preserve what remained of his legacy. The words of South America's greatest-ever statesman are today etched onto the wall of the outbuilding where he died. I take out my notebook and note them down:

'I aspire to no other glory than the consolidation of Colombia. You must all work to the inestimable good of the union: the people offering their obedience to the current government in order to save themselves from anarchy.'

Conflict-ridden Colombia had clearly failed.

I jump on a bus to Venezuela and the home of the 'Bolívarian Revolution'. Maybe there I will have more hope of finding the dreams of the Liberator realised?

9

OPERATION BOLÍVAR

Venezuela and revolution

The fundamental principle of our system demands that equality be immediately and exclusively established and put into practice in Venezuela . . . We have the right to expect that happiness will be the legacy Venezuela bequeaths her citizens.

SIMÓN BOLÍVAR, 'THE ANGOSTURA ADDRESS'

Los Rastrojos

Lourdes has spent a lifetime of dusk-filtered evenings just watching. Several years ago, when cataracts began eating away at his sight, they packed him off to Cuba. The eighty-one-year-old was bundled onto a charter flight to Havana, hosted for a week without charge and examined by a bevy of eye surgeons dressed in creased white lab coats.

Unfortunately, his octogenarian eyes ended up being too deteriorated to operate on. Lourdes' ability to see is shrinking by the day. Yet the old man is philosophical about growing blind. He's already seen a lifetime of seasons come and go, he says. What's another springtime? He can hear the larks and smell the jacaranda blossom. Besides, he's happy to have been on an aeroplane before he dies.

Habits being what they are, Lourdes still sits out on his porch to watch the world go by. His outdoor haven constitutes a narrow strip of crumbling concrete, no wider than a pavement. A large, inverted oil drum occupies the far end. Its spherical bulk looks to be anchoring his prefabricated house to its moorings. Strewn across its surface lies a colourful collection of half-empty glass bottles. Their labels are blanched yellow by the sun. The writing suggests that the functions of the upended barrel extend to medicine closet and drinks cabinet too.

The last scarlet rays of the day glint off the face of his cheap wristwatch. The reflection catches my eye as I pass by, and I look up towards his rudimentary home. There, by the oil drum, the blind watchman is sitting in his habitual spot. He's slumped in a plastic rocking chair, his thin frame crumpled inwards as if someone's just vacuumed the air out of him. A cloud of midges is buzzing around his hairless forearms.

I wave at him from the road in front, not yet knowing about his fogged vision. The gesture is wasted, but he hears my footsteps and greets my blur with a cheerful *buenas tarde*s. I respond in kind, and he beckons me over to join him. Four mucus-yellow teeth lodged into a set of mud-brown gums grin in my direction. Aside from the dental catastrophe, his smile is kind and welcoming. There's only one other chair. I take a seat.

We talk for an hour or so. Lourdes has lived in the same one-street hamlet of Los Rastrojos all his life. Down the highway is Sabaneta, a two-bit town in the third-rate province of Barinas. This is the heart of the *llanos,* Venezuela's ground zero, miles and miles of flat savannah broken up by nothing except fields of dry corn and starved-looking cattle. In Bolívar's day, bands of outlaws had ridden across these dusty grasslands. Today, it's dented pick-ups that trawl the dusty highways.

I've come for clues about Hugo Chávez, the boy from the back-waters. Little Hugo had spent his early years under these same sun-scorched skies, fighting the midges and listening to *joropo* country dances played out on a five-stringed banjo.

After hearing all about Lourdes' cataracts and his Cuban adventure, I inquire if he'd known the president as a boy. The Los Rastrojos old-timer smiles. I suspect he'd been anticipating the question, waiting patiently for me to get round to it.

'Of course. All us oldies round here remember him well, me more than most. I was friends with his father. He was the local school-master here for a while. *El Maestro,* as good a man as they get.'

The schoolhouse is long gone, replaced by a brick-built agricultural college. The Chávez family home has also ceased to be. A roadside lot full of weeds is all that's left. *El Maestro* moved on decades ago. Shortly after his son came to power, he changed jobs too. Lourdes' former friend became governor and moved into the walled mansion in the state capital. He's since passed on the gubernatorial keys to his eldest offspring, Adán.

Falling quiet for a minute, the *llanero* retrieves a distant memory from half a century ago. He locates it and dusts it off. Like its owner, the anecdote is mottled with age.

'It must have taken place about this time in the evening. No, a little later perhaps. The sun had set. Anyway, I was sitting out on the porch when I saw a small boy tearing down the road. He was riding an oversized bicycle with no stabilisers.'

The absence of supports identified him immediately as the schoolmaster's son. Young Hugo never once used the beginners' wheels, according to Lourdes. The detail appears important to him. It's as if the future president was impatient with his youth, anxious to be done with it and on to the chapters of his adult life.

The storyteller continues.

'He was alone, pedalling hard down the bumpy street. I stepped off the porch as he approached and put my hand up for him to stop, like this.'

Lourdes holds up an outstretched palm as a traffic policeman might.

The rest of the scene plays out like the final frames of a timeworn cine film.

'The little scoundrel didn't have any brakes so he jammed his heels in the mud. He pulled up just short, almost knocked me over. "Hugito, does your father know that you are out by yourself in the dark?" I ask him. He was always charging around, you see, day or night. Always had a broken bone or a wrist in a sling. Do you know what the little man said to me? Fired back with it, quick as a flash. I remember it clear as day. "Why, Don Lourdes," he replies, "I'm not alone." "And how might that be, Hugito?" I inquire. He jumps back on his bike and shouts over his shoulder: "Don Lourdes, I'm not riding by myself. God and Bolívar are at my side."'

*

Every revolution requires a sense of destiny. Yet destiny is an unfulfilled promise, a legal contract that awaits signing. Without a signature, it's as useless as a winning lottery ticket squirrelled away on a shelf. Simón Bolívar was the man to step forward. As a twenty-two-year-old tourist on the slopes of Rome's Monte Sacro, the unknown South American aristocrat put his name to paper, in the presence of his childhood tutor, Simón Rodríguez.

'I swear by the God of my fathers, I swear on their graves, I swear by my country that I will not rest body or soul until I have broken the chains binding us to the will of Spanish might!'

The oath might well have been a commandment from on high so religiously did he observe it.

It takes a special kind of man to heed the call of Providence. Many millennia before, Moses had been called upon by the same God to speak before Pharaoh. The tremulous prophet begged off as a poor public speaker.

Not so the young Venezuelan revolutionary. He jumped at the task of history-making. No power, neither in Heaven nor on Earth, could divert him from his mission. Even when an earthquake prised open the streets of Caracas and swallowed up the vestiges of the First Republic, Bolívar's confidence did not budge. He stood above the rubble and wrung his fists: 'We will fight Nature itself if it opposes us, and force it to obey.'

Loss in battle did nothing to diminish his faith. He fed his armies with the same fervour. Twice the patriot forces claimed Venezuela as theirs, and twice the Spaniards stole it back. Only confidence in the ineluctability of fate persuaded them back a third time.

Knowing he was the right man at the right time enabled Bolívar to believe in the insuperable. His legendary proclamations on independence, visionary epics in which he mapped out the future of the continent – 'The Cartagena Manifesto', 'The Jamaica Letter', 'The Angostura Address' – were all written with the ink of defeat. 'Success will crown our efforts,' the Liberator wrote after the fall of the Second Republic, 'because the destiny of America is irrevocably fixed.' The vanquished general was holed up in a rented garret at the time, so broke he had to scrounge money to pay his landlady.

Hugo Chávez shares that spirit of destiny. He has renamed the country over which he presides as the Bolívarian Republic of Venezuela. Noam Chomsky in hand, the big shot from Barinas sees himself standing at the apex of history. Civilisations are clashing. Class wars are waging. The dawn of a second independence is awaiting its claimant. A twenty-first-century Bolívar is rising from the ashes.

Maracaibo and Coro

My first sighting of Hugo Chávez on Venezuelan soil occurs in the ground-floor room of a love hotel. It was mid-morning on a Sunday, and I'd just found the remote for the padlocked television set.

It had been an eventful Saturday night, though not one that would typically end up in a by-the-hour motel room. A long-distance bus had deposited me in the oil town of Maracaibo. It was well after dark when the Caracas-bound driver unceremoniously dumped me on an artery road miles from the centre of town. Disorientated and without a cent in my pocket, I'd flagged down the first taxi that passed.

For the next hour and a half, Diego took me on a tour of the city's cash machines. To my increasing dismay, each turned out to be empty or unwilling to recognise my foreign bank card. Eleventh time lucky, I found one that worked. By this stage, we'd lapped the city twice, and Diego's bill covered a good percentage of the extraction.

The change would see me through a night at an *económico* hotel. Diego recommended the Hotel Caribe and duly dropped me at the front door of the rundown joint. The luminous neon sign with its flashing coconuts should have alerted me. But it was 2 a.m., and I was dog-tired. I paid the grizzled rent-a-thug at the counter ('Yes, a full night please' – strange question?), crossed the hall and unlocked the door to my windowless double room. Within seconds, I was asleep.

Only the next morning, in the starkness of the bare strip light, do my suspicions about the Hotel Caribe's true credentials begin to grow. The clues are not hard to spot: the disproportionate-sized bed, the plastic under-sheet, the continual comings and goings outside the door, the faint grunting echoing through the vent pipes.

Confirmation comes at the touch of the remote. Onto the television screen flashes a graphic close-up of a copulating couple. There's no dialogue, just grinding. I flick channels. The only alternative is *Aló Presidente*, Hugo Chávez's weekly chat show. Hardcore porn or soft-core politics? I switch off the set.

My night tour with Diego and subsequent sleepover is enough to persuade me not to tarry long in Maracaibo. An unsubtle blend of concrete gristle and industrial grime, Venezuela's second city dedicates itself to oil: to drilling it, collecting it, refining it and selling it. Beneath the Orinoco Belt sit billions of barrels of thick crude. This is the fuel for the revolution, the black gold bankroll that keeps Chávez & Co. on the road.

I shower, change and take a second cab to the bus station. Through the smudged window of the taxi, Maracaibo's flyovers and charmless streets look as uninviting by day as they did by night. The buses are all booked, and twenty minutes later I'm sitting shot-gun in a loaded 1967 Ford Mustang, heading east along the coast to the colonial town of Coro.

The car's gears crunch noisily and its fan belt whines, but the road stretches straight and flat, and I'm soon asleep again. I awake three hours later to see my fellow passengers dismounting. We have arrived. Checking my accommodation listings for a hotel free of stained bedding, I choose a mid-range place near the town centre and flick on the television.

There's no more grinding, but to my surprise I find the president still on air. The man has been at it for over five hours. Picking up my notebook, I sit down to watch.

Like Bolívar, he's no looker. His forehead is too flat, his nose too pendulous, his eyes too piggy, his teeth too spaced, his cheeks too flaccid, his neck too thick, his hair too wiry. But there's a magnetism about him that keeps me watching. Two hours later, I'm still there.

The show's format is relatively straightforward. The president is shown in close-up, usually behind a simple desk. He dresses casually, always the same shirt of revolutionary red. His style is conversational and unscripted, a rambling monologue of ideas and anecdotes, policy commitments and the occasional military threat. When the urge takes him, he's wont to break out in song as well – snippets from the *boleros* of his childhood. The spectacle is part cabinet meeting, part cabaret performance and part chat on the porch.

Each week, a loose theme runs through the show. Today's episode happens to focus on farming. As viewers, we're taken on a tour of a 'socialist' cooperative. The camera tracks slowly across a field of happy workers toiling with hoes and ploughs. An earthy folk song plays softly in the background. The voice of an off-screen narrator then starts disparaging land-snatching monopolies and 'vile estates'. We hear how the soil of Venezuela is a battleground for justice. We're told about the flag of 'Land and Free Men', an abstract ensign that's sowing sovereignty up and down the fatherland. Smiling farmhands pop up to share their thoughts on the joys of 'agrarian socialism'.

From the pre-recorded tape, we flip across to a live two-way between farm manager and president. Phone-ins, audience questions and other daytime-TV staples fill the remaining gaps.

Aló Presidente is ostensibly dedicated to nurturing the roots of the revolution. Inextricably and intentionally, it also operates as propagandist publicity for its host. The Chávez caravan appears to be everywhere. This week, we find him in a grassy meadow in Sabaneta. Next week, it could be a mountain summit or the beach. This is the president with his people.

Audiences of everyday folk are bussed in to fill the temporary studios: bakers, teachers, road sweepers, cleaners, factory workers. All are dressed in the same revolutionary red, all ready to laugh and cheer on cue. The show's front man talks their language and asks their names. With every episode that passes, the image of *mi Presidente*, '*my* president' – the leader with the people's touch, the champion of the common man – inflates a little larger.

The seven-hour marathon eventually draws to a close. Chávez's face fades from the screen and the credits roll. In homes across the nation, people get up from chairs to put on supper. Only in the Hotel Caribe do they stay in bed, televisions presumably still grinding.

Adrián Navarro's office in Coro's Town Hall is cluttered with political paraphernalia. The national pennant hangs limp from a flagpole in one corner. On the wall in front of the entrance door hangs an official photo of Hugo Rafael Chávez Frías. The president is dressed in a dark suit with a carnival queen's sash neatly slung over his right shoulder. A truncated portrait of Bolívar in dress uniform sits next to it.

A far larger painting depicting a white-haired naval officer dominates the main wall. The artist's subject cuts a swashbuckling figure in a tailcoat of gold trim. A dress sword dangles from his waist in a silver sheath. The stout Señor Navarro is ensconced proudly behind his desk in his government-branded puffa jacket and *Chavista* baseball cap.

'General Francisco de Miranda,' says the Town Hall's general director, following my eye to the painting. 'The first great liberator of Venezuela.'

A full and thorough biography of the chivalrous revolutionary is accorded to all Coro newcomers. Señor Navarro does the honours. A veteran of the French and American Revolutions, a friend of William Pitt and lover of Catherine the Great, Francisco de Miranda lived a romantic life in a romantic age. Liberating South America constituted the last of his great adventures.

Miranda landed on the shores of Coro in 1806 at the head of a voluntary force of five hundred would-be liberators. The scheme did not go quite to plan. He freed the town, but few residents rallied to his call. Meanwhile, the Spanish mustered their garrison at the city gates and sent for reinforcements. Playing the odds, Miranda set sail before his ships were scuttled. The occupation was a fiasco, but the ball of independence was set in motion.

Five years later, the revolutionary chancer would be back, this time with an inexperienced Bolívar at his side. The two had met several years earlier at the older man's Georgian town house in London's Bloomsbury district. A meeting place for South America's political exiles, it was there that Bolívar is reputed to have first heard the idea of a continental confederation, a sort of European Union of the former Spanish colonies.

Failure again marked Miranda's steps. For persistence if not success, the pony-tailed poseur is heralded as the precursor of Venezuelan's independence. The municipality of Coro today carries his name and the town centre his statue.

The ring of the telephone breaks off the history lesson: '*Hola?* Yes, good thanks, *Coronel.* Here in the office, fighting the good fight.'

From the jovial tone of the conversation, I wonder if it's a real colonel on the other end of the phone. Using military terms has become the vogue ever since Chávez, an ex-paratrooper, entered the Presidential Palace.

During his early years in power, the Venezuelan head of state was fond of dressing up in his military fatigues for the cameras. Viewers were reminded of the young Chávez, the idealist army officer who once headed a bold, but bungled, *coup d'état*. The image also fits well with his idol Bolívar, the wartime general and peacetime president. But too much boot polish also dredged up memories of the murderous military juntas of South America's recent past. The public-relations people hinted at a change of outfit. Today, the bomber boots and jumpsuits are kept mostly in the closet.

The man can be taken out of the army, but not the army out of the man. Hugo Chávez's Bolívarian Revolution is run like a military operation. The president's office in Miraflores Palace acts as Command HQ, a war bunker from which executive communiqués are dispatched and political strategy devised. Paintings of Bolívar in his general's garb spread across the walls. The Liberator's protégé is even said to have kept a chair empty for the military mastermind's wandering spirit.

No war for independence, figurative or otherwise, can go without an army. The Bolívarian Revolution keeps the rule. During the Chávez administration, the armed forces have been stockpiling their arsenals and training their troops. *El Comandante,* as the president likes to be named, once warned the 'Venezuelan oligarchy' not to fool themselves into thinking that a 'peaceful revolution is an unarmed revolution'. Sabre-rattling against his neighbours in Colombia and the forces of Yankee imperialism are also commonplace. Latent, but lurking, is the military threat in Venezuela.

So far, the fight has kept to the ballot boxes. Even so, soldiers are in the streets. The ex-military strongman believes in putting the army to work. Not that yesteryear's dictators kept their armies idle. Running death squads and meeting arbitrary arrest quotas all took time. But Venezuela's restyled National Bolívarian Army sees its civic duties differently. Toolkits, not torture techniques, are its newfound speciality.

Under 'Plan Bolívar', the country's soldiers are educated to become caring combatants. When they're not on military exercise, they're out in the community fixing potholes and manning market stalls. The tactic of 'civic-military union' went down so well with the public that *El Comandante* effectively militarised the rest of government too.

Public services are now planned and plotted like battleground manoeuvres. The main vehicle for attack are the missions, a sort of multi-insurgent offensive against Venezuela's prevailing ills.

One of the earliest assaults set out to annihilate illiteracy. Reinforced by a battalion of Cuban teachers, Mission Robinson dispatched crack education detachments to root out those in need of their ABCs. The coded title owes its origins to Bolívar's eccentric tutor, Simón Rodríguez (who later changed his surname to Robinson after reading the adventures of Daniel Defoe's shipwrecked sailor). No aspect of the Liberator's life is too insignificant for the marketing-minded missions. Mission Negra Hipolitá, for example, a meals-on-wheels service for the hungry and destitute, takes its name from Bolívar's wet nurse.

Señor Navarro puts down the receiver, turning his mind from history of the revolution to its paperwork, towers of which pile precipitously on the edge of his desk.

Sensing he wants to get on with his day, I cut to the purpose of my visit and explain that I'm interested in visiting some of the missions.

From under a stack of papers, he retrieves a directory. Only marginally thinner than a copy of the Yellow Pages, he drops it on the desk with a thud: 'Where do you want to start?'

I leave the Town Hall five minutes later with an abbreviated list of suggestions and a map of the grid-marked town. In Bolívarian terms, I have in my hand the coordinates of the revolution's infrastructure: its supply depots, its field hospitals and, above all, its training grounds.

My first appointment behind allied lines takes me downtown to the grubby market district. Unlicensed vendors hawk week-old vegetables and stale-looking meat from stalls along the roadsides. Set back from the street are the headquarters of Mission Mercal, the poor man's supermarket. Its subsidised goods are stacked up along the aisles of a characterless warehouse.

There's no car park, no shopping trolleys and no automatic sliding door to facilitate entrance. Instead, there's an iron-grille gate and a uniformed guard. Each waiting shopper is handed a numbered chit. Mercal works on a one-in, one-out system. The guard monitors the barred door, shouting out a number every few minutes like a bingo caller and allowing the next in line to scuttle through. The heavy metal door clangs shut behind them. It reminds me of visiting day at Asunción's Tacumbú prison.

Once inside, the supermarket sweep begins. Consumers have no special two-for-one deals to tempt them. Everything in Mercal is on permanent rock-bottom offer. Products are packaged in simple, nondescript containers. Some aren't wrapped at all. Shoppers come to buy the larder essentials: meat, flour, milk, sugar, cheese, salt, rice, cooking oil. These are the rations of the revolution.

I conduct a spot of market research in the queue outside. Mercal's customers all seem elated with the bargain-basement store. The women I speak with (there are only women in the queue) have no word of complaint. The chicken might come with a few feathers, one young mum concedes, but she can pull those off. Fresh milk is sometimes scarce, an older lady comments, but her husband prefers the powdered stuff anyway. No one moans about the three-hour wait outside or about the total absence of customer service. Thanks to *El Presidente*, they can now put food on the family table. If it means standing in the scorching sun all afternoon, so be it.

Out at the Barrio Adentro clinic on Avenida Ramón Antonio, a similar satisfaction reigns. Waiting by the entrance door, I come across twenty-nine-year-old Migales. An unemployed single mum, she is waiting to see a doctor with her energetic four-year-old, Juan. She came by this morning, but the queue was too long and the attending nurse told her to come back later. The reception desk is temporarily empty.

Migales unsuccessfully grabs at her young son, who has slipped onto the floor and is now crawling under the waiting room's row of cupped plastic chairs: 'They think he might be suffering from a pelvis problem. We're here to get some X-rays.'

Tacked onto the wall beside us, behind transparent plastic sheeting, read the various services available at the clinic: ophthalmology, electrocardiography, radiography, intensive therapy, ultrasounds, endoscopies. Staffed by Cuban medics, the clinic forms part of a network of smaller Barrio Adentro health centres dotted around the town's poorer neighbourhoods.

'Before, the health services were pathetic,' Migales says in response to my question about the impact of Barrio Adentro, the Government's flagship medical mission.

'You used to have to pay for operations and medicines up front, and the doctors were always very unfriendly. In the normal public hospitals, it's still like that.'

Juan delivers a heavy kick to the bottom of his mother's chair. I have a hunch his pelvis is fine, but Migales wants the doctor's assurance. Like the ladies at Mission Mercal, she doesn't mind the wait. Besides, as with everything else at the clinic, the X-rays are free of charge.

In addition to the social work of the missions, Señor Navarro had thought it worth adding an educational element to my tour as well.

Class is out when I climb the stone stairs of Cecilio Acosta High School. The crest on the door dates the institution back to 1833. Coro's oldest school has seen more changes in recent years than the rest of its history put together: class hours and teaching days have been extended to maximise learning opportunities; competitive rankings are off limits; entrance fees have been abolished; exams can be re-sat until the student passes; group work is replacing individual study; and the tuck shop has been replaced by free, healthy lunches in the canteen.

The most substantive changes are in the curriculum, Iván Primera, the school's coordinator, tells me. 'Trans-disciplinary' is the new buzzword for Venezuela's educationalists. The laws of gravity and the periodic table now sit side by side in one homogenised subject called 'science'. French and English, meanwhile, are merged together in one Esperantoesque 'language' class.

Bolívar's own ideas on teaching had their quirks. In a letter about the education of his twelve-year-old nephew, he specified the subject areas he judged worthy of study. The list includes classes in good manners, botany, dance, civil engineering (optional) and 'the enjoyment of cultivated society where the fairer sex exerts its beneficial influence'.

By the same token, the Liberator also decreed that primary schools be established with public funds, a visionary measure for the time. His appetite for innovation is often credited to Simón Rodríguez, whose edict on life Bolívar learned by rote as a boy: 'Either we invent or we err.' In recognition, Venezuela's new Bolívarian kindergartens are now known as *Simoncitos,* 'Little Simóns'.

The serious Mr Primera finishes with a lengthy discourse on the philosophy behind all the turnarounds. 'Pragmatics' have dominated the teaching handbook for too long. More 'humanism' must be brought to bear: 'What's most important is putting an integrated vision of the individual at the centre of our education system.'

On my way out, I pass a pair of smooching teenagers on the school steps. Their tongues are closely examining one another's larynges, while their hands run over the remainder of the anatomy syllabus. Cecilio Acosta's students seem to be taking to the notion of integrated learning with enthusiasm.

In a *Simoncito* just around the corner, I find fifty-one-year-old Héctor, his knees squashed beneath a miniature wooden desk. The electrician is at the other end of the revolution's learning cycle. Every day after work, he attends a three-hour evening class. Héctor and his twenty classmates are swotting up on affidavits and contract law in the hope of qualifying as lawyers.

The extra-curricula lessons fall under the rubric of Mission Sucre, a programme designed to give mature students a crack at university. An equivalent initiative, Mission Ribas, is aimed at adults who never obtained their high-school diplomas first time round.

In the Bolívarian Revolution, family outings with grandpa and the kids are fast going out of fashion. If Mum isn't waiting in line, then everyone is busy with their homework.

Feeling my personal mission in Coro has run its course, I book myself onto the evening bus to Caracas and go in search of something to eat. In the colonial city centre, across from the spot where South America's first Catholic Mass was celebrated, I stumble on Club Bolívar.

A former private members' club for Coro's great and good, the town landmark lay vacant for decades until the bicentenary celebrations for Miranda's invasion earned it a revamp. The one-storey building now gleams with fresh paint. Inside, it houses an exhibition space for local artists, a bar area and a boutique restaurant.

I push open the restaurant door and find it empty except for a group of three diners. The conversation is being led by a woman in a pale blue suit, who is talking loudly to her two companions about the dessert before them. She turns out to be the chef and inventor of the macaroon-encrusted sweet.

'Some chocolate mousse cheesecake?' she asks, offering up a tempting slither of her calorie-rich creation.

Thanking her, I try a forkful: 'Wow. *Que rico!*'

'I trained in Belgium,' she replies, smugly.

I'm presented with a full portion and an invitation to join them. The sight of so much cream cheese persuades me to take a chair. Even in a Marxist-inspired republic, I should have guessed there's no such thing as a free lunch.

For the next thirty minutes, Virginia, Club Bolívar's head chef, holds forth on the unassailable benefits of Venezuela's cooperative movement. In her kitchen, worker solidarity rules: 'Chefs and waiters on an even keel, I say.'

Not only does capitalism turn workers into slaves, she pontificates, it brings us Subway and McDonald's. She scrunches her cordon bleu nose at the words: 'Our children should be eating food that contains something, some feeling, of where they belong.'

To make her point, she clicks her fingers, and the waiter comes running.

'Be a doll, bring us some *Cocuy de Pecaya,* would you?'

For an egalitarian enterprise, she runs a tight ship.

The 53-per-cent-proof liqueur is with us in seconds. Transparent and evil-looking, the local tequila equivalent is concocted from the spiny leaves of an indigenous cactus plant. Glasses are passed around.

'A toast?' Virginia suggests.

I wince as the smell of neat alcohol reaches my nostril.

'*Patria, socialismo o muerte, venceremos,*' one of her companions shouts. 'Fatherland, socialism or death, we shall conquer.'

And down it goes. A fit of explosive spluttering immediately overwhelms me. My mouth on fire, I lunge for the water jug. Everyone bursts out laughing. Socialism or death, indeed.

Caracas

Gato Negro metro station in west Caracas is awash with the revolution's foot soldiers. Men and women bunch together on the sidewalk, uniformly dressed in the same shade of red. Political slogans adorn their T-shirts and baseball caps. '*Rumbo al socialismo*', runs the official favourite of the day. 'Towards socialism'.

This is the *Chavista* army. Drawn from the vast well of modern-day Bolívarians, these citizen volunteers are committed to defending the presidential project tooth and nail. Today, *El Comandante* is due to inaugurate a bridge on the way to the airport. The rank and file received their call-up, and here they are.

I join the queue at a food stall along the roadside. A tall man in wrap-around sunglasses is waiting in front of me. He orders himself two fried *empanadas* and a thimble of steaming black coffee.

'The same for me please,' I say to the street vendor.

Lingering over his breakfast at the stall's rusty counter, the man with the dark glasses asks if I'm intending to go to the inauguration. I tell him I am. My accent and blue shirt single me out as an outsider. Either from curiosity or courtesy, he invites me to tag along with him and his friends.

'Sure,' I reply, glad of the company.

'Great. My name's Ramón, by the way. Where're you from . . . er?'

'Oliver, my name's Oliver,' I clarify. 'I'm from England.'

The information meets with his approval:

'Was in England myself many years ago. Liverr-poul. Fixing one of our ships. Used to be in the navy. *Mucha música*. Beatles, Lennon and all that. Good times. Follow me. I'll introduce you to my mates.'

We leave the wheeled *empanada* carts and head down the busy pavement towards a park entrance. Ramón's obligatory red T-shirt barely fits his muscular frame and generous girth. Repeated washing has faded the scarlet red into an off-crimson, and the cotton lining around the neck has begun to fray.

The T-shirt bears the logo of the Simón Rodríguez National

Experimental University, an alternative further-education institution for the underprivileged. Through Mission Sucre, the ex-navy deckhand undertook a two-year course in electrical engineering. Ramón has struggled to find a job though. El Valle, the district of southern Caracas where he lives, is better known for its gang violence than its graduate openings. Despite a year out of work, he remains upbeat about his new career opportunities: 'I'm waiting for the State to designate me a job. They've plenty to go around.'

It's a reasonable expectation, for a militant *Chavista*. Ramón recently acquired a government grant for several thousand dollars. 'For essential house repairs,' he winks. The money went towards remodelling his bathroom.

A block away, lounging against the park railings, we find Ramón's five friends: 'Meet Oliver, from the land of the Beatles' [pronounced "Beet-léss" in Spanish].' They look at him blankly. 'From *Inglaterra*, you morons!'

My guide for the day introduces me to the group. There's Guillermo, a short man with a pockmarked face and the rough hands of a veteran labourer; Jonny, a gangly black man with a goatee beard and the unimaginative nickname of 'Negro'; Edgar, who is scrawny, moustached and the spitting image of an Indian rickshaw-wallah; Julio, the group joker, who has a plastic Venezuelan flag sticking out from beneath his red bandana; and, finally, Elizabeth, a wiry-haired *mulatta* with rounded thighs who's wearing an unflattering angler's fly jacket. As with Ramón, all are in their late forties or early fifties. I go round shaking everyone's hand.

The introductions done, Jonny reaches down into a plastic carrier bag between his feet and retrieves a bottle of rum. It's wrapped in a brown paper bag. 'One for the heat?' he suggests. A plastic shot glass makes the rounds of the seven of us. I check my watch. It is just after 9 a.m.

'Time we were off, no?' advises Edgar, nodding his head in the direction of the two-lane highway at the corner of the block.

Julio falls into step with me as we make our way to the road and the waiting transport. His voice grows in volume as he speaks.

'This bridge being opened today is just one of heaps of projects that this government has enacted. Schools, hospitals, train lines, power plants, you name it. Previous presidents just used to pocket the money or share it around among their cronies. You should see the millions they've got stashed away in *gringo* bank accounts. Chávez is different. He cares about Venezuela. He wants to make us great again!'

Everyone nods in agreement. The affirmation of his audience buoys him up, and he continues.

'Venezuela is a country facing many threats. International capitalists want to keep the poor like us in chains. We won't stand for it, I tell you! Not to mention the United States. Bunch of terrorists, always meddling in our internal affairs and insulting our sovereignty. Damn Yankees, they can just sod off, that's what we say.'

'Yeah, too right, *compañero*,' an overweight man shouts from further down the pavement. 'Socialism or death!' another joins in. There's a festive atmosphere to the day already.

We reach the bus stop just as Julio is finishing up his public discourse. His audience has grown from our small group to the entire bus queue.

'In our battle for socialism, we are fighting against the tide. But we are confident that our president can achieve victory for us. He's an honest man, a strong man, a true Bolívarian leader!'

The rousing finale earns the crowd-pleaser the applause that he's looking for. It's impossible to tell how much Julio actually agrees with what he's saying. But he plays the part of political apparatchik to a tee. Here, in the trenches of the revolution, that's all that really matters.

'All aboard,' Guillermo hollers. As the oldest of our number, he's the unofficial leader of our small unit of *Chavista* loyalists.

I climb up behind Ramón onto the waiting minibus. The driver revs his engine impatiently, sending up a cloud of black smoke from the exhaust. The smell of diesel leaks through the open windows. The air is muggy and stale-smelling, a tendency that increases as the vehicle fills inexorably.

I find a seat at the back. Elizabeth hands me a bottle of water that she'd extracted from a large ice-filled barrel on the kerbside. I put it into my bag and thank her.

'Think nothing of it,' she says, handing out bottles to everyone else in the group. 'It's free. This country produces a lot so it can pay for stuff like this.' I'm reminded of the unsightly oil refineries outside Maracaibo.

Ramón and his friends have grown used to 'free stuff'. How long the gravy train will last depends largely on world oil prices. Not that they're complaining about the government's short-termism. None of them has a salaried job exactly. They are all volunteer members of an ill-defined 'committee'. Their task is to invigilate the delivery of foodstuffs, medicines and other government-subsidised goods in their neighbourhood. By hanging around the stockrooms, employees are supposed to be dissuaded from stealing. There's still a substantial deficit in the stock-list every month. Despite never having caught anyone, the team collects an 'incentive' for its vigilance. The monthly stipend conveniently tallies with the national minimum wage.

'*Vamos! Vamos! Vamos!*' the animated busload begins yelling.

The driver slides the free bus service into gear, and we pull off. Mexican hip-hop is blasting from the minibus radio. A popular track comes on, and the bus begins to rock as everyone joins in with the chorus. Five minutes into the journey, we run into traffic. The delay inspires a violent spate of horn-pounding from our driver. A cacophony of irritated klaxons responds. The passengers treat the racket as a test of their vocal power and begin screaming the song lyrics.

Wedged between two corpulent women who are bulging out of their seats and onto mine, I begin to feel slightly queasy. Now we've slowed to a crawl, there's no longer a breeze to offset the stultifying heat and humidity. The sun is beating through the rear window and my shirt is growing damp with sweat.

I begin to regret the *empanadas* back at the metro station. The taste of bile rises to the back of my mouth. I think I might vomit.

357

I scan the bus for an open window. The nearest is two rows ahead. To reach it would require manoeuvring around a trio of busty middle-aged ladies. They are dancing along the row in a violent form of sedentary salsa. Arms and arses are flailing everywhere. I prepare to lunge.

Seconds from take-off, my mind flicks back to the free water. Immediately I thrust a desperate hand into my bag and grab the bottle. It's still cold to the touch. I flip the cap and take a swig. It's so refreshing it makes my toes curl. I close my eyes and take another gulp, cherishing each icy rivulet as it rolls over my tongue. The nausea passes. If Ramón had handed me a recruitment form for the *Chavista* army then and there, I would have willingly signed up.

Eventually the heat begins to get to the other passengers as well. In a commanding voice, Guillermo demands that the man at the wheel let us off. The door slides open, and we all pile onto the melting tarmac. Weaving between the hooting cars, it's a fifteen-minute walk to the bridge. Hundreds of others are also making the pilgrimage.

In the sea of red, Ramón and I manage to get separated from the rest of the group. After a long but fruitless search for them, we press on. As we near the inauguration point, the security increases. Military police mix with civilian law-enforcement officers, their arms locked together in an impenetrable wall of Robocop riot gear. They steer us along with the help of volunteer stewards.

To the left of the bridge runs the old highway. It curves down the gorge of a precipitous valley. Above straddles the imposing concrete bridge that we've all collectively gathered to admire.

Looking up across the ravine, I spot a brightly painted shanty settlement sitting high on a distant hill. The residents are just visible on their rooftops, tiny stickmen and stickwomen standing out against the cobalt-blue sky. From their scrappy hilltop escarpment, they have an eagle's view of the events below. There, on the barren slopes of Caracas, in tens of thousands of colourful matchboxes, live the residents of the *Chavista* heartlands.

It was from hillside shanties like this one that the poor and marginalised swarmed down into the city streets at the end of February

1989. Ostensibly annoyed by a rise in bus fares, they ran riot through the capital for two full days. Barricading themselves inside their homes, the middle classes looked on in horror as shops were looted and cars set on fire.

El Comandante is fond of pointing to the so-called *Caracazo* as the Miranda moment of the Bolívarian Revolution, the time when the people stood up and demonstrated their desire for change. It would take ten years, one failed coup attempt and a prison sentence for the modern-day Bolívar to take power. Now that he had, the streets were teeming once again.

'It looks like there's a clearing over there,' Ramón says above the crowd. 'Perhaps we'll get a view of the others?'

We edge off to the left, away from the ravine and the bridge, towards steep bank running along the roadside. At its edge runs a pipeline, yet another reminder of the liquid gold propping up the new bridge and mega-projects like it. We climb up onto the hulking metal tubing, which stands about three feet off the ground. It feels good to be briefly out of the swirling sea of people, but there's no sign of Guillermo and company.

'You wait here, I'll have to go look for them,' says Ramón, after unsuccessfully scanning the crowd for a few moments.

I watch him climb back down and disappear, swept up by the tide of human bodies. Back up the road, six white drums are floating downstream on the surface of the crowd. From a distance, they look like giant buoyancy aids. As they bob closer towards me, a band of tousled drummers comes into view beneath them. Eventually, the drums' owners escape the swell and wash up in the clearing beneath me.

They brush themselves down and, after a quick conflab, kick off their set. In an instant, the rally-goers quit their pushing and begin clapping and dancing to the percussion's energetic vibe. The beat of the drums drowns the voice of the event's official announcer, who's finding infinite ways to thank *El Presidente* for the gift of the bridge.

A television cameraman on the roof of his crew van swivels round to catch the action, and the drummers pick up the tempo.

The pulsating beat spreads through the crowd, setting bottoms wobbling and arms waving. In the centre of the throng, the band-leader blows repeatedly on a whistle. The sound rents the air like piercing shards of high-pitched shrapnel. On the pipeline beside me, a jiving black woman with bleached peroxide hair thrusts a plastic flag into my hand. Then the man on my other side throws an arm round my shoulder. He's jumping up and down in time to the rhythm. Soon the flag woman is joining in too. Before we know it, an improvised line dance is rippling down the elevated oil duct.

'Oliver, have you gone *loco?*'

It's Ramón. Having miraculously located his friends, he's come back to collect me. I half thought I'd never see him again, and I wave down to him enthusiastically. The *Chavista* cheerleader is pointing a rotating index finger at the side of his head, a sign of my alleged dementia. I release myself from the grip of the unknown spectator next to me and climb down to the roadside. Immediately, another revolutionary reveller fills my space on the party pipeline. If Chávez's supporters care half as much about politics as they do about partying, the Bolívarian Revolution can but grow.

'They've got front-row seats, overlooking the ravine,' an animated Ramón tells me.

We wade back into the roaring current, emerging flustered but unscathed on the highway's far bank ten minutes later. Julio welcomes me with a mock salute. Jonny, who's now onto his second bottle of the day, offers me a drop of rum, 'for the heat'. Meanwhile, the rest of the group occupy themselves laying into Ramón for getting lost and criticising his scouting skills.

Sharing our rocky outcrop above the ravine is a legion of civil servants from the Ministry of Education. They've been given the morning off work to attend the opening. Excited to be on a day out, the work colleagues snap giggling photos of themselves on their mobile-phone cameras.

An hour after the scheduled arrival time, with the sun at its highest, three small specks emerge on the horizon. A woman from the Ministry of Education spots them first. 'It's *him*,' she squeals overexcitedly. An animated buzz passes through the crowd. Eyes shaded behind dark glasses look up towards the approaching celestial cohort. Fingers point. Banners unfurl. Cameras are retrieved from belt-holders.

The far-off dots grow in shape and form until finally the insignia of the President's helicopter is visible to the naked eye. The two support choppers branch off, leaving the skies empty for Chávez. Alone, he flies circular laps above the crowd.

'There he is, there he is,' Elizabeth is screaming. Others join in the bedlam. 'Chávez! *Viva mi Presidente!*'

Above our heads, the ex-paratrooper is standing in the open door of the helicopter's hold. He leans forward, suspended on the ledge by a safety harness. The presidential Action Man salutes the multitude, sending thousands of waving arms shooting up in response. Three times he circles the swaying reed bed of people below.

Another woman from the Ministry of Education is crying unrestrainedly beside me, beyond herself at the sight of her real-life hero. '*Te amo, mi Presidente, te amo*,' the star-struck pen pusher is shouting hysterically: 'I love you, my president, I love you.' These are not rent-a-crowd tears. Her emotion is visceral and mildly scary.

The ceremony itself passes in a haze. The President lands at the bridgehead, gently lowered to earth like a *deus ex machina* in an ancient Greek stage play. The descending helicopter drowns the retinue of waiting dignitaries in a cloud of dust. Then a priest intones a solemn blessing, a ribbon is clipped and a trail of red balloons is released into the indigo blue sky.

From our high-up vantage point, we watch the ceremony unfold like battlefield generals on a far-off hilltop. The presidential cavalcade sets off across the bridge, pressed in from behind by a slow-moving phalanx of toy soldiers. President Chávez rides in an open-backed jeep. A contemporary Caesar, he waves imperially at his faithful foot soldiers from the rear of the diesel-powered chariot. Engulfed by security staff and carnivorous press photographers, it's almost impossible to catch a glimpse of him. Back at the bridgehead, the helicopter makes a stealthy take-off and arcs back across the ravine. Leaving his blades turning, the pilot is ready to whisk away *El Comandante* as soon as the victory march is done. A final wave and the president is duly off, chasing after the balloons towards the rocky horizon.

Our regiment of the *Chavista* army is left suffering in post-orgasmic deflation. 'Would have been good to hear him speak,' mumbles Julio.

Ramón shoots him a stern look: '*El Presidente* is a busy man. Have some respect. He has a whole country to run and don't you forget it.'

There are no free shuttle buses for the return leg. We prepare to walk back up the highway, already awash with other footsore soldiers returning from the front.

The crying bureaucrat has grown calmer now. Dry-eyed, she's sitting on her haunches observing the flow of spectators crossing the bridge above the ravine.

'It's so beautiful,' she's murmuring repeatedly to herself. 'End to end, a sea of red.'

Jonny wanders over and pulls out his bottle of rum. He's been saving the last drops for the trek back up the hill to the metro. Bending his lanky legs down to her level, the tall black man touches the woman paternally on the shoulder. 'Go on, *compañera*,' he bids in solidarity. 'For the heat.'

She takes the bottle from him, a benign smile across her upturned face. Slowly she raises it to her lips. Drip by drip, his final measure trickles away. Both of them, in their own way, silently savouring the revolution.

In an Italian restaurant across town, the taste of change has a more bitter edge.

'Can ya speak up?' a loud voice in American English hollers from the back of the room.

Amid the bustle of waiters and food trolleys, Bárbara Pugliese's gentle voice is difficult to make out. Wearing a dark suit with a chiffon scarf, the attractive law graduate is the face of the revolutionary enemy.

Bárbara is used to fighting to be heard and raises her voice as requested. Along two long trestle tables sit her evening's audience, the forty-member Seattle Peace Chorus.

For the past three weeks, the amateur singing troupe has been travelling through Venezuela spreading harmony and love. Their performance repertoire includes such classics as 'I've Got Peace like a River,' 'Circle Round for Freedom' and 'Peace Salaam Shalom'. Before leaving home, they mugged up on some songs in Spanish too. 'Todos Somos Americanos', 'We Are All Americans', an up-tempo tune with accompanying hand actions, has emerged as the undisputed hit of the tour. Their West Coast drawl makes the title lyrics sound like a group request for black Americano-style coffee. Back in Seattle, it could lead to a mix-up. Here in Venezuela, where the tentacles of Starbucks have yet to reach, their revolutionary fan club does not suffer such confusion.

When not out waging peace, the choristers have spent their time on a guided visit around *Chavezlandia*. They're but one of a steady stream of politically motivated tour groups coming to see the 'Bolívarian experiment' for themselves. With a disproportionately high number of teachers and care professionals among their number, the non-violent activists were especially anxious to see some schools and to familiarise themselves with the missions. Their tour coordinator also organised a factory visit, a trip to a cooperative farm and a singing contest on the Isle of Margarita. Bárbara has been pencilled in right at the end, a token contrary voice before the chorus packs up its song sheets and flies home.

'I am here to represent Primero Justicia, Venezuela's largest opposition party,' the pretty dissident hollers. 'As you might be able to tell from my surname, my grandparents are from Italy . . .'

No one in the audience seems to care too much about the party spokeswoman's parentage nor, for that matter, about her politics. She struggles on for ten minutes in a vain attempt to explain how Primero Justicia would change the country for the better.

As representatives of a young party, they aren't afraid to try 'radical, new policies', she says. Cutting taxes, encouraging foreign investment and reducing bureaucracy are the way ahead for Venezuela apparently. The manifesto of uninspired economic orthodoxies has the unmistakable ring of the US grant-maker that helps fund her party. The choir isn't buying it.

Dennis, a nonconformist pastor and tenor bass, turns from his shrimp risotto and whispers something to his wife. The tail end of the phrase is loud enough to carry across the table to where I'm sitting: 'This woman is more Neocon than the Neocons.'

Wisely, Bárbara gives up on her efforts to build a constructive case. She does what all opposition parties do best: she looks around for mud to fling.

Crime is on the up. Did we know forty-six people are killed in Venezuela every day? The government hides the true figures. Were we aware that six in ten Venezuelans live in sub-standard housing? Or that the only way to apply for a passport was through a website that's permanently crashing? Had we heard what a mess the economy was in: inflation running out of control, millions lost through public mismanagement, scarcities of basic foodstuffs? Companies are even moving their operations to Colombia – 'I mean, they prefer the violence of the guerrillas to working with Chávez!'

Bárbara recalibrates her verbal assault weapon, adding extra firepower for her attack on the missions. Barrio Adentro is little more than 'basic first aid', degrees from the new Bolívarian universities aren't worth the paper they're written on, and Mercal is 'positively Third World'. As for claims that Venezuela is now an 'illiteracy-free territory', the government's own statistics indicate one million people still can't read or write.

Bellowing from her soapbox, there's certainly no problem hearing her now.

'Every one of Chávez's good ideas is just a rip-off from previous governments. All the government does is repackage old ideas and make them look new. So now we have the "tribunal" rather than the "court" and the "National Assembly" rather than "Congress".

But they're all basically the same thing. And as for changing the name of the country to the *Bolívarian* Republic of Venezuela . . . frankly, it's just embarrassing. Can you imagine how much it cost to change all the bank notes?'

'More risotto anyone?' a bored Dennis inquires of his table companions. Ten weary heads shake back at him.

Bárbara will have to shift tack again if she's to convince the chorus that the Bolívarian Revolution is not the best thing since sliced, gluten-free bread. She's astute enough to realise.

'Do you know that democracy is under attack here in Venezuela?'

The rhetorical question touches a nerve. The choir's attention is briefly wrested away from the dessert menu.

'Under Chávez, power has become increasingly centralised. Congress and the Supreme Court are packed with government sympathisers. What the president decides, they rubber stamp. Anyone that disagrees is branded a "counter-revolutionary".'

A muffle of concern greets her use of Cold War terminology, a throwback to a trip the choir made during the Communist era to Moscow, Leningrad and other Soviet hotspots.

Spotting a chink in her audience's resistance, the refusenik pulls out one of the big guns from her arsenal.

'How many of you know about the Tascón List?'

A few doubtful hands go up, but the question draws a blank from most.

Bárbara fills them in. Understand the list, we're told, and we'll get an idea of how democracy works in Venezuela. On paper, the country's newly revised constitution could be lifted straight from Plato's theory of 'rule by the governed'. Any voter, however lowly, can decide an elected official is not up to scratch and call a no-confidence vote. All it takes is for a fifth of the electorate to agree to it.

At the beginning of Chávez's second term, the opposition used their new-found constitutional powers to try and unseat the very president who'd introduced them. To do so required the collection of two and a half million signatures. Armed with clipboards and biros, the anti-*Chavista* mutineers went door-knocking.

It was the last play of a fast emptying hand, a fact Bárbara neatly skips over. In the full version of events, mention would also be made of the opposition's less libertarian tactics. First, they tried the traditional route. Their palace coup saw businessman Pedro Carmona take the throne. His tenure lasted two days, earning himself the unkind epithet of Pedro the Brief. Next, they attempted to starve the president out. For four months, the Maracaibo 'mafia' turned off the taps at the oil wells. The situation hung in the balance for a moment, but ultimately the lockdown didn't work either. *El Comandante* just came out stronger.

Bárbara's rebel colleagues had no more luck with the democratic option. They managed to force a referendum but succeeded in losing the vote. Chávez would stay in power, and the 'betrayers' would pay the price. The president charged Luis Tascón, a respected congressman, with collecting the names, addresses and identity numbers of every last signatory. Somehow, the list made its way onto the Internet. A later version came out on CD-ROM with a fully searchable database.

'It was amazing how often people on the Tascón lists fell victim to bureaucratic bungles and lost cheques in the mail,' Bárbara says sarcastically.

'People like me were branded. We were like the Jews in Hitler's Germany being made to wear the Star of David. Those of us who aren't *Chavistas* are now denied everything: jobs, credit lines, public health care, you name it. Where's the democracy there, eh?'

The choral singers shift in their seats, temporarily discomforted.

Dominic, a floppy-haired postgraduate student and tenor, has a question. His tone is ultra-polite, but the left-leaning chorister is clearly rankled.

'I might be mistaken, but as I understand it, Venezuela's old *representative* system of democracy has been replaced with a *participative* model. Isn't that all rather progressive?'

In answer to his own rhetorical question, diffident Dominic recounts a visit the chorus made to a *consejo comunal,* a communal council. They'd been told – 'and, please, correct me if I'm wrong' –

that these neighbourhood councils empower everyday people to determine what needs doing locally. The council they'd visited had received funds to have the water tank fixed, for example. Others are asphalting their street or having playgrounds built in the square.

'Now democracy doesn't – umm, err – get much more grass-roots than that, surely?' says Dominic, who stutters to a stop after thanking Bárbara for listening and apologising if she thinks him rude.

Bárbara, who's used to having far worse things said to her, is not flustered in the least. Instead, she launches into an immediate counter-attack.

'It's essential to remember that the communal councils remain new and untested. The participants are totally ill-prepared for managing budgets and designing projects. It's all very well getting the people to involve themselves, but you can't just pass on the responsibility of local government overnight.'

Her scarf becomes dislodged in the harangue to the tremulous tenor. Brushing it back over her shoulder like a tank commander in a desert squadron, she loads up for a second round of fire.

'You should know there's a darker side to these councils too. They developed out of what were known as "Bolívarian circles", groups of residents who went around at election time getting people to vote for Chávez. They're like nasty little soldiers. And do you know where the idea came from?'

Dominic did not.

'From Cuba. Yes, it's true. Chávez's mentor Fidel came up with the idea first. There, they serve as an extension of his spy network. Here, it'll be just the same.'

If we want a sign of things to come, Bárbara pronounces, we need look no further than the RCTV case.

'Anyone heard of it?'

A roomful of hands go up. The chorus has been watching their CNN.

'Good,' continues the indefatigable Bárbara, 'then you'll know that Chávez ordered our longest-running TV channel to be closed. And why, you ask?'

367

Nobody is actually asking, but she carries on just the same.

'. . . because he didn't like its editorial content. Closing down hostile press is what dictators do, or am I wrong?'

Dominic had retreated to his shell, and none of the other choristers had the appetite to enter the fray. Coffee had just arrived, and the elderly audience were thinking about pyjamas and bed.

In Bárbara's defence, the RCTV case sparked widespread disquiet throughout the country. Technically, the channel's broadcasting licence wasn't 'closed' as such. It simply wasn't renewed after it ran out. Still, intellectuals inveighed against the attack on freedom of speech. Students staged massive rallies in the street. More nerve-racking for the regime, the masses were upset.

Editorial considerations had nothing to do with the proletarian disquiet. The revolution had climbed into their homes and had taken away their soap operas. The sofa-sitting polity wanted their *My Cousin Ciela* back. In the weeks after its closure, thousands would turn up to see public viewings of RCTV's hit show, now only available via costly satellite channels. But television viewers are a fickle bunch. A new favourite *telenovela* and the whole affair soon passed into history.

A waiter comes with a bill for each table. The chorus fumble with their wallets. After three weeks, Dennis and his wife are still having problems calculating the dollar equivalent of the funny-looking bolívar notes in their pockets. Their cause isn't helped by the parallel exchange rate or escalating inflation.

As the choir prepares to go, I'm struck by the irony of the evening: Bárbara, the young, intelligent Venezuelan law graduate, so desperate for her country to be more like the USA, and the US citizens of the chorus, who'd pack Venezuela's socialist-inspired revolution into a suitcase and take it home with them if they could.

Another paradox hangs unrecognised, or at least unaccredited, over the event. Here is Bárbara, wheeled in to play her part as the political dissident. Yet there, opposite her, itching to be back in their hotel, sit the passport-holding representatives of the real enemy. In the revolution's ranking of evil, Primero Justicia is a blob on the radar compared to the mighty *imperio* of the USA.

Revolutions breed two types of enemies: internal and external. Bolívar spent the first decade or more of the War for Independence fighting against the second. With the Spanish foe finally smitten, a spate of civil wars forced him to turn to the first.

Likewise, the Bolívarian Revolution is a war on two fronts. Outside its borders is the entire capitalist world. At its head rules the 'evil empire', that brooding, conniving, jealous oppressor to the north. The US government and its multinational minions are painted as the master manipulators, always lurking offstage, ever stirring the pot. An order from Washington is all it takes for democratically elected presidents to come toppling down: Jacobo Guzmán in Guatemala, Velasco Ibarra in Ecuador, Salvador Allende in Chile. It doesn't take much to persuade loyal *Chavistas* that their man is next in line.

Rarely does Bolívar's heir allow an opportunity to pass without denouncing the enemy at the gates. A typical example took place on *Aló Presidente* the previous week. *El Comandante* used his Sunday spot to present an unpublished manuscript to the nation. Its pages, we were informed, contained a fly-on-the-wall exposé of the Central Intelligence Agency, the enemy's international Gestapo. A handwritten note ran across the title page, which the show's presenter kindly read out to us.

'For Hugo, so that you might know the machine of terror . . . Fidel Castro.'

Chávez, like his Cuban mentor, revels in the idea that US-sponsored assassins are out to get him. He's even coined a term for it, 'magnicide'.

Later in the programme, the defender of the Bolívarian Revolution leaves no doubt in the public's mind where the chief danger lies.

'Our principal enemy is the most powerful empire that has ever existed on Earth, and it does not rest, nor will it rest, from trying to derail movements that seek social justice, independence, sovereignty.'

Regrettably, the chorus didn't catch the episode.

Timing has certainly helped in casting the USA as the arch-oppressor. For much of his second and third terms in office, Chávez had the perfect whipping boy in the White House. In George W. Bush, the Venezuelan showman never ran short of material. Over the years, *El Comandante* came up with a catalogue of insulting pseudonyms for the man who 'walks like John Wayne'. *Terrorista* (terrorist), *burro* (donkey) and *alcohólico* (drunkard) featured among the favourites, but 'Mr Danger' was the one that stuck. Chávez would blame his Texan nemesis for everything from genocide in Iraq to global climate change. 'More dangerous than a monkey with a razor blade,' he once said of him. Empire-bashing goes down well at home. If the Seattle *Americanos* are anything to go by, it also has its fans behind enemy lines.

The revolution's internal enemies are now amassing as well. Bolívar knew the pernicious power of domestic infighting.

'It was your brothers, not the Spaniards, who ripped out your hearts, shed your blood, set fire to your homes and forced you into exile,' the Liberator argued in his 'Manifesto of Cirúpano'. The man who had freed half the continent, who had defeated a very real, flesh-and-blood empire, could not get the measure of his local rivals.

On the eve of Venezuela's independence, with the Spanish on the run, he wrote to his minister of foreign affairs about his fear of 'peace more than war'. Ultimately, the unremitting squabbles between opposing factions squeezed the life from him, sending him to his grave depressed and demoralised.

Chávez has proved a master strategist at outmanoeuvring the enemies within. But the Bárbaras of the revolution are persistent. Several months after my visit, they'd succeed in voting down *El Comandante*'s idea for a radical overhaul of the constitution. If passed, the text would have technically allowed him to be elected indefinitely. The idea of a president for life wasn't new. It first appeared almost two centuries ago, in the Liberator's own draft charter for Bolivia.

For now though, Bárbara is wrapping up warm and preparing to head out into the chilly Caracas evening. She's running late for a date with her girlfriends. There's a Hollywood blockbuster they all want to catch. She'd ask the chorus but senses it'd be too all-American for their tastes.

Merida

In Mérida's central square, a bronze Bolívar sits astride a splendid stallion. Legend has it that beneath him is buried the right hand of Lope de Aguirre, a brutal conquistador who took the unwise step of rebelling against the Spanish king. When the forces of his royal employer finally got their hands on him, they dismembered him and distributed him in little pieces across Venezuela. His body parts were supposed to be a visible lesson for others not to do the same.

The history of South America is constructed on the plinths of its *plazas* and the leading actors of its legends. The continent's authorities know the past is too important to be left to the academics. Better the sculptors and storytellers be allowed to tell it. That way, everyone's favourite heroes and villains get to stay centre stage. But monuments and myth have their limitations as tools of history. They are to the past what horoscopes are to the future: never dull, rarely factual and always open to manipulation.

Nowhere is history more at the beck and call of its modern masters than Venezuela. Chávez recently assigned his vice-president and nine cabinet ministers to head up a scientific commission into Bolívar's death. For two centuries, received wisdom held that the Liberator died from tuberculosis. Now his bones are being exhumed to prove that assassins hired by the 'oligarchies' bumped him off.

Poor old Christopher Columbus is bearing the brunt of these changing winds. The European adventurer is held responsible for introducing the New World to the Old, a fateful encounter that makes him *persona* very much *non grata*. His birthday is now celebrated as the Day of Indigenous Resistance. In Caracas's Plaza

371

Venezuela, his statue has been shrunk. Sculptors are currently working up a miniature replacement. Above him, dominating the spot where the discoverer of America used to stand, the image of a gigantic indigenous warrior is planned. In Mérida, they've gone one step further. Someone has lopped off Columbus's head. All that's left of the man who once sailed the ocean blue is a bare plinth with a severed neck.

A picturesque university town perched on a river plateau in the folds of the surging Andes, Mérida has always understood the significance of historical symbolism. Its citizens were the first to recognise Bolívar by the name 'Liberator'. The move was a testament to foresight. The vagrant general and his ragtag army of New Granadians were still eight years short of fully liberating Venezuela. Its burghers were also the first to erect a statue in his honour, twelve years after Bolívar's death.

I'd travelled down to Mérida on an uncomfortable night bus from Caracas to speak with José Sant Roz. A mathematician by training, he's also author of half a dozen books on Bolívar and the independence period. We meet in the coffee shop of an out-of-town shopping centre.

'Bolívar has been a passion for me all my life,' the white-haired academic says up front, fussing over the removal of his Barbour jacket. 'Even now, when I read his journals and his letters, it sometimes makes me cry.'

I try and picture the learned university professor sitting in his study with Bolívar's collected works in front of him and a damp hanky at his side. The image stays with me as we talk.

Like Chávez, Dr Sant Roz's perception of history is coloured by his politics. The sentimental statistician is one of the few avowed government sympathisers on campus.

'What is it that attracts you so much to Bolívar?' I ask, anxious to orientate the conversation back towards Venezuela's founding father.

His reply is long and convoluted, as all true stories of infatuation should be. Like every schoolboy, it was the Liberator's dashing exploits on the battlefield that first grabbed him. As he grew older, he found inspiration in his hero's intellect and political vision.

'Bolívar's genius was too profound for the country in which he found himself,' he says, a curious mix of awe and disappointment in his voice.

In his later years, it's been Bolívar the man that moves him most: his spirit of adventure, his single vision, his sense of destiny, his indefatigable energy and, of course, his many trials. Spaniards have no concept of tragic-heroism, the Bolívarian enthusiast maintains. *Don Quixote,* the great heroic epic of Spanish literature, is saturated in comedy; 'Bolívar, in contrast, is a character directly from the pages of a Shakespearian tragedy.'

'And what of President Chávez? Are the comparisons that people make between him and Bolívar fair?' It's the question I'd travelled down to Mérida to ask.

The beep of an incoming text message postpones the academic's answer. For a few moments, he fumbles in his jacket pocket in an attempt to locate his mobile. I feel my question lingering in the air, like courtroom nerves before a verdict.

The mathematician places the retrieved phone beside his empty coffee cup. The contents of the message seem to have flustered him. He's lost track momentarily. 'Sorry, what was the question again?' he asks.

'Chávez and Bolívar,' I repeat. 'Are they similar?'

'Yes, yes, of course, I remember now.' He pauses, weighing his reply. Again, he comes to his answer in a roundabout way:

'No politician has ever understood the thinking of Bolívar. They want to be like him, that's the problem. But none of them have the capacity.'

He cites the example of Antonio Guzmán Blanco, a despot from the late nineteenth century. Keen to show himself a true patriot, the right-wing military president officially deified the Liberator. A vast painting of this glorious apotheosis still hangs on the wall of Bolívar's childhood house in Caracas. It goes without saying that Blanco occupies a prominent spot in the picture's foreground.

'But Chávez is the only one that's different,' Dr Sant Roz maintains. '*El Presidente* is the one politician who has the personal
qualities to become the new Bolívar. He has intelligence, bravery,
charisma, knowledge. He understands how the other half live.'

There's something of the zealot in the professor's eyes as he marks
off the historical similarities: both men know what it is to suffer;
both have shown they can bounce back from defeat; and, most
strikingly, both are consumed by the pull of destiny.

'Bolívar knew political independence was just the first step.
Chávez is likewise aware that our struggle will not end with him.
His destiny is to establish a milestone, to start *la lucha,* the fight.'

The coffee house has grown busier since we started talking, and I
request a refill of coffee to keep the hovering waitress at bay.

'What fight exactly?' I ask, as the waitress shuttles off to another
table.

There's no hesitation this time.

'Our fight is the fight to win back justice, to win back our values,
to stop this ridiculous consumerist race to possess more and more.
It's the fight of twenty-first-century socialism.'

I can almost sense his mathematician's brain buzzing with political
theorems and historical equations: Bolívar raised to the numerical
power of Chávez equals the logarithm of the Bolívarian Revolution.

'And how long will the fight take, do you think?' A straightforward question, I judge, in search of a straightforward reply. The
hypothesis proves incorrect.

The professor's answer comes back like a bad lesson in prob-
ability.

'No one knows. Perhaps fifty years. Maybe one hundred. But we
feel that we are close. It's as if we are swimming in the ocean and we
can see the shoreline. Many people now sense we are arriving
towards the beach. We feel we can save ourselves.'

Our coffees are brought over by the waitress, who listens in to the
professor but pretends not to. He ignores her and continues.

'What's preventing us from getting to the coast faster are the millions of opponents that get in the way. Sometimes there is also a

cloud that stops us from seeing the shoreline. Chávez is the one that clears the mist for us, the one who shows us north from south.'

The historical field is more exacting. Before leaving for Mérida, I'd paid a visit to Caracas' prestigious Central University. In place of ivory towers, I'd found a series of square concrete blocks dotted around campus. The man I'd arranged to interview was sitting in the musty, first-floor staffroom of the History Department.

Miguel Hurtado, a sinewy professor with a smoker's cough and a close-cropped beard, has been teaching Bolívarian thought for five decades. Far from welcoming the renewed interest in his subject matter, the lecturer was horrified.

'Today's Bolívar has nothing to do with the historical character, the Bolívar of flesh and blood.'

He went on to cite copious examples of quotations taken out of context and ideas twisted to fit with Chávez's socialist thinking.

The use of Bolívar for political propaganda had particularly offended his academic scruples.

'He even turns up in your soup these days!' Professor Hurtado had complained, in reference to the Government's habit of stamping political messages on food packaging. The Liberator never claimed to speak for ever, the history purist had continued. The questions of his own day, not those of the future, were what bothered him. Bolívar never even wrote a coherent political theory.

Not that the academic traditionalist could complain too vigorously. Today, his department counts over six hundred undergraduates. His own matriculation class at the Central University had had nine.

Walking back to the town centre after our discussion, I reflect on the differing historical perspectives of Dr Sant Roz and Professor Hurtado: the *Chavista* mathematician, with his romantic, utilitarian view of history and the classical historian, with his admonishments and his desire for 'Bolívar to be left to rest in peace'. Which, I wonder, is the most valid?

I'm still toying with the question when I reach the central square. It's late, and I'm surprised to find a group of labourers still at work.

They've fenced off the statue of Bolívar with plastic tape. Venezuela is due to host the Copa América, a continent-wide football competition, and Mérida is desperately trying to spruce itself up in time. I sit briefly on a bench and watch a workman buffing up the bronze Bolívar and his stallion.

In the man's dusting cloth and tin of polish, I locate what appears to be an answer. As far as historical documentation goes, Professor Hurtado's archivist approach has the undoubted upper hand. But a thousand of his academic journals will never make one of Dr Sant Roz's statues. Symbolism and science are two divergent lines running across the same page: one is set on making history, the other is happy to record it. With revolutions to fight, the first is what really counts.

There's no question on which side of the line *El Comandante* falls. The seer from Sabaneta is inspired more by the morals of history than its methodologies. In Bolívar, he's discovered the ultimate heroic figure: idealistic, revolutionary and malleable.

'Bolívar is not just a man,' the president once recounted to Aleida Guevara, Che's daughter, in a lengthy interview. 'Bolívar is a concept.'

This conceptual Bolívar isn't bound by the rigours of history. The president's version of the Great Liberator would have been a socialist, for example, if only Karl Marx had been born earlier. He would presumably have been a twenty-first-century Bolívarian too. Nor would reincarnation pose a problem. In the presidential chair, Chávez's Bolívar would find an exaggerated replica of himself.

Legend has it that the Liberator will rise again.

'I awake every hundred years when the people awake,' Pablo Neruda wrote in his poem, 'A Song for Bolívar'. To be certain, Venezuela's contemporary replacement sent the earth removers in to dig him up. In Chávez's mind, his life and that of his hero weave into one another. The fates have built a bridge across the ravines of history. His description of the Second Republic's fall displays this habit of historical schizophrenia.

'Bolívar had the greatness required to reflect on the defeat, to understand it, and then to go back and unite with the black and olive-skinned Venezuelans, the people of the plains; he won the people's support, their admiration. He removed from himself all vestiges of oligarchy . . . and joined with the marginalised sectors of society.'

The story is pure Chávez: the failed coup in 1992, the brief years in prison, the political comeback, the electoral victories, the man of the people. It's history rewriting itself into the present. It's Bolívar being born again. It's Sant Roz's shoreline being reached.

For Venezuela's Bolívarians, the second War of Independence is at last taking shape. Fortunately for future generations, Professor Hurtado's students are at hand to write the chronicle.

Ciudad Bolívar

Ciudad Bolívar is celebrating Independence Day. The distinguished citizens of the riverside town are gathered around their elegant square. Each is in their finest attire. They sit in the plastic seats assigned to them by protocol. The Governor looks to have waxed his bushy moustache especially for the occasion. Occupying pride of place beside him sits a stiff-backed general. Military medals cluster together across his lapel.

Those in the second row look over the shoulder of the dignitaries in front – some scheming how to sit up front the following year, others honoured to have made the invite list at all. Above everyone's head, the tropical sun beats down. The ceremonial flags hang limp and heavy in the absent breeze.

The representatives of Venezuela's security forces stand to attention in the square: soldiers, sailors, airmen, police and civil guard, all in neat formation. Together they fashion a regimental semicircle of clipped haircuts around the Liberator. Perched high on his plinth, overlooking the terracotta rooftops of the colonial town, the sword-brandishing Bolívar endures the formal speeches along with the rest of us. The flowered wreaths and cathedral bells would please his wandering spirit more, were it passing. A pigeon lands on his head, scans the pomp below and flies away.

Nineteen decades before, Bolívar and his patriot army had found refuge in this tropical town on the banks of the river Orinoco. They were invading Venezuela for the third time. Isolated and outnumbered, the Liberator convoked a congress to discuss a constitution for an independent republic – an eventuality the self-proclaimed 'plaything of the revolutionary hurricane' saw as inevitable. He wrote a lengthy letter to the congressional delegates, in which he highlighted the best and the worst of the world's political systems. 'Let us not aspire to the impossible,' the pragmatist in him cautioned, 'lest in reaching for the ring of freedom we fall into the abyss of tyranny.'

Claiming liberty, Bolívar knew, would be no easy task. His South American compatriots were still 'numbed by chains' and 'their sight dimmed in dark dungeons'. Like a good general, he laid out the terrain ahead.

'Our weakened citizens will have to strengthen their spirits mightily before they succeed in digesting the healthful nourishment of Freedom . . . Will they ever be capable of marching with firm steps toward the august temple of Freedom?'

The twenty-six delegates met in the Governor's residence opposite the cathedral. Around its columned garden cloister and over its hardwood floors Bolívar paced as the representatives discussed his counsel. At the conference table, they toyed over the political lessons of Greece, Rome, France, England and North America. After two days' talking, the final document was ready.

Wandering over to the congressional meeting house, now a museum, I find a shady step on which to sit and watch the remainder of the ceremony. The speeches show no sign of letting up. Switching off from the official sermons, I reach into my bag for my copy of Bolívar's collected works. The book is dog-eared and worn after its trek around the continent. As guide and companion, it's served me well. I open it to 'The Angostura Address' and begin reading. The Liberator's words to his delegates have a pleasant familiarity to them, like the creases in the leather of a favourite armchair. I reach the conclusion as the last of the wreath-bearers are having their photographs taken:

'Flying from age to age, my imagination reflects on the centuries to come . . .'

The dignitaries are slowly cooking under the midday sun. Valiantly, the military band strikes up. Their trumpets and cymbals surprise the pigeons, which disperse in a flock of frantic flapping. Bolívar dreams on.

'I look down from such a vantage point . . . I feel a kind of rapture, as if this land stood at the very heart of the universe, spread out from coast to coast between oceans separated by nature . . .'

The uniformed semicircle disbands, marching off unit by unit from the civic parade ground. The Liberator, the voice of past and present, continues to contemplate the splendour of his beloved South America from his pedestal above.

'I see her seated on the throne of liberty, grasping the sceptre of justice, crowned by glory and revealing to the old world the majesty of the new world.'

A local politician in a dark suit closes the act. The dignitaries' wives reach for their handbags. '*Socialismo o muerte! Venceremos!*' 'Socialism or death! We will conquer!' Ciudad Bolívar erupts. The square begins to empty, but the band plays on. Above the rooftops, the Liberator and the pigeons are listening.

Conclusion

HASTA LA VICTORIA, SIEMPRE

Cuba

A single revolution engenders a thousand others.
SIMÓN BOLÍVAR, LETTER TO GENERAL JUAN JOSÉ FLORES, NOVEMBER
1830

Havana

Bolívar docked briefly in Havana at the beginning of his adventures.
The fifteen-year-old child of privilege was on his way to Madrid. A
lifetime lay ahead of him. I arrive in the Cuban capital after a year
on the road, my journey around South America now at an end.

Where Bolívar and his fellow liberators had gone, I'd done my
best to follow. Their quest for independence had taken me from the
heights of the Andes, up the banks of the river Plate, down the tributaries of the Amazon and to the coast of the Caribbean.

Panama also made the list, courtesy of my transit flight to Cuba.
Bolívar had gone there too, in 1824. He'd invited representatives
from across South America to join him. The plan was to talk
through his dream for a continental union. The Liberator even sent
a courtesy note to the White House. Unlike the pan-American free-
trade summit in Mar del Plata, the delegate for the USA never made
it. In both cases, the conferences came to naught.

As I flew into Havana's José Martí airport, I made a quick calculation of the numbers involved in my twelve-month trek: sixty-
seven long-distance buses, eighteen flights, nine thousand five
hundred and seventy-eight photos, one hundred and five hotel beds,
twenty-nine notebooks, hundreds of local buses, scores of metro
stops, sixteen tram journeys, dozens of taxi rides, eleven trips by
rickshaw, innumerable interviews, eight nights in a tent, five days in

a canoe, four boat rides, three trips by cable car, two lost memory sticks and one dinner of boiled Bolivian sheep's head.

Compared to Bolívar, my expedition had the ring of a day trip. By his fortieth birthday, the great adventurer had covered over twenty thousand miles on horseback, fought in more than three hundred battles and skirmishes, liberated six countries, occupied three presidencies, led an army, spent a personal fortune and orchestrated the independence of an entire continent. In a colonial house of sand-blast stone along Old Havana's Calle Mercaderes, I discover the story mapped out in ceramic.

As with most public buildings in the Cuban capital, the Simón Bolívar Museum has about five uniformed employees for every one visitor. A panel of bored faces looks up as I pass through the carriageway entrance of a sugar baron's former home. From the central courtyard, a parrot squawks a welcome. No one else speaks.

The idling staff greet my presence by glancing disinterestedly at one another. Eventually, their collective eye falls on Lupe. An attractive brunette with a low-cut blouse, she resignedly pushes herself up from her chair, brushes the creases out of her conscription navy trouser suit and asks if I want to be shown around. Her guided tour consists of switching the lights on and off as I make my own way through the museum.

Funded by the Venezuelan Embassy in Havana, most of the displays are devoted to local pottery pieces and handicrafts of middling quality. My eye is drawn to a vivid stained-glass mural. The historic landmarks of modern South America illuminate the coloured, molten landscape, beginning with Columbus's portentous armada and ending with the bearded Fidel Castro. In the centre, dividing history, swaggers the mighty Bolívar, proud as a peacock in a pair of tight, white jodhpurs.

Not until I've lapped the two-storey house in silence does Lupe point me towards the ceramics. Each representation is exhibited on individual rectangular columns under a cube of transparent glass. There are twenty-eight pieces in total, filling two low-ceilinged rooms. According to the earthenware biography, the Liberator was born with sideburns and a full head of curly orange hair. Hipólita, the bulging-lipped wet nurse, is waiting at the bedside. She holds a Venezuelan flag in which to wrap the illustrious infant.

Lupe hovers by the doorway as I stroll leisurely through the subsequent chapters of the legend's life. The artist brings a graphic humour to her tale. Presiding over Bolívar's school life is a naked, baton-holding Simón Rodríguez. The well-endowed tutor sets up his young pupil for an amorous adolescence. By a stone well in Spain, we see him plucking petals to test if his darling María Teresa truly loves him. Later, long after the wilting of that innocent daisy, he's off on a deserted beach romping in the sand with the libidinous Manuela. His general's jacket and sandals lie discarded beside his unclothed body. It's a scene worthy of the Hotel Caribe.

Every Bolívar story, even this comedy version, has its morals: there's Bolívar the Emancipator unlocking the ankle-chains of his slaves, Bolívar the Archetypal Citizen playing guitar around a campfire and eating cornbread *arepas,* Bolívar the Reformer dancing with his black sergeant at a ball for snobbish aristocrats, Bolívar the Thinker writing truisms about justice at his desk and, naturally, Bolívar the Liberator flying through the sky on a white stallion above an adoring crowd. Closing the show is Bolívar the Immortal, sitting cross-legged on a park bench in Heaven, chewing the cud with a ginger-bearded Jesus.

'Finished yet?' Lupe wants to know, her finger pressed to the light switch.

I take the hint and wander through a connecting doorway into the final section of the exhibition. Drenched in sunlight, the expansive room looks out onto the street. Along the outside wall, a group of schoolchildren is noisily queuing. Their harassed teacher numbers them off to check none have gone missing en route to the museum.

Occupying this last room is a second account of the Bolívar epic, this time delivered in blocks of bilingual prose and stapled onto a row of free-standing presentation boards. After the light-heartedness of the ceramicist, the narrative version feels dry and pedagogic. The stiffness of the English translation doesn't help. The man who inspired a continent is described as having 'actuated mechanisms for greater understanding,' while his master-plan for South American unity is judged worthy of study 'with respect to its essential lineaments'.

Back in the doorway, Lupe is chewing her fingernails. I begin skim-reading the text, conscious that the voices of the beleaguered teacher and her charges are growing closer. The pupils have just discovered the parrot in the balconied courtyard. They're yelling at it to say something, but the formerly hospitable bird is stubbornly not playing ball.

I reach the concluding blocks of text. The story's end dedicates itself to the Liberator's legacy. As his climax nears, the uptight narrator unwinds a fraction. I note down his more elaborate musings about the revolutionary role model:

' . . . he wished to emancipate not just nations, but minds; not only with the sword, but by word and example'

' . . . raising high the torch of liberty, democracy, independence and human rights, he illuminated ever larger areas of the South American continent while dispersing the darkness to the decrepit institutions of the old regime'

' . . . to say "Simón Bolívar" is to exalt the values of liberty which are imbedded in the heart of every individual and which inspire all civilisations'

' . . . much of what he planned and proposed is still undone'

A form's worth of five- and six-year-olds hurtles into the room. I notice that Lupe has slunk away from her guard post by the door. Her 250 *peso* (£5.50) monthly salary doesn't cover crowd control.

' . . . he is symbol, reality and myth'

The author's broad-brush finale escapes the attentions of the unruly primary-school pupils. Bolívar is not going anywhere though. They have a lifetime ahead with him.

I'd come to Cuba ostensibly to cover the parliamentary 'elections'. Reporting in the world's longest-running socialist state has its difficulties. Press departments don't exist, people in the street rarely open up and most dissidents live ninety miles away in Florida.

Theoretically, any foreign journalist entering the island state should apply for an official media pass. Hardly any do. The bureaucratic hoops are so convoluted that only the permanent press pack bothers to tackle them. I'd snuck in on a tourist visa. Every year, two hundred thousand Brits fly into the revolutionary republic. Most are immediately carted off to all-inclusive hotels in resorts such as Varadero or Cayo Largo. With all-you-can-eat wristbands slapped on their wrists, they spend their days on the beach and their evenings in the bar sipping mint mojitos and listening to the hotel band play endless renditions of 'Guantanamera'. I figured one more Caribbean sun-seeker wouldn't trouble immigration.

I skip the beach resort and catch a cab to a *casa particular* in the heart of Old Havana. Renting a room to foreign tourists represents one of the few legitimate ways Cubans can turn a profit. I'd found details of Sergio and Miriam's apartment block through Google. In a country where less than 2 per cent of citizens have access to the Internet, having a website is an achievement in itself. I booked in for a week. Located on Calle Luz, their building proves straightforward for the taxi driver to find. Recently renovated, it's the only property on the block to have seen any modification since the 1959 revolution. A sapphire-blue Buick, half a century old, is parked outside.

The elections take place on a Sunday. My lack of formal press credentials turns out to be only a minor inconvenience. In Cuba, the media is invited to take a back seat at polling hour. There are no campaign rallies to attend and no pollster surveys to cover. Nor is there any doubt about the result.

Voters are invited to choose from a list of closely vetted representatives. They learn about their delegates from a mugshot and a short biography, which are diligently posted around town by the Election Commission. I stop a moment outside a dollar store on Calle Obispo. A dozen photocopied profiles stare out from behind the glass frontage. They remind me of 'Wanted' signs. Several of the candidates even look like felons. Their summaries paint a very different picture. All are upstanding citizens and signed-up members of the Community Party. Around half are politicos with existing experience. The remainder are drawn from the arts, education and other civic-minded fields.

Alongside their career information, the carefully crafted curricula vitae pull out salient facts to bolster their individual candidacies. Antonio Orestes, for example, is credited with joining the National Revolutionary Police Band in 1959. He also holds a medal for culture, issued to him by the government of Zaire. The précis of Carlos Crenata, on the other hand, boasts of 'military missions overseas'. Where these covert forays might have occurred and what they involved remains tantalisingly vague. Taking the revolution to foreign lands is not a prerequisite. Eusebio Leal, for example, is singled out for his voluntary efforts in the community. He's also a blood donor.

Neatly, there are six hundred and fourteen pre-selected nominees for six hundred and fourteen seats. In the election history of the Cuban Revolution, no candidate has ever obtained less than the 50 per cent margin required to take office.

I persuade Miriam to take me with her to the polling station. We don't have far to walk. Votes are cast in the primary school across the street. Along with free health care, universal education is one of the much-heralded triumphs of socialist Cuba. No pupil in Havana has to walk more than a few blocks to be in class.

Cristina, a big-haired woman with a matriarchal disposition, is loitering by the door when we arrive. The two women live in the same apartment building, and Miriam stops briefly to chat. I overhear her asking if foreigners are allowed inside. Cristina sees no problem.

'Go right on in,' she tells me loudly, motioning me towards the door with a 'be my guest' sweep of the arm. 'Take some photos if you like. We don't want people saying that Cuba isn't a free country.'

Miriam's neighbour isn't being ironic. A senior representative for the Committee for the Defence of the Revolution, she follows her duties to the letter. She won't have anyone bad-mouthing Cuba or its election practices: every citizen is fully consulted throughout the selection process; millions of dollars aren't wasted in election campaigns; voting is secret and voluntary; parliamentarians aren't paid and therefore crooks don't apply.

'The foreign media is always accusing Cuba of not having free and fair elections. As you can see, the system here is really very democratic.'

Except for the absence of opposition, that is. Not that Cristina dwells on the issue. Instead, she's looking down her residents' list for Miriam's name. Finding it, she ticks her off, another loyal foot soldier for the revolution.

Not all Cuban officialdom shares Cristina's lack of irony. The Museum of the Revolution in central Havana is a positive monument to satire. Housed in a sumptuous neoclassical mansion, it started life as opulent headquarters for the province's politicians and civil servants. Enamoured with its mirrored ballrooms and marble staircases, the wife of the then president decided she'd have it for herself. When the revolution came four decades later, the Presidential Palace was requisitioned a second time. Now it houses a permanent exhibition to the demise of Cuba's property-seizing plutocrats.

The curators share the building's ironic spirit. In its last room, museum visitors are treated to the derisively entitled 'Cretins' Gallery'. Beside an enlarged caricature of Fulgencio Batista, the former Cuban dictator, is nailed a plaque of appreciation: 'Thank you cretin for helping us make the revolution.' On the exhibit wall beside him hang two similar cartoon images, both of US presidents. Decked out as a Hollywood cowboy struts Ronald Reagan. Prancing next to him is a Caesaresque George W. Bush, clothed in sandals and a toga. Arch-defenders of the US embargo against Cuba, the cartoon pair are graciously thanked for their commitment to 'strengthen' and 'consolidate' the revolution.

Most ironies in modern Cuba tend to be less intentional. Some end up being amusing, such as the socialist bookseller in the Plaza de Armas who had somehow allowed an English edition of *Market-Driven Management* to slip between his tracts on Communist economics. Yet, the majority veer towards the tragic, like an island people banned from owning boats. Or a universal free health system that lacks basic medicines. Or trained professionals who work as waiters because the tips pay ten times their salary.

'*Votó!*' exclaim the two school pupils commandeered to man the polling booth. 'She voted!'

They salute Miriam as she submits her ballot paper. Like always, she's put a 'yes' beside every name on the ballot paper.

Monday's edition of *Granma,* the government's official newspaper, indicates my host wasn't alone in block voting. The six hundred and fourteen delegates were jointly elected with an overwhelming 91 per cent of the vote. A landslide victory for Cuba's democracy, the state-sponsored press declares.

Bolívar had his own reservations about modern democratic methods. He feared that the 'untrammelled liberty' of people power would lead to anarchy. At the other extreme, he dreaded an obsequious citizenry, as in Cuba, 'whence come usurpation and tyranny.' The idealist in him always strove for a balance between the two. No South American country ever achieved that illusive equilibrium in his lifetime. Nor has any since.

The election results could have ended any which way. Only one political position exists in Cuba: the presidency. Omniscient and omnipresent, its holder rules over all. For forty-nine years, Fidel Castro had doggedly occupied that seat of power. He acted like a cricket batsman at the crease, slowly building up his score with single after single, waiting for that elusive last run to reach his half-century.

I catch the totemic revolutionary in the twilight of his career. Recovering from major intestinal surgery, the original *El Comandante* hasn't been seen in public for eighteen months. The streets of Havana are awash with rumours. The party faithful readily predicted his gradual recovery and imminent return to office, a verdict based more on the habit of having him there than any medical evidence. After all, seven in ten Cubans have never known another leader. Others whisper about retirement and regime change. Some even doubt he is still alive. As with everything in Cuba, only Fidel really knows the truth.

Illness and speculation beleaguered Bolívar during his last days in power too. Plagued by insomnia and weakened by fits of fever, the Liberator set himself on a course for Europe and exile. His departure was repeatedly delayed – first for want of a passport, then for the absence of a ship, then for poor weather, and finally on doctor's orders. By the end, even his personal entourage speculated whether he ever truly meant to leave.

As his health deteriorated so did his optimism. His mood worsened when he learned of the assassination of Antonio José de Sucre, his intended successor. In a letter to General Juan José Flores, creator of Ecuador, Bolívar gave vent to his disillusion. Twenty years of leadership had led him to the following morbid conclusions: '(1) America is ungovernable, for us. (2) Those who serve the Revolution plough the sea.'

Acerbic at the best of times, the Liberator's humour became positively acidic as death approached.

'The only thing to do in America is emigrate,' he chided his fellow general.

The ailing Bolívar had more caustic ink in his pen. So criminally debased would South America become, he wrote, that 'the Europeans won't bother to conquer us'.

As so often the case, history proved him right.

Sitting in the Plaza de la Catedral on my last day in Havana, I meet someone suffering under a cloud even darker than Bolívar's. José Quiñones is a man bereft: his son just fled to the USA; his wife works every hour in the hospital for next to nothing; and he himself has fallen foul of the authorities. He has a word for the revolution too: 'fossilised'.

The outburst leaves me suspicious. Innuendo. Words unsaid. Muffled grumbles. This is as much as I'd obtained from a week of enquiries. Out of nowhere, a stranger sidles up to me in a touristic part of town and starts deriding the regime. It was all too easy. Could he be Cuban Secret Service? I'd had the sensation of being watched several times in Havana. Could he be setting a trap for me, tricking me into revealing myself as an unlicensed journalist? I'd been warned that I'd be deported if caught. Or was I being paranoid? Didn't Fidel's police have better things to do? I swallowed my doubts and agreed to his suggestion that we meet later that evening.

As I walk towards our rendezvous point, I've still not made up my mind about the mysterious Señor Quiñones. A large part of me still strongly suspects he's a stooge. By way of back-up, I rope in two young British travellers who are also staying at the *casa particular* to act as my wingmen. They have instructions to call the British Embassy should I suddenly disappear into the back of a police van. A smaller part thinks he might be a charlatan, in which case I wager he won't turn up at all. The remaining fraction hopes he might be a genuine dissident.

'Over here,' the man from the square shouts as we enter the veranda bar at the Hotel Inglaterra. He's changed his T-shirt for a well-pressed polo top. A half-drunk beer sits on the table in front of him.

I introduce my companions, who take a seat at the next table. They order strawberry daiquiris and watch the long-legged Cuban girls chatting up foreign businessmen at the bar.

'So, what do you want to know?'

His directness catches me off guard, but I do have a question. I've been carrying it around ever since listening to Chávez in the football stadium.

Across South America, people are striving for change. The battle lines for a second independence, for a final liberation, are being drawn. Behind it all hovers Fidel, the revolutionary magus sitting in his Havana hermitage, watching the 'historic events' play out on satellite television. His protégé is turning Venezuela upside down in Bolívar's name. The ripples of José Martí's 'second independence' are spreading from the City of Women to the Casa Hadewijch, from the Vigario Geral *favela* to Bolivia's Presidential Palace. Here in Cuba, in Fidel's backyard, what lessons are there for the Liberator's heirs? What could half a century of revolution teach them to expect?

Still keeping to my tourist alibi, I try crystallising my query into something an interested visitor might ask: 'What's it like living the revolution?'

Señor Quiñones cracks the knuckles on his left hand. I notice the grime under his fingernails. Back in the square, he'd told me he'd lost his job as a government lawyer and now worked illegally as an odd-job mechanic. Perhaps he was telling the truth, after all? He swigs down his beer and I order him another.

'Here in Cuba things aren't allowed to change,' he answers, adopting the judicious tone of the courtroom. 'Everything just goes round and round and round.'

For the next hour and a half, he's occupied with the trials of living in a modern socialist republic: the food shortages, the lousy wages, the high prices, the inability to travel abroad, the ban on moving house, the restrictions on free speech, the farcical voting system.

'Here I am, forty-six years old, never having owned my own car,' he says at one point. 'Just think about it: I have a beautiful beach less than half an hour away from my house, and I haven't visited it for three years because I can't afford the transport.

'Here in Cuba, we're taught that capitalism is bad,' he continues, 'that it brings crime and beggars and social unrest. Sure, there is social inequality in Europe and other countries, but there's nothing like the general poverty that we have in Cuba.'

I ask the alleged dissident if it's not dangerous for him to voice such opinions. Señor Quiñones doesn't care who knows what he thinks. I could be one of Fidel's informants for all he knows. The idea amuses me. I hadn't thought about our meeting from his perspective.

He takes out a brown envelope from his bag. It has a letter inside and a postcard with a sequence of photographs of Che. I'd told him I was heading back to Argentina in the morning, and he wonders if

I might send the package to a friend of his in Patagonia. The six-line address is written diligently in thin blue biro on the front.

'It's for a woman I know,' the married Señor Quiñones tells me. 'She came here looking for answers after her marriage broke up.' He doesn't elaborate on their relationship.

Cautiously, I take the envelope from him. As I do, I'm struck by the feeling that a chapter of an altogether different conspiracy is beginning to unfold.

The stranger from the square gets to his feet, reaching out a hand stained with engine oil. I stand, and we shake. His grip is firm, as if conveying sincerity in its touch. My palm remains in his, suffering the heavy press of his fingers. *Is it really sincerity? Or could it be a threat?* I still can't decide who this unknown Cuban with his sub-versive opinions and his black fingernails really is.

Our palms still clasped, he takes my elbow with his other hand. Two dark hazel eyes stare straight into mine. He leans forward until I smell the stale whiff of beer on his breath. His voice is low and confidential.

'I was brought up believing in the revolution. But then the *grandes* defrauded us.'

His fingers squeeze mine one last time before letting them go.

'Now I feel like a *real* revolutionary. History will absolve me.'

Further up the street, a dapper-looking group of theatre-goers emerges from an evening at the ballet. Soviet-style taxis cough grat-ingly towards them. A beautiful Cuban girl slips out of the Inglaterra bar with a Westerner on her arm. Then Señor Quiñones turns and walks off into the sticky Havana night.

I return to Buenos Aires to hear Fidel has resigned. Old and infirm, the octogenarian revolutionary has at last handed over the reins. A pundit on the radio news is predicting great changes ahead for Cuba. Another comes on to disagree. I leave my house and walk to the post office to buy stamps for the letter in my pocket. Will the revolution outlast its leader? In the short term, most probably. Will capitalist counter-revolutionaries overrun the island with Burger King and advertisements for car insurance? In time, perhaps.

Revolutions aren't static affairs. They change and mutate and adapt to circumstance. From Bolivia's coca-farmers to Venezuela's Bolívarian reformers, South America's present generation of liberators had taught me that. And Cuba has been stationary too long, trapped in a time warp, starved of the oxygen to fight.

'Nothing is so dangerous as to leave power in the hands of a single citizen over long periods of time.' The words once belonged to Bolívar. They still do. But now the present owns them as well. And the future too. As with all true revolutionaries, the idea outlives the individual. Symbol, reality and myth: the most powerful triumvirate of them all.

Two centuries on, the liberators continue to speak. This vast, magical, enchanting continent seeps and seethes their voices. Listen, and they're to be heard trickling up river ways and murmuring through marketplaces, bouncing down mountainsides and, when the hour's right, surging through the Earth's crust. As long as there are ears to hear it, the *viva!* of liberation will carry on the wind.

The storm clouds are gathering. Hundreds of thousands of South Americans are today laying claim to their second independence. The continent's citizens are undergoing a 'collective exorcism', to steal a phrase from Eduardo Galeano, the Uruguayan author recently brought to prominence by Hugo Chávez.

'Huge multitudes from many different pueblos are involved in ridding themselves of the demons derived from the culture of colonialism,' he'd told me over a bottle of local beer in his favourite bar in Montevideo's Old Town.

'The worst aspect of our colonial traditions is the culture of impotency. It's a culture that says "this would be good, but it can't be done. And it can't be done because you're not able to do it. You can't walk on your own two feet. You can't think with your own head. You can't feel with your own heart."'

He'd looked up from his beer at that point. He stared at the neo-classical columns of the Teatro Solis across the street. A thought seemed to be playing in his head. It drew a wistful smile to his face. He pointed to the adjacent Plaza Independencia. A week or so before, he'd fronted a public demonstration against Uruguay's prohibition of abortion. The results of a public referendum had just been published. He'd lost. He was used to losing.

'Win or lose, I don't really care. What's important to me is to keep fighting.' A steely, humourless determination fixed upon his mouth and jaw line.

Señor Quiñones and Galeano share little in terms of their political perspective. But they are men of the same spirit. To them and others like them, la lucha, the 'fight', is what counts. On an individual scale, such struggles may appear the flailing of drowning men. Their full impact can only be seen on a collective scale. They challenge and chaff at the powers that be. Together, they cause walls to crumble and foundations to shake. In these years of bicentenary, they breathe life into the past. Into the future, they bring the hope of change.

I lick the back of the stamps, paste them onto the top of the envelope and then drop it into the post box. The words are on their way. Across the grassy pampas they'll fly, a missive from another world. In the wilds of Patagonia, a lone recipient awaits unknowingly. Another story is unfolding. Revolution or resignation, it's hers to decipher. But the message is in the post.

Postscript

VIVA SOUTH AMERICA

'When I contemplate this immense reunited country, my soul mounts to that height demanded by the colossal perspective of a picture so wonderful. My imagination takes flight toward future ages and admiringly observes from them the prosperity, the splendour, and the life, which will exist within this vast territory.'

SIMÓN BOLÍVAR, 'THE ANGOSTURA ADDRESS', 1819

I find myself in Central London on a cold Saturday morning, seemingly a world away from the events of this book. I am lined up, single file, in a ragged queue outside Congress House, the rain-grey headquarters of the Trades Union Congress. The line is short, no more than eight or ten of us. We stand alone in diligent, British silence. The woman on the other side of the glass door avoids eye contact. She holds the keys and obviously has instructions not to let us in before 9.15am precisely. We are two minutes short. She continues to stare elsewhere and pretend we don't exist.

I look around. Traffic is quiet. A straggle of pedestrians shuffles past in the direction of Oxford Street, heads down, chins pointed into chests. Several of the passers-by wear large, spherical headphones that look like bulbous ear-warmers. Encased in a private, beat-beat world of iPod tunes, they pass us by without the slightest acknowledgement. To them, we're invisible. On a weekday, the streets would be full of hurrying office workers and shop assistants. Today, Londoners are taking a break from their work-bound rushing. The buses, like the pavements, are virtually devoid of people. So too the black cabs that trail them, like hungry crows behind a tractor plough.

I have come in the hope of reconnecting with South America, which, as I look up at the cloudy London sky and across to the empty street, suddenly feels impossibly far away.

Five years have passed since I wrote this book, and two years since I packed my bags and relocated home to the UK. What was meant to be a brief sojourn had turned itself into semi-permanent residency. Our children both held Argentine passports. Our network of friends had come to feel a little like a surrogate family. Yet it felt the time had come to reconnect with our roots again, with old friends and our real-life family. It was the right decision, but leaving South America was not an easy one. It felt like we were deserting in a way, or, at the very least, reluctantly cutting off a lengthy love affair. Even at the time, I knew it was a move that would be laden with future longing and complicated by 'what ifs?'

Although I no longer live in South America, I feel a part of me remains there. I try and stay in touch with the continent, by which I mean abreast of its more macro tooings and froings. Sadly the micro now largely escapes me. For the act of not being there means missing the anecdotal and seemingly incidental. I no longer get tit-bits from the newspaper vendor at the *kiosko*, for instance; no longer hear the dinner-party gossip or bar-room chatter; no longer see the fresh-painted graffiti on the subway or the headlines in the 'yellow tops'. All those things that give you a feel about the place you live in; everyday things that never find their way into newsprint but which define much of how people think and see and conceive of the world they inhabit.

Regrettably, I have not had much success in remaining in touch with the majority of those who appear in the pages of this book either. For many, our meeting was only ever fleeting. Others have changed their phone numbers or moved on. Social media wasn't as big then as it is now, so suggestions to connect through Facebook and the like occurred less often. Of course, I often find myself wondering what happened to the various characters whose stories populate these pages. Certain individuals come to mind with particular clarity. Basillo, the *Devil's Miner*, in Potosí, is one, which is slightly strange as I didn't even meet him in the end. Yet images of his family in their hut at the mineshaft come back to me now with intense vividness. Louis in the Asunción prison is another. Is he still there?

If he got out, where is he now? Similar questions come back to me about Blanca in the battered women's home in Concepción, and Alvaro in Colombia. I regret that I'm not in a position to provide an update on how their stories evolved. Whatever the case, for now, it's my hope they've been able to wrest back control over their lives and to '*seguir para adelante*', to keep going, as my friend Enrique in Lima would say.

In fact, Enrique is one of the few exceptions when it comes to keeping in contact. Some time after the book came out, he appeared out of the blue on my doorstep in Buenos Aires. He'd taken up the offer of a job, made via his cousin, with a shoe manufacturer. The term 'manufacturer' makes it sound rather grand. From what I could tell, the place conformed to what by most criteria could be described as a 'sweat shop': the employees almost all illegal immigrants, everything managed in cash, no contracts, no benefits, no set hours. He initially lived on the factory site, which was located near La Salada, a vast commercial market on the outskirts of the city that sells counterfeit goods by the truckload. Things didn't go well. Enrique turned out to be all fingers and thumbs when it came to shoe making. His pay was meagre and based on how many shoes he could produce, which meant extra hours if he was ever to escape working penury. Furthermore, some of his wages were deducted against food and lodging. For the initial months, a fee was also withheld to cover the cost of his three-day bus ride from Peru.

We'd see him on Sundays, the one day off he had all week. He'd go to church in the morning, then call round at ours. We'd give him a meal and ask how he was getting on, but he spoke little. All he wanted to do was eat, use the shower and slump in front of the television. Last thing at night, he'd wave goodbye and head back home on the bus. He grew increasingly more insular as the weeks passed. A poor diet of highly processed food saw him put on weight quickly. He ballooned. When his ground-floor box room flooded after a spate of heavy rain, he hit a real low. He was still reluctant to quit, however. Without official papers, he was in a poor negotiating position not only with his immediate employer but with future employers too. A dozen other Peruvians would happily take his job, his boss kept telling him. What weighed on him more heavily, however, was the prospect of returning home empty-handed. He had come to '*hacer América*', to live the dream. In the end, it took a month of arrears with his pay to eventually persuade him that it was time to walk out.

He didn't leave La Salada, though. For the best part of a year, he picked up temporary jobs in and around the unlicensed market. All of them were exploitative and all, without exception, miserably remunerated. We tried to arrange casual work for him as a handyman with friends, but it never worked out. He'd turn up one day and not the next. Or he wouldn't return their calls. It was a two-hour bus ride to the central neighbourhood of town where we lived, which, in balance, probably made it an unattractive proposition. As his second winter in Argentina approached, his health began to decline dramatically. He'd turn up at the house on Sundays looking ever more miserable, always with a cold and a worryingly persistent cough. After much discussion, he eventually resolved to return to his family in Peru. It was tough saying 'goodbye'. In reality, his job prospects were equally grim at home. But he could be with his mother and could see his child, both of whom I knew he sorely missed. Today, we're in touch through Facebook. He's living up in a mountainous region east of Lima, where he's volunteering for a church. He tells me he's doing well.

To stay in touch with South American affairs more generally, I'm almost entirely dependent on a network of intermediaries. I rely on friends, for the most part. We communicate via email or Skype, although on a fairly irregular basis. Most of my closest contacts are based in Argentina, as we were, and our conversations rarely reach beyond that particular country's borders. For a wider perspective, I follow coverage in the international press. Yet foreign reporting from the region is generally so scant and often so skewed, it's difficult to get a full picture. To supplement this rather muddied trickle, I sign up to various email newsletters. Most are run by civil society groups, almost all of which are cash-strapped types that wear their politics on their sleeve. Latin American Bureau is one of my favourites. Whenever its regular mail-out pops up in my inbox, a chunk of my working day is lost clicking through to links about everything from land grabs in the Colombian countryside to indigenous protests in Patagonia. South American commentators litter my Twitter feed too. I read books, of course. Fiction in the main. It was the writers of the Latin American 'boom' – Gabriel García Márquez, Mario Vargas Llosa, Julio Cortázar, Carlos Fuentes, and so on – who did so much to kindle my original fascination in the continent. Now I'm back in the UK, and can't feel the vibe on the street for myself, I enjoy the ability of fiction writers to take me from my armchair and deposit me amid the sights and smells of far-away lands.

Since returning, I've developed a rather curious habit too. There's no delicate way to put it really: I've become prone to *thrusting* myself on South Americans whom I come across. They might be friends of friends, or people I meet through work, or just random strangers – a Colombian working in a bar, say, or a Brazilian student on a bus. It doesn't matter. I feel impelled to introduce myself and then find myself scrabbling around for ways to kick start a conversation. I want to hear them speak Spanish, want to guess from their inflection where they might be from, want to learn why they've come to the UK and to hear what lives they've left behind. My British friends think this is all very peculiar. So do I, I guess, now I sit here and reflect on it. I'm not an especially gregarious person; not one for generally bounding up to people I don't know. Fortunately, most South Americans are somewhat different. My uninvited attempts at engagement have always been met with warmth, my inquiries always treated with openness and generosity. Perhaps that's what I miss the most? The easy way of South Americans, their willingness to treat strangers as friends, the pleasure they derive from social interaction.

Of course, to speak of 'South Americans' as a homogenous group is to invite accusations of simplification and stereotyping. There are grumpy Sudamericanos, just as there are unabashed, talkative Brits. A 'propensity towards' – openness, sociability, revolution, whatever the descriptive noun – may be a more accurate way of putting it, although still not entirely satisfactory. The trap of generalities is a simple one to fall into, and one that I am guilty of more than once in this book. There are throwaway comments about places or descriptions of whole people groups that, on re-reading, feel abrupt at best and perfunctory at worst. For these, I apologise.

In my defence, let me say that my abiding concern throughout the book was to bring the reader along with me, to invite them to 'walk in my shoes', so to speak. Too many qualifications and detailed explanations would, I felt at the time, steal from the pace and vividness required for that endeavour. The researcher in me considered adding footnotes to this new edition, but I resolved to keep to my original mission. Indeed, the only alteration that I've made for purposes of clarification is in the sub-title of the second chapter, which now refers to 'gender' rather than 'women', in keeping with the wider themes discussed. The lack of other tweaks will, I hope, be balanced out by the in-situ style and speed of this kind of reportage form. It should be said that a number of factual errors were weeded out in the second edition. You will find no sightings of lemurs referenced in the Paraguay chapter, for example. Such mistakes that remain are, as stated in the preface, mine and mine alone.

The structure of the book lends itself to some unavoidable shortfalls. I'm thinking primarily of the charges of oversight and subjectivity, a niggly pair for sure. I chose to use an individual country as a canvass to discuss separate topic areas because it was the only way I could see of giving meaningful focus to continent-sized questions. The cost of this wider ambition is, in some ways, to shrink the frame. Ecuador has more to it than indigenous issues, for example, just as Paraguay is more than a human-rights dead zone. Likewise, a degree of interchange between country and subject area would have been perfectly feasible. Religion is a patently transferable theme, for example. Every country on the continent was touched by the same Catholic heritage as Peru, just as they were by pre-Christian belief systems and as they currently are by modern variants of Protestantism. Similarly, economic exploitation is by no means unique to Bolivia. Nor is violent machismo particular to Chile.

Again, in an attempt to marshal some arguments in my favour, I'd maintain that the issues ascribed to each country hold particular prevalence in those national settings. Located at the heart of the Spanish empire, for instance, Peru served as a centrifugal force for the promotion of the cross as well as the slashing of the sword. Chile, on the other hand, had elected its first female president at the time, putting gender politics on the map in unprecedented fashion. Meanwhile, few countries have been plundered over the centuries quite so spectacularly as mineral-rich Bolivia.

Such prevalence persists, I'd argue, as events since the publication of this book bear testament. Chile provides one of the clearest, and saddest, cases in point, with a spate of brutal attacks against young gay men over recent years. The most notorious was the gruesome murder of Daniel Zamudio, who was set upon by a gang of four thugs in a Santiago park. His assailants carved swastikas on his skin and branded him with cigarettes, then urinated on his body before leaving him for dead. Shortly afterwards, another gay man, Wladimir Sepúlveda, was left in a coma after a similar unprovoked attack. Incidences like these are forcing this *machista*, military-minded country to face up to the existence of entrenched homophobia. Today, murmurings of a same-sex marriage bill suggest that such a process could be beginning to happen.

Paraguay has undergone a series of regrettably predictable events over recent years too. The landlocked nation appears adamant to prove that its historic disregard for good governance continues at pace. Fernando Lugo, the 'red bishop', never got to fully enact his scribbled manifesto, being summarily ousted before the end of his presidential term. In Ecuador, meanwhile, the indigenous struggle to protect their traditional territories has won international attention of late. Back in 2007, environmentalists in Quito had told me about a bold plan to keep the Amazon's oil reserves under the ground. The deal rested on the international community putting up half the value of the untapped resource, equivalent to around US$3.6bn. After six years, only a dribble of pledges had been made and President Rafael Correa called an end to the idea. The first licences for exploration in the Yasuní National Park have since been dealt out. Traffic into the jungle homelands of Guinto and his fellow Huaoraní promises to get much busier in the years ahead. As for Colombia, displacement has steadily grown in political significance over recent years, with the government signing into force land restitution measures under a new Victims' Law. As with previous legal rights to state support, however, most of Colombia's displaced millions have yet to feel any effect of the legislative change.

Elsewhere in the region, the same issues keep cropping up, albeit away from the international spotlight. News from Bolivia is scant at the best of times, yet Evo Morales remains in power (for now) and, as with Bechtel, continues to rescind the contracts of foreign companies deemed antithetical to his nation's interests. The most recent to find their assets seized by the state were two Spanish-owned electricity distribution firms. In Argentina, the Peronists continue to squabble and fight among themselves, although they still cling to power in their inimitable way. Evangelical Christianity appears to continue to grow in Peru, on the other hand. Tens of thousands recently attended a weeklong conference held by the Movimiento Misionero Mundial church. The organisers had to hire a football stadium to accommodate them all. As for Brazil, the absence of a widespread debate about the silent marginalisation of the nation's black community speaks for itself. Expect to see plenty of Afro-Brazilian dance and music on show during the 2014 FIFA World Cup, plus black athletes on the field at the 2016 Rio Olympics. Just don't expect an Afro-Brazilian to be heading up the Central Bank or challenging for the presidency any time soon.

The one massive development since this book first appeared, of course, is the death of El Comandante. The passing of Hugo Rafael Chávez Frías in a Cuban hospital came in March 2013. After a prolonged fight with cancer, his death was widely expected but it came as a shock all the same. He'd dominated the South American political stage for so long, for him to suddenly be gone, for the tiger in Miraflores to have fallen silent, seemed altogether too odd and too abrupt.

Not all were puzzled, however. Many met the news of his death with tears of genuine sadness, others with triumphant cheers of joy. It was one of those rare moments that the world's media shifted away from its usual concerns and focused its lens on South America. On those terms alone, it puts Chávez's death on a par with the Brazilian World Cup and the Rio Olympics, the only other events (sparing a tsunami-type natural disaster) where such blanket coverage is guaranteed. True to form, newspapers reported his passing through the prism of their own worldview. 'A dictator dies', the *Washington Post* predictably wrote. From the other political extreme, the *Socialist Worker* came out with the headline: 'The outsider who became a legend.' Uncharacteristically, the *Guardian* toed an ambivalent line, describing Chávez as a 'populist leader' and 'charismatic hero to the poor' in the same breath.

I never felt it was the role of a reportage-style book like this to provide a detailed analysis of Chávez's administration. On the tentative evidence available to me, it would be difficult to avoid the trap of partiality and personal opinion. Even among the accounts of seasoned Venezuelan observers – of which many have found their way to print since El Comandante's death – few could ever be said to be balanced and ideology free. That's understandable. Neutrality is an almost impossible note to strike when discussing such a polarising figure. The ex-soldier from Los Llanos fed off controversy. He wasn't interested in people sitting on the fence. With his bombastic rhetoric and unapologetic manner, the Venezuelan leader virtually compelled people to take sides.

For me, the more interesting facet of his leadership lay in the political impulse he gave to citizens in Venezuela and across the continent. For millions of everyday people, he stood for something. That something was difficult to define and would change from person to person, from country to country, but it centred around certain enduring themes – themes like justice and self-assertion, empowerment and sticking two fingers up to the powers that be. Chávez chose to define this loose jumble of political tenets as 'Bolivarian'. What Bolívar himself would have made of this remains anyone's guess, but it was a shrewd piece of political positioning.

Chávez's supporters, both home and abroad, interpreted his mission variously. For some, he stood for anti-imperialism and South American sovereignty. For others, he embodied the fight for modern-day socialism and the enduring plight of class struggle. For others, it came down to the principles of participative democracy and civic empowerment. Chávismo was (is?) a wonderful, hydra-like catchall that could bend and twist according to the political winds. And therein lay its potency for so many. Television pundits can fight over whether Venezuela is now better or worse for the Chávez years. The writers of history books can squabble over his status as a true democrat or an authoritarian thug. For me, however, what I'm more intrigued by are the passions he unleashed and the hopes he gave rise to. What has happened to those?

The clock ticks to 9.15 and the lady behind the glass reaches for her keys and unlocks the double doors. We edge towards the entrance of the TUC's conference rooms, eager to get inside and into the warmth. A group of South Americans, meanwhile, chattering in Spanish and nursing cups of hot coffee, emerge from the soft-chaired lobby area next door.

Down a flight of stairs is a registration desk. It's then that I realise that I've forgotten my ticket. I'd booked the *Adelante!* conference online and the paper ticket had been sent to me in the post. On it had read the explicit message: 'Presentation of ticket required for entry.' I explain my oversight and, in true Latino rule-breaking spirit, the lady behind the desk gives me a wink and hands over a guest ticket. South America feels closer already.

Through the next door, into the lobby, and the continent looms up before me, laid out on stalls laden with colourful posters and politically motivated books, with fair-trade artisanal crafts and t-shirts depicting Che and Chávez. Flags serve as tablecloths; boxes of political pamphlets act as doorstops. I peruse the wares on offer. The Venezuela Solidarity Campaign is selling bright red, Bolivarian embossed baseball caps. I pick one up and I'm reminded of my day with the Chavista supporters at the inauguration of the bridge outside Caracas.

As I weigh up whether to buy one, a lady from the Cuba Solidarity Campaign stall opposite touches my elbow and invites me to sign a petition for the 'Miami 5' – a group of Cubans arrested in the US on charges of espionage. She wants a photo too. I happily agree.

The room fills up gradually. We're a mixed crowd: part students, part British trade unionists, part South American exiles and visitors, and large part placard-carrying activists from the hard Left. 'I remember stuffing envelops in your basement,' I overhear a man with a grey beard and wooly jumper saying. He's speaking to the salesperson at Housmans, a self-proclaimed 'radical' independent publisher which runs a 'Boycott Amazon' campaign and keeps itself afloat with hefty sales of Noam Chomsky and Karl Marx. It's not immediately clear what the envelope stuffing was motivated by. The Falklands War, maybe? Monsanto's introduction of genetically modified cash crops in Paraguay, perhaps? '1973, it was.' Ah. The bloody overthrow of Salvador Allende in Chile. It's a date that resonates with everyone in the room: the downfall of South America's first Marxist government.

I cross over to the Zed Books stand, another left-wing publisher. Before I get there, a lady in a bright yellow jacket thrusts a pamphlet in my hand. It concerns the destruction of the Ecuadorian Amazon by US oil company Chevron. Depicted graphically inside are images of ponds and water courses oozing with silvery, black crude. The pamphlet, like the campaign itself, is sponsored by the Ecuadorian embassy in London. I try to imagine the British embassy in Quito doing something similar, and the preposterousness of it makes me smile. I'm reminded afresh of why this continent of protesting presidents and everyday agitators excites me so much. Softened, I end up giving my train money to the nice lady at Zed. In exchange, I shove a compilation of essays about South America's social movements and leftist governments into my bag.

The conference kicks off with a call to arms in the TUC's main auditorium. But before it does, we're all asked to stand. Nelson Mandela has just died. The news is still fresh and the conference organisers call for a minute's silence. While on our feet, we are invited to remember the 'sad and untimely' death of Hugo Chávez as well. As the hubbub dies down and quiet settles over the room, a TUC official on the panel urges us to recall Chávez's contribution to building 'the new Latin America'. We do as we're bid. It's only afterwards that I get to wondering what the lady had meant by 'new'. It's a strange word in a way, supposing, as it does, the passing of one historical era and the emergence of another. For me, it brings to mind the José Martí quote about the coming of the 'second Independence' of the Americas, which I'd first heard long ago at the Mar del Plata summit. Is that what the TUC representative had in mind? Is it this epoch-making shift that's whirling through the heads of my fellow conference delegates as they take to their feet?

I'm left to ponder the question as the introductory speakers take to the podium. Each gears us up in turn for the day's big themes: the continued economic blockade of Cuba; the insatiable advance of neo-liberalism; the 'Gilbert and Sullivan farce' of British claims to the Falklands, to use the words of George Galloway, MP for Bradford West and a close friend of Chávez. And then it's off to the break-out seminars that run through the course of the morning.

The first session I attend is focused on economic alternatives. The assumption is that South America offers something that we in the world's industrialised economies can learn from, slavishly beholden as we are to capital markets and the private interests of multinational corporations. It's true that South America as a whole rode rather well through the 2008 banking crisis and subsequent recession. It's slightly less clear whether those countries pursuing more unorthodox economic policies, such as Ecuador, Bolivia, Venezuela and Argentina, are exemplars for others to follow. The panel certainly thinks so. A combination of state interventionism (including price fixing and the nationalisation of private assets), economic redistribution through government spending and public ownership is beating down poverty and delivering fairer societies, it is argued. Poverty has fallen by a third in Ecuador under Rafael Correa, one speaker notes. Venezuela's gross domestic product grew at 5.6 per cent in the last year of Chávez's administration, cites another. In the same year, El Comandante's Bolivarian Republic built 200,000 social homes for its poorest citizens.

Conventional economists will, with varying levels of hubris, line up to disagree. Inflation is running riot in Argentina, they say. Foreign investors are wary about Ecuador and positively dismissive of Bolivia. Their real punch bag is Venezuela, of course, where corruption and mismanagement are held up as utterly ruinous. The economy might be growing, but nothing like it should be for a country recently rated as having the largest certified oil and gas reserves on the planet. Meanwhile, critical analysts wag a finger at Venezuela's rampant inflation, its electricity blackouts and its supermarket shelves that are ever more empty. At the time of my visit, nearly a decade into Chávez's experiment in '21st Century Socialism', the unofficial dollar exchange rate was running at twice the official rate. Since then, the Bolivar has been strengthened, only to collapse over the monetary cliff a second time round. Today, the black-market dollar rate is six times what you'd get if you were to walk into a high-street bank in downtown Caracas, prompting a pending balance-of-payments crisis and general disgruntlement. Foreign currency reserves are shrinking fast, it's said, while infrastructure investments lie unloved or unfinished. In short, the picture is of a country at the edge of a precipice. The question critics ask is not *if* the Venezuela left behind by Chávez will collapse, but *when*.

The number of zeros on some of the macro-economic figures may have increased and some critical percentage points might have shifted, but the core arguments haven't changed since I wrote this book five years ago. The suits on Wall Street have forever been predicting the demise of the Venezuelan economy and others like it. That doesn't appear to have happened. Not yet, anyway. By hook or by crook (or, more precisely, by Asian demand for raw materials), they have proved resilient.

Likewise, the obedient students of free-market economics – Chile, Peru, Colombia and, especially, Brazil – are growing moderately, although not nearly as madly as previously predicted. Furthermore, redistribution in the most marginalised groups remains problematic for these countries. In Brazil, poverty has halved over the last decade or so. The expansion of the country's social welfare programmes and progressive tax policies have helped more than 28 million people out of poverty since the Workers' Party came to power under Luiz Inácio Lula da Silva in 2003. His successor in post, President Dilma Rousseff, has since introduced new welfare initiatives, such as the multi-million dollar 'Brazil Dem Miseria' (Brazil Without Misery) programme. Even so, disparities in wealth remain huge. Brazil is now the world's sixth biggest economy. Yet on a per capita earnings rate, it slips back to 100th place, behind Iran. Brazil's own statistics bureau estimates that 16.2 million Brazilians still live on less than R$70 (around £18) per month – the same amount that low-budget travellers 'can probably scrape by on' per day, according to the *Lonely Planet* guide. And while the statistics office declines to reveal the racial balance of the country's entrenched poor, you can bet that Afro-Brazilians continue to make up a fair slice of those at the bottom of the ladder.

What has gradually dawned on me since coming back to the UK is how little these arguments have to do with what's actually happening on the ground. Opinions about South America are forged first and foremost on ideological preference. If reality gets a look in, it's very much as a distant third (after who's got the best national football team). Perhaps that's always been the case? Half a century ago, successive US administrations convinced themselves that South Americans, man and boy, were all budding Communists. Today, right-wing commentators are equally quick to denounce as suspect the likes of Morales, Correa, Fernandez de Kirchner and anyone else with the temerity to question the dominant capitalist dogmas of the day.

Of course, it's the global political Left rather than the Right for whom the symbolic importance of South America is really paramount. For a generation of leftists that grew up watching, reading and listening to Fidel, Che and Allende, the region's prominence is long-standing and self-evident. This collective consciousness passes on to newer generations too. It's a political inheritance of sorts. This strikes me powerfully towards the end of the day when a young panelist recalls how his parents had taken in exiles fleeing Pinochet's Chile. He couldn't have been long out of nappies at the time, yet the memory and its significance was clearly seared into his political thinking as an adult.

I'm more than aware that those looking for overt political lessons from this book will encounter a degree of disappointment. The contents are too individually specific, too non-schematic and, very possibly, too contradictory for such tastes. The picture of the region that emerges is a messy one. There is no neat pattern between political reforms and social outcomes. I don't apologise for that. Everyday life is itself a messy affair, and it is everyday life that primarily interests me. In each country that I visited, it was the people and their stories that captivated me, not so much the policies of their respective governments. Naturally, the two are intrinsically linked. Politics and policy-making feed into people's lives. And to that extent, accounts of those lives can provide insights into the political climate of the day. But to extrapolate from the individual to the collective is a dangerous game, and one I feel instinctively reluctant to play.

To reiterate, I feel my primary job – the primary job of any writer engaged on a project of this type, in fact – is to provide a faithful chronicle of events as they unfold. That's not to say I haven't used (although hopefully not abused) the writer's prerogative to select and interpret. Of course, the book is not without its own goals either – to explore South America's contemporary struggles and its people's fights for independence. But a goal is not an agenda, at least in the strictly political sense. As ambitions go, the reporter's remit is more modest than that of the treatise-maker or history writer, but it's one that I'd like to think serves – within its own parameters – a valuable, illuminative purpose of its own.

South America's leaders don't help attempts to steer an even course. Chávez was unparalleled in his mastery of political rhetoric. Give him a topic, any topic, urban sanitation, say, or the price of poultry, and he could use it to find fault with US imperialism or evidence of domestic oligarchy. Few may be able to rival his rhetorical fluency, but that certainly doesn't stop them trying. Take Cristina Fernández de Kirchner. I listened to dozens of her speeches in the aftermath of her successful 2007 election (and subsequent re-election). Rarely does Argentina's first-elected female president miss an opportunity to set the mundane day-to-day affairs of state within a wider ideological arc. Hence, the continual references to Eva Peron, especially during her early days in office. The question of Falklands' sovereignty too, an iconic issue that gives any Argentine free rein to show old-style colonialism lives on (which well it may). More recently, her 'K' faction of the Peronist party has found a new hero in her husband, Néstor Kirchner, who died suddenly in 2010. Overnight, his image began popping up everywhere: always depicted as a defender of the poor, a champion of the oppressed – qualities more evident in death than in life, many would argue.

Alternatively, look at Rafael Correa in Ecuador. He peppered his successful presidential campaign in 2013 with references to the hundreds of schools, hospitals and new roads built during his time in office. This impressive track record would be enough for most presidents. And most voting publics too. But South Americans like their politics to come theoretically packaged, not just practically delivered. Hence Correa's promise to keep building a 'Citizens' Revolution' in Ecuador.

Power to the people. It's a bold, progressive, perennially seductive promise. Sceptics might sneer and decry such claims as cynical populism, but none can deny their potency.

Where it's easy to slip up is to read such rhetoric as reality. It's not a mistake South American politicians themselves make. As an outsider looking in, it's often difficult to determine just how far the orator in front of the camera differs from the dealmaker behind closed doors. Again, much comes down to one's own political beliefs. I, for one, would like to think that Chávez meant much (if not all) of what he said. I find it hard to believe that his missions were a calculated exercise in political expediency. I struggle to convince myself that his marathon speeches were nothing more than manufactured pap to feed the masses. Yet I've listened to many who would swear blind that this was entirely the case.

The art of politics as theatre is seen in sharp relief in humble Uruguay. Ironically, given its almost wholesale absence from the book, it's the country I've come to follow most closely of late. In a spate of enthusiasm following my return to the UK, I signed myself up for a post-graduate programme in Latin American Studies. The course is based around a research case study, and, for reasons that I won't bore you with, I chose to go with a Finnish timber investment near the Uruguayan day-tripper town of Colonia. You'll perhaps recall the Botnia mill near Gualeguaychú that Guru and his wind-surfing buddies objected to so strongly. Well, the US$1.9bn Punta Pereira pulp project is much the same, only even bigger and arguably more ugly. The fifty-kilometre drive from Colonia to the mill site passes the president's official *estancia*. José Mujica, the country's head of state during the mill's construction, was an irregular visitor. Known as 'Pepe' to most Uruguayans, the former Tupamaro guerrilla leader and long-time political prisoner prefers to spend his time at his own modest farmhouse near Montevideo. On the rare occasions that he visits the official residence, he eschews security teams and travels under his own steam, in a battered Volkswagen Beetle.

In Mujica's case, his austerity is genuine. Chávez once turned up to a voting booth in a Caracas slum driving a Beetle, but no one – even ardent Chavista supporters – imagined it was anything other than a publicity stunt. Visit Mujica's farm, however, and you'll see his clapped-out VW parked in the driveway. The Uruguayan premier suffers no whispered allegations about grand mansions in Miami or vast cash deposits in Swiss banks. The same can't be said for other leaders in the region. This is the man who reputedly gives 90 per cent of his presidential salary to charity, and who the BBC once described as the 'poorest president in the world' (a title that apparently grated on him).

Mujica's rhetoric fits his image. His speech at the United Nations' 2012 Rio Earth Summit is often presented as an archetypal example. Down with 'hyper-consumption', he cried. Let's bring an end to 'market societies', he pleaded. Enough with rampant globalisation, 'it's time to start fighting for a different culture,' he said. Nation states should be ruling over the market, not vice versa. The whole performance served as a homage to a genuinely sustainable model of human (not just economic) development, to a way of living that fits within the planet's material means. Mujica's message resonated with millions around the world. Almost immediately the ten-minute talk became an Internet sensation.

Little of such clear-minded thinking ever made its way onto the statute book, however. That's not to say that Mujica didn't push through a range of progressive social measures. Marijuana, abortion and same-sex marriages all became legal under his watch, for example. That's no mean feat. Yet the fundamental economic model on which modern Uruguay relies has survived untouched. So the mill owners gain tax breaks by the dozen, while the fiscal burden on national workers edges ever upwards. The same market-beholden system is changing the shape of the countryside too as traditional smallholders lose out to high-tech farmers and grazing lands disappear under commercial forest plantations. When a British-based extractive firm proposed creating the country's first open-pit mine, Mujica's government made its support clear. Why? For the same reason he refuses to dismantle the laissez-faire logic to which the majority of South America is now dutifully bound: 'Because [my] people ask for more and more.' Mujica, a former Marxist, can do little to rebut the material desires of his people. Indeed, if he forced his countrymen to live like he does, he admits that he'd have a revolution on his hands – and not the kind the hard Left has in mind.

Political pragmatism is, and always has been, the quiet companion of discursive idealism. Quiet but compelling: so Mujica's Uruguay teaches. Chávez, as ever, provides the exception. With global oil prices soaring for a substantial period of his term, the 'petrodollar president' found himself in the rare position for a South American leader of enjoying a budget surplus. With oodles of cash coming in, offending international bankers didn't bother him. Indeed, he seemed to enjoy it. ExxonMobil, the world's largest energy company, meanwhile, could up sticks and leave, and Chávez could afford to sit back and cheer.

No other leader has that luxury, certainly not a comparative minnow such as Uruguay. Ecuador is in a similar boat. Hence the first country in the world to confer constitutional rights to Nature is now actively pillaging its rainforests for oil and gas. Peru's Ollanta Humala is pursuing much the same strategy. A convincing argument can be made to suggest that his close association with Chávez and his Bolivarian agenda cost the ex-military man the 2006 election. Humala wisely softened his stance and edged towards the political centre. In 2010, a more moderate Humala carried the day. Dressed in the presidential sash, he now toes a market-friendly line. Economic analysts are queuing up to praise Peru for its prudent fiscal spending and pro-investment policies. Of course, it's a game that centre-left governments in Chile and Brazil have been playing for years. For the *Adelante!* audience, however, these are backward steps, more akin to Blairism than Bolivarianism. For critics on the Right, on the other hand, it's evidence of political populism at its worst.

So what does this all tell us about the dreams of Bolívar? To me, it seems obvious: if they are ever to be realised, if a second independence is ever to come, it'll arrive from outside formal electoral politics. Progressive constitutional reforms such as those in Bolivia, Ecuador and Venezuela provide welcome and essential building blocks. Yet the struggles on the street are where the authentic action lies, where political passions pump fastest, and, I'd argue, where the legacy of the Bolivarian Revolution really resides. Voters mobilising against corrupt officials; citizens taking on bullyboy businesses; factory workers fighting for fair pay: this is where the spirit of freedom is found at its fiercest and most feisty. And it's happening. Look at Chile and the long-running student protests that drew tens of thousands onto the streets of Santiago. Recall the 'Brazilian Spring' of 2013, when popular frustration at poor public services and political mismanagement finally boiled over into mass marches and riots. These are the big stories we hear about, but there are others – plenty of others – besides.

Chávez's legacy forms the centerpiece for several sessions during the conference. The first features the screening of a documentary by Aleida Guevara (daughter to Che and an Argentine diplomat under Cristina). The film's celebratory style is indicative of the general tone of the day. I attend a later event hosted by the Venezuela Solidarity Campaign. A picture of Chávez at a rally, rain splashing against his upturned face, is projected onto the whiteboard. Posters are pinned either side of it. '¡Victoria Presidente!' reads one. 'Chávez: corazon de mi patria', reads another: 'Chávez: heart of my homeland.'

I'm readying myself for a litany of unparalleled achievements. One of the speakers, a former adviser to the Venezuelan premier, provides just that. The new constitution is 'our utopia', he tells us. Democracy is up, poverty down. The only 'unfinished task' of the Chávez regime is the failure to wean the economy off its dependency on oil. As political confessions go, it's not much of a myth-buster.

The second speaker is a retired university lecturer. She is no less a fan of El Comandante, but she approaches the question of his legacy from an altogether different tack. We hear less about Chávez the Politician, and more about Chávez the Man. The candour with which she expresses her personal feelings for the former Venezuelan president is refreshing. 'I miss his voice,' she admits upfront. That's not all she misses. She misses his willingness to break the rules of 'elite, pompous discourse'. She misses his 'graspable' way of explaining complex ideas and his penchant for telling jokes. He was just a 'kid from the streets', which is why he was so deeply loved as well as so viscerally hated, she argues. Chávez's appeal was more a matter of gut reaction than intellectual response. To her mind (and to millions of Venezuelans, she asserts), he spoke not only for the people, but to people. His voice, his charisma, his unique ability to connect: as a collection of attributes, Chávez the Package is impossible to replicate. That's problematic when it comes to considering questions of legacy. Indeed, in terms of gut-level politics, his death is nothing less than a 'complete loss', she laments.

I wonder if we're about to lose her too. At the start of the session, the moderator had signalled that the lecturer would have to leave early. There's a People's Assembly in South London this afternoon. The burghers of Lewisham are gathering to protest against government austerity measures. Her attendance is requested. She'd given her word.

She doesn't end there though. She has one last thought to share before scooting off. It's about voice again. Although not Chávez's voice this time: it's the voice of the people she wants to talk about. Political analysts have come up with a number of impressive terms for Chávez's form of people's power. 'Constituent power' is one she likes best. 'Protagonistic democracy' is another. 'But what was at issue . . .' She corrects herself. Legacies live on, we shouldn't forget. Let us not slip into the past so quickly. 'But what is at issue [in Venezuela] is a real attempt to articulate the voices of grassroots and social movements together with the voices expressed through electoral democracy.' As political experiments go, it's a knotty one, she concedes. It's also unfinished. Indeed, its very unfinishedness is part of the politics of the Bolivarian Revolution. Its internal tensions are what gives it life, what keeps it real, what instills it with energy and verve.

It's a neat idea, and one that goes down well with her audience. Bringing the marginalised into the mainstream. Fixing the system so as to include the excluded. Giving a voice, at its most basic, to the voiceless. And all with the state at the centre: fair, benign, acting accountably in the service of the 'common weal'. I like the ideal. I even wish it could be true. But even if they can't, are these ideas worth fighting for? Are they principles that men and women will roll up their sleeves for, will stuff envelopes for, will put their necks out for? I'd like to think so. Far more importantly, I'd wager Bolívar and his fellow liberators would like to think so too.

The day ends with a plenary back in the main hall. A different set of speakers from the morning takes to the stage, but their message is essentially the same. We must take heart from the example of South America. The unipolar world that was supposed to take root after the downfall of the Soviet Union never materialised. The Washington Consensus is losing ground. Social democracy is holding on. So we must take note of the alternatives that this continent of mavericks and *militantes* has to offer: alternatives to corporate capitalism, to Yankee domination, to compulsive consumerism, to structural poverty and, most of all, to political disengagement. And we must do more besides. We must learn, we must copy and above all we must resolve to keep fighting. That's how we keep the legacy of the Bolivarian Revolution alive. That's how we show our solidarity with South Americans. Ultimately, that's how true independence, how real freedom, will come into bud and will one day blossom into flower.

The final speaker of the day is a Member of Parliament and a long-term advocate for the Cuban Solidarity Campaign. He's spoken at the *Adelante!* conference every year since it kicked off a decade ago. 'When was the first time we shared a platform together?' the bearded moderator asks him. The question provokes amicable laughter between the two. 'Must be thirty years at least', comes the reply. The audience smiles as one, wanting in on the fraternal bonhomie. The MP goes on to deliver a barnstorming speech. This year, his focus falls on the perils of a proposed free trade agreement between the European Union, Colombia and Peru. It's all a sham, he insists: cooked up by vested business interests on either side of the Atlantic. Last year, the specific subject under scrutiny was different. Just as next year it will be different too.

The point is that *la lucha*, the struggle, doesn't go away. Freedom, justice, equality: these are perennial ideas. Yes, progress is made, but setbacks are incurred, which merely goes to show that the story is far from linear. South America's recent past evidences that, oscillating from left-wing revolutions one minute to right-wing militarism the next. This book caught a moment when the political mood favoured change.

Moods themselves change, however. Ironically, the slow but steady success of South America over recent years has taken some of the sting out of the region's radicalism. Material comfort, after all, is a great downer for political agitation. So too is formal politics, with all its power plays and party bickering. I understand why the international Left desires to present Bolivarianism as inspiration for nation states elsewhere. It's good to know that other alternatives are possible. Yet as soon as counter-movements become part of the formal fabric, their essential character inevitably and indelibly shifts. Being anti-mainstream while in the mainstream is nigh on impossible. Unless the whole mainstream shifts, of course. That's yet to happen anywhere in South America, even in Venezuela. Just as material comfort is still a distant dream for many. So expect others to pick up the banner of Bolívar, and the grassroots' fights described in this book to continue.

The conference closes in widespread applause. When the clapping eventually dies down, I hear a British lady chatting to her South American companion in the seat behind me. She's late middle-aged. He's old and frail. I guess she might be his carer. Either way, the closing speeches appear to have left her a little stunned. 'That Chevron thing is terrible isn't it?' she remarks to her companion, audibly aghast. He mumbles a reply that I don't catch. She presses on. Others around us are getting up to go. Amid the noise of scraping chairs and chatter, I catch only snippets. 'It's because they don't have them in their pockets . . .' Her companion merely nods. 'So much money . . .' she says, followed by something about 'damaging the government'. It's only when she takes the elderly gentleman by the arm and prepares to leave that I catch another full sentence. 'If you don't come along to things like this', she's telling her companion, 'you wouldn't have a clue what's going on really, now would you?' The two walk off. Confusion rather than conviction is the dominant expression in her voice. Even so, that's proof enough she's had a taste of South America – of what it means and, indeed, what it could mean.

I pick up my coat too and retrace my steps back through the lobby and out of the glass doors. The street is busy now with weekend shoppers. My new book on social movements coupled with the pile of pamphlets I picked up during the day are weighing heavy in my bag. Head down, I make my way towards Oxford Street, the echo of the final rally still ringing in my ears. I resolve to return next year, to check on how the revolution is progressing.

ACKNOWLEDGEMENTS

A special thanks to all those cited in this book, without whom both my travels would have been a great deal less colourful. Thanks also to the hundreds of unmentioned others who opened their hearts and their homes to me across the continent.

Approaching a book of this nature without local contacts would have been impossible. For opening doors and pointing the way, I am particularly indebted to the following: in Bolivia, Liliana Poquechoque, Julie Noble and the Alcazar family; in Chile, James Palmer and Jonathan Franklin; in Argentina, René Mally, Ignacio Padilla, Daniel Schweimler and the ever generous Bustamante clan; in Paraguay, Andrea Machain and Javiera Rulli; in Brazil, Jonathan Wheatley and Tom Phillips; in Peru, Ricardo Cubas, Mauricio Novoa and Andrew Parkins; in Ecuador, Roberto Salazar, Eugenio Naranjo and Kempery Tours; in Colombia, Sibylla Brodzinsky, Jerry McDermott and the folk at UNHCR; in Venezuela, Rory Carroll, Benedict Mander and James Ingham; and in Cuba, Anita Snow.

Thanks are also due to Liz O'Donnell and Victoria Hutchinson for their little red pens; to Walter Donohue at Faber and Faber for a blank sheet on which to write; to Nick Davies for his timely advice; and to Georgina Capel and her team for their unflagging enthusiasm.

I am particularly grateful to the following authors and books: Robert Harvey, *Liberators: Latin America's Struggle for Independence*; John Lynch, *Simón Bolívar: A Life*; Duncan Green, *Faces of Latin America*.

Finally, I would like to thank my parents, Douglas and Vanessa, for giving me the space to find my own way; to Emma, for helping keep both my feet and our fortunes on an even keel; and to Seth, whose arrival into this world provided me with the most immovable and most joyous of deadlines.

The occasional name has been changed for reasons of privacy or security. Every effort has been made to ensure that all other information is a faithful representation of the facts. Any failure in this respect belongs entirely to me.

INDEX

Also by Oliver Balch

ff

India Rising

India is in transition. With its door thrown wide open to the world, New India is muscling in alongside the Old. Aspiration and ambition are in the air. The middle classes are expanding and the cityscapes enlarging. But who are the people behind this transition, and what impact are these changes having on everyday life? Oliver Balch meets with everyone from self-made entrepreneurs and wannabe actors to rag-pickers and tea wallahs in his search for answers. In telling the stories of everyday India across the length and breadth of the country, *India Rising* presents a fresh and vivid account of India in transition.

'Oliver Balch brings a zestful, youthful approach to a sub-continent as ancient as history but young in the perpetual reinvention of itself.' Iain Finlayson, THE TIMES

'Oliver Balch's writing is impassioned, vivid and illuminating.' FINANCIAL TIMES

'The commitment and skill of the author are never in doubt: *India Rising* is a paean to this extraordinary nation and to the power of a well-told tale.' Craig Jeffrey, TIMES LITERARY SUPPLEMENT